Hegemony and Revolution

WALTER L. ADAMSON

HEGEMONY AND REVOLUTION

A Study of Antonio Gramsci's Political and Cultural Theory

UNIVERSITY OF CALIFORNIA PRESS
Berkeley • Los Angeles • London

University of California Press
Berkeley and Los Angeles, California
University of California Press, Ltd.
London, England

First Paperback Printing 1983
ISBN 0-520-05057-6
Printed in the United States of America

1 2 3 4 5 6 7 8 9

Library of Congress Cataloging in Publication Data

Adamson, Walter L.
Hegemony and revolution. Antonio Gramsci's political and cultural theory.

Bibliography: p.
Includes index.
1. Gramsci, Antonio, 1891-1937.
2. Gramsci, Antonio, 1891-1937—Political Science.
I. Title.
HX288.G7A58 320.5'32'0924 79-64478

To my mother and father
and to the memory of
my grandfathers

Contents

Acknowledgments

SOME PASSAGES in this book have already appeared, somewhat differently arranged, in the following journal articles: "Towards the Prison Notebooks: The Evolution of Gramsci's Thinking on Political Organization, 1918-1926," *Polity* (Fall 1979); "Beyond Reform or Revolution: Notes on Political Education in Gramsci, Habermas, and Arendt," *Theory and Society* (November 1978); and "Marx and Political Education," *Review of Politics* (July 1977). I am grateful to the editors for permission to reprint.

My greatest debt is to George Armstrong Kelly, whose patient reading and telling criticisms were invaluable when a manuscript remotely resembling this one served as a dissertation in the History of Ideas Program at Brandeis University in 1976. Thanks are due as well to Gerald Izenberg, who also read the manuscript at that time and offered many valuable suggestions.

I am grateful to the Andrew Mellon Foundation and the Harvard-Mellon Fellowship Program in the Humanities and its director, Richard M. Hunt, who put the resources of Widener Library at my disposal in 1977-78. Without this help the book would not yet be written. I would also like to acknowledge the generosity of the Research Committee at Emory University for a grant which greatly aided me in preparing the final manuscript for publication.

Finally, I thank Lauren, whose intellectual, logistical, and personal support was absolutely indispensable and far greater than she will ever realize.

Atlanta
June 1979

Introduction

THE POLITICAL and cultural theory of Antonio Gramsci rests on a triple irony. Committed during his lifetime (1891-1937) to political and journalistic activity as a "unity of theory and practice," he began to achieve his greatest recognition as a theorist only in 1947, long after his tragic death had shattered this unity. What gave him this recognition was the publication of his *Prison Notebooks*, written mostly in the early 1930s, smuggled to Russia upon his death, and returned to Italy at the war's end. Though enormously diverse in content, these notes are shot through with a desire to free Italy from fascism. Yet, as a second irony, it must be conceded that without fascism's victory and his resulting imprisonment, Gramsci might well never have undertaken any such sustained theoretical reflection. And thirdly, while this reflection remains bound to the problems of his epoch and his people, by the time his work appeared it was appreciated less for its historical value than for the suggestiveness of its categories for the politics of a new post-fascist and "technological" society. Indeed, his continent-wide and even transatlantic acclaim has been born only in the 1970s and by events of which, in most cases, he had not the faintest inkling: the demise of a theoretically impoverished New Left, the increased skepticism about the wider applicability of Eastern "roads to socialism," and the apparent emergence of a *sui generis* "Eurocommunism."

In Italy, Gramsci's postwar popularity was self-consciously generated and nurtured by the Italian Communist Party (PCI), which elevated him to the level of a patron saint. Each of its many factions pressed hard to appropriate him for its principles and programs. Extra-parliamentary groups flanking the PCI on the left and socialists (PSI) on its right later joined the fray, in many cases seeking to use Gramsci as an ideological wedge against the PCI. Even Benedetto Croce, the dominant force in Italian letters for half a century and a political liberal, could not resist referring to him as "one of us" after reading the first volume of the *Prison Notebooks* in 1947.[1] The result is a dizzying array of perspectives; indeed, a major sector of the Italian publishing industry has built its foundation on Gramsci studies—and on contemporary political debates cast in surrogate form as Gramsci studies. As writers elsewhere on the continent have swelled the industry, a rich knowledge of the man and his work has become possible, though it must be disentangled from a number of partisan contexts.

In contrast, English-language studies of Gramsci have been relatively few, though increasingly frequent in recent years. John Cammett's pioneering study of a decade ago approached Gramsci as part of a larger history of the PCI, which Gramsci helped to found in 1921.[2] More recent devotees of this approach, like Martin Clark[3] and Gwyn Williams,[4] have much expanded our knowledge of the 1919-20 revolutionary wave in the Italian North and Gramsci's involvement in it. In addition, we have several biographies[5] and lengthy selections from the *Prison Notebooks* and the pre-prison journalism.[6] Enough of this had appeared by 1974 to allow the English historian Eric Hobsbawm to venture then that Gramsci is "probably the most original communist thinker produced in the twentieth century West" and "a political theorist, perhaps the only major Marxist thinker who can be so described."[7] Yet what we have always lacked, and what seems likely to be of the greatest long-term importance, is an interpretative study which gives some substance to Hobsbawm's estimation of Gramsci, and which offers a thorough reading of the *Prison Notebooks* in particular. This is the task I have set for myself in this book.

Three motives lie below the book's surface. As I have reflected on the history of Marxist theory, I have become steadily more convinced that there exists an unambiguous (though widely scattered and never practically realized) tradition of what Merleau-Ponty called "Western Marxism." This tradition stands in sharp contrast to the shape that Marxism received in the hands of Lenin, Stalin, Mao, and other orthodox "Marxist-Leninists." Its representatives would certainly include the "Hegelian-Marxists" of the 1920s,[8] Gramsci, Georg Lukács, and Karl Korsch; Frankfurt School theorists like Theodor Adorno, Max Horkheimer, Herbert Marcuse, and, more recently, Jürgen Habermas; French existential and phenomenological Marxists like Jean-Paul Sartre and Maurice Merleau-Ponty; and the Eastern European "revisionists" of the 1960s like Adam Schaff, Leszek Kolakowski, Karel Kosík, and Mihailo Marković. One can also make good arguments for including "anticipators" like Antonio Labriola and Georges Sorel. Yet, on any such accounting, it is striking how historically confined such theorizing has been. Apart from the first flowering of this tradition from 1919 to 1926 (the year of Stalin's ascension and the consolidation of Italian fascism's totalitarian turn), most of its expressions have come only since 1956 (the year of the Hungarian Revolution and the critique of Stalinism at the Soviet Communist Party's Twentieth Congress). To launch an historical inquiry into the reasons for this relative dearth would be a fruitful project but one beyond my own knowledge and energy.[9] What does concern me is the more modest task of ascertaining (1) how it was that Gramsci's own intellectual development saved him from the perdition of a positivist or historically determinist and "totalitarian" Marxism, and (2) how—or better, to what extent and with what consequences—he was able to theorize a first version of the "Western Marxist" alternative.

My second motive has been to discover why and how Gramsci's Marxism took such a uniquely political direction. If Lukács and Korsch had reacted just as forcefully against the philosophical sterility of Second International Marxism, Gramsci alone had recognized the need for a political response which analyzed the contemporary Western state and the possibility of posing an activist and essentially educational politics against it. Central here was the problem of political legitimation—or what, in the Marxist tradition generally, has been called the problem of "consciousness." Efforts to deal with this problem have had a long, if not very fruitful, history. Marx himself half knew that class consciousness sufficient for revolution could not be generated merely through what he once called the "school of labor."[10] His writings on history and practical politics often suggested the need for a much more actively directed proletarian education. But the prestige of his economic analysis, and the reassuring image of inevitability which it seemed to promise, tended to perpetuate the notion of a "spontaneous" development of class consciousness until the crisis of the First World War shocked international socialism out of its theoretical and practical lethargy. Before then, the only well-known challenges to this "spontaneism" came from Bernstein, who rejected it along with the economic analysis in which it was grounded, and from Lenin, whose tough-minded sense for the exigencies of practical politics led him, in effect, to rediscover Marx's private doubts. Yet Lenin's radically "voluntarist" solution of the vanguard party was more a sidestepping of the problem of class consciousness than a confrontation with it. Nowhere did he suggest how the worker's self-construction of the world through social labor might be combined with a specifically political education to fuel the revolutionary movement and create the consciousness necessary for socialist society. Nowhere did he consider the possibility of creating genuinely proletarian institutions of *both* an economic and political nature which might serve an educational function. These were the areas in which Gramsci would offer some of his most original insights.

Finally, I have been concerned with ascertaining in what ways Gramsci's theory is bound by the intellectual horizons of his age, and in what ways it speaks to ours. In part this is a matter of sorting out issues, like that of the "totalitarianism" sometimes attached to Gramsci, which were only just dawning in his era and which have since become embedded in a wealth of analysis and historical experience that he knew nothing about. Even more fundamentally, we need to establish precisely what the ideological interrelationships were in Gramsci's political milieu. How illuminating is it, for instance, to think of his theory as part of a wider Hegelianized Marxism? What was his relation to Lenin and Bolshevism? What were the polemical divisions on the Italian left over which he had to make the personal choices which ultimately shaped his theoretical outlook? How did the larger developments in the political and economic history of his period shape this outlook as well? A brief look at some of these questions will be useful.

The suggestion I have made that Gramsci was an Hegelian Marxist and part of an Hegelian Marxist flowering harbors hidden complexities. There is no doubt that he shared with Lukács and Korsch certain philosophical affinities. Each of them defended the then shocking proposition that materialism is revolutionary not because it asserts the primacy of matter over mind, but because it centers theory around the concept of praxis taken as the dialectical unity of being and consciousness, matter and mind, theory and practice. Each of them attacked positivism for its determinism and its objective-materialist theory of history. Each opposed the model of a mechanical relationship between an economic substructure, understood as the forces and relations of production, and an "ideological superstructure," understood as an epiphenomenon or mere "reflection" of the substructure. Each paid scarcely any attention, in comparison with their forebears in the Second International, to matters of political economy. Each argued instead that the objective conditions for revolution had been created in Western Europe by the twin debacle of the Great War and the Russian Revolution, but that what was still lacking was the decisive political action necessary to engage the "subjective factor."

Yet the differences among the three theorists are almost as striking. While Lukács followed Hegel in his appraisal of the "alienation" inherent in bourgeois "civil society," and then went on to develop a highly original theory of "reification" based on certain hints in Marx, Gramsci had no such problematic and was consequently able to embrace the rationalization of industrial labor with few apparent qualms. While both Lukács and Korsch were condemned by the Comintern as "theoretical revisionists" and mere "professors,"[11] Gramsci was on the whole revered by the

Bolsheviks and cooperated fully with them except for a brief period in 1921-22. Later in the 1920s, while Lukács repudiated his Hegelian-Marxist leanings and fell in line under Stalinist orthodoxy, and while Korsch deserted Marxism altogether, Gramsci alone continued on a relatively smooth political and philosophical course.

Thus, while I believe that it is still appropriate to speak of an Hegelian Marxism common to the three theorists in the early 1920s, one must also insist on their differences. This point has too frequently been ignored in contemporary political debates on the value of Leninism. In these debates, those who have portrayed Gramsci as the Hegelian Marxist have too often smoothed away the tensions in his theory, and between his theory and practice, so as to overemphasize the historical continuities in the anti-Leninist "Western Marxist" tradition; while those who have attacked this characterization have sought to assimilate Gramsci to Leninism as further evidence for its adaptability and political virtues.[12] There may be merit in the debate, but it has contributed little to a thoughtful appraisal of Gramsci.

The related issue of Gramsci's Leninism seems to me to have been badly posed. Those who have denied that he owed any debt whatsoever to Leninism have simply adopted some strict definition of the term and then shown that Gramsci never parroted such a view, even if, by his own admission, he was greatly influenced by at least certain of its features. This interpretation has the considerable merit of reminding us of the stark contrast between Gramsci and Lenin on a philosophical plane, and it is no accident that those who seek to assimilate Gramsci to Leninism tend to forget about *Materialism and Empirio-criticism* and to proceed on a more political level. Yet the more sophisticated among them are able to parry the philosophical issue by treating his work as a "creative and critical development" of classical Leninism.[13] The result is a stalemate from which an appreciation of the true complexity of Gramsci's relation to Lenin cannot emerge. The same must be said concerning other rubrics—like Croceanism or Bordiganism—under which his theory has sometimes been discussed in some or all of its phases.[14] While these terms will be raised in this book where they are relevant to particular points under discussion, and while I will certainly express some strong views of my own, I hope that the reader who follows the argument through to the end will concede that my reading is not distorted by them and that I plead no partisan cause.

Navigating around caricatures and through partially submerged political debates is not the only difficulty confronting the student of Gramsci. By any accounting, the *Prison Notebooks* are a vast enterprise, a panoramic sweep across Italian political and cultural history and a mining of some of the least explored but potentially richest veins in Marxist theory. Taken as a whole, the four thousand manuscript pages can appear forbidding. As one exasperated student put it: "What kind of Marxist was it who could compare the Marxism of his own day to the Reformation in its cruder ideological formation and who looked to the philosophy of Croce (a latter-day Erasmus) to transform it into a culture of the classic stature of Greece or the Renaissance as a preliminary to the reunification of human life in an 'integral Humanism'?"[15] Moreover, not only is this writing theoretically rich, but its disordered presentation can make it extremely difficult for the unwary reader who plunges in. These are literally just notes, written without the aid of a great number of reference books and under the duress of prison conditions in which Gramsci's always precarious health steadily deteriorated.

From this derive a number of acute methodological problems. As Gramsci himself observed in considering the practice of intellectual history: "A work can never be identified with the raw material collected for its compilation. It is the definitive choice, the way the component elements are arranged, the greater or lesser importance given to this or that element of those collected in the preparatory phase, which are precisely what constitute the effective work."[16] Unfortunately, in Gramsci's own case, to take this caveat literally would be to abandon any hope of understanding the man and his work. The best one can do is to observe it in spirit, by allowing him to speak for himself as much as possible, by avoiding the practice of establishing a major point with only a single or a few quotations, and by suppressing the tendency to impose intentions and rigorous formulations where they may not exist. I have tried to keep such cautions continually in mind, even though at times they have made my interpretation somewhat less sharp and decisive than one might like.

A second problem concerns Gramsci's intellectual development. I am convinced that one cannot understand the political and cultural theory of the *Notebooks* apart from a creative reconstruction of the 1914-26 period, especially at those junctures in which he made critical decisions or shifted his point of view. Specifically, one must come to terms with how he understood Lenin and the Bolshevik Revolution; how and why he theorized a politics of worker councilism in Turin, 1919-20; why he committed himself to a new PCI in 1921; how he understood the nature of fascism and its appeal as it made its first appearances on the Italian scene; how his sojourn in Russia (1922-23) led him to new perceptions of the necessary differences between revolutionary politics East and West; and how he promulgated a new direction for the PCI in the years of his chairmanship, 1924-26. This background is fascinating in itself; where it has been told before, it has not always been told well, and I offer many new interpretations. But most importantly, I have tried to place it in a new light as the essential prolegomenon to the political and cultural theory of the *Notebooks*, one which establishes how their themes are connected to an unfolding human project. I must caution, however, that I have not intended this as biography or even intellectual biography; happily, the reader can turn for these to other sources.[17]

Gramsci himself called attention to the need to interpret an author's works against the background of his life, "above all as regards his intellectual activity."[18] In this way he thought one could gain a feeling for the author's "*leitmotiv*, for the rhythm of the thought as it develops" rather than just his "single casual affirmations and isolated aphorisms."[19] However, there are other reasons as well for undertaking the analysis of Part I. One is that it gives me the opportunity to indicate the nature of Gramsci's practical achievements as well as what their shortcomings already reveal about the limits of his theoretical imagination. Another is that it allows me to present the overriding continuities in Gramsci's political understanding and so to avoid any mechanical confrontation between the "early" and "late" Gramsci, figments of the interpretative imagination created by those writers who construct a closed version of the "mature" work (the *Notebooks*) and then confront it with those early writings that seem to be at odds with it. Still another reason is to offer the reader enough sense for what Gramsci's pre-prison interests really were so that the balance and plausibility of Part II can be fairly judged. Thus, to some extent, I have tried in Part I to let Gramsci's own emphases provide the weighting for mine. This is one reason why, for instance, I have had to pay close attention in Chapters 2 and 3 to the relatively obscure party disputes of the 1920s. These disputes reveal an approach to practical politics that is strongly related to his theoretical arguments at many points. And, by a tortuous path, they lead to his 1923 reassessment of the meaning of revolution in the West, an understanding of which is crucial background to the *Notebooks* and central to any legitimate claim for placing Gramsci within the "Western Marxist" tradition. But, above all, these disputes embody the issues which most preoccupied Gramsci in the years before his arrest, and which must therefore be considered in any account which strives to comprehend his basic motives and concerns.

From what is essentially a study of intellectual formation, we move into a somewhat different realm of discourse when we take up the political and cultural theory of the *Notebooks* in Part II. Here problems of interpretation revolve not so much around the extrinsic relations of theory and practice or work and life, as around peculiarities in the mode of composition itself. Thus, the extreme interconnectedness of Gramsci's conceptual universe makes it difficult to discuss any single concept without introducing them all. In ordering my exposition, I have therefore had to resort numerous times to the device of introducing a concept in a preliminary and unsatisfactory way while postponing a fuller discussion of it until somewhat later.

Another problem is Gramsci's somewhat idiosyncratic way of formulating concepts. Whether because of polemical intellectual formation or simply as a methodological preference, his linguistic universe was self-consciously "dialectical"—i.e., his concepts are almost always formulated in tandem like so many mental double stars. In fact, it is unlikely that one has understood a Gramscian concept until one has recognized the implicit syntagmatic relationship it is intended to evoke.

This raises several important complications. First, a concept may be contrasted with more than one partner, and it will have a different (even opposite) meaning in each case. *Hegemony*, for instance, is sometimes compared with *domination*, in which case the reference is to the process of gaining legitimate consent within the functional universe of civil society, as opposed to simply holding it together through a monopoly on the means of violence. At other times, *hegemony* is compared with *economic-corporative*. Here the reference is to two historical phases of bourgeois development, the former representing a higher stage than the latter. Thus, in an important sense, Gramsci had not one but two concepts of hegemony, a point which has eluded nearly all of his interpreters and which has led to the common misunderstanding that he was inconsistent in his definition of the term. We will return to this point in Chapters 6 and 7.

Secondly, Gramsci will sometimes define a pair of concepts with respect to one another, then offer an historical generalization about their usage, and then finally incorporate that generalization into the definitions themselves. Thus, "war of position," in its most restricted sense, means a tactic of informal penetration required when open warfare or "war of maneuver" (i.e., armies across borders) is impossible. On the basis of historical generalization, Gramsci then links this with a particular sort of social movement—a "passive revolution" as opposed to an active one. Then, through a further generalization, time becomes linked with space: Gramsci argues that a "war of position" in "passive revolution" is applicable to the contemporary West, while a "war of maneuver" in active revolution is more appropriate for the less developed East. From this point forward, Gramsci will use the term "war of position" defined simply as the revolutionary tactic appropriate in advanced societies.

Finally, sets of Gramscian conceptual double stars sometimes form a constellation. Consent (as opposed to force), hegemony (as opposed to domination), organic (as opposed to conjunctural), civil society (as opposed to political society), and passive revolution (as opposed to complete revolution) are all more or less related. Moreover, Gramsci will sometimes take an opposed pair and synthesize it as one definition. Thus "force/consent" becomes "the dual perspective"; "civil/political society" becomes "the state"; and "structure/superstructure" becomes an "historical bloc." As these examples suggest, and as all readers of the *Notebooks* quickly discover, Gramsci worked with a continually expanding network of concepts which he never effectively encompassed or delimited. We can only surmise that he would have brought his vocabulary and thought under more effective control had he lived to write the books which the *Notebooks* outline.

Yet even in its unfinished form, Gramsci's theory is enormously provocative and speaks to a number of problems in contemporary political theory. He was among the first to suggest, for instance, that the realms of civil society and government, if roughly separate in the "nightwatchman state" of nineteenth-century liberalism, had become inextricably intertwined in advanced capitalism. From this perception he reasoned that economic crises would not necessarily be experienced immediately as political crises; on the contrary, at least strong governments could deflect the impact of an economic crisis through their ideological and cultural hegemony. Indeed, in anticipation of a thesis that Marcuse would later put forward, he even suggested that such crises could encourage the expansion of the state's hegemonic apparatus and thus strengthen its position. In this sense, the state had become "relatively autonomous" from the economic substructure—a formulation which has received intensive scrutiny in recent discussions of the state by Nicos Poulantzas, Ralph Miliband, C. B. Macpherson, Jürgen Habermas, and many others.

In view of this contemporary interest, I draw out the implications of Gramsci's theory of the state in Chapters 5 and 7 and the Conclusion; yet at the same time I hope I have preserved a sense of the historical context which frames Gramsci's writing. For he was both a brilliant theoretical innovator and a child of his time whose political and philosophical formulations, like those of his contemporary Georg Lukács, may sometimes appear innocent to readers in the more skeptical climate on the far side of Hitler and Stalin.

Part One

CHAPTER ONE

The Formative Years

> Some whimper miserably, others curse obscenely, but nobody, or only a few, ask themselves: if I too had done my duty, if I had tried to impose my will, make my advice heard, would things have turned out as they have. . . . I live, I am a partisan. This is why I hate those who do not take sides; I hate those who are indifferent.
>
> (February 1917)

WITH THE ONSET of the First World War in August 1914, the socialism of the Second International entered into the acute phase of a crisis from which it would never recover. From its birth in 1889, the International had been plagued by a multiplicity of allegiances, both ideological and national, which did not always find common cause as easily as their shared internationalist pretensions suggested they should have. Yet few Europeans in or out of the International had predicted the speed and fervor with which these socialists would rally around their respective national flags once the war arrived. The Italian Socialist Party (PSI) was an exception to this trend for a variety of political and ideological reasons.[1] Not the least of these was the tremendous increase in popular support that the party had gained by adopting a firm antimilitarist stance in the wake of the 1911 Libyan War. Indeed, in 1912, the party's left-wing or "maximalist" faction had wrested the leadership away from the reformism of Leonida Bissolati and Filippo Turati largely through its greater ability to manipulate the antiwar appeal. Through the spring of 1914, this appeal was the object of competition among all factions of the Italian left: syndicalists, maximalists, reformists, republicans, and anarchists. Only with the defeats of "Red Week" in June did some elements of the left, particularly the syndicalists, begin to drift toward the "interventionist" camp.[2] When the war arrived in August, the governing Liberal Party was confronted with an inflamed and divided electorate, and it could not make up its mind to enter the war until the spring of 1915. The intervening months witnessed a rancorous debate between two rather strange assemblages: the nationalist and futurist avant-garde, syndicalists, republicans, and the extreme left and right fringes of the PSI favoring intervention, versus the majority of liberals, Catholics, reformists, and maximalists calling for neutrality. It was in this highly charged atmosphere that a hitherto unknown 23-year-old Sardinian made his national journalistic debut.

Gramsci's article, "Active and Operative Neutrality," appeared in the Turinese socialist weekly, *Il Grido del popolo*, on October 31, 1914. The previous edition had featured a passionate rebuttal by the leader of the Turinese Young Socialist Federation, Angelo Tasca, to an article which had appeared on October 18 in *Avanti!* by its editor, Benito Mussolini. Leader of the maximalists since their triumph at the Reggio Emilia Congress in July 1912, Mussolini was already showing many signs of the tactical cunning and personal dynamism which he would later display as the founder and leader of Italian fascism. His article had jolted the still predominantly unquestioned internationalism of most of his readers by recasting the argument against neutralism in a new and revolutionary light. His style was rhetorical and overwrought, but the questions he raised were clear enough. Might not national proletariats everywhere gain by exploiting the political weaknesses in their governments created by the wartime crisis? Or to put it the other way around: might not these proletariats lose out on a unique historic opportunity for revolutionary change by defining their position dogmatically as "impartial spectators"? Tasca's answer was to condemn such questions as irrationally opportunist: the proletariat was still too weak to control events, and any attempt by it to do so could only end in catastrophe. Gramsci's article attempted to mediate these views, though at least on the surface it sided much more with Mussolini. This is interesting in itself, yet the article reveals a great deal more about the political and intellectual currents then influencing Gramsci.

First of all, Gramsci chided Tasca for his dogmatism and "naive Buddhist contemplation."[3] Tasca had allowed himself to be blinded and even incapacitated by a slogan; a policy of "realist concretism" would have to pay much closer attention to events. Early in the crisis, when the point was to establish credibility as an internationally united proletarian class, the slogan of "absolute neutrality" had made sense. The war had to be revealed for what it was—the struggle of rival imperialist bourgeoisies—and the proletariat had to be blocked from any temptation to indulge in the bloody reveries of the "useless slaughter." But, by now, that point had been made, and the initial chaotic situation had passed. Absolute neutrality could now only favor the reformists, whose political position would be enhanced by a proletariat of docile, "impartial observers." Revolutionaries "who conceive of history as the creation of their own spirit, made by an uninterrupted series of lacerations of other active or passive social forces, and who prepare the best conditions favorable for the final laceration (revolution), must not be satisfied with the provisional formula of 'absolute neutrality' but ought to transform it to another: 'active and operative neutrality.'"[4] Only through such a transformation could the PSI begin to rid itself of all the "bourgeois incrustations" which had, unfortunately, plagued it from the beginning. Only then would the party be able to make full use of the educational value of a war that had laid bare the "imperfect form of a civilization" which must "overflow" into a "more perfect one."[5]

Several attitudes important for understanding Gramsci at this early stage lie embedded in this analysis. Its idealist language—"history" as the "creation" of human "spirit"—announces a bold activism uncomfortable with the pettiness and lack of imagination and courage in a mechanical, rule-following, or determinist politics. Revolutionaries seize history; they can never allow it simply to unfold. Here already lies the basis for the charge which would never be far from Gramsci's later Marxism: that of "voluntarism" or "idealism" or "Bergsonianism." And in this early period the charge had much merit (excepting perhaps the Bergsonian label);[6] even in the *Prison Notebooks*, Gramsci did not entirely avoid a highly qualified form of voluntarism.[7] Ironically, however, he was at the same time far more down-to-earth and pragmatic than the bulk of his critics. For, like Mussolini, he was shrewd enough to recognize that any measure which increased the likelihood of an Austrian attack on Italy would be advantageous for a proletarian politics of mass mobilization. And the only politics worthy of being called proletarian was one which sought, in Gramsci's phrase, to build a "potential state"—a notion which he would later develop with great originality.

Also in this view was an emphasis, common to much of the Italian left since Mazzini, on "preparing" and "educating" a class for political ascendancy. Much of the mainstream political debate in prewar "liberal" Italy revolved around the question of the extent to which the large mass of Northern workers and Southern peasants might be brought into active political participation. Writers like Gaetano Salvemini, who argued the optimistic case, predicated their optimism on the power of public education—if, that is, the present liberal elite would only institute it.[8] Evidently, Gramsci was much in sympathy with this view despite its somewhat "liberal" colorations in Salvemini.

A further indication of political pragmatism is evident in the position the article takes on the "national question." The task of the "potential state" is to "prepare" the Italian nation for international socialism, but "in the unfolding of this function, it is autonomous and . . . independent of the International. . . ."[9] That the final goal was internationalism was consistent with Gramsci's socialism; that the immediate goal was national was consistent with his admiration for Salvemini, his conception of the PSI, and his emotional disposition towards political activism.

It was also consistent with his general approval of Mussolini's position. Again this revealed something which would later become characteristic of the Gramscian style: the ability to go against the grain, to adopt an independent position if this was where analysis led. Rarely did this fail to attract criticism; yet the criticism in this particular instance was especially embarrassing, since Mussolini was expelled from the PSI only several weeks later. Gramsci's support had not been unequivocal: he had acknowledged that Tasca might have been right to criticize "Mussolini the man," but thought it would have been wiser to have kept Mussolini's arguments separate from this estimate. Furthermore, he readily conceded that Mussolini's statements were "somewhat disorganized" and that he could not be sure if he had "developed them along the same lines as he [Mussolini] would have done himself."[10] Yet the thrust of the article placed him unmistakably in Mussolini's camp. This was short-lived, yet it is worth noting that the irony of his later debt to fascism was foreshadowed so early. Moreover, the article was ironic in an immediate sense as well. For what apparently attracted Gramsci to Mussolini were his intense activism and the "Italy-first" attitude this activism implied. In terms of the cultural ambience of the time, this associated them both with the new, Nietzschean avant-gardism in all its many manifestations—nationalist, syndicalist, futurist, etc.—that had emerged in the previous decade. Yet as we will shortly see, Gramsci's relationship to this avant-garde, or "rejuvenation movement" as one historian has called it,[11] was ambiguous. While he seems to have embraced some of its features, especially in the prewar period, he did so in a rather atypical way, and his posture toward it soon became more detached and skeptical than this article would lead one to believe. Before turning to the larger themes in his early writing, then, we will do well to investigate their cultural context in some detail.

Culture and Politics in Post-Risorgimento Italy

The starting point for any assessment of the intellectual and cultural life in which Gramsci's early political outlook took shape is the particular character of the Italian political unification achieved during the Risorgimento (1848-70). As Gramsci himself would later argue, Italy's unification had been brought about largely through the diplomatic finesse of Cavour, who extended the control of one of her provinces, Piedmont, over all the rest. It had not been a genuine social revolution out of which a political mandate might have grown, and it was bound to have an artificial ring to the Mazzianian wing of the Risorgimento, which had romanticized the Italian project so deeply and for so long. Consequently the political culture of post-Risorgimento Italy was profoundly, though of course not uniformly, hostile to its narrow and weakly institutionalized system of governance. Though many, perhaps most, Italians accepted the view that the age of heroes must give way to a more classical spirit based on the quiet and steadfast pursuit of social and economic progress, intense criticism of the system was to be found even among conservative realists like Gaetano Mosca.[12] Still more threatening was the highly vituperative, if somewhat less numerous group which, following Mazzini, refused entirely to give up heroic imagery, felt that they had been betrayed by the Cavourian triumph, and either welcomed the war when it came or at least felt their own politics to have been redeemed by it.[13] At the forefront of this group after 1870 was Giosuè Carducci. His self-proclaimed successor in the next generation was the far more militant and lofty irrationalist, Gabriele D'Annunzio. It was D'Annunzio who, more than anyone, was responsible for the vast increases in size and fervor registered by this group after 1900.

To come fully to grips with the nature of this cultural "rejuvenation movement" in Italy, one would have to trace its interrelationship with similar movements arising elsewhere in Europe in this period. Nothing so ambitious can be attempted here. Suffice it to say that what was most specifically manifest across European culture as the new century arrived was an attack on positivism, both as a philosophy and as a style of life without a spiritual dimension.[14] As Croce shrewdly observed, "industrialism and Bismarckianism," however potent as modernizing forces, had been unable to create a "new and satisfying religion."[15] This failure prepared the ground for surrogate philosophies of "intuition, pragmatism and mysticism" which, coupled with a nationalist political appeal, stood in the way of the "sounder and truer rationalism" he thought should have been provoked.[16] In Italy the advance of these new philosophies was further facilitated by the relative weakness of any positivist tradition. The dominant intellectual traditions of the Risorgimento had been idealist, and specifically neo-Hegelian, and this hegemony had been only partially eclipsed during the last third of the century.[17] If, as has been plausibly argued,[18] this puts Croce, Gentile, and even Gramsci in his early idealist moods, into a tradition which begins with Vera, De Sanctis, and the brothers Spaventa, then D'Annunzio was the Nietzsche for Croce's Hegel.

In his novels, poetry, and plays, D'Annunzio reveled in nationalist and imperialist themes, in sensuous and violent historical imagery like the Renaissance of the Borgias, and in irrationalist philosophy and futurist aesthetics which constantly betrayed the influence of Nietzsche, however little he actually understood him. Yet if D'Annunzio was instrumental in creating the cultural atmosphere out of which the Italian National Party was born in Florence in 1910, he was slightly too old and had too much the aura of literary dandyism to appeal to this movement as a leader. Instead they turned to Enrico Corradini, a writer and publicist who had edited the flamboyant journal *Regno* during its short life from 1903 to 1905. Corradini ridiculed D'Annunzio as "an effeminate Franco-Russo-Abruzzese novelist,"[19] but these are the words of a political rival. The only real difference they expose is that Corradini's interest was closer to the concrete political world. Like D'Annunzio, he glorified war entirely on literary and psychological grounds (the Russo-Japanese clash particularly caught his fancy). More originally, he argued that revolutionary struggle was not between classes but between nations, proletarian and bourgeois nations, and he continually evoked the memory of Imperial Rome to goad Italians toward greater displays of national power which neither liberals nor socialists had had the courage to take. Varnished over this nationalism was a futurist aesthetic—modern machine warfare as a new source of earthly beauty—which he proclaimed considerably in advance of F. T. Marinetti's 1909 *Futurist Manifesto*. If he was less the Nietzschean devotee, he put Carlyle to much the same use; and like D'Annunzio, his hatred was more for liberalism and rationalism than for socialism. Thus, while he could not have accepted every proposition in Sorel's *Reflections on Violence*, he could at least have applauded the psychological exaltation of violence it put forth.

While it is fair to say, then, that the rejuvenation movement generally took a right-wing direction, even its most reactionary writings had a revolutionary tinge which was entirely foreign to classical conservatism. As an early American student of it has written:

> Dissatisfied with the current state of affairs, the contributors to the above-named reviews [*Il Leonardo, La Critica, Il Regno, La Voce, Lacerba,* and *La Ronda*] wished to arouse their fellow countrymen to a proper realization of the political and cultural problems that lay before them. They wanted the people to forget the past, to overthrow the old order of things. . . .
>
> The young critics of the new generation began to visualize the ship of

civilization already heading for the rocks of destruction, as long as blind materialism and selfish individualism were at the helm.[20]

Prior to 1911, these emotions and ideals allowed nationalists, futurists, syndicalists, advocates of the South, and some socialists to write for the same journals. Only with the Libyan War did previously latent left-right cleavages become significant enough that the latter three groups were forced to split off from the other two.[21]

Among the more progressive of rejuvenation movement writers were those who served as advocates of the Southern Question. Of all the problems faced by Italian governing elites after 1870, this was surely the most intractable. Nonetheless, most Northerners were ignorant of the real desperateness of conditions in the South, and this ignorance was only compounded by the widespread practice of co-opting Southern landowners rather than facing the issue squarely. Most Northerners preferred the comfortable assumption that whatever real problems the South had would work themselves out naturally over time. The widely disseminated legend that the South was a naturally rich region which had declined only because of Bourbon political abuses and indigence among the natives appeared to bolster the plausibility of this assumption.

Advocates of the South had little difficulty discrediting such views. A socioeconomic survey by Leopoldo Franchetti and Sidney Sonnino had done this as early as 1878.[22] But national politicians nonetheless paid little attention to the problem until after 1900. Among those most responsible for this turn of events was Salvemini, a deft writer who knew very well how to exploit the sentiments of the growing post-Risorgimento opposition on the South's behalf.

Salvemini's argument was always vehement in its analysis but patient and pragmatic in its prescription, at least until 1909. In the 1890s, he advocated federalist reform aimed at eradicating the then widespread practice of appeasing the few powerful Southern politicians with tax deals in exchange for inaction on the Southern Question. He also campaigned for universal suffrage and tried to promote his ideas through membership in the newly formed

PSI. When the party ignored his cause, Salvemini began to expound his views exclusively through journalism, first in *La Voce* (probably the most radical and widely read of Italian rejuvenation movement journals), later in *L'Unità*, which he founded in 1911. These views became increasingly strident. In his frustrations both with the socialists and with Prime Minister Giolitti's coy sidestepping of the Southern issue, he began to advocate violence by 1910.[23] Only through the use of violence, he thought, would universal suffrage ever be granted. When Giolitti finally succumbed to the pressures for a widened franchise and signed a bill for near universal suffrage in June 1912, Salvemini wrote that he felt like a man served a huge and delicious meal for breakfast: what his mind desired his stomach could not digest.[24] While his prescriptions remained essentially "liberal," he nonetheless welcomed the war as a way of shaking Italy loose from Giolittian cynicism and complacency.

Another left-wing challenge to the political culture of the post-Risorgimento grew out of the anarchist tradition and later from the socialists who split off from it.[25] When Bakuninist anarchism arrived in Italy in 1865, the ground for it was already well prepared by a native radical tradition. Spontaneous revolts of major proportion had occurred in 1820, 1837, 1848, and 1860. Moreover, a radical federalism similar to Proudhon's in France—and an advocacy of direct action through spontaneous revolt to achieve it—was already being theorized in the 1840s by Carlo Pisacane and Carlo Cattaneo. Pisacane was widely celebrated for his formula, the "propaganda of deeds," and Cattaneo had been a leader in the major uprising of the period, the Five Days of Milan in 1848. Mazzini's romantic yearnings for a new Italy and Garibaldi's alliance with the Sicilian peasants in the 1860 revolt on the island were also grist for the anarchist mill. By 1866, Bakunin's influence was gathering momentum, and many of the intellectuals who had previously been Mazzinians succumbed to it during the next decade. Anarchism never achieved an extensive mass base, however, and its influence faded in the late 1870s as European Marxist currents began to penetrate Italy. The shift was well exemplified by Carlo Cafiero. As a Bakuninist in 1878, Cafiero had led the peasants of San Lupo in the burning of the land register. By 1880, he was advocating for Italy something like what the German Social Democrats had spelled out in the Gotha Program.[26]

Nonetheless, this penetration was slow and the shift was more often gradual than sudden. As Croce was later to write, Karl Marx had little early following in Italy because he was "too critical, too much the economist, too sarcastic, and too much lacking in human sympathy"[27] to appeal to those who had been nurtured on Mazzinian fare. Thus, while the unexpectedly cordial reception given the prominent Marxist Benoit Malon when he visited Italy in 1874 may have been an omen, it was not until the 1890s that Marxism hit Italy in full force. In theory this was mostly the work of Antonio Labriola, who, Croce tells us,[28] discovered Marx in 1890 and became an avid student of the early works, especially the *Deutsch-Französische Jahrbücher* of 1843, the *Heilige Familie* of 1845, and the articles in the *Neue Rheinische Zeitung* of 1848. Through his writing and his Rome lectures, Labriola disseminated a popularized though highly articulate Marxism. It was also a Marxism of a deeply Italian character. The vagueness of Mazzinian romanticism is gone, but the humanitarian idealism which inspired it and which fueled the post-Risorgimento opposition is continually evident. Moreover, Labriola's Marxism had strong Hegelian resonances. While Marx is counted as the great economist of his age, Labriola sharply repudiated the "vulgar" and "positivist" Marxism which, paying no heed to Engels's qualifications, explained all history on the basis of the "economic factor."

On the practical level, Marxism gained its first strong foothold in Italy when the socialists split with the anarchists in 1892 and formed the PSI. From the beginning the party was badly divided between reformist and revolutionary wings, but even Turati, the arch-reformist, had "humanitarian" as well as "scientific" pretensions. Though his own orientation could best be described as "positivist,"[29] a lively and multifaceted debate on the merits of a positivist Marxism was a regular feature in *Critica Sociale*, the journal he founded in 1891 and edited thereafter.[30] Moreover, *Critica Sociale* revealed a deeply Mazzinian streak in its continual suggestion that, when accorded a "proletarian education," workers have the political capacities for democratic self-governance.[31]

For their part, the revolutionary wing recalled even more the style of the radical left during the Risorgimento, however much they declared their adherence to Marx and Engels. The rebelliousness they showed in the Milan May Days of 1898 self-consciously recalled the Milan of exactly fifty years earlier. After the turn of the century, the syndicalist movement, which Fernand Pelloutier had founded in France, made a large impact among Italian revolutionary socialists in part because it seemed to be a creative transformation of the anarchist and Cattaneo's federalist traditions. It scored an important success in the general strike of September 16-20, 1904, which spread like a contagion from Milan across Italy. And syndicalism reached even greater heights in subsequent socialist politics until it was eclipsed by the reformist congresses at Florence in 1908 and at Milan in 1910.

The revolutionary and direct-action impulses in Italian syndicalism were reflected in its decided preference for the writings of Sorel over those of Pelloutier. Sorel, whose *L'Avenir socialiste des syndicats* was translated into Italian in 1903, was attractive for his voluntarist emphasis on struggle, violence, heroes, and myth, as well as for avoiding the drier virtues of the *Bourses du Travail*. Indeed, to syndicalist intellectuals like Arturo Labriola and Enrico Leone, Sorel seems to have represented a kind of left-wing version of the life philosophies of Bergson and Nietzsche. Under this influence, Labriola wrote some suggestive passages on the nature of alienation under capitalism, which, though never fully developed, anticipated in many ways the brilliant formulations of Lukács in the early 1920s.[32] If the political power of the syndicalists was relatively fleeting, the revolutionary socialists who emerged from Reggio Emilia in 1912 owed much of their far greater success[33] to the style and tactics the syndicalists pioneered.

Together, Italian syndicalism and Mussolinian socialism provide convincing evidence for Croce's observation that, after 1900,

> the socialist ideal . . . no longer attracted the youth of the day, nor even those who had been young at the period of its ascendency. This was partly due to the criticism which had undermined the Marxian apoca-

lyptic, partly to the gradual absorption of socialism into liberalism, partly to the reforms which were rapidly bringing into effect the "minimum program" in its entirety.[34]

It was also partly due to the fact that an increasingly attractive replacement for Marxism had been located in the irrationalist frenzy of D'Annunzio and the Italian futurists. In this cultural climate, the Marxian currents which retained their appeal were those which learned to exploit the same sentiments as these new rivals were exploiting. The syndicalists did this with some success; Mussolini was a virtuoso at it.

One might, of course, object that Mussolini was not always clear about how he stood in relation to D'Annunzio, Corradini, and Marinetti, even in his early socialist phase. Yet Leone and Arturo Labriola could be counted as progressives, at least in this period, and one finds this same tendency to exploit D'Annunzian appeals even in writers who held him in contempt. Salvemini, for instance, never embraced the nationalists even when his hatred for Giolitti reached its most anguished depths, yet he also recognized the psychic vitality missing from nineteenth-century Marxism, advocated violence as a means of restoring the political passion necessary for dramatic change, and welcomed the war along with the nationalists as one step toward this end.[35]

Between Croce and La Voce

With this cultural milieu in mind, we may now return to the question of Gramsci's intellectual formation. A glance at his boyhood years suggests both that he would likely have been attracted to any radical appeal which was also pro-Southern and that he lived in an extremely isolated world. Until the age of eighteen, he had never been very far from the rural Sardinian hamlet of Ghilarza, where he was born in 1891. His early years had been hard; later he recalled "the sewer of my past"[36] which had shown him only the "most brutal aspect of life."[37] His father had been arrested for an "administrative irregularity" when Antonio was six;[38] and as the second oldest male of seven children, he had had to go to work. Even very hard labor, however, barely improved the family's position. By age eleven he was trading ten hours of work for wages which could buy only a loaf of bread each day.[39] His education suffered as a result, and his resentment was intense. "From my youth on I had an instinct for rebellion against the rich because I, who had made 10s in every subject in elementary school, had been unable to continue studying, while the sons of the butcher, pharmacist and tailor had gone on."[40] Only at eighteen did he have the opportunity to attend a *liceo* in the Sardinian capital of Cagliari. He spent three years there and did well enough to win a modest scholarship to the University of Turin for the fall of 1911.

We know very little about Gramsci's political thinking and activity during his years in Cagliari. His older brother Gennaro was already a militant in the local socialist youth club; and according to an old friend, Daniele Putzolo, Antonio spent a good deal of his spare time there too.[41] What is more certain is that he was already an avid reader of anti-regime authors. While he later confessed to having already read "some things by Marx . . . out of intellectual curiosity,"[42] his principal preoccupation was with Giovanni Papini, Benedetto Croce, and Gaetano Salvemini, all of whom contributed heavily to *La Voce*.[43] He also read numerous Sardinian writers, and subscribed to the newspaper of the Milanese establishment, *Domenica del Corriere*, as well as to Milan's syndicalist journal, *Il Viandante*, in which the articles of Arturo Labriola regularly appeared.[44] An early school essay, "Oppressed and Oppressors," bears the imprint both of this reading and of his early years of life. "The French Revolution," wrote the young Sardinian, "has abolished many privileges and raised up many oppressed; but it did no more than replace one ruling class with another. Yet, it has left us a great teaching: that privileges and social differences, being the products of society and not nature, can be overcome."[45]

If these words already suggested the emphasis on political education which was to characterize every phase of his mature theory and practice, there was as yet nothing particularly Marxist or socialist about them. What they did seem to reflect was the influence of Salvemini's writings, which were heavily concerned with political education from a pro-South standpoint.[46] Indeed, all of Gramsci's reading at this point was conspicuous for its combination of emancipatory and pro-South perspectives. From its birth in 1908, *La Voce* had devoted much attention to the Southern Question. An entire issue was devoted to it in 1911, a fact that Gramsci later recalled in the *Notebooks*.[47] Both Croce and Salvemini were Southerners; and in Sardinia, which was considered Southern both for geographic and economic reasons, popular manifestoes commonly combined Salveminian ideas with separatist or federalist and sometimes revolutionary sentiments. Gramsci seems to have shared very deeply in this.[48] Palmiro Togliatti remembers him, upon his arrival in Turin in 1911, as someone who was "frankly and proudly pro-Sardinian, even Sardinian nationalist. He felt very deeply the common resentment of all Sardinians at the wrongs suffered by the island; and for him, too, such resentment turned easily against continentals, and against the continent itself."[49]

This Sardinian nationalism may have been one of the reasons for Gramsci's apparent coldness toward Turinese socialism in his first two years at the University. Though he had been sympathetic to Sardinian socialism,[50] he encountered in the continental version a predominantly "positivist" style which persisted in explaining the Southern Question in terms of the biological inferiority of Southerners. He reflected on this fact in his later essay on the Southern Question:

> It is well known what ideology is propagated through the multifarious forms of bourgeois propaganda among the masses of the North: the South is a lead weight which impedes a more rapid civil development of Italy; the Southerners are biologically inferior beings, semi-barbarians or complete barbarians by natural destiny; if the South is backward, the fault is not to be found in the capitalist system or in any other historical cause, but is the fault of nature which has made the Southerner lazy, incapable, criminal, barbarous, moderating his stepmother's fate by the purely individual outbursts of great geniuses, who are like solitary palms in an arid and sterile desert. The Socialist Party was very largely the vehicle of this bourgeois ideology among the Northern proletariat; the Socialist Party gave its blessing to the whole "pro-Southern" literature of the clique of so-called positivist writers like Ferri, Sergi, Niceforo, Orano and their minor followers, who in articles, sketches, stories, novels, books of impressions and memoirs repeated in various forms the same refrain; once again "science" had turned to crushing the wretched and the exploited, but this time it was cloaked in socialist colors, pretending to be the science of the proletariat.[51]

So intense was his resentment that Gramsci in 1913 appears to have had far more admiration for Papini's futurism than for any version of socialism. Though their authorship cannot be verified with absolute certainty, two articles openly embracing Papini appeared in the University press that spring signed by "alfa gamma," the *nom de plume* Gramsci frequently used later in *Il Grido del popolo*.[52]

Of course, even if he had been attracted by the PSI in this period, he might well have been hesitant to participate for personal reasons as well.[53] His health had never been good: he had suffered from occasional internal hemorrhages and a probably congenital hunchback condition since he was four. Now his condition became aggravated because of his student poverty, which did not even allow him to buy a winter coat to face the severe Turinese winter. To be sure not to lose even the modest scholarship he had, as well as to compensate for his "provincial" background, he felt he had to study very hard. Togliatti reports that even his spare time was spent attending additional lectures "whenever there were professors dealing with essential problems in an illuminating way...."[54] Moreover, the anxieties created by his deformity and the social and intellectual transition from life in the provinces tended to reinforce what from all reports was a natural shyness and thus to make his existence an extremely lonely one. So it is not surprising that two years should pass before Gramsci became identified with socialist politics, and that when he did so it should be an outgrowth of his political concern for Sardinia.

When he returned there for a vacation in the summer of 1913, the island was in the midst of an election campaign under a newly expanded franchise which had increased the rolls from 42,000 to 178,000.[55] Gramsci quickly perceived that to win this new vote for their candidates, local landowners had shed their Sardinian nationalism and had accepted the aid of elite power brokers on the continent.[56] He therefore participated actively on behalf of the socialist candidates and signed the pro-South anti-protectionist petition which was supported by socialists and later reprinted in *La Voce*.[57] His friend from Turin, Angelo Tasca, later recalled that Gramsci

> had been very impressed by the utter change caused by the participation of the peasant masses in the election, even though they had not known how to make proper use of their new weapon. It was this experience, and

his own reflection on it, that finally made Gramsci into a socialist. When he returned to Turin at the start of the following session, I had fresh evidence of just how decisive these events had been for him.[58]

One concrete step he took was to join the PSI.[59]

There is little doubt, then, that Gramsci was initially attracted to socialism because he perceived it as the most efficacious way of dealing with the Southern Question. Yet for some time thereafter, his identification with socialist politics in Turin remained uneasily allied with his partisanship for the South. The tension was central to his article on the war, since the "absolute neutralists" were often the most doctrinaire, even "positivist" socialists, while the "interventionists" could count Salvemini and other progressive Southerners among their number. The tension also continually arose in Gramsci's practical politics. When, in 1914, one of Turin's parliamentary representatives died, Gramsci proposed Salvemini as the socialist candidate to replace him even though he was neither socialist nor from Turin. The point, as Gramsci later expressed it, was to demonstrate the solidarity of the Turinese workers with the Apulian peasants:

The workers in Turin know that in the general elections of 1913 the overwhelming majority of peasants of Molfetta and Bitonto supported Salvemini; the administrative pressures of the Giolitti government and the violence of the gangs and the police prevented the Apulian peasants expressing themselves. The workers of Turin do not ask for pledges from Salvemini, neither of Party program nor of discipline within the Parliamentary group; once elected Salvemini will answer to the Apulian peasants, not to the workers of Turin, who will carry on their propaganda according to their principles and will not be at all committed by the political activity of Salvemini.[60]

Salvemini declined but, ironically enough in view of his later intense anti-fascism, proposed Mussolini in his place.

In the winter and spring of 1915, Gramsci was deeply absorbed in his fourth and final year in the Faculty of Letters. From his prison letters we can surmise that he was led to still further reading of Croce and Salvemini, and that he began to master Dante, Machiavelli, Hegel, and De Sanctis as well.[61] He also apparently took one course in Marx's dialectic.[62] By late 1915 he had become involved in anti-nationalist polemics in *Il Grido del popolo* and elsewhere.[63] Shortly thereafter he also apparently lectured on Marx before a socialist student group.[64] Clearly, he was far beyond "Active and Operative Neutrality" in this period. Yet it is unlikely, as has sometimes been suggested,[65] that any of this can be taken as evidence that he had already turned to activist socialism by virtue of a commitment to Marxism. The large body of journalism which he published in 1916 shows no significant debt to Marx and rests instead on an idealism and a preoccupation with "culture" influenced above all by Croce.

In "Socialism and Culture," one of the earliest and most interesting of these articles, Gramsci defined culture as "the organization, the disciplining of one's inner self; it is the appropriation of one's own personality; it is the conquest of a superior consciousness whereby it becomes possible to understand one's own historical value, function in life, rights, and duties."[66] Man is "above all, spirit"; he is an historical creature who appropriates his personality through "intelligent reflection"; and he transforms society by means of "cultural penetration." Yet the article showed little of his later sense for "culture" as an arena of class conflict; it posed the socialist mission entirely in personalist and utopian terms, bolstering the argument with quotes from Novalis and Vico.[67] A year later in the short-lived PSI Youth Federation journal, *La Città Futura*, he could still write:

> Socialists must not replace order with order. They must bring about order itself. The juridical norm that they want to establish is the *possibility of the complete realization of one's human personality for every citizen.* With the realization of this norm all established privileges collapse.[68]

Again the emphasis is on men as the makers of history, on the personal responsibility of each citizen to become concerned, on the moral and strategic importance of imposing one's will on events, and on the ability of men to transcend themselves through thought. To crown the argument, Gramsci set forth as his ideal a very Crocean concept of liberty: "maximum liberty with a minimum of [individual] constraints."

One is therefore not surprised to learn of Gramsci's own later characterization of himself in this period as "rather Crocean in tendency."[69] Croce's four-part system was complete by 1916, and Gramsci would have been acquainted with at least its first three parts—especially the all-important volume on *Practice* (1908)—from his university studies. He also seems to have read Croce's *Cultura e vita morale*, to have followed his journal, *La Critica*, and to have studied the Croce-Gentile debate of 1913, part of which appeared in *La Voce*.[70] Yet despite his heavy indebtedness to Croce's theoretical formulations, it was not so much in the precise details of the system that Gramsci was a Crocean. As we will see shortly, his appropriation of Croce was intensely critical, and he did not agree with all of Croce's formulations nor take his entire intellectual orientation from this source. What was Crocean about his writings of 1916-17 was that they breathed with the same style, spoke the same language, and, above all, confronted a common set of intellectual and cultural antagonists.

Croce wrote in his *History of Italy, 1871-1915*[71] that already in 1902 he was in a two-front war with "positivists, empiricists, and 'philologists' on the one hand, and pseudo-geniuses, mystics, and *dilettanti* on the other." With respect to the latter group, this was slightly exaggerated, for to fight the positivists, Croce often joined forces with the new wave, writing for its journals and siding with it on many issues. Yet, to the large extent that the statement was true, it was also true for Gramsci, especially after 1914. He had learned to distrust the first group not only from Croce but also from Antonio Labriola[72] and nearly everything he read in *Il Viandante* or *La Voce*. As we have seen, the feeling was deepened by his intense commitment to the South. But, like Croce, he too seemed to favor a "sounder and truer rationalism"[73] over any sort of mysticism, spiritualism, or glorification of violence and the irrational. Croce admitted that he lacked the taste for the latter philosophies because he was too old to have grown up in the "D'Annunzian atmosphere, in the grasping, pleasure-loving spirit of the new industrialism."[74] Though far removed from this continental atmosphere until almost 1912, Gramsci was young enough and, in part through a generational attachment, probably went farther in this direction than Croce had. Yet the embrace with Papini's futurism had been brief, if it occurred at all, and in the war years his taste in literary criticism was for the classical

Francesco De Sanctis, much out of favor with the new wave but very dear also to Croce.[75] Also unlike this new wave, Gramsci lacked a well-developed psychology. This was a deficiency common to all Marxists prior to the generation of the Frankfurt School, but it was particularly notable in Gramsci, since so much of his reading might have goaded him toward one. He seems instead to have thought that the proletariat was immune to the current spiritual and cultural malaise and that it could create a genuine culture integrated with industrialism by the wholly rational means of political self-education.[76] "For socialists," wrote Gramsci in 1917, "the problem of an initiative which produces value is not resolved in psychology but in history."[77]

In short, Gramsci's early writing expressed a staunch opposition to the post-Risorgimento from a Southern, socialist point of view, and probably from a rejuvenation movement point of view, though he was always Crocean enough to avoid the latter's excesses. As he wrote later in the *Notebooks*:

> De Sanctis fought for the creation *ex novo* in Italy of a national high culture, in opposition to the traditional older ones, rhetoric and Jesuitism (Guerrazzi and Father Bresciani). *La Voce* fought only for the dissemination, in an intermediate stratum, of this same culture, against provincialism, etc. *La Voce* was an aspect of militant Croceanism, because it wanted to democratize what was necessarily "aristocratic" in De Sanctis and maintained as "aristocratic" in Croce.[78]

In this period, perhaps the best way to understand Gramsci is as a "militant Crocean," one who drew on the new wave for its democratic temper but who still located himself in the long, neo-Hegelian stream of Italian high culture.[79] This was possible largely because the left-right cleavage of prewar Italian political and intellectual life was very much overshadowed and even confused by other, more dominating cleavages between North and South, positivist and anti-positivist, Marxist and anti-positivist radical, and rationalist and irrationalist. On each of these divides, Gramsci stood on the same side as Croce.

Of course, part of the reason for referring to Gramsci as a *militant* Crocean is that he also drew much inspiration from elsewhere, especially, in 1916-17, from the romantic socialist but non-Marxist or at least nonorthodox sector of the French intelligentsia: Romain Rolland, Charles Péguy, Henri Barbusse, and Georges Sorel.[80] What all these writers had in common was an intense preoccupation with the category of "will" and a moralism aimed at renewing the "consciousness" of the masses through education and culture. Marx and prominent Italian Marxists like Antonio Labriola and Rodolfo Mondolfo may also have been "militant" influences on him in this period.[81] Yet, as will be argued in the next chapter, Gramsci came to Marxism finally only through the Russian Revolution, an "idea-force" which merged his activist and idealist leanings with Marxist ones, or better, transcended the former in the name of the latter. Unlike Lukács, he did not come to Marx at the end of an essentially intellectual quest. He came to Marx as he had come to socialism: in search of answers to practical political problems.

Organizing a Collective Will

However, before turning directly to the question of the Russian Revolution and Gramsci's road to Marx, we need to explain the tensions in his Croceanism and his Southernism in the 1917-18 period, tensions which reflect a coming to grips with Marx but which have to do more directly with the practical problem that he had posed in *La Città Futura*:[82] how to organize the "collective will" necessary for an active and potent socialist left in Italy. This was a constant concern well prior to his inspiration from, or knowledge of, what was going on in Russia.

The principal issue over which Gramsci showed his critical distance from Croce was that of "prediction." While he could not accept the positivist presumption that prediction could and should achieve a factual description of the future, neither could he swallow Croce's absolute denial of that presumption. The problem, as he put it in *La Città Futura*, was that "in order to operate, man must be able to predict to some extent. . . . It is impossible to conceive of a collective will without a universal, concrete aim."[83] Two years later, he expanded on the point in a lucid passage which strikingly anticipates his view of prediction in the *Notebooks*:

History is continually being made and is therefore essentially unpredictable. But that does not mean that "everything" is unpredictable in the making of history, that history is arbitrary or irresponsible caprice. History is both freedom and necessity. Institutions, in whose development and activity history is incarnated, are drawn up and maintained because they have a task and a mission to realize. They draw up and develop the determinate objective conditions of the production of material goods and of the spiritual consciousness of men. If these objective conditions (which due to their mechanical nature are almost mathematically commensurable) change, then the sum of the relations which regulate and inform human society along with the degree of human consciousness changes also. The social pattern is transformed, traditional institutions are impoverished, they are inadequate to their tasks, and they become cumbersome and defunct. If in the making of history the intelligence were incapable of establishing a rhythm, of stabilizing a process, civilized life would be impossible. The political genius recognizes precisely this capacity of appropriating the greatest possible number of concrete terms which are necessary and sufficient for the purpose of examining a development process and therefore for anticipating the future both in the short and long run. On the basis of that intuition he sets up the activity of a state and ventures the fortunes of a people. In this sense Karl Marx was by far the greatest modern political genius.[84]

To use the language which Gramsci drew from Labriola and used in the *Notebooks*, history must be canvassed for "laws of tendency" which can then be exploited by a class acting on the basis of a collective will. In this earlier period, Gramsci seemed to be transcending Croce and approaching Marx by means of Gentile's doctrine that "man and reality, the instruments of labor and will, are not dissolved but identified in the historical act."[85]

The trouble with Croceanism, ultimately, was that in denying any possibility for knowledge of the future—for vision—it established the philosophical basis for reformism.[86] A true historicism, Gramsci thought, must forge the analytical basis for vision, and thus for revolution. "I am a revolutionary, an historicist," he wrote to a friend in 1918;[87] and in this revolutionary historicism, history is not an "idea" but an "idea-force."[88] History was indeed "contemporary" history, but in a different way than Croce had imagined.[89] Contemporary history meant a practical approach to political activism, that is, an approach which purges itself of all *apriorisms* through a continuous study of past events in the light of present needs.[90]

By 1918, Gramsci was also attacking Salvemini for his political idealism, which lacked firm grounding in an historical analysis of existing class relations. Yet, as in the case of Croce and historicism, Gramsci's early essays on the Southern Question owed a great deal to the man he would soon criticize. His first essay, "The South and the War," which appeared in *Il Grido del popolo* on April 1, 1916, retraced familiar ideas on the origins and political and economic character of the North-South split.[91] He argued that its cultural origins went back to Roman times, but that these had been of little practical consequence until the unification. What really made life in the South miserable from then on was the national policy of protectionism which supported Northern industry at the expense of the South. Accompanying that policy was the "unjust accusation" by Northerners that the South had suffered only because of a "lack of initiative." Gramsci was quick to note, however, that the inverse of this attitude would prove no better. The South did not need "special laws" or "special treatment." It needed equal power within the government to assert its priorities in the formation of national policy.

None of this was very different from Salvemini's long-held position. It is noteworthy that Gramsci did not link his discussion at this point with any specific political solution, revolutionary or not. But two months later, his central suggestion was for a policy of free trade.[92] How seriously he took this as an overall solution to the Southern Question is hard to tell. Certainly it is very much at odds with the "intransigent" socialism that he was moving toward at this time.[93] Yet there is some evidence that his attitudes toward the South and toward the proletariat were partially inconsistent even in his own mind. What sort of state is it that can be asked to institute free-trade "*liberismo*" and which nonetheless must be politically boycotted by the socialists? Gramsci attempted an answer in these terms: "The problem of the post-war era ought to be resolved not through class compromise but through a bourgeois initiative under the class stimulus of the proletariat."[94]

This was a hazy and precarious formulation, and by late 1919 he had overthrown it in favor of the more straightforward and politically tenable assertion that the Southern Question could only be resolved through a revolution establishing a communist state.[95] But even by June 1918, there were strong indications as to the direction his advocacy of the South was taking him. In an article entitled "The Politics of 'If,'" he lashed out at Salvemini for a utopianism which failed to confront the terms of the current class struggle.[96] Salvemini's was a "Protestant" view of history as progressive revelation, a view which "abstracted from the concrete form of economic and political life" and created "absolutes outside of time and space" which stymied practical political advance. Gramsci was also sharply critical of what he called Salvemini's "infinite faith in the efficacy of discussion and propaganda" united to an "organized social energy" which could really act as a political educator. Salvemini had divided the cultural and the political spheres so that he was not fully able to see either the political force of education or the necessity for the democratic participation of Southerners in institutions integrated with their culture. It was only a small step from this to his later insight that the solution to the Southern Question was proletarian revolution in the North.

What, then, was Gramsci's choice as the practical vehicle for organizing a "collective will"? The answer in the years before 1919 was simply the PSI. Of course, since the "intransigent" faction which he supported was in the minority and imposed its views only occasionally, his casting of the PSI for a role as the "active coefficient of Italian history"[97] was primarily by default. When the "intransigents" did control a national congress, as they did at Rome in September 1918, he could speak optimistically of how the party might educate the proletariat by "forcing the bourgeoisie to assume total responsibility for its actions. . . ."[98] On such occasions, he would stress the value of a party which, in developing precise definitions of its boundaries vis-à-vis the bourgeois state, could begin to create the proletarian "potential state" that he had advocated as early as 1914. More often, he was reduced to describing a much less radical PSI; and yet there were elements in its approach to politics of which he certainly approved. One was its internal democracy,[99] a value he never denied even when popular support for the "intransigents" was at its lowest ebb. Another was its idea that the party must be an organic expression of, and not an imposition on, the proletariat: "The socialists are not the commanders of a proletarian army, they are a part of the proletariat itself. . . . The socialists cannot be placed in a dualism with the proletariat."[100] Like other PSI factions, the intransigents would and should attempt to gain a consensus supporting their views. But this should be a natural consensus, a unity without tyranny.[101]

The emphasis on democracy, on "organicism," and on unity without tyranny were hardly the mainstay emphases of intransigence as seen by most of the faction, and certainly not by its leader, the Neapolitan Amadeo Bordiga. To understand Gramsci's mixed attitudes, it is necessary to describe the sources of "centrist" maximalism as well as of intransigence. The latter was rooted in Mussolini's 1912 triumph at Reggio Emilia, where the reformists were ousted from party leadership. The idea of establishing a separate proletarian identity through the party which Mussolini then put forward also tended to mean tight party organization at whatever cost to democratic procedures. Gramsci stood firmly behind the first half of this attitude, as was demonstrated by his article on the war and by his later practical support for the intransigent faction led by Bordiga after the Florence Conference in 1917. But he could not accept the latter half. When Mussolini abandoned the socialists for the greener pastures of nationalism, Giacinto Serrati took over the editorship of *Avanti!* and became one of the new PSI leaders. His new "centrist" emphasis was on establishing a well-formulated party program as a basis for proletarian education rather than on simply preparing for revolution through the internal discipline of intransigence. Mussolini had ridiculed "programs" and "education" on the grounds that proletarian understanding was always amorphous and rudimentary. Gramsci sided here very definitely with Serrati, despite the "economistic" and reformist character of his general position. Indeed, his major criticism of Serrati was that his stress on political education had not been great enough. Without activist political education the party could too easily become an oligarchic bastion, which, according to some contemporary pessimists like Michels, was always its inherent tendency.[102]

Like Bordiga's intransigents, then, Gramsci insisted on the necessity of a politics of proletarian autonomy vis-à-vis the bourgeois state. Yet his preoccupation with organizing a collective will through a politics of education was much closer to Serrati's view. This put him in the uncomfortable position of supporting a faction with which he disagreed in some important respects, and the result was a bifurcation in his political practice. Since he believed both in democratic mass politics and in the need for intransigent leadership of the proletariat, he could not abandon the party. Yet, inspired by Croce and Salvemini, he was committed to a politics of proletarian education which no faction of the party could satisfy.

The tension would persist until 1919, when he began to implement his ideas on proletarian education through the nonparty channel of workers' councils. But his writings already discussed the value and methods of proletarian education. As early as December 1916, he wrote a detailed article on it for the "School and Socialism" column in *Avanti!*[103] Applauding the effort to revitalize a "humanist current" in worker education, he nevertheless pointed to the danger of making this just a scholastic exercise. The danger would be especially great if one attempted to pursue proletarian goals by revamping traditional education. The schools would then remain what they had always been: "bourgeois institutions in the worst sense of the word." In existing schools, "the proletarian, even if he is intelligent, even if he has all the grades necessary to become a 'man of culture,' is compelled to waste his talents in other activities or to become an obstinate or self-taught person." A genuinely proletarian education, on the other hand, can avoid the dilettantism and narrow technical emphasis of the education that the worker receives from the bourgeoisie. The proletariat can and must create "a free school where initiative can be taken freely, not a school based on slavery and mechanization." But Gramsci did not yet see how to yoke this theoretical prescription to a socialist practice, and he contented himself with what must have later appeared to be a hopelessly romanticized image. The proletarian school, he suggested, should restore the Italian humanist tradition and seek to create the educational basis for twentieth-century "Renaissance men."

Only Gramsci's purpose was clear at this point. He hoped to overcome the sterile mechanicity of bourgeois-dominated life not simply by injecting a little "culture" into it from the outside, but by stimulating the worker himself to integrate cultural experience within his daily life. Having articulated this objective, he at least had a potent critical weapon against the educational norms of the bourgeoisie as well as against some of the "proletarian" educational experiments then being launched. One of these was the *Università popolare* of Turin.[104] This was a well-intentioned but misguided effort based on the same theoretical mistake that Gramsci had seen in Salvemini and for which he would later criticize Tasca—namely, dividing the cultural from the political and economic spheres. Culture could not be created and disseminated in isolation from everyday life; the *Università popolare* was simply too remote. It had equated education with a conventional curriculum in natural science, Italian literature, and philosophy. Except for the worker audience and the self-consciously "proletarian" point of view, it might easily have been mistaken for just another local night school.

In Gramsci's impatiently revolutionary view, the *Università popolare* looked "neither like a university, nor like a popular one."[105] A real proletarian university would be linked to the development of the revolution, for socialism is nothing if not "the future which is organized potentially in the present," and socialist education is nothing if not the "first nucleus" of the future society.[106] These phrases, which were fairly typical of Gramsci throughout the war years, show that he had already grasped the notion that present proletarian education, the coming revolution, and the future socialist society are all inextricably linked as one process. As we shall see, his understanding of the Russian Revolution helped to make this notion concrete, so that by 1919 he was able to institutionalize his idea of education in the worker council movement. There was, however, already a small anticipation of this shift.

In December 1917, Gramsci established his *Club di vita morale* dedicated to the educational advancement of some young socialist workers in Turin. His method was entirely Socratic and open-ended: "I . . . assign a paper to some young person, a chapter from Croce's *Cultura e vita morale* perhaps, or Salvemini's *Problemi educativi e sociali*, or his *Rivoluzione francese* or *Cultura e laicità*, or the *Communist Manifesto*, or a critical note from Croce's

Critica, or something else related to the contemporary idealist movement. . . . Then I or someone else replies." Apart from their inherent pleasure, these sessions were intended to illustrate how even a modest educational enterprise could answer those intransigents who thought the proletariat incapable of education. "In Turin we do not think it is enough just to preach verbally the principles and moral maxims to be realized in a socialist civilization. We have sought to organize this preaching, to give a new example (for Italy) of how to work together."[107] Discipline, proletarian autonomy, democratic political control, culture through education, and the democratic transmission of knowledge are all organically related in Gramsci's intransigence. No educational elite "towers above," for the Gramscian intellectual acts only to enter into a dialectic with the democratic organization of the masses, which itself has been founded on political and intellectual self-activity.[108] The *Club di vita morale* revealed the desirable pedagogical relationship in microcosm; the Russian Revolution had portrayed the revolutionary possibility of this strategy on the world stage. The Bolsheviks had won because they had organized a collective will through an "active pedagogy."[109] Moreover, they had done this not "through a definitive myth crystallized in an external formula" (a Sorelian stratagem that Gramsci belittled) but through the "self-determination [*auto-decisione*] of the governed."[110]

By 1918, then, Gramsci's understanding of political education was composed of the following interrelated ideas: a substantive "humanism" aimed at developing the whole proletarian person; a pedagogical activism which would mobilize the masses for revolution through their own self-activity; democratic participation with no special class of intellectuals and no "external formula"; a conceptual integration of culture, politics, and economics; a class-based education; and a cultural organization which acts as the "first nucleus" of the coming socialist society.

In addition, one can see already emerging an idea which will become of decisive importance in the philosophical standpoint of the *Prison Notebooks*. This is the idea that, through its own self-education, the proletariat is bringing about a cultural integration of the human race in industrial society:

It is through the critique of capitalist civilization that the unified consciousness of the proletariat is formed or is forming. Here *criticism* signifies *culture*, not spontaneous, naturalistic evolution.[111]

Effective criticism is the building of an alternative culture, one through which the values and aspirations of a class can be expressed. The bourgeoisie had developed such a culture in the medieval city states.[112] Unlike the bourgeoisie, the proletariat has never had an independent geographical base for the formation of its culture, a factor which has held back its development. But Gramsci would soon argue that it has an equally powerful alternative: to organize an autonomous and integrated culture around the proletarian institution which advanced industrialism has created—the factory. It was to this idea above all that, in 1919, he dedicated both his new journal, *Ordine Nuovo*, and the council movement that it theorized and promoted.

CHAPTER TWO

The "New Order" and Its Collapse

Marx did not write a nice little doctrine, he is not a messiah who left a file of parables. . . . His only categorical imperative, his only norm is "Workers of the world unite!"

(May 1918)

WITH THE nineteenth-century political world reduced to ashes by the First World War, the Bolshevik Revolution appeared to be the phoenix-like expression of a new political destiny for all of Europe.[1] Sympathetic or not, few observers in 1917 could avoid the suspicion that Marx's day might finally have arrived, if not quite in the way he had anticipated. "The war changed everything," wrote one disillusioned Hungarian who had served in the moderate postwar government overthrown by Bela Kun. "Bolshevism is simply the revival of the doctrine of the *Communist Manifesto* in an environment in which all the conditions of the Marxist prognosis are combined, not as Marx expected, through the free development of economic forces, but by an external factor, the war."[2]

The spectre which had haunted Europe seemed finally to be conquering her. Bolshevik-backed governments had brief triumphs in Germany, the German state of Bavaria, and Hungary. More moderate social-democratic or peasant socialist parties took over briefly in Finland, Poland, Austria, Bulgaria, and the Ukraine. Even in England, Lloyd George noticed that "the shock that came from Petrograd passed through every workshop and mine and produced a disquiet which made things difficult in recruitment and munitionment [of the army]."[3] By 1919, the British Socialists had already held a convention at Leeds which announced their intention to "do for Britain what the Russian Revolution has accomplished in Russia" and which passed a resolution calling for the establishment of worker and soldier soviets.[4]

This action was typical of the revolutionary fervor which gripped European socialism during the two years after the armistice that Italians dubbed the *biennio rosso*. Even in 1917, however, leftist journals in France and Italy spoke incessantly about the Russian events. Certainly no one growing up socialist then in those two countries could have avoided being affected by them (although, as we shall see, they were perceived rather differently than in later historical accounts). Gramsci was no exception; indeed, the Russian Revolution was the decisive experience of his early years. With dramatic suddenness it brought vitality and concrete meaning to his political activity. Against the Italian horizon, the revolution appeared as a sparkling mythic image of a possible future, one that would inspire him long after he was forced to abandon the immediate methods and strategies that he thought he had adapted from it.

Gramsci's Russia and the Road to Marx

In Gramsci's earliest writing on Russia, the events of March 1917 served as a kind of prism through which he could refilter and reassess his acquired philosophical conceptions and ideals. The test was not very fair, for he knew hardly anything reliable about Russia until July, when a delegation of Bolsheviks led by Joseph Goldenberg arrived in Turin.[5] Even several months after that, his information was still so sparse, and the distortion in the Italian press so great, that he would mistakenly take Chernov as the great world-historical figure in command.[6] Nonetheless, he was sure that the Russian events reaffirmed his overall political outlook. Thus, on April 29, 1917, he wrote an acid polemic against the "bourgeois press" for suggesting that the revolution could be adequately understood as a power play by the rising bourgeoisie to wrest the state from a crumbling autocracy.[7] To Gramsci this was an inapt attempt to locate the historical meaning of the Russian events through an analogy to the French Revolution of a century before. The Russians were not "Jacobins" bent on conquering a political majority through violence. Bourgeois revolutions were necessarily elitist because they represented only the interests of a class and lacked a universal program. The Russian revolutionaries, in contrast, "pursue an ideal which cannot be only for the few." They propose a fundamentally new society, one from which a whole new man can be born:

> As a result of the Russian revolution the man who was a common criminal has turned into the sort of man whom Immanuel Kant, the theoretician of absolute ethical conduct, had called for—the sort of man who says: the immensity of the heavens above me, the imperative of my conscience within me. What these brief news items reveal to us is a liberation of spirit, the establishment of a new moral awareness. It is the advent of a new order, one that coincides with everything our masters taught us.[8]

Through such idealist and romanticized language, Gramsci was able to forge a powerful myth which reinforced his own prior view of proletarian revolution as the steady ascension of a mass-based, educated, and organized collective will in which the final seizure of power is merely the climactic act of a broader process. In this process, proletarian power was revealed as something more than high wages and worker rights: it was a new society and a new man. Moreover, as he put it in a celebrated article, this was a "revolution against *Capital*," a concrete demonstration of the importance of "will" in history.[9] "The Bolsheviks repudiate Karl Marx, and their explicit actions and conquests bear witness that the canons of historical materialism are not as rigid as might have been and has been thought."

Of course, Gramsci's real enemy was not Karl Marx, not even the Karl Marx of *Capital.* His real enemy was the vulgarized Marxism which had become prominent in the Second International. Writers like Kautsky in Germany or Achille Loria in Italy had made a mockery of *Capital* by treating it almost as a mathematical equation for revolution. In an article written several weeks after "The Revolution against *Capital*," Gramsci argued that "the new generation" of Italian socialists "wants to return to the genuine doctrine of Marx. . . ."[10] Here he suggested implicitly that Marx himself would not have accepted the dogma which his celebrated treatise had become in the hands of its inheritors. The Bolsheviks had escaped the fate of being "Marxists" (just as Marx had declared he was not a "Marxist") because "they live the thought of Marx." Theirs was not an "external doctrine of dogmatic, indisputable statements" but a "continuation of Italian and German idealistic thought which in Marx was contaminated with positivist and naturalist encrustations." In this Marxism the central figures of history are not inanimate economic facts but flesh and blood men "who have together developed a collective, social will, who comprehend economic facts, evaluate them and adapt them to their will. . . ."[11] Marx could not be faulted for failing to predict the unpredictable. No one had foreseen a war of a length and intensity sufficient to create popular revolution in Russia. The Bolsheviks had simply been flexible enough to take advantage of an unforeseeable opportunity. The result was a full-scale proletarian revolution while socialists in the developed nations of Europe merely looked on.

Later articles added many details to this argument, but the basic contention that the revolution vindicated a politics of organized collective will was repeated again and again. The revolution was a world-historical pageant which had shown how the energy and imagination common to syndicalism, *La Voce*, Salveminian pedagogical politics, and Rolland's "optimism of the will" could be organized and disciplined. By 1918, Gramsci was picturing the Bolsheviks as revolutionary "historicists" who grasped politics in the proper context of its "historical development."[12] And he credited Lenin with having proved the historical decisiveness of political as opposed to economic factors in crisis periods, a contention he turned against Loria's crude positivism.[13] But the truly decisive influence of the revolution on his own political practice began to dawn only as the new shape of the Russian socioeconomic structure came to be somewhat more fully described in the Western press of 1918.[14]

The Bolsheviks, he then saw, had not simply conquered state power, they had substituted for it. "The essential fact of the Russian Revolution is the installation of a new type of state: the state of the councils [soviets]."[15] The Bolsheviks had used the "soviet" as an organizational base during their rise to power and then as the central organ controlling state power through direct producer representation.[16] Representation in the soviet was direct because it grew out of the institutions where people worked (factories, army regiments); it was democratic because soviet members were freely elected and could be recalled immediately for misconduct in office.[17] As this latter feature suggests, the historical model for the soviet was the Paris Commune, which Marx had eulogized and which Lenin's recent *State and Revolution* had made the model for socialist politics. Unlike the bourgeois state which Machiavelli theorized, the soviet was founded on the spontaneous expression of the masses, not on "the dictates of a 'hero' who imposes himself through violence."[18] The soviet was the concrete utopia which had eluded the liberals because of their alliance with capitalism. It expressed well how an essentially economic institution could go beyond its formal purpose to serve as the foundation for a reconstruction of the political process in proletarian terms. This fusion of economics and politics also provided ideal terrain for a proletarian education in which "criticism" might become "culture."

However, Gramsci was not immediately able to translate the theoretical advance represented by the Russian soviet into Turinese practice. He filled the 1918 issues of *Il Grido del popolo* with his first sustained discussions of socio-economic policy and organization before settling on the formulation we will come to shortly. What he did see immediately, however, was that Italy and Russia shared class structures and socioeconomic backgrounds similar enough to allow their revolutions to be waged in the same terms. Both countries had large peasant masses preserved from the feudal era for lack of commercial development linking town and country. Moreover, both peasantries had been profoundly radicalized by the war and were ready for a tactical alliance with the proletariat. And in a striking anticipation of his later emphasis on the importance of "organic intellectuals" in the development of an insurgent class, Gramsci argued that while both these proletariats were relatively small, each had produced or attracted intellectual classes which were potentially revolutionary since, unlike the developed states of Western Europe, neither Russia nor Italy had a bureaucracy strong enough to co-opt them.[19]

Armed with faith in this parallel, Gramsci set out to construct an Italian equivalent of the "soviet" in 1919. But before turning to that project, let us review Gramsci's road to Marx and comment briefly on his understanding of Lenin in this period. We have seen that Gramsci turned to socialism in 1913, though far more for its efficacy in dealing with the Southern Question than for any "proletarian" or Marxist commitment. We have also seen that he studied Marxism at the University in 1915 and lectured on the topic in 1916. But his early writing reveals a predominantly Crocean orientation, even if it is an increasingly critical and "militant" Croceanism which he may have been trying to reconcile with a Marxist perspective. This is suggested, for instance, by his reading of Marx and Labriola in 1917 as well as by his reading of Gentile, whose *Philosophy of Spirit as a Pure Act* (1916) could well lead to a Marxism conceived as a philosophy of the "impure act."[20]

Yet what I want to suggest is that it is only with the arrival of the Russian Revolution that Gramsci turned squarely toward Marx. Even then he was careful to qualify his commitment in a generational sense: his was the "genuine Marx" of the new generation, not the hobbled and bifocaled positivism of Turati, Treves, and their reformist fellows. His Marx, like his Croce, was a "master of spiritual and moral life,"[21] not of political economy. Much of Gramsci's writing on Bolshevism, as we have seen, was an attempt to identify them with "German and Italian idealist thought." The question, then, is not one of relinquishing idealism but of transcending it in a dialectical *Aufhebung* (a canceling, preserving, and overcoming, all at once). Marx himself must be purged of his "positivist and naturalist encrustations"—perhaps one source of Gramsci's long hesitation in embracing Marx—in order to bring fully into view what is truly important and distinctive about his philosophy:

> Marx did not write a nice little doctrine, he is not a messiah who left a file of parables pregnant with categorical imperatives, of absolute indisputable norms independent of time and space. His only categorical imperative, his only norm is "Workers of the world unite!" The duty of organization, the propaganda for the need to organize and align should be the factors used to separate Marxists from non-Marxists.[22]

As a master of spiritual and moral life, Marx had insisted on the imperative to organize as his fundamental teaching. The Bolsheviks had learned this lesson, built soviets, and waged a revolutionary war which reconciled the idealist emphasis on will and historical creativity with socialist politics.

There is, however, some room for misinterpretation here, since this is not to suggest that Gramsci came to Marx through Lenin, or that he was "Leninist" and therefore "Marxist." No one doubts that Gramsci's friend and fellow activist, Piero Gobetti, was right when he wrote that "the figure of Lenin appeared to him [Gramsci] as a heroic will of liberation."[23] But the Lenin whom Gramsci knew in 1917-20 was hardly the purveyor of orthodox "Marxism-Leninism" admired by Stalin and Mao. As the articles by Lenin that Gramsci reprinted in *Ordine Nuovo* make abundantly clear,[24] Gramsci's was a most libertarian Lenin, a democrat, an organizer of soviets, and a leader of a mass-based party conscious of the need for the political education and cultural autonomy of the proletariat.[25] To be sure, Gramsci knew of *What Is to Be Done?* at least by late 1919, but he passed it off as an "old thesis of Lenin's on the 'qualified' revolutionary."[26] Lenin's important works were his contemporary ones like *State and Revolution*, which Gramsci characterized as "indispensable to an understanding of the Bolshevik revolution."[27]

This impression of Lenin was widespread in Europe at this time and seems to have been fostered by Lenin himself. Whether owing to a newfound "anarcho-syndicalism"[28] or to a shrewd sense for socialist diplomacy (or both), Lenin's writings in the two years after his speech at the Finland Station were very different in style and argument from those which had accompanied his rise to power. Now he exalted the soviet as a replacement for the bourgeois state, even though his earlier writings show that he had not expected the soviets to arise either in 1905 or 1917 and that their "anarcho-syndicalist tendencies" were to be deplored.[29] Apparently, he had private misgivings about them even in 1917. In July he told his fellow Bolsheviks: "Soviets may appear in this new revolution, and indeed are bound to, but *not* the present soviets. . . . The present soviets have failed, have suffered complete defeat, because they are dominated by the Socialist-Revolutionary and Menshevik parties."[30] But in his articles written for foreign consumption, such as those printed in *Ordine Nuovo* or his "Letter to American Workingmen," which Gramsci very likely read as well, Lenin underscored both the importance of the soviets and their highly democratic character. Apparently, what was domestically suspect was internationally useful; but whatever the source of the discrepancy, the point is that Gramsci could not have been aware of it.

The "New Order" in Turin

When the Bolsheviks proclaimed the triumph of the revolution from Red Square, workers in Finland, Germany, Bavaria, Holland, Poland, Austria, Hungary, and England responded with the spontaneous generation of local "soviets." Mirroring the political systems in which they were situated, these soviets varied widely both within and between nations. Though not generally insurrectionary in England, they played a major role in organizing the abortive Spartacist Revolt in Germany.[31] But in every case they expressed a generic opposition to the conventional wisdom of the European socialist parties that one creates the new society only after the seizure of political power. Thus, in organizing soviets or worker councils in Turin, "the Italian Petrograd," Gramsci was not only participating in a Europe-wide phenomenon, but he was also attaching himself to a particular ideological orientation which grew logically from his earlier theoretical and practical outlook and which received an unusually full, as well as a distinctive and imaginative, formulation in his writings. Our concern here, however, will not be to explore these historical interrelationships or even the history of the councils in the *biennio rosso* itself, which is well treated elsewhere.[32] Nor am I particularly concerned with a critical estimate of the historical efficacy of Gramsci's council strategy. It may well be that he treated the councils in a transhistorical manner when they were in fact rooted in a particular and very transitory "productivist" moment in the history of European labor.[33] Even within that moment they shared the sad fate of the rest of their genus. Whether they would have been able to buck this fate had party-council relations been carried out according to Gramsci's design remains as unanswerable a question as it was in 1920.[34]

What we are concerned with here is a careful reconstruction of Gramsci's *Ordine Nuovo* vision in its totality as a theory of political and economic organization. We will then be in a position to understand it as an emerging stage in his political and cultural theory, one which already incorporated many of the key ideas that will appear later in the *Notebooks.* For as the last part of the chapter will show, Gramsci did not abandon this *Ordine Nuovo* vision when he helped to found the new PCI at Livorno in January 1921. On the contrary, he accepted the new party as the necessary complement to the councils which the *Ordine Nuovo* vision had always entailed but which the PSI had never fulfilled.

What, then, was this "new order" proclaimed by Gramsci and his Turin comrades? Perhaps the best place to begin is with the journal itself. *Ordine Nuovo* was established in May 1919 just as Italy's postwar political crisis was intensifying amid strikes, food riots, and strident demands for a new constituent assembly. The four former Turin University students who founded it conceived it as a "weekly review of socialist culture." Now twenty-eight, Gramsci was their natural leader. Unlike the others—Angelo Tasca (twenty-seven), Umberto Terracini (twenty-four), and Palmiro Togliatti (twenty-six)—he had been disqualified from military service and had been active as a journalist throughout the war. Long infatuated with the idea of a proletarian *La Voce,* he had tried two years earlier to turn *Il Grido del popolo* into a "journal of culture" and had written most of the short-lived *La Città Futura.*[35] Tasca, however, had been the one to raise the 6,000 lire necessary to start publication; and though Gramsci was always formally listed as editor, he claimed that Tasca's views had prevailed at the beginning. As a socialist with long-standing ties to the trade union movement, Tasca was suspicious of promoting Italian worker councils, and Gramsci said later that the first six issues of the review expressed nothing but a "vague passion for a vague proletarian culture."[36] Early in June, Gramsci and Togliatti, backed by Terracini, "plotted an editorial coup d'etat." Gramsci took full control of the seventh issue and used it to analyze "the problem of the factory committees."[37] From then on his editorial model was the French journal *Clarté,* edited by Henri Barbusse.[38] Like Lunacharski's *Proletkult* in Russia, Gramsci thought *Clarté* had tried "to find a gathering point between the working class and the intellectuals," a literary marriage of theory and practice.[39] With this as a guiding precept, Gramsci achieved considerable notice. Circulation remained largely restricted to Turin itself, but it reached 3,000 in the first year and almost 6,000 in the second.[40] *Ordine Nuovo* published articles by numerous well-known foreign writers such as Lenin, Romain Rolland, Anatole France, Sylvia Pankhurst, and even Walt Whitman. Moreover, it earned Lenin's commendation as "fully in keeping with the fundamental principles of the Third International."[41]

Gramsci's criticism of Tasca was the familiar one that he had leveled at Salvemini and the *Università popolare*. Tasca had divided culture and education from the worker's political and economic experiences. He had made *Ordine Nuovo* "a journal of abstract culture and abstract information" which could just as easily "have come out of Naples, Caltanisetta or Brindisi."[42] Gramsci's object was to make it a journal in which workers

> found something of themselves, their own better selves. . . . The articles in *Ordine Nuovo* were not of cold intellectual construction but flowed out of our own discussions with the best workers and set forth the feelings, wishes, real passions of the Turin working class of which we had partaken and which we had stimulated.[43]

This was only possible because of the activity shared by the workers and the young intellectual editorship: the formation and management of the workers' councils. In rejecting the councils, Tasca had failed to appreciate the meaning of political education.

We have said that the major inspiration for the new worker councils came from Lenin and the Russian experience. One might also cite the influence of Daniel DeLeon, Max Eastman's *Liberator*, and the English shop-steward committees whose structure Gramsci studied in 1918.[44] And given the existence of the Italian "internal commissions," established in 1906 under French syndicalist inspiration, Gramsci's problem was not creation *ex nihilo*. Nonetheless, what he proposed in his June 1919 article, "Workers' Democracy," was dramatically original.[45] Given his intense concern that the new councils be a direct outgrowth and active expression of proletarian life, he suggested an organizational structure based in part on the factory and in part on geography. Ward committees within Turin would establish themselves, first by surveying the worker population of their zone and then by ensuring that each production unit of each factory within the zone elected a ward delegate. While these elections would vary according to ward size, the aim would be one delegate per fifteen workers. These delegates would then elect from among themselves an overall factory council in such a way that each craft within the factory would be represented. The final ward council would be made up of one member from each factory council and one member from each distinct group of unorganized, non-factory workers (e.g., waiters, railway workers, clerks, etc.) within the district.

Once the ward committees were operating smoothly, Gramsci hoped it would be possible to create Turin-wide "urban commissariats."[46] One can thus begin to see how the council network, when brought into rapport with party and trade union structures in ways we will soon specify, could appear to Gramsci as the "potential state" that he had spoken of in 1914. However, though the emphasis here is on large-scale and encompassing structures, later articles would increasingly emphasize local factory councils as the real basis for worker democracy. Such councils were conceived as public, not private, institutions; the worker participates in them "as a producer, i.e. as a consequence of his universal character . . . and in the same way that the citizen participates in the democratic parliamentary state."[47]

Since the network of councils is a "model of the proletarian state,"[48] growing beside the present state and challenging it, Gramsci from the beginning insisted on the importance of its educational function. Within each factory, elected "commissars"[49] ran "labor schools" aimed at discovering the full meaning of being a producer as opposed to a mere wage-earner. On one level these schools were concerned with increasing worker skills within each craft area. Even here the pervading spirit was highly idealistic: workers were encouraged to think of new ways to increase productivity and skill in workmanship, even if short-run profits did accrue to the capitalist owners. The "School of Culture and Socialist Propaganda" operated at a second level. Through lectures and discussions, usually held at night, the worker was introduced to the idea of councils as an emerging proletarian state which would obliterate the distinction between "bourgeois" and "citizen" that had preoccupied progressive political theory from Rousseau onward.[50] Through his activity in the factory, the worker could become both a producer of public welfare and a self-governing person.

Did this system of political education also have a more immediate goal? There is no doubt that Gramsci hoped to use the "School of Culture and Socialist Propaganda" along with *Ordine Nuovo* itself as a means of shoring up the working class's self-confidence in its own ability to direct society. Yet, beyond this the intention is less clear. Some commentators have argued that Gramsci perceived a deeply "alienated" condition within the working classes.[51] As a commodity in the labor market, "every citizen is a gladiator who sees in others enemies to be destroyed or to be subjugated to his will; all the higher links of solidarity and love are dissolved, from the artisans' corporations and classes to religion and the family."[52] Education toward a socialist culture serves, in this view, the essentially restorative purpose of resoldering the collective linkages which capitalist society has torn asunder. Others have suggested that, far from championing the need to overcome worker "alienation," Gramsci was an advocate of Taylorism, the "scientific organization of labor."[53] Taylorism was not concerned with the worker-as-exploited but with the worker-as-producer, one who must learn to be still more efficient and, in this sense, still more competitive. Taylorism sought "to produce a new type of worker, sober, disciplined, industrious, and monogamous," a person capable of revolution but also of industrial management.[54]

If Gramsci, as a Marxist, necessarily had a keen sense for the deprivations of the working class under capitalism, it is also true that he never developed a systematic analysis of "reification" as a total cultural system, as the young Lukács would do in 1923.[55] Gramsci's instincts were always more puritanical than culturally liberating in an expansive and nonrepressive way. Though he himself never declared openly for Taylorism (or "productivism") in the early writings, he gave it tacit support by publishing a series of articles praising it in *Ordine Nuovo*.[56] Certainly he had no illusions about the degree of diligence and instinctual sacrifice that would be necessary if workers were to run the state, as is indicated, for instance, by his later support for American Prohibition.[57] Yet it is equally a mistake to assimilate Gramsci's "productivism" to the theories of industrial management so popular with the PCI in the post-World War II era.[58] For while productivism in the latter context has become essentially an end in itself, Gramsci's version was always a means to the higher end of a new proletarian culture. The education of the worker councils as we have outlined it involved both the inculcation of "skills" and an emancipatory thrust aimed at fostering genuine "creativity." For the councils were not merely the pulsating nodes in a cost-efficient bureaucracy; they were the crucial ethico-political mediations of an emerging proletarian state and a new, integrated cultural totality.

What, then, of the relations between the councils and the other parts of the state such as the party and the trade unions? In his article on "Workers' Democracy," Gramsci had suggested that the "urban commissariats" might be "controlled and disciplined by the PSI and the craft federations."[59] It is difficult to tell precisely what he meant by this, and the article, which is only exploratory, does not clarify it elsewhere. Perhaps it was only a diplomatic concession or reassurance to the more traditional working-class leaders. This seems likely with respect to the craft federations, since Tasca's objections must have been in the forefront of his mind in this, the very first issue after the "editorial coup d'etat." Moreover, Gramsci reversed himself on this point once the councils were established.[60] In the case of party control and discipline, however, it seems more likely that he was seeking to theorize the mutual dependence of mass will and socialist consciousness, of workers and intellectuals. Prior to 1919, Gramsci had envisioned the organization of a collective will within the mass democratic setting of the PSI. Now that the primary mass organization would function outside the party and include many non-socialists, he saw that the PSI should take on a new dialectical role as the embodiment of "vigilant revolutionary consciousness."[61] This is why he argued in the same article that "precisely because the party must carry out this task [of Communist education], it cannot throw open its doors to an invasion of new members who are not accustomed to the exercise of responsibility and discipline."[62] Only a disciplined party could provide a successful counterpoint to the broadly based organizational hierarchy of the councils. Without it the mass will created by the councils might never seize on a single purpose and might dissipate instead into factionalism.

However, Gramsci was not very precise at this point about the organizational arrangements that he advocated for the party. One must therefore be careful in labeling his view. Certainly it represented more of a "vanguard" organization than he would previously have accepted, yet this is the very opposite of a "Leninist vanguard" as the phrase is conventionally understood. For Gramsci, both the council-party as well as the council-union relationships must, in essence, be based on council dominance. Parties and trade unions, having arisen "in the sphere of bourgeois democracy and political liberty,"[63] can never be the central organizational components of a revolutionary process. In contrast to the public character of the councils, they are private, voluntary organizations and can only play a secondary role as "the direct and responsible agents of the successive acts of liberation."[64] Ultimately their significance will fade entirely, since the revolution is to produce "a world organized on the model of a large engineering works, a Communist International in which every people, every part of humanity acquires a characteristic personality by its performance of a particular form of production and no longer by its organization as a state with particular frontiers."[65] The factory council is described as the "first cell" of this process; union and party have no place in it.

How, then, did Gramsci characterize the organization and activities proper to party and union as revolutionary "agents"? With respect to the party, the answer is essentially this: the party is to "guide" the revolution by educating the proletariat in a passive, representational sense. It is also to guide it militarily toward the seizure of power. But it is not to "make" the revolution even by playing an active role in the formation of councils.[66] Gramsci was heavily critical of the German Social Democrats for having intervened so directly in the formation of the German council movement.[67] Their policy had been based on a major theoretical mistake. Thinking they needed to be both democratic internally and capable of "dominating history," they "forced the process of the German proletarian revolution violently into their own organizational forms." The artificiality of this solution compromised both goals. The solution was not democratic because when they did create councils, they created them by fiat in order to have "a secure majority of their own men in them." But it was also incompatible with revolutionary efficiency, since in casting their own organizational net so wide, they could not help but "shackle the revolution and domesticate it."[68] What Gramsci now saw was that if the relationship between council and party were correctly construed as highly interdependent, both proletarian democracy and revolutionary efficiency could be achieved at higher levels than in the traditional democratic party approach to revolution. Democracy would be much increased because by basing it in the councils it would include *all* workers, would be much more participatory, and would be directly linked to everyday life. Revolutionary control would also be enhanced because the party would include only dedicated socialist militants, would give up its impossible task of trying to coordinate the activities of all proletarian organizations, and would therefore inspire and guide proletarian consciousness with a singular purpose.

Of course, even in theorizing such a dialectical view of organization, Gramsci did not deny the advantages in gaining a majority of communists within local councils. He simply thought it would be in the party's best interest to seek this only through indirect acitivity.[69] A good first step would be to get its own house in order. Where Gramsci thought the "intransigents" were right was in insisting upon the creation of a revolutionary program which by its very existence would "deny the bourgeois state apparatus its democratic basis in the consent of the governed."[70] The intransigent program, with its stress on proletarian autonomy, had created the possibility of undercutting what Gramsci would later call the "hegemony" of the bourgeoisie, i.e., its social, political, and cultural legitimacy. Such a program was extremely important in creating the political climate in which a system of councils could be seen as an alternative state.

But in terms of its organization, Gramsci's conception of the party was not "Bordighist" any more than it was "Leninist." As the leader of the intransigents, Bordiga had become obsessed with the formation of an all-powerful vanguard steeling itself for the task of carrying out what was essentially a revolution from above. Gramsci ridiculed such a party as "a collection of dogmatists or little Machiavellis . . . which makes use of the masses for its own heroic attempts to imitate the French Jacobins."[71] In contrast, his conception is poised delicately between popularism and elitism. The party does not "make" the revolution, yet it is composed exclusively of dedicated militants and is, in this broad sense, an elite. Gramsci's new integrated theory of political organization must be grasped as a dialectical relation between the formation of critical consciousness in the councils and the symbolic and military guidance entrusted to the party.

What about the trade unions? Could they also exercise a revolutionary function? To a surprising degree, Gramsci answered this in the affirmative despite his generally contemptuous attitudes toward the legalism and reformism of existing unions. In part this was because many Italian workers, even in Turin, were not yet organized in any form; joining a trade union was a helpful, if only a first step in the development of a socialist consciousness. More importantly, Gramsci recognized that unions were instrumental in the intellectual and technical formation of what he would later call "organic intellectuals," i.e., intellectual products of class-specific, in this case proletarian, activities.[72] And, most important of all, the "centralized and absolutist character" of the union structures meant that they could play the same role vis-à-vis capitalist industry that the party was to play vis-à-vis the capitalist state. Just as the party was to symbolize the political embodiment of socialist consciousness, unions could symbolize its industrial embodiment by presiding over the new socialization of industry.[73] The Russian experience, Gramsci believed, had shown how important unions could be in directing the work forces of a communist society.[74]

However, prior to revolution, Gramsci recognized a very strong tendency in trade unions to function as "an integral part of capitalist society."[75] Unions represent workers yet live in the compromise status of "industrial legality."[76] They necessarily treat workers as wage-earners, not as producers, and are thus "competitive not communist."[77] In each of these ways they contrast directly and unfavorably with worker councils. Councils are "the negation of industrial legality";[78] they organize producers, not wage-earners; and they are "based on the organic and concrete unity of the craft as it is realized in the discipline of the industrial process," rather than simply on the "individual" members of the craft.[79] As creators of the "producer mentality," councils allow a self-realization which overcomes the false dichotomy of bourgeois and citizen.[80] Yet their ability to do this is predicated upon their autonomy from all institutional collaboration with capitalism. Both unions and councils have a role to play in organizing the new society, but these roles must be exercised autonomously. In the end, the only olive branch that Gramsci was willing to hold out from the councils to the Tascas of Turin was his hope that "the majority or a substantial number of the electors to the council would be organized in unions."[81]

Gramsci's insistence on the subordination of party and union to council in his "new order" was hardly designed to promote its popularity. Certainly there is room to argue that his political strategy was unduly divisive as well as somewhat vague in its formulation. Yet there is also a tension in it which no amount of diplomacy or specification of details could have alleviated. One sees this tension in the party itself. As Gwyn Williams has written: "The operation called for, however—a toughly centralized and communist party, operating in a *completely libertarian* manner in the heart of the whole mass of the working population—was to say the least, dialectically delicate!"[82] Yet this tension between educational and military functions characterizes not only Gramsci's conception of the party but his vision as a whole. Gramsci's metaphors for the proletariat's path continually alternate between the educational and the military. The factory councils would be "a magnificent school of political and administrative experience" that could "effect a radical transformation of the worker's mentality." As such they are the key to organizing what he would later call the alternative "hegemony" of the working class. But the workers are also an army. "Each factory would make up one or more regiments of this army, which would have to have its own N.C.O.'s, its own liaison services, officer corps and general staff, with all powers being delegated by free election and not imposed in an authoritarian manner."[83] Clearly, Gramsci was seeking to reconcile the principles of education and democracy with those of efficiency and control. That he never achieved a successful blend became tragically apparent to all in the spring and fall of 1920.

The tension was reflected in a still deeper ambiguity in the way Gramsci theorized the nature of revolution itself. We have seen that he had always conceived of revolution not as some specific event or set of events but as a "dialectical process of historical development."[84] Revolution was the building of an alternative system of economic and political institutions which could substitute for the existing bourgeois state. Indeed, a successful seizure of power prior to the proper institutionalization of an alternative would leave the new regime paralyzed and "incapable of anything except repeated and desperate attempts to create by fiat the economic conditions it needs to survive and grow stronger."[85] Yet, in drawing the parallel between the socioeconomic conditions of Italy and those of Russia, Gramsci had also suggested that the possibility of a proletarian seizure of power was close at hand. The devastation wreaked by the war, he believed, had substituted in Italy, as it had in Russia, for the full development of capitalist contradictions as the "objective conditions" for revolution.[86] Once the council movement was flourishing in 1920, he became obsessed not with the institutional but with the military aspects of revolution. During the September occupation of the factories, when the PSI seemed incapable of taking the initiative to become revolutionary and seize power, Gramsci was outraged. "Revolution is like war," he wrote in a blistering reprimand to Serrati and others in the PSI leadership. "It must be minutely prepared by a working class general staff, just as a war is by the Army's general staff . . . ," and it "must be led without prior consultation, without the apparatus of representative assemblies."[87]

Four years later, Gramsci would isolate the source of this ambiguity in his overestimation of the parallels between the Russian and Italian situations.[88] And though he would continue to explain the Italian proletariat's defeat largely in terms of the political incapacity of the PSI, he would also note the isolation of the insurgents in Turin. Certainly, Turin was distinctive in its proletarian zeal, and the revolutionary aspirations of the worker movements even in other Northern Italian cities paled in comparison. Yet if in his enthusiasm for worker councils and for Turin he had held the Southern Question in abeyance, Gramsci had not entirely forgotten the South and the peasantry even in 1920. Several articles in *Ordine Nuovo* show his preoccupation with it, and he even suggested the formation of peasant councils.[89] Largely through his influence, the Turin worker councils had actually set up study committees in 1920 to investigate the possibility of better relations with the peasants.[90] Yet the failure of the "new order" to spread across Italy was symptomatic of the still more serious problem of its failure to gain the adherence of either of the major left-leaning factions in the PSI.

Both Bordiga and Serrati viewed the activities of Gramsci's *Ordine Nuovo* group (the *ordinovisti*) with a measure of circumspection and distrust which sometimes lapsed into open hostility. Though they may privately have approved of the revolutionary passions that the councils were exciting in Turin, neither of them would offer *Ordine Nuovo* any public support. Bordiga argued that the factory councils embodied an old reformist mistake in new dress—namely, "that the proletariat can emancipate itself by winning territory within economic relations while capitalism still holds political power through the state."[91] This was quite ironic in view of Gramsci's efforts to distance the councils from trade unionism and the sharp attacks that his stance provoked from reformist leaders like Turati.[92] But from his vantage point in Naples, Bordiga thought that the advanced industrial conditions prevalent in Turin had led to a placing of the cart before the horse. Even if *ordinovismo* worked there, it would never be realistic as a national formula for revolution.

Serrati's objections were more confined to a defense of the party mainstream against what he regarded as an unwelcome rival. On the one hand, he was anxious to subordinate the councils to the PSI: "The only possible dictatorship of the proletariat is a conscious dictatorship by the PSI."[93] Careful not to cross swords with Lenin, he insisted on the absolute difference between the political leadership of "soviets, the political organs and governing powers of a victorious revolution" and the "syndicalism" of councils, "technical organs of production and industrial organization."[94] On the other hand, he was unyielding in his opposition to any transformation of the party (such as the expulsion of the reformists) which might increase the potency of its revolutionary leadership.

The three-sided controversies between Gramsci, Bordiga, and Serrati are extremely involved and will be touched on below only insofar as they illuminate the nature of Gramsci's response to the events of 1920.[95] Yet, before turning to this question, it will be helpful to reflect on the charges of reformism and syndicalism made against Gramsci in light of what we have already seen of his new order.

Bordiga's contention that the worker councils were nothing but "reformist experiments"[96] reveals at least as much about Bordiga as about Gramsci and the councils. From his formation of the "intransigents" in 1917, to his insistence on "electoral abstentionism" in 1919, to his call for a purely Communist Party in 1920, Bordiga had been fixated on the single goal of forming a tight-knit revolutionary elite which would stand in stark opposition to bourgeois politics. Any socialist tactic which failed to place prime emphasis on this goal struck him as "reformist" because in one way or another it was cooperating with, or at least recognizing, the existing political system. This prejudice prevented Bordiga from ever really understanding Gramsci, even though there was a germ of truth in what he said. Gramsci, by his own admission, had been influenced by the reformist emphasis on political education, particularly as articulated by the French journalist and essayist Charles Péguy.[97] And if one compares Gramsci's writings with those of Eduard Bernstein on this point, one can easily perceive a superficial resemblance. Both seemed to be arguing that a properly socialist manipulation of institutions in bourgeois society could generate what Bernstein had called "levers for the socialist emancipation."[98] Yet the "levers" that Bernstein had in mind were institutions that he himself conceded were "bourgeois": parliaments, cooperatives, trade unions, and so forth.[99] The point was simply to get workers involved in participatory activities so that they would want to play a more active role in bourgeois political affairs and thus become capable of reshaping these affairs to correspond more with their own class interests. Gramsci's worker council vision, as we have seen, was designed to overcome bourgeois political processes at the same time as it prepared workers for revolution. Only someone unwilling to see such a vast difference could possibly have ignored it.

Serrati's claim that Gramsci was "more inspired by the English syndicalism of the shop-steward movement than by the Russian example [of soviets]"[100] is more penetrating, for Gramsci himself acknowledged such an influence along with those of DeLeon and Sorel. Apparently, the respect was mutual. Though DeLeon died in 1914 and thus could never have heard of an Italian soviet, Sorel once told an interviewer that:

> Rather than asking Kautsky and his emulators for the design of the city of the future, let [the workers] carry out their education by conquering more extensive powers in the factories. This should be the work of the Communists! The experience they are undergoing in the Fiat plants is more important than all the writings published by *Neue Zeit.*

To thwart some of his critics, Gramsci proudly quoted this remark in *Ordine Nuovo.*[101] Clearly he was influenced by Sorel's view that the proper task of the workers was to organize the factory and then to use it as a base for organizing the whole of social life. Yet he left no doubt that he lacked the stomach for the often mindless and undialectical fixation of syndicalists on violence and direct action, as well as for their tendency to conceive of the self-governing factory severed from all interaction with centralized, guiding institutions. "We do not accept the syndicalist theory," he wrote. "We have no sympathy for those unbridled habits and glittering mental vanity which syndicalist theory has introduced into our country."[102] Reflecting back on syndicalism in 1926, however, Gramsci explained its historical experience in Italy rather sympathetically. Syndicalism was the "instinctive, elementary, primitive but healthy expression of the working-class reaction against the bloc with the bourgeoisie and in favor of a bloc with the peasants, *and especially with the peasants of the South.*"[103] Given Gramsci's own early enthusiasm for *La Voce* and his advocacy of the South, he may well have been recalling an early attachment to syndicalism as well. Yet these reflections also make clear why he eventually had to separate from syndicalism. What it lacked was a political theory, and specifically a theory of political organization, which could have led beyond the "new liberalism"—"more energetic, more aggressive, more pugnacious than traditional liberalism" but no more imaginative in its choice of institutions—which it necessarily adopted by default.[104] While Gramsci struggled for several years before eventually locating an acceptable alternative through Marx and the Russian Revolution, the more impulsive syndicalists had "passed over to nationalism; in fact the Nationalist Party was originally constituted by ex-syndicalist intellectuals."[105] This was a tragic failure for which the only compensation was that it was one of imagination and not of the will.

Revolt in the PSI

Unfortunately for Gramsci, the existing PSI was not playing the role his *Ordine Nuovo* designs required, nor did it show much sympathy for them. Though Gramsci had never supported Serrati's leadership, he had in 1919 been entirely preoccupied with the councils, and his criticisms of the party were left largely unvoiced. The silence ended in December 1919, as the political consequences of the PSI's surprisingly strong showing in the November national elections were becoming manifest.[106] He now openly attacked the PSI both for its increasingly collaborationist attitude and for its arrogant new sense of self-sufficiency, which it dressed up with the "revolutionary myth that equates proletarian power with the dictatorship of the system of Socialist Party sections."[107] Had these last words been written two months earlier, they might plausibly have been read as a criticism of Bordiga's program of electoral abstentionism, elite revolution, and party dictatorship, from which Gramsci had carefully distanced himself in 1919. Then, Bordiga had symbolized the very real danger of a narrow, sectarian PSI, isolated from creative contact with the working masses. But this danger was put to rest by the elections, and, as Gramsci's references to German Social Democracy made clear, he was now retargeting his principal attack on the amorphous ensemble which Serrati, the Italian Kautsky, was already commanding. This PSI was "utopian" and "disastrous" because it refused to perceive that "the revolutionary process can only be identified with a spontaneous movement of the working masses brought about by the clash of contradictions inherent in the social system . . . of capitalist property."[108] Presciently, in view of the events of 1920, he complained that any party which attempted to organize revolution entirely on its own, without links to workers organized in the factory, "would unconsciously become an organ of conservatism."[109]

During the postal-telegraph and railway strikes of January 1920, to which the PSI had given little visible support, Gramsci lashed out at Serrati in no uncertain terms:

> The country is racked by feverish spasms, the forces eroding bourgeois democracy, and the capitalist regime continue to operate implacably and ruthlessly, and yet the Party does not intervene, does not illuminate the broad masses of workers and peasants, does not justify its activity or its non-activity, does not launch slogans to calm impatience, check demoralization, and maintain closed ["*serrati*"] ranks and strong links between worker and peasant armies. The Party, which had become the greatest historical force in the Italian nation, has fallen prey to a crisis of political infantilism and is today the most crippling of the social weaknesses of the Italian nation.[110]

Yet, serious as this diagnosis is, Gramsci's prescription at this point was only that communist workers should increase their militance within the Party to "prevent the petty-bourgeois opportunists from reducing it to the level of so many other parties in this land of Pulcinella."[111]

By May, his taste for such sardonic prodding had been worn thin by the PSI's refusal to support the April General Strike in Piedmont, which had consequently been lost. In "Towards a Renewal of the Socialist Party," which appeared in *Ordine Nuovo* on May 8, Gramsci offered much the same analysis as in January, but he now linked it to a new threat and a somewhat refurbished prescription for "renewal." If the Party could not "impress upon the masses the conviction that there is an order within the terrible disorder of the present," if it could not "counterpose a *de facto* revolutionary power to the legal power of the bourgeois state," then "another party" would have to be constructed to replace it.[112] Yet his proposals for immediate action left no doubt that the present aim was still conceived of as a "renewal": from below as always through the councils, but now also from above by eliminating non-communists from the Party.[113]

However, while essentially a challenge to Serrati, the article also made clear Gramsci's continued opposition to Bordiga. Gramsci argued, for instance, that the Party leadership should reorganize itself on a dialectical basis in which, on the one hand, it would "become the motor center of proletarian action in all its manifestations," while on the other, it would keep "constantly in touch" with its local sections. These sections would in turn become involved in an interactive education with "factories, unions, cooperatives, and barracks."[114] He also proposed the issuing of a Party manifesto which would reaffirm its commitment to mass-based revolution. Clearly, Gramsci had become involved in a delicate and subtle three-way contest. The problem was how to create a more potent revolutionary leadership, a party of communists, while still holding fast to an image of mass-based revolution. Serratian maximalism might debilitate the movement through its theoretically rationalized passivity, but control by Bordiga might weaken it fatally by splitting it in two.

Early in July, on the eve of the Second Comintern Congress, Gramsci made his two-front war still more explicit.[115] He denounced Bordiga and his fellow "abstentionists" as a "collection of dogmatists or little Machiavellis" who impede what the revolution needs most—proletarian institutions which can substitute for bourgeois state power—and who cling to a conception of an autonomous Communist Party which is nothing but an "hallucination."[116] Such extreme language, even for Gramsci, was very likely a product of his failure to win the Bordigans away from their "abstentionism" at their Florence Conference in May. While he had always been sympathetic to the "intransigence" within Bordiga's program because of his own commitment to a proletarian "potential state," he now seemed to suggest that Bordiga's abstentionism, far from being the logical outgrowth of intransigence, was in fact at odds with it:

> Can the Party abstain from participation in electoral struggles for the representative institutions of bourgeois democracy, if one of its tasks is the political organization of all the oppressed classes about the communist proletariat, and if to obtain this it must become the governmental party for those classes in a democratic sense, given that it can only be the party of the communist proletariat in a revolutionary sense?[117]

To fail to be intransigent in this way was to deny that the revolution was a "single dialectical process of development" and therefore to divide it artificially into two stages, one before attaining power, one after. And, he hastened to add, "since Russia, all other two-stage revolutions have failed."[118]

When the Second Congress convened, almost everyone in the PSI was surprised to discover that Lenin concurred with Gramsci rather than with Serrati or Bordiga. Gramsci, who did not attend the congress, publicized this fact widely once he learned of it.[119] Yet what is interesting about Lenin's support is that, in the Italian context at least, Gramsci was not so much a Leninist as Lenin was a Gramscist.[120] The May 8 proposals for "renewal" had grown out of a fight internal to the PSI and without foreign influence. Even Lenin's vituperative criticisms of Bordiga's "abstentionism" in *Left-Wing Communism—An Infantile Disorder* reached Italians only after the Second Congress had begun.[121] Bordiga, who did attend, backed away from his "abstentionism" as gracefully as he could, but he took the "21 Points" to heart and left with a renewed determination to form an Italian Communist Party without the Serratian center.[122] For his part, Serrati pledged to support the 21 Points and promised to call a special congress of the PSI to have them approved, a move that would have required expelling Turati and the reformists. The congress was never convened.

Now that the prestige of the International was solidly behind the formation of a communist PSI, Gramsci endorsed the idea without hesitation. "The communist faction of the PSI," he declared, ". . . must become in name and in deed the Communist Party of Italy."[123] And with the "abstentionism" issue now cast aside, he proceeded to make definite conciliatory gestures toward Bordiga in the hopes of uniting the PSI left. In August he launched a "Communist Education Group" explicitly designed to improve relations between the two factions.[124] However, unfortunately for Gramsci, the move was not very popular among his fellow *ordinovisti.* Before the Second Congress, in the tension-filled atmosphere of the abortive April strike, he had refused to side with Togliatti and Terracini in what he regarded as a petty organizational dispute within the Turin section.[125] His relations with Tasca had been strained ever since the "coup d'etat" the previous spring, but they also worsened in this new dispute and reached the boiling point even before Gramsci published his scathing attack that August on Tasca's whole conception of

Ordine Nuovo.[126] By this time he had also effectively split with Togliatti and Terracini, who would not follow him in his courtship of the Bordigans and who even persisted in using the Turin section to carry on an anti-Bordiga crusade. In describing their behavior later, Gramsci wrote that they had "rejoined Tasca" in this period.[127]

Given this disunity, Gramsci attracted only seventeen members to the Communist Education Group; and if we judge by this factor alone, his rapprochement with Bordiga must be deemed a disaster. Yet even had this rapprochement succeeded, Gramsci's continued efforts at PSI "renewal" might have gone awry, since they were predicated on the additional gamble that the Serratians would accept an openly Communist Party at the PSI Livorno Congress in January. This was a gamble that he was prepared to take (his only other choice was to desert the PSI in favor of Bordiga's minoritarianism), since it was his last hope that a "new order" might be brought to fruition. But the dramatic events of the early autumn did not cooperate with this design. Early in September, councils in the Turin metallurgical industry began to occupy their factories, and the movement quickly spread through the city and thence to much of the rest of Italy. Given the scale of the insurrection, the PSI leadership paid it some lip service, but in Gramsci's estimation, which was widely shared, they avoided every opportunity they had to take control of events. Giolitti, who had once again become premier the previous June, played a cool waiting game which ultimately succeeded.[128] Indeed, he was doubly successful: the occupation ended and the left became irreparably divided. In this climate, a reconciliation with Serrati was all but impossible, and when Serrati did refuse to back a Communist PSI at Livorno, Gramsci had no choice but to accept a new PCI. For it followed logically from his original *Ordine Nuovo* design that some disciplined working-class party was necessary, and if the PSI could not be revitalized to fulfill this role, then the torch had to pass to some other party that could.

Two mistaken conclusions are commonly drawn in assessing these changing Party commitments. One, drawn notably by John Cammett, is that Gramsci abandoned the renewal image by late July and had become a "Leninist" by September.[129] While it is true, as just suggested, that he assumed the risk of a PSI/PCI split in his decision to court the Bordigans, the evidence indicates that he was continuing to pin his hopes on renewal as late as October 24,[130] and that he did not openly relinquish these hopes until December 18.[131] The passage Cammett cites to deny this, which pictures a new party "rising from the ashes" of the PSI, seems rather to suggest a phoenix-like rebirth.[132] Moreover, Cammett's attribution of "Leninism" is left completely undeveloped, and the evidence cited is limited to one quotation, which does not mention Lenin and which was delivered in the heat of the September factory occupation. What is historically certain is that from early 1921 to late 1922 Gramsci publicly supported Bordiga, and thus opposed Lenin, in each of their many disputes over PCI policy.

It is this fact, apparently, that has prompted the rival and more formidable interpretation that Gramsci had become a Bordigan by mid-1920 or, at the very latest, 1921.[133] The problem is complex. Certainly he had been pushed into a corner by the political maneuverings of 1920 in which the choice he was forced to make between Serrati and Bordiga was made in favor of Bordiga. Moreover, once committed to a PCI led by Bordiga, he had stood by this decision with characteristic resolve. His beloved *Ordine Nuovo* now became the Party daily, and many of the themes for which it had become famous were partially eclipsed. Moreover, as we will see in the next chapter, he rarely used it to express a view that Bordiga opposed and he never openly criticized Bordiga's leadership. Nevertheless, Gramsci's practice must be understood in the context of his own intellectual development; it does not justify the assumption that his *theory* was also Bordigan.

What prevented his theory of political organization from being realized in the Italy of 1920 was, he believed, the aloofness and lassitude of the PSI. As his every effort ended in failure and as the Turin workers met defeat after defeat, he could not help becoming embittered toward the PSI. This appears to have led him by the fall of 1920 to an obsession with the need for a properly constituted revolutionary party. But this is not to say that he became a Bordigan. For while Bordiga had long held a new Communist Party to be a self-evident necessity, Gramsci viewed it as a likely source of division but as his only choice given the PSI failure. Moreover, while Bordiga viewed the new party as self-sufficient in carrying out its revolutionary task, Gramsci continued to treat it as just one, if a very important, element in his organizational program. Though the councils had been thoroughly defeated in 1920 and completely destroyed by April 1921, he continued to emphasize their importance well after that, and there is no evidence to suggest that his theory of organization changed in this period.[134] He simply worked to perfect the institution that in his view would have led the councils to success in 1920 and which was now the only viable institution left.

One other factor contributed to Gramsci's analysis of the "revolution that failed." The councils, though extensive and effective in Turin, had not spread in significant numbers to other cities or to the Italian countryside. As Gramsci confided to Leonetti in 1924: "We did not create a fraction nor try to organize it throughout Italy for fear of being called *arrivistes* and careerists."[135] In truth, as we noted earlier, he had proposed peasant councils for both North and South in 1920, but he had not pressed the matter. Now the importance of such action was driven home by the new political phenomenon that began to appear late in the year: the squads of *fascisti* who soon roamed almost at will across the Northern countryside.

CHAPTER THREE

Fascism and Revolution in the West

Our pessimism is increasing, but our will is undiminished.
(March 1921)

The determination, which in Russia was direct and drove the masses into the streets for a revolutionary uprising, is complicated in Central and Western Europe, by all those political superstructures created by the greater development of capitalism.
(February 1924)

If we succeed in organizing the Southern peasants, we will have won the revolution.
(November 1925)

As EARLY AS May 1920, Gramsci had written ominously that "the present phase of the class struggle in Italy is the phase that precedes either the conquest of power on the part of the revolutionary proletariat . . . or a tremendous reaction on the part of the propertied classes and governing caste."[1] This sense of being at a major historical watershed, and of the promise and dangers inherent in it, was to prove profoundly accurate in the wake of the defeated factory occupation. Two years after that, it would be apparent to all that the late fall and early winter of 1920-21 had witnessed a transfer of political legitimacy and vitality from the socialist left, now deeply embittered and divided, to the black-shirted *squadristi*, whose violence and populist bravado pushed them suddenly into the national spotlight.

Gramsci was among the first political observers and activists in Italy to sense the potential and the danger in fascism, but he was less quick to recognize the tremendous, perhaps irreversible, damage that the Italian left had inflicted upon itself at Livorno. His journalism of the next year and a half remained obsessed with the desire to complete the *Ordine Nuovo* design by building a new Communist Party capable of leading a mass revolution organized in the factories. When the worker councils died in the spring of 1921, his reaction was not to question the efficacy of the design in which they were grounded but rather to mount an increasingly rancorous campaign against the "Barnum's Circus" that the PSI had become.[2] Yet the objective circumstances in which his politics were now situated could not help having a profound impact on him. For the first and only time in his public life, he found himself working predominantly within an institution which he was not leading and which was pursuing an overall policy direction not always consistent with his own aims and judgments. His old institutional attachments were either gone, as with the councils, or changing, as with *Ordine Nuovo*. Though he remained the paper's editor, its new function as a daily and a party mouthpiece made his position far more administrative and far less creative than it had been.

In these threatening and unfamiliar circumstances, Gramsci looked to the new PCI for all his emotional and spiritual sustenance, and the degree of his loyalty to Bordiga's leadership, as evidenced by the public display of ideological unity that they were able to sustain, is quite remarkable, especially given the intense Comintern opposition to the PCI, which cast them both in the role of left deviationists at the end of 1921 and in 1922. What Gramsci and Bordiga shared above all was an implacable hatred for the PSI, which they each blamed for the demise of their very different revolutionary designs in 1920. Yet, from the beginning of their collaboration, differences between the two were continually apparent, if almost never openly acknowledged. As the national elections of May 1921 approached, Bordiga, despite the formal retraction of his "abstentionism" at the second Comintern Congress, assumed his customary coolness toward them,[3] and it was mostly through Gramsci's efforts that the PCI participated in the campaign. Through editorials in *Ordine Nuovo*, he spearheaded a propaganda drive aimed not so much at the government as at the PSI, which he accused of being "essentially a petty-bourgeois party," allied to "counter-revolutionary" trade unions,[4] and propagators of a socialist culture filled with "ideology, sentiment, aspirations, and incoherent dreams."[5] Unfortunately for Gramsci, the PSI was able to overcome these limitations and to outpoll the PCI by a stunning margin of 1,600,000 to 290,000.

These results served as a painful reminder of the need for the Party to take the construction of its mass base more seriously. Though Gramsci himself had not been particularly remiss on this point, few others in positions of leadership could be counted along with him. Just prior to Livorno, he had pleaded for "an alliance between the industrial workers of the North and the poor peasants of the South."[6] In the ensuing months, he had called for closer links to the socialist youth movement, a PCI initiative on daily-life issues like the price of bread, and PCI support for the interparty *arditi del popolo* in the resistance against fascist aggression.[7] In April he even made an effort to confer secretly with D'Annunzio, apparently in hopes of gaining his cooperation in an anti-fascist campaign, or at least of wooing his legionnaires away from Mussolini.[8] The attitude which all this activity reflected was well summed up by Gramsci himself when he remarked, paraphrasing Rolland: "Our pessimism is increasing, but our will is undiminished."[9]

Yet, as the International opened its Third Congress in June, Gramsci had little but disappointments to show for these efforts,[10] and it was clear to the Russians that the PCI was riding the downward crest of Europe's postwar revolutionary wave. Their response was to formulate a "united front" policy for Italy, which in essence would have committed the PCI to tactical alliances with all other "parties of the proletariat," i.e., at the very least the PSI, and perhaps even the Italian Populists (PPI). In his resolute opposition to this, Gramsci stood solidly behind Bordiga. Though he could court D'Annunzio, he could not bring himself to a reconciliation with the PSI. In large part this was due to his emotional revulsion at such a prospect; yet this was not all that was involved, and a closer look at Gramsci's thinking on this issue is essential to understanding his politics of 1921-22.

United Front and Fusion

To the Italian Communists who had lived through the political paroxysms of 1920 which culminated at Livorno, the proposal of a united front with the PSI must have appeared incredible, if not insane. How could the Comintern even contemplate an alliance with a group that dedicated Communists like themselves had fought continuously for over a year, a fight that had ended in a bitter divorce now only six months old? Lenin appears to have appreciated the irony, but nonetheless scolded Bordiga for his short-sighted recalcitrance.[11] Much later, Gramsci saw the logic in the Comintern position and formulated it brilliantly:

> Comrade Lenin summed up what should have been the meaning of the split when he said to Comrade Serrati: "*Separate yourselves from Turati, and then form an alliance with him.*" We should have adapted this formula to the split, which took place in a form different from the one foreseen by Lenin. That is, we should certainly have separated ourselves from reformism, and from maximalism (which represented, and still represents, no more than typical Italian opportunism in the working class movement). It was indispensable and historically necessary to do so. But afterwards, and without giving up our ideological and organizational struggle against them, we should have attempted to build an alliance against reaction. To the leadership of our Party, however, every attempt by the International to make us adopt this line appeared as an implicit disavowal of the Livorno split. . . .[12]

Even in 1921, however, Gramsci himself was not oblivious to such logic. Indeed, Togliatti recalls that Gramsci had frequently questioned Bordiga's blind rejection of a united front in private conversation.[13] Yet Gramsci's public posture, like Bordiga's, was to maintain that "talk of an abstract united front is a manifestation of verbalism."[14] When the issue came to a head at the Party's Rome Congress in March 1922, he made a strong statement in support of Bordiga's position.[15] This statement made it clear that his opposition was based on a contempt for the PSI and, to a lesser extent, on his fear that the Party might lose its proletarian identity by being drawn into defensive alliances with essentially peasant parties like the PPI.

However, he also joined Tasca in drafting theses which advocated a united front at the trade union level. At Gramsci's insistence, they even included a strong endorsement of factory councils as the essential core of a revolutionary movement:

> To achieve autonomy in the industrial field the working class ought to go beyond the limits of union organization and create a new type of

organization, representatively based and not too bureaucratic, which embraces the whole working class. . . . The system of factory councils is the concrete historical expression of the proletariat's aspirations for its own autonomy.[16]

Despite this statement, and despite Bordiga's much cooler attitude on the whole question of a united front "from below," the trade union theses passed at the Congress.[17] Tasca then went on to propose a more moderate position on united front generally, one designed to reconcile the Party with the Comintern. In refusing to take this step, Gramsci thus appears to have planted himself between the Party's left and right wings, though somewhat closer to Bordiga than to Tasca.

This interpretation is strengthened by Gramsci's own later reconstruction of the Congress, in which he claimed to have "accepted the theses on tactics only for the contingent reason of party organization."[18] This "contingent reason," according to Togliatti, was the threat from the Party's right wing, particularly Tasca.[19] Unwittingly, the Comintern had played right into Tasca's hands. By virtue of his own power base in the unions and his close relations with the PSI left, Tasca was much more favorably disposed to any form of united front than were the other PCI leaders. Gramsci was thus pushed into a situation not unlike the one in which he had found himself during the summer of 1920. Then he had tried to hold together the center and left of the PSI; now he was trying to reconcile the various ideological tendencies of the PCI. In both cases he had recognized the absolute indispensability of Bordiga's group (the only Communist faction with a national following) for a strong Communist Party. In neither case did he have any significant power base of his own; and in 1922, being in particularly bad health, he was in no position to organize one.

After the Congress, Gramsci was appointed PCI representative to the Comintern, and he left for Moscow in June. Shortly after his arrival, he collapsed from nervous exhaustion, and a rest cure was arranged for him at a Russian sanitorium. He spent four months there and was released just as news was reaching Moscow of the fascist March on Rome and of the PSI's October Congress, at which the reformists had been expelled.[20] Gramsci traveled quickly to Moscow, where the Fourth Congress of the International was about to convene. The Russian Party (CPSU) was already making it clear that a "fusion" of PCI and PSI in a "workers' government" should take place now that the PSI had put itself fundamentally in accord with the 21 Points. When Bordiga and Tasca heard of this upon arriving from Italy a few days later, their breach widened into an open dispute. Apparently, Gramsci's intermediate position was widely perceived; one Comintern agent actually suggested that he overthrow Bordiga as chairman, since he could undoubtedly do so with the International's backing.[21] Yet throughout the pre-Congress discussions, Gramsci sided entirely with Bordiga and was condemned for this by Zinoviev and Trotsky. This was followed by a stern letter from the CPSU Central Committee which warned the PCI leaders not to express their dissenting views at the Congress itself.[22] Bordiga's reaction was defiant: he declared that he would remain silent at the Congress and thus took a big step toward the international Trotskyist opposition that he would openly embrace just two years later. Gramsci's reaction was less extreme. At first he advocated a limited fusion not with the PSI as a whole but only with the so-called *terzini* faction, Serrati's left-wing group which had now declared itself in complete support of the Third International. When this was rejected by the CPSU, Gramsci was persuaded to participate on the fusion implementation committee in place of Bordiga, who refused. However, according to the Comintern secretary overseeing the committee, Gramsci remained deeply skeptical and made a series of demands designed to obstruct the merger.[23] Though these were accepted by the PSI representatives on the committee, the PSI rejected the fusion proposal at its Milan Congress in April 1923.

Thus, when understood in terms of the united front controversy, Gramsci's political behavior in this period bears striking resemblances to Bordiga's while also camouflaging important differences. With the objective collapse of the "new order" in Turin, Gramsci needed Bordiga; and in their hatred of the PSI and their fear of Tasca, they shared sympathies which led them both to a resolute opposition to the idea of a united front. Yet if, for Bordiga, an anti-front policy was in keeping with his minoritarian image of revolution, for Gramsci it was a continuation of his *Ordine Nuovo* design. His concern with organizing a mass base for revolution is evident throughout the period, and, as the trade union theses presented at Rome make clear, he was still committed in principle to building this base in the factories. He was therefore able to accept the idea of a united front at the trade union level, or at the level of civil defense (the *arditi del popolo*), or among youth organizations. But, in keeping with the *Ordine Nuovo* principle of a disciplined party symbolizing the critical consciousness of the proletariat and leading it militarily, he simply could not embrace a united front with the PSI or PPI. This is why his behavior could be all but identical with Bordiga's while not in any sense expressing "Bordiganism."

However, to describe Gramsci's political behavior in this way is still to overstate somewhat his overall similarity with Bordiga in this period, for not all of this behavior had to do with party congresses and united fronts. Indeed, perhaps his most interesting efforts in this period concern the analysis of fascism that he was developing in the pages of *Ordine Nuovo*. Here he was miles beyond Bordiga in the sophistication and direction of his thinking. And, as we shall see, this analysis played a very significant role in leading him toward the Comintern and away from Bordiga in 1923. Ultimately, this shift in loyalty can be seen as part of a larger reassessment of the revolutionary process, one which grounded his political designs of 1924-26 and the political and cultural theory of the *Prison Notebooks*.

The Meaning of Fascism

Bordiga's official conception of fascism in the two years before the March on Rome was that of a simple "class reaction" of the bourgeoisie which, however, had no interest in destroying the appearance of formal democracy. The real danger was the formation of a social democratic government posing as an antifascist united front.[24] In contrast, Gramsci had taken the fascists much more seriously; as Trotsky would note in 1931, he had been the only Italian Communist to foresee a possible fascist dictatorship.[25] When he began to write about it late in 1920, however, he saw only "the latest 'performance' offered by the urban petty bourgeoisie," silently directed by the capitalist class and Giolitti's government. Like D'Annunzio's "pathetic" Fiume adventure, fascism was only a kind of last gasp: "the most important episode of inner dissolution being experienced by this class of the Italian people."[26] But the full complexity of fascism did begin to dawn for Gramsci shortly after the new year as a wave of fascist violence of unprecedented intensity swept across the Italian North.

Fascism, he was recognizing by February 1921, had not one but two faces: a radical one represented by the unemployed veterans, nationalists, and legionnaires who supported D'Annunzio's invasion of Fiume; and a more conservative one represented by Mussolini's diverse but more middle-class and more organization-minded urban constituency.[27] Six months later, Gramsci was drawing the consequence that, since fascism was not a unified bloc, the proletariat should seek to locate its fissures precisely and split them open still further.[28] Even by April, he had taken the extraordinary step of trying to confer with D'Annunzio. A few days later, he had penned "Forze elementari," a startlingly sophisticated examination of fascism and one of the most provocative single articles on it that he ever wrote.[29] Consider the following:

> It has by now become evident that fascism can only partly be assumed to be a class phenomenon, a movement of political forces conscious of a real goal; it has overflowed, it has broken loose from every organizational framework, it is superior to the will and intention of every regional or central committee, it has become an unleashing of elemental forces which cannot be restrained within the bourgeois system of economic and political governance. Fascism is the name for the profound decomposition of Italian society which could not but accompany the profound decomposition of the state and which can today be explained only with reference to the low level of civilization which the Italian nation has reached in sixty years of unitary administration.[30]

Here in two long sentences, written a year and a half prior to the March on Rome, lie many of the features that would come to distinguish Gramsci's analysis from Bordiga's and from the Comintern clichés of later years. Fascism is based on a cross-class appeal and cannot be explained merely in class terms; it is bound up with a profound decomposition of civil society and parliamentary government in Italy. Fascism also appeals, as the article's later reference to a "barbaric and anti-social psychology" makes clear, to irrational elements in the human psyche. Yet—and this is a crucial point for grasping Gramsci's entire intellectual outlook —he was unable now or later to explain this irrationalism in anything but the most rationalistic of terms. Here the resort was to a national character argument about the "human immaturity" of the Italian people, an affliction, apparently, to which the working class was entirely immune.[31]

Ultimately, "Forze elementari" is perhaps best understood as an effort to grasp the full meaning of Italy's still unresolved national crisis, in order to fathom the means by which the proletariat might still play the role of a national savior. Gramsci hardly wavered in his view that this remained the overwhelmingly likely outcome of the crisis. In June and July his articles did turn repeatedly to an image of a fascist *colpo di stato* (a possibility to which the socialists were blind because of their "pseudo-Marxism").[32] Yet this image was abandoned when the "Pact of Pacification," signed August 2, 1921, by Mussolini and representatives of the PSI, quickly backfired and opened still wider the breaches within the fascist ranks. While careful not to underestimate the fascists, Gramsci's response was his most sustained probe to date into the historical sources of the "two fascisms."[33]

The early, war-generated *fasci di combattimento*, he recalled, were essentially of petty bourgeois orientation, given their support base in the various associations of ex-servicemen. This made them hostile to the PSI, which was, of course, working-class in orientation and which had opposed the Italian intervention in the war. This anti-socialism gained the *fasci* some support among "the capitalists and the authorities" but also, and primarily, among the "agrarians," i.e., the small and medium farmers and large latifundists—everyone in the countryside, in fact, except the landless peasants. Fascism's problem was that this origin ultimately contradicted the direction of its expanding strength, which was predominantly in the Northern cities, where those attracted to it ("the *ceti medi* [middle strata], employees, and small businessmen and industrialists") were more parliamentary and collaborationist in orientation. Discomfort with the political style of fascism's rural wing was also evident among the capitalists who gave the movement financial backing and even among the local authorities who looked the other way during outbursts of fascist violence.

To guarantee his political future, the always alert Mussolini had recognized early the necessity of building ties with at least some industrial capitalists. "The reality of the world," he was fond of saying, "is capitalist."[34] Yet, as Gramsci clearly perceived, Mussolini could not take such ties for granted.[35] If the industrialists feared fascism's instability, Mussolini and his cohorts were uneasy among the industrialists and, or so it appeared to Gramsci, incapable even of understanding the nature of their new industrialism. Mussolini's economic conceptions remained mired in the "pre-war years, the period before the 'trusts' and the concentration of industrial capital in banks."[36]

Yet despite all these weaknesses, Gramsci's proletariat-to-the-rescue scenario became steadily less plausible over the fall and winter of 1921-22. Gradually, Mussolini managed to patch over the schisms within the movement and to restore its vitality, while at the same time the fortunes of the PCI continued to wane amidst incessant bickering with the PSI and a prevailing disillusion among the urban working classes. By spring, Gramsci had come to recognize that a fascist victory was all but a matter of time. His last article before leaving for Russia spoke darkly of those who will "pay in person for having disgraced themselves with crimes" of "opposition to proletarian unity" and "vain compromise."[37]

In his article on fascism for the Fourth Comintern Congress of November 1922, Gramsci was led back to a still deeper search for the origins of this now victorious movement.[38] As in his later, more extended discussion of these origins in the Lyons Theses, the essay on the "Southern Question," and his prison discussions of 1930,[39] he found his starting point in the character of the Italian Risorgimento. Unlike France and Britain, Italy had never really experienced a bourgeois, democratic revolution. The Risorgimento was a revolution from above, successful largely because of Cavour's skillful diplomacy; and the resulting political system, though parliamentary in form, was in practice based on a system of inter-elite collaboration known as *trasformismo*. While they had some input into this collaboration, bourgeois elements were in no position to "defend the unity and integrity of the state against the repeated attacks of the reactionary forces, represented above all by the alliance of the great landowners with the Vatican."[40]

Prewar liberal leaders like Giolitti had coped with their situation by forging an alliance between some of the Southern landowners and the Northern industrial bourgeoisie, and by coopting the working class with political and economic concessions while altogether neglecting the politically impotent rural masses. But this was an inherently weak solution which broke apart under the strains of the war. Though a strengthened, left-wing, populist opposition, led by the PSI, and in 1919 by the PPI, did emerge from the war crisis, its leadership was never properly consolidated. Thus the revolutionary moment which existed in Italy above all in 1919 was missed, and the groundwork was laid for a powerful right-wing reaction. The following year saw the formation of a centralized organization of industrialists, the *Confindustria*, which crushed the Turin labor movement in every encounter, and the rapid expansion of the *fasci di combattimento*. Given the disarray on the left and the loss of all confidence in parliamentarism, the fascists, Gramsci now seemed to suggest, were the only political force capable of filling the vacuum.

One upshot of this account is that Gramsci already explicitly rejected any identification of fascism as the "agent" of the bourgeoisie. Moreover, the thesis that fascism is a form of "Bonapartism" was rejected as well, at least as it was propounded by August Thalheimer and others a decade later in Germany.[41] Fascism is not the product of a standoff between the bourgeoisie and the proletariat, but of the proletariat's outright defeat in a political setting where the bourgeoisie is dominant despite the intrinsic weaknesses of its political institutions. In prison, Gramsci would use the concept of hegemony to develop this insight into a highly original theory of fascism as a form of "Caesarism."

From the perspective of politics in 1922, however, what is noteworthy in the account is that it made no allusion to the relatively optimistic analyses of fascism's weaknesses that he had made in 1921. Nor did it draw out the new strategic implications of fascist victory for the PCI. In his strategic assessments of 1921,

Gramsci had usually focused on the divisions in the fascist movement upon which the proletariat might capitalize, and he had assumed that Italy remained in a revolutionary situation roughly parallel to Russia's in 1917.[42] Hence the basic premise of his *Ordine Nuovo* design did not have to be questioned. Moreover, reflection on Giolitti's prewar politics seems to have magnified his prevailing skepticism about the wisdom of a united front with the PSI. For any alliance that might be perceived as strengthening the working class and the left wing of the industrial bourgeoisie at the expense of rural workers and peasants would very likely backfire in the way that liberalism's alliances had. Thus, while Bordiga had feared a united front because it might take over, Gramsci seems to have rejected it, in addition to the other reasons which have been pointed out, because it would "accelerate the fascist coup."[43]

However, one might have expected Gramsci to alter, or at least to question, this strategic assessment as fascism moved toward power in 1922. He does seem to have recognized an increasingly counterrevolutionary situation at least by spring; and if his rationalist psychology prevented him from fully grasping fascism's public appeal,[44] he had long recognized it as a cross-class movement commanding a powerful set of social and cultural forces. These forces might not be able to solve the crisis of post-Risorgimento politics and postwar capitalism in Italy, but they were certainly demonstrating the capacity to undercut the crisis's revolutionary tendencies and thus to draw it out to very great lengths. Now at the Fourth Congress, Gramsci was acknowledging how decisively the fascists had been favored by postwar circumstances. The implicit corollary to this was that the past few years had not been a revolutionary situation after all. Though he did not yet question his "new order" or fundamentally shift his views on the united front, events in Italy would soon shock him into a complete reassessment of his political outlook and commitments.

A Revolutionary Reassessment

On February 3, 1923, only weeks after their return from Moscow, Bordiga and several of his closest associates were arrested by the fascist police. As Terracini concluded in a letter written ten days later, the fascists had apparently

> unleashed the long announced anti-communist round-up. In a week the police have arrested more than 5000 comrades, including all our area secretaries, all the communist trade union organizers, and all our local councillors. Moreover, they have succeeded in seizing all our party funds, and thus in delivering what is perhaps a mortal blow to our press. . . .[45]

When Gramsci received the news in Moscow a month and a half later, he was, in his own words, "badly shaken." As he reflected on what had transpired, he found himself "compelled to admit" that the Party would have to be reorganized "with cadres nominated by the International itself."[46]

That this was the catalytic event which transformed his November analysis of fascism into a more general political reassessment became clear in April. In a speech to the Central Committee of the Comintern (EKKI), Gramsci argued that fascism had blunted the revolutionary crisis at least for the moment, and he grudgingly conceded that the Party needed to adopt a defensive tactic that could cement an anti-fascist unity of the progressive classes.[47] Meanwhile in Italy, Bordiga, undaunted by the arrest, issued a manifesto from prison attacking the Comintern and defiantly reaffirming the essential correctness of his anti-united front and anti-fusion positions.[48] When Togliatti wrote to Gramsci in May asking him to sign the manifesto, Gramsci refused and thus broke publicly with Bordiga for the first time since 1920.[49] In June, when the enlarged EKKI adopted the slogan of a "worker and peasant government" for Italy, Gramsci endorsed it without hesitation.[50]

These events prompted a full year of intense debate within the PCI. Through this debate Gramsci was able to articulate his new political outlook for himself as well as for others. In September, he called for the establishment of a new working class daily, to be devoted to "a special stress on the Southern Question" and on a "federal republic of workers and peasants," to be run jointly with the *terzini*, and thus to be called *L'Unità*, a name which also recalled Salvemini's prewar publication.[51] Several months later, after Bordiga had been released from prison and had issued still another "manifesto," Gramsci again separated himself sharply from the Neapolitan, this time declaring: "I have another concept of the party, its functions, and the relations it ought to establish with the non-party masses, i.e., with the population in general."[52] In February, the first issues of *L'Unità* appeared, and this was followed in March by another non-party journal, a resurrected *Ordine Nuovo*, now planned as a biweekly. In May, at a clandestine conference in Como, Gramsci engaged in some sharp exchanges with Bordiga; and though the latter's faction remained visibly larger, Gramsci won many important converts, including Togliatti and Mauro Scoccimarro. His "centrist" faction gained the Comintern's endorsement at the Fifth Congress in June, and Gramsci was officially installed as Secretary-General of the PCI by the end of the summer.

This, in bare outline, is the political behavior through which Gramsci's new political orientation was disclosed to his comrades. Taken as a whole, his various communications can be seen as a new vision of the mass organization of workers and peasants required to confront and counter the fascist state. What this new vision entailed will be described shortly. But we must first attempt to reconstruct the larger theoretical shifts which Gramsci made during the second half of his sojourn in Russia. While the documentation we have for Gramsci's thinking in Russia is weaker than for any comparable period in his adult life, it seems clear that his analysis of fascism eventually led him to address two fundamental issues: relations between the PCI and the Comintern, and the nature of a "Western" as opposed to an "Eastern" revolution.

Much of Gramsci's first nine months as permanent PCI representative to the Comintern were spent in resisting it, yet he was at least developing a firsthand feeling for its inner workings. The boy from Sardinia who had yearned to become an Italian had now achieved a truly international horizon. But in the latter half of his tenure, after the fascist purge of the PCI, he seems to have recognized the full importance of the principle of proletarian internationalism which the Comintern symbolized. What his politics of 1921-22 had lacked, it now appeared, was an adequate sense for the international dimension of proletarian struggle; he had become parochial in his single-minded effort to build up the

PCI. The victory of fascism showed that the narrowness of this project, though designed to overcome the problems of 1920, had, if anything, contributed to further defeats.

Thus, by the spring of 1923, Gramsci was criticizing Bordiga centrally on the grounds that his politics were not sufficiently internationalist. As he wrote of Bordiga's manifesto:

> In practice, given the conditions prevailing, to follow Amadeo would mean engaging in open struggle with the Comintern; and to be outside it would mean losing its very powerful material and moral support, while we ourselves would be reduced to a very small group held together almost entirely by personal ties. We would very soon lose all real influence on the course of the political struggle in Italy, and might be completely annihilated.[53]

And in notes written in June, he criticized his Party for its "equivocal attitudes towards the Comintern: while the value of maximizing formal discipline is affirmed verbally . . . , [the Party's] actions leave the impression of trying to do everything possible to evade the orders laid down by the Executive and the congresses."[54]

Quite possibly this new sense of commitment to the Comintern was intensified by Gramsci's strong emotional identification with the Soviet Union, which, as a 1924 letter to Zino Zini revealingly suggests, had become his only source of optimism "about our country and its future."[55] Yet it would be a mistake to portray him one-sidedly as the "leftist turned dedicated Comintern man." His study of fascism had given him good independent reasons for closing ranks with the International and against Bordiga, as he reassessed the peculiar nature of the obstacles to revolution in the West.

So long as Gramsci compared nations exclusively in terms of their relation to the system of international capitalism, Russia and Italy could be considered similar in revolutionary potential. The parallel guided him in 1919-20, and he persisted after 1923 in stressing Italy's "relative backwardness."[56] But this was no longer the whole story nor even the crucial part of the story. What fascism had demonstrated, Gramsci now perceived, was that states also had to be compared in the light of relations between state and civil society. In 1919-20, he had foreseen a Russian-style revolution in which a preparatory "revolutionary process" would, at some acutely contradictory point, explode in a "revolutionary act," which would then be subsumed within the process.[57] The series of "moments" could be envisaged as continuous,[58] yet Gramsci clearly expected that the preparatory moment for Italy would be short and the moment of seizure dominant.[59] Giolitti's government was "exhausted and worn out. . . . Only the proletariat is capable of creating a strong and respected state."[60] Now, in 1924, he was forced to conclude that this image had been misconceived. Fascism had demonstrated that the bourgeois state in Western Europe had far greater adaptive capacities than he had previously been willing to concede.

This had far-reaching implications for a political theory of state and revolution that would only be fully confronted in the *Prison Notebooks*, and not finally worked out even there. Though it is doubtful that Gramsci ever accepted the vulgar Marxist view of the state as the mere dictatorial instrument of the ruling class, he had believed that under proletarian guidance the state could wither away into a society modeled on "a large engineering works."[61] Now he began to see that the state had instruments of control far more subtle and effective than dictatorial force, that the threat of such force was only one of a number of state functions, and that variations in the legal-political forms of the state were highly significant.[62] As he wrote to Togliatti in February 1924:

> The determination, which in Russia was direct and drove the masses into the streets for a revolutionary uprising, is complicated in Central and Western Europe by all those political superstructures created by the greater development of capitalism. This makes the action of the masses slower and more prudent, and therefore requires of the revolutionary party a strategy and tactics altogether more complex and long-term than those which were necessary for the Bolsheviks in the period between March and November, 1917.[63]

In this passage, Gramsci for the first time drew a clear connection between the nature of Western revolution and the character of the Western state as revealed to him by fascism. He had long recognized that revolution is a single, unified process of historical development, but now he abandoned any notion of a culminating "revolutionary act" or "simple assault" on the state, at least in the West.[64] Communists here were faced with a defensive situation; though revolution did not have to be abandoned, it would have to be retailored for these circumstances. Western revolution would be a "slow and prudent" construction of alternative "superstructures," i.e., an alternative "hegemony" in civil society, which would come finally to encompass the state only in the very long term. This image too, as we have seen, was anticipated in earlier writings, but now the concept of hegemony as the consensual and institutional basis of proletarian power is explicitly introduced.[65] And while Gramsci offered here no theoretical elaboration on this conception of revolution, it is clear that this is the "war of position" that he would propose in the *Notebooks*.[66]

But if revolution is to be conducted as the construction of an alternative hegemony, then what will be its institutions and who will be the proletariat's allies in this process? This was the question that preoccupied Gramsci in 1924. On this question he would make a genuine theoretical advance in this period, one that depended on his conception of Italy as a Western "peripheral state" with "intermediate strata." Again the insight would grow from his analysis of fascism, and this time specifically from the Matteotti Crisis of 1924.

In June of that year, Italians were stunned by the assassination of Giacomo Matteotti, a particularly vocal opposition deputy in the Italian parliament. Immediately, fascism was plunged into its deepest crisis since gaining power. Gramsci leaped to the offensive, arguing in *L'Unità* that the regime's legalistic facade was crumbling, that its inner essence as an "armed dictatorship" was being exposed, and that it was in danger of collapse. What interested him most was how quickly fascism's support seemed to be evaporating among the urban petty bourgeoisie and middle classes.[67] Many of their parliamentary representatives had walked out and formed the alternative "Aventine Parliament." Calls for a new, broadly based "constituent assembly" were widely voiced. Gramsci himself was suspicious of this movement at the time, and when he recognized in November that another revolutionary moment had passed, he sought to blame "the influence of democrats and social democrats."[68] Only much later would he come to embrace the idea of an anti-fascist constituent assembly.[69] Yet the very important lesson that he had already learned from the crisis was that fascism's appeal was unstable and that the level of popular support for it could be expected to fluctuate widely.

In 1926, he would expand the point into a more general historical analysis of the fascist appeal. In the two years prior to the March on Rome, he argued, fears of the proletariat among the urban petty bourgeoisie and the bourgeoisie had led them in a reactionary direction. But beginning in 1923, "the most active elements of the middle classes" had shifted toward the left, eventually providing the backbone of the Aventine opposition. New fears of proletarian extremism, however, soon drove them back toward the regime, and they tended to support Mussolini's assumption of dictatorial power in January 1925. Uncomfortable with this by 1926, the middle classes seemed to be swinging back toward liberalism, or so at least Gramsci perceived, and he held out great hope that they might now become allied with a more disciplined and pragmatic proletarian left into a viable counter-fascist bloc.[70]

How was this shifting to be explained? The closest that Gramsci could come to a direct answer based on fascism's appeal was to point to "fears of the proletariat." Yet he managed to develop another more interesting, though still partial, answer by formulating a comparative analysis of European regimes.[71] A tendency toward middle-class fluctuations roughly similar to those in Italy could also be discerned, he suggested, in the politics of Spain, Portugal, Poland, and the Balkans. What might explain this commonality was that all these states had "peripheral" status within the structure of international capitalism. Since in more advanced states like Czechoslovakia and France one found instead a relative continuity of the left bloc, it seemed to follow that Italy's peripheral status and the vacillating political allegiances of its middle classes were somehow related.

Gramsci nowhere pursued the inner logic of this connection, but he seems to have been operating with the following typology of European states:

	Western	Non-Western
Advanced Capitalist	Great Britain	————
Transitional	France	Czechoslovakia?
Peripheral	Italy, Spain	Russia?, Poland

What Western states shared were the complex superstructures which required that revolution be waged as alternative hegemony. What peripheral states shared in terms of their social structures was "a large stratum of intermediate classes" poised "between the proletariat and capitalism."[72] While Gramsci referred to them loosely as "middle classes," the particular stratum he had in mind was mostly of the older petty bourgeois type that had been conserved or even expanded because of what would now be called the uneven development of the peripheral state. In politics these classes tended to conduct themselves as an independent bloc "with ideologies that often influence large sections of the proletariat but which are particularly suggestive to the peasant masses."[73]

Here, then, were the allies which Gramsci was seeking and which, according to this analysis, were also seeking him. The problem was to institutionalize the basis for a consolidation of what had so far only been a series of ephemeral leftward movements. From this perspective, the Southern Question gained new and still greater significance for the pursuit of proletarian politics. Prior to 1923, Gramsci had tended to conflate the Southern Question with the call for worker-peasant alliances, even though, given fascism's relative lack of appeal among the Southern masses, the need for the latter was more directly a Northern matter. Now he could see the importance of the South in terms of its "intermediate classes," proletarian support for which could help to awaken the Southern masses and to catalyze a significant counter-fascist bloc of workers and peasants. Here are the "democratic intellectuals" of Gramsci's 1926 essay on the Southern Question and the source of his concern with this theme in the *Notebooks*. Other strategic implications of this analysis had already been anticipated in 1924-25, as will soon become apparent.

Chairman Gramsci and the Southern Question

It followed from Gramsci's analysis of fascism and his corresponding reassessment of Western revolution in 1924 that three new elements had to be incorporated into PCI strategy: (1) strong ties to the Comintern (embracing its policy of "Bolshevization" adopted at the Fifth Congress); (2) a cultural and educational effort aimed at rechanneling the consensual support for fascism into an alternative hegemony; and (3) a careful reassessment of the advantages that the proletariat could draw from Italy's status as a peripheral state. These elements were difficult to mesh smoothly, and the first two especially were contradictory in some important ways. For while the first required very tight control from the leadership downward, the second implied the mass-based, bottom-up (and in this sense democratic) "organization of a collective will" through "political education" that had so typified Gramsci's thinking in the *Ordine Nuovo* period. As he wrote in April 1924: "Our present program ought to reproduce, within the situation existing in Italy today, the position we had reached in 1919-1920."[74]

In practice, however, Gramsci used the "new order" parallel only as a rough guide. For while he did not deny himself a certain nostalgia, he also did not confuse nostalgia with reality, nor model with program. He knew that a spirit of self-creation was necessarily the driving force behind any worker council movement and that one could not revive such a spirit from above.

Gramsci's strategy for the defensive revolution he proposed was essentially this: At its center was to be a mass party,[75] flexible in tactics[76] but "centralized" and firm in internal discipline.[77] Its roots in everyday life were to be secured through cell organization at the level of the workplace (not territorially, as Bordiga advocated)[78] and through a cross-class membership of workers and peasants.[79] Its major function was to institutionalize "a dialectical process in which the spontaneous movement of the revolutionary masses and the organizing and directing will of the center converge." The new dialectic of political education, in other words, would have to operate primarily within the party rather than between party and council.[80] This was a defensive measure required by fascism, yet difficult to implement given Bordiga's influence on the local section level, which remained strong until 1926.[81]

At the same time, three complementary policies were to be pursued. First, Gramsci again called for the establishment of "worker and peasant committees" which, as "elective, representative organizations," would serve as the basis for the creation of the worker councils in the future, and presently as a united front of "communists, maximalists, unitarians, populists, republicans, and all other parties in the fight against the fascist regime."[82] In addition, he proposed a "National Association for the Defense of Poor Peasants."[83] Neither of these efforts was implemented very successfully, but Gramsci initially held out high hopes, especially for the latter.[84]

Secondly, he proposed a class alliance with the peasants and other oppressed groups, which would grow out of the "worker and peasant committees" and culminate, hopefully, in a nationwide "anti-parliament" cementing a mass base for revolution and exposing the "nullism" of the Aventine.[85] Given Gramsci's unwillingness in this period to move from an anti-parliament of the working classes to a constituent assembly of the entire anti-fascist opposition, one may doubt the depth of this commitment, and he certainly seems to have demanded any such alliance on terms most favorable to the PCI. Yet, as his efforts on behalf of the National Association for the Defense of Poor Peasants once again showed, his concern for the Italian peasantry was genuine and deeply felt.

Finally, Gramsci suggested that these politics of a united front be actualized on the journalistic front in *L'Unità* and *Il Seme*, the latter to be devoted entirely to the peasants, and on the educational front as a new "party school" with correspondence courses for workers and peasants.[86] Again the attention to the peasantry indicated that his concern for the Southern Question, which he had identified in 1921 as "the central problem of Italian national life,"[87] had, if anything, intensified. In February 1924, Gramsci confided to Togliatti and Terracini: "I have always been persuaded that the *Mezzogiorno* [South] could be fascism's grave, but I also believe that it will be the major reservoir and marshalling-ground of the national and international reaction if we do not study the question adequately and prepare ourselves for everything before the revolution."[88] By late 1925, he had formulated this ambivalence much more precisely:

> In Italy the situation is revolutionary when the proletariat in the North is strong; if the proletariat in the North is weak, the peasants fall in behind the petit-bourgeoisie. And reciprocally, the Southern peasants represent an element of force and revolutionary impetus for the Northern workers. The Northern workers and the Southern peasants are therefore the two immediately revolutionary forces. . . . Hence if we succeed in organizing the Southern peasants, we will have won the revolution.[89]

If, however, this imperative is ignored or faced without success, the consequences for the revolution are apt to be grim indeed.

These were some of the hopes and fears behind the Lyons Theses, a major statement of program that Gramsci wrote with Togliatti in the fall of 1925.[90] The Lyons Theses were Gramsci's first and last attempt at a document which could match the stature of, and therefore replace, Bordiga's Rome Theses of 1922. They contained some of Gramsci's clearest statements on the organizational design that he had in this period, and they offered one of his earliest discussions of the need to undercut reactionary intellectual influences in the rural areas. As he argued verbally during one of the sessions: "The realization of the worker-peasant alliance in the struggle against capitalism presupposes the destruction of Vatican influence over the peasants particularly in Central and Northern Italy."[91] Yet not until his essay on the Southern Question did he nurture this idea into full bloom.

By late 1926, when this essay was written, Gramsci realized that only a major cultural revolution led by intellectuals could hope to disaggregate the existing tie between old customs and new political forces in the South. As he observed toward the essay's close:

> The proletariat will destroy the Southern agrarian bloc to the extent to which, through its party, it succeeds in organizing ever larger masses of peasants in autonomous and independent formations; but it will succeed to a more or less large extent in this obligatory task according to its

capacity to break up the intellectual bloc which forms the flexible but very resistant armor of the agrarian bloc.[92]

The essay pictured the *Mezzogiorno* as "an area of extreme social disintegration."[93] Though in "perpetual ferment," the peasants had no inner cohesion as a class and were therefore easily manipulated. By and large, this manipulation was exercised by what Gramsci called "the big property owners and top intellectuals." The manipulation was easiest in the "ideological field," which was why "Giustino Fortunato and Benedetto Croce . . . represent the keystones of the Southern system and, in a certain sense, are the two greatest figures of Italian reaction."[94] Their power had been enhanced by the absence in the South of an organized tradition of what Gramsci loosely called "democratic intellectuals" of the peasantry or petty rural bourgeoisie.[95] Southern intellectuals were generally of the "old type" associated with "a society based on peasant and artisan."[96] They were aloof, affiliated entirely with the rural bourgeoisie rather than the peasantry, and disposed toward

a strong aversion for the peasant laborer whom they look on as a living machine that must be worked to the bone and can easily be replaced in view of overpopulation. They also develop an atavistic and instinctive feeling of crazy fear of the peasant and his destructive violence, and hence a habit of refined hypocrisy and a most refined skill in deceiving and breaking in the peasant masses.[97]

Two separate problems emerged from this analysis. One was to find a way to attack the hegemony of the top intellectuals directly. This became one of Gramsci's major preoccupations in the *Notebooks*, but he did not explore it in this essay. The second problem was to find an effective way of organizing "democratic intellectuals" in rural areas. Although Gramsci advanced no overarching formula for accomplishing this, he left a number of hints throughout the essay. In the North he seemed to suggest the creation of a Socialist-Christian dialogue, since the Northern priest was usually the son of an artisan or peasant and had good rapport with the rural population.[98] This would not be possible in the South, however, since the Southern priest was corrupt and totally lacking in popular respect. Two other possibilities would have to be explored there. One would be to offer encouragement and support to those few "democratic intellectuals" who had already organized. A recent example of such a group was the postwar "ex-servicemen's movement, in which peasant-soldiers and intellectual-officers formed themselves into a more united bloc which was to some extent antagonistic to the big landowners."[99] A second possibility might be to support "small and medium reviews" and "publishing houses around which average groups of intellectuals gather."[100] At the time, these were almost nonexistent, since potential "democratic intellectuals" had been forced to go North to seek work.

In this sense Benedetto Croce has fulfilled a supreme "national" function: he has detached the radical intellectuals of the South from the peasant masses, making them share in national and European culture, and by means of this culture he has caused them to be absorbed by the national bourgeoisie and so by the agrarian bloc.[101]

Now that they had recognized this fact, the socialists were obligated to reverse it.

In all this attention to cultivating a mass base, one senses the *Ordine Nuovo* mind at work, even if *ordinovismo* itself was only remotely translatable into the new circumstances. What was always constant in Gramsci's approach to politics was the notion that the "subjective factor" must be just as developed as the "objective conditions" if revolution is to take place. A "collective will" or mass base must therefore be "organized" through appropriately institutionalized forms of political education. In both the 1919-20 and 1924-26 periods, Gramsci conceived this organization as a relationship of three interconnected parts. At the apex stood the institution charged with overall tactical coordination, the initiation of revolutionary action, and the exemplification of proletarian consciousness, though not with political education directly. In the *Ordine Nuovo* scheme this was the disciplined party; now it was to be the central committee within a mass party. Political education was the responsibility of "democratic" or "organic" intellectuals and workers linked, in the earlier period, in worker councils, and in the later period, primarily at the lower levels of the party. Whenever possible, educational activity in the latter case was to be infused into worker and peasant committees and the various institutions of class alliance. But Gramsci knew that such activity was necessarily limited in a defensive situation, and his elaborations of this organization in the *Notebooks*[102] were entirely concerned with the relationship of "middle-level cadres" and masses within the party.

One must be careful, however, not to press this organizational parallel too far. "*Ordinovismo* in a defensive situation" is in some important respects no longer *ordinovismo*. For in recognizing the necessity of crowding nearly all his organizational design under the common roof of the party, Gramsci paradoxically took a large step toward abandoning the "new order" even as he was seeking to revive it. The new order was a genuinely popular expression because of its grounding in worker councils and because these councils were expressly designated as the dominant institutions in the overall design. Political education remained a central commitment of the party under Gramsci's leadership; indeed, given his insight into Western civil societies, it took on still greater importance than in the earlier period. But its incorporation into the bureaucratic structures of the party could hardly avoid choking off much of the participatory style and spontaneous self-activity that had characterized the councils. Moreover, the problem was exacerbated by the particular kind of party which the PCI had of necessity become. For the new party was not only a mass educator, it was a "Bolshevized" organ of the Comintern, a "party centralized nationally and internationally."[103] Gramsci could sometimes bend Comintern directives to local conditions and to his own principles and purposes.[104] In general, however, his commitment to the Comintern, which he recognized as crucial to PCI survival, left him no choice but to exercise considerable control over public discussion in the Party—a policy which, by his own later account, was inimical to any genuine program of political education.[105]

Already in the spring of 1923, when PCI survival was very much in doubt, Gramsci was writing that

> from the whole experience of the Russian Revolution it appears that the absence of unanimity on important public votes creates special attitudes in the midst of the great masses. The political opposition coalesces into a minority. It expands and generalizes its position, conspires to publish manifestoes, programs, etc., . . . and carries on an all-out effort of agitation which can become extremely dangerous at a certain moment.[106]

The point was clarified in the Lyons Theses:

> Complete ideological unity is necessary for a communist party to be able to carry out continually its function as a guide for the working class. Ideological unity is an element of party strength and of its political capacity, and it is indispensable in making it a Bolshevik party.[107]

And in keeping with this defense of a Bolshevized party, Gramsci bent over backwards to defend the CPSU in all its activities until the fall of 1926. What finally caused him to question the commitment to ideological unity had nothing to do with any sacrifices he was making in its name, but rather with the accumulating evidence that the CPSU itself was no longer living by any such "Bolshevik" spirit.

In a letter addressed to the Central Committee of the CPSU in October 1926, Gramsci criticized their recent activity on precisely the same grounds that he had defended them over the previous four years.[108] The CPSU and the Comintern, he had argued in this period, were important for Western revolution, above all because they symbolized proletarian solidarity and thus gave concrete focus to the idea of an alternative proletarian hegemony. But this function was now being negated by the "sharpness of [recent] polemics within the CPSU." These polemics might well have dangerous "international repercussions," especially in a society like Italy "where fascist state and party organization succeed in suffocating every notable manifestation of the autonomous life of the large worker and peasant masses."[109] Thus, while Gramsci did not stray from the principle of proletarian unity but rather posed as its great defender, he was also, paradoxically, expressing a dissenting viewpoint for the first time in nearly four years.

Four years later, in 1930, this incident would appear as the first episode in an evolving political self-criticism. For as Stalin consolidated his leadership in a highly authoritarian manner and, after 1928, moved international communism away from the defensive tactics that Lenin had advocated in his last years, Gramsci became increasingly critical of his leadership.[110] While we cannot pursue here an analysis of Comintern and PCI politics in the 1926-30 period,[111] it is clear that Gramsci's reaction to these politics stimulated a self-critical elaboration of his program as chairman that involved at least the following three points.

First, he appears to have recognized that the ideological unity he had demanded was excessive. In a prison conversation, he characterized the costs of inadequate internal discussion in these terms:

> Too often in our Party . . . there is fear of all those ideas not sanctified by inclusion in the old maximalist dictionary of clichés. . . . Any tactic which does not correspond well with the subjectivism of these dreamers is considered a deviation from proper revolutionary strategy and tactics. Then one ends up discussing revolution without having any very precise notion of what is to be done to realize it. . . .[112]

Later, in the *Prison Notebooks*, he would explicitly advocate open discussion within the Party.[113]

Secondly, he seems to have reacted to the Comintern left turn not simply by upholding his political position of 1924-26 but by deepening his commitment to a defensive alliance against fascism. Thus, as Paolo Spriano has argued, Gramsci's greater openness to a "constituent" in 1930 was almost certainly a self-critical reflection on the 1924-26 period.[114]

Finally, after 1926, he turned decisively toward a critique of authoritarian leadership in both the Party and the Comintern—indeed, wherever it appeared. In the *Notebooks*, he referred to authoritarianism as "Cadornism" (after the general who had been blamed for the Italian defeat at Caporetto in 1917), but he may well have been thinking of Stalin. For a "Cadornist" is one who fails to win the consent of those he is leading and who believes "that a thing will be done [merely] because the leader considers it just and reasonable that it should be done."[115]

None of this, however, should lead us to think that, in opposing Stalin privately, Gramsci would have been forced out of the Party had he not been in jail or that he was moving toward the Trotskyist opposition. In his 1965 biography of Gramsci, Giuseppe Fiori claimed, on the basis of an interview with Gramsci's brother Gennaro, who served as an intermediary between Gramsci and Togliatti in 1930, that Gramsci would almost certainly have been expelled or harshly condemned for his dissent on the "left turn."[116] But, as Spriano has recently shown, there is conflicting testimony which casts considerable doubt on Gennaro's account.[117] Moreover, while Gramsci did oppose the "left turn" in no uncertain terms, he was just as staunchly opposed to "fractionalism." Thus, it is by no means clear how far he would have carried his "dissent," and, given his long-standing practice of serving as a mediator between political extremes in the Party, it is doubtful that he would have seen any useful purpose in declaring his differences publicly.

As to Gramsci's relations with the Trotskyist opposition, one must begin by recognizing that he never held Trotsky in very high regard either as a political theorist or as a tactician. In 1924, he had criticized Trotsky for an "attitude of passive opposition, similar to Bordiga's," which has created a "crisis" that "puts in danger the very conquests of the revolution."[118] And he certainly did not agree with the analysis of Trotsky and Bordiga that the post-Fifth Congress Comintern had deviated from the principles of Leninism and the Russian Revolution.[119] When the third volume of Trotsky's *History of the Russian Revolution* appeared in 1924, Gramsci dismissed it as "revisionist" and wrote approvingly of its censorship by the Soviet government.[120]

Yet clearly it was the Trotsky issue which stood behind his 1926 letter to the CPSU. There he separated himself sharply from the view that Trotsky should be ousted because of his differences with Stalin. Indeed, he explicitly defended Trotsky, along with Zinoviev and Kamenev, as having "contributed powerfully to our education in revolution."[121] And after the Comintern Sixth Congress, when Gramsci retreated from the uncompromising internationalism of his politics as PCI chairman,[122] he may not have sided with Trotsky, but neither were their respective critiques entirely dissimilar.[123]

Apparently aware of this, Gramsci sought permission to read Trotsky's works in prison but was granted access only to *My Life*. From this work, and from citations he found elsewhere, he seems to have concluded that his earlier assessments of Trotsky's abstract and mechanical tendencies were essentially correct. In what is clearly a reference to Trotsky's theory of "permanent revolution," he cautioned in 1933 that "the line of development is, to be sure, towards internationalism, but the point of departure is 'national'—and it is from this point of departure that one must begin."[124] Trotsky was not sufficiently attuned to contemporary history; his political ideas branded him "in one way or another . . . a political theorist of frontal attack in a period in which it only leads to defeats."[125] Trotsky had failed to appreciate what Gramsci believed Lenin had seen late in life: that revolution in the West would have to be waged in a fundamentally different fashion than the frontal attack strategy which had been applied victoriously in the East.[126] Thus, Leonetti seems justified in concluding that Gramsci's post-1926 opposition, if it must be labeled, was not Trotskyist but "Bolshevik-Leninist,"[127] in the sense that it remained wedded to the pre-turn strategy of mass politics and antifascist class alliance. Gramsci's many admiring references to Lenin in the *Notebooks* are best understood in this context.

Before turning to the political theory of the *Prison Notebooks*, then, we need to make a summary assessment of Gramsci's relation to Lenin over the entire course of Gramsci's active political life. It was suggested in the last chapter that, prior to 1921, Gramsci admired the Lenin who had organized and won the Russian Revolution, who had written of soviets and democracy in *State and Revolution* and other shorter pieces since 1917, and who had come to symbolize for a whole generation the kind of dedication and will necessary to lead the international proletariat. Except in the case of the worker councils, however, Gramsci did not model his ideas and projects after Lenin's but rather used him as the crucial ally for sustaining conclusions that he had arrived at quite independently of Lenin's influence. Thus, Lenin's practical commitment to the role of human will in history served to buttress Gramsci's fight not only against scientistic Marxism but against all forms of positivism which he had been taught to suspect by Croce, Gentile, Labriola, Papini, and Sorel. Likewise, Lenin served Gramsci in the summer of 1920 as an important ally in his fight to free the PSI from the passive and mechanicist extreme represented by Serrati on the one hand, and the sectarianism and elitism represented by Bordiga on the other. Even in the case of the worker councils, Gramsci was indebted to Lenin less for any organizational design than for the flash of inspiration which alerted him to the need for building the political-economic structures that prefigure a new socialist society.

What I would argue about the 1921-26 period is that, even as

Gramsci gained far greater knowledge of Lenin's work, he continued to use him as an ally in much the same way as before. Thus, in 1921-22, when Lenin was of little use to Gramsci because of their quite fundamental disagreements, Gramsci had no qualms about expressing what these disagreements were. Though he had never been anyone's loyal disciple and had never adopted anyone else's notions without giving them his own personal stamp, these years offer a particularly dramatic example of Gramsci's independence of mind. Yet, in 1924, when Gramsci came to loggerheads with Bordiga over the nature of fascism and Western revolution, Lenin once again became important for Gramsci as an ally and, eventually, as the legitimation for the direction of his new leadership.

We see this alliance manifested in at least two ways. On the theoretical level, Gramsci now turned to Lenin's concept of "hegemony."[128] Though Lenin had distinguished himself at "Eastern" revolution, the concept of hegemony was well suited to conceptualizing the present need in the West for a patient nurturing of class alliances into alternative states. As we will see more fully in Chapter 6, Gramsci went far beyond Lenin in developing this concept, and yet continued to insist on Lenin's essential authorship of it. As in the case of his advocacy of worker councils, Gramsci's "Leninism" here served to legitimize a theoretical position which later orthodox "Marxist-Leninists" would probably regard as "idealist."

On the practical level of organization, Lenin's canonical warrant aided in promoting a centralized yet mass-based party which could serve as the vehicle for the class alliances and popular political education that the coming Western revolution presupposed. At the same time, Gramsci's politics remained largely free of the sort of "Leninism" which had actually brought the Bolsheviks into power or which was later enshrined by Stalin and Mao. As we will see more fully in Chapter 7, Gramsci's concept of revolution was very different from Lenin's. In line with this conception, he believed to the end in the capacity of and need for workers to define their socialist consciousness through production-based institutions of their own creation. His writings revealed no obsession with the party for its own sake, no interest in creating a professional elite to manipulate the masses, no limiting of political education merely to an instrumental role in revolution, and certainly no passive and undialectical "copy theory of perception" as the philosophical grounding for his pedagogy.[129] When at one point he defined "Leninism" for himself, he stressed only its general commitments to Marxism, proletarian activism, political realism, party discipline, and internationalism.[130]

On the evening of November 8, 1926, Gramsci was summarily arrested and thrown in jail despite the immunity guaranteed him as an elected parliamentary deputy. After this he would be shuffled from prison to prison, brought to trial finally in May 1928, and then sentenced to jail for twenty years, four months, and five days. "We must prevent this brain from functioning . . . ," the prosecutor had declared at his trial,[131] and it was a remark that would prove both ironic and tragic. Eight months later, in the isolation of a prison cell at Turi, Gramsci began the notebooks that would gain him considerable posthumous acclaim. But while he continued to express his political opinions to the few who could hear him, he would never again enjoy a public audience or participate actively in public affairs.

Part Two

CHAPTER FOUR

Philosophy as Political Education

A man of politics writes about philosophy: it could be that his "true" philosophy should be looked for rather in his writings on politics.

(1932-33)

THE ENFORCED isolation of prison, though never entirely removing Gramsci from the world of concrete politics, did force him to think out its issues as part of a larger historical panorama. He was himself fully conscious of this when he wrote to his sister-in-law in 1927 that he wanted now to accomplish something "*für ewig.*"[1] The reality of Stalin's left turn after 1928 could only have reinforced Gramsci's sense of isolation. While we have seen that he did not flinch from confronting this development, his most sustained and thoroughgoing critiques of it were philosophical rather than programmatic. If the Comintern was taking a "mechanistic" and "economistic" route like the one which led the Second International to a shipwreck on the shores of World War I, then surely nothing less than a full-scale philosophical reconstruction of Marxism as a "philosophy of praxis" would suffice to set it back on course.

Our purpose in this chapter will be to explore the epistemological underpinnings of Gramsci's "philosophy of praxis" as it is articulated in the *Prison Notebooks.* It must be kept continually in mind, however, that for Gramsci a true "philosophy" is never an isolated branch of study but rather "contains in itself all the fundamental elements needed to construct a total and integral conception of the world . . . and everything that is needed to give life to an integral political organization of society."[2] This point is reflected in his very definition of Marxist orthodoxy: the view that the "philosophy of praxis" is "general" and "sufficient unto itself."[3] Thus, just as Gramsci's politics led him to philosophy, so his philosophy was thoroughly political.[4] This is true not only of its practical intention (it is no accident that his critique of Bukharin was initiated at the same time that he led prison discussions about Comintern politics and theorized the concept of a "war of position")[5] but also of its internal character. The key to grasping the full import of Gramsci's epistemology is to recognize how fully entwined it is with considerations on political education. This connection is affirmed very early in the *Notebooks* and repeated many times thereafter.[6]

In positing this connection, however, Gramsci inherited a whole range of problems within the Marxist tradition. We saw initially that his early intellectual horizons were largely confined to Italy and France. His critical appropriation of Marx was partial, came relatively late, and was heavily mediated by the discussions of Labriola, Croce, Gentile, and Sorel. This mediation remains continually evident in the *Notebooks*; but given the breadth of his reflection, a fuller and more direct confrontation with Marx and Marxism was also necessary. Before turning directly to Gramsci, then, we must look more closely at the connections between Marx's philosophy and his conception of political education. Indeed, we will need to begin by situating both Marx and Gramsci in a larger tradition of philosophical discourse.

Plato, Hegel, and Marx

Among the most fundamental assumptions in Marx's theoretical enterprise is the idea that human reason could become a "material" or life-transforming force able to shape human character and direct it (or reveal its movement) toward the "good life." Stated in this way, it is obvious that Marx participated in a Socratic tradition of political philosophy, even if he also believed that his "unity of theory and praxis" could dialectically transcend this tradition. In Plato's classic expression, politics and philosophy were conceived in the same terms; the goal was to rationalize the political order according to the results of philosophical reflection and to institute the search for philosophical knowledge as the major principle of political order. Yet this is hardly the only way that philosophy has been conceived, and, on the whole, it is distinctly out of favor in the modern world. Already in Aristotle we find a denial that there exists any *theoria* about politics;

though the characteristically Greek insistence on the "good life" as the end of the state is retained, politics is conceived entirely as praxis, which depends as much on good habits as clear thinking.[7] With Descartes and Hobbes, even the political ideal of the "good life" or "ethical state" is denied, and philosophy becomes entirely the private province of the individual inquirer.

The Platonic tradition remained the subject of creative transformation by some philosophers. The Renaissance utopians (More and Campanella), Rousseau, Kant, Fichte, and Hegel are certainly among this company; and I would argue that Marx and Hegelian Marxists are in it as well. Yet even in this tradition, the critique of the classical conception of philosophy remains fundamental. A central section of Hegel's *Phenomenology*,[8] for instance, is concerned with a critique of the view that politics can be entrusted to the heroic leadership of philosopher-kings. Such a conception is part of an aristocratic ideal of service which Hegel found not just out of date but out of tune with human nature.[9] In setting himself apart from the pursuit of wealth that material labor makes possible, the philosopher *qua* noble public servant denies his own creative needs, assumes an artificial posture toward the world, and risks inner spiritual discord. Hegel thought that the final bankruptcy of this "heroism of dumb service" revealed itself historically when it devolved into the "heroism of flattery" and eventually into the "base consciousness" which it had originally sought to educate.[10]

Apart from its direct political implications, the significance of this critique lies in its recourse to historical reflection. Hegel's point was both the shameful smallness of individual rationalization, given the larger pattern of historical development, and the educative value of history when reappropriated through critical reflection. Indeed, his overall view of history led him even further: history, not "philosophy," is the great cosmic tutor of mankind. The philosopher's role is not to bring the ideal state into being, but as we learn in the *Philosophy of Right*, to strive for a comprehension of how men acting in history have brought it into being.[11] The entire thrust of Hegel's philosophical effort was to show how the real and the rational have become wedded in the historical present.

Marx's conception of philosophy may be understood as a

simultaneous critique of both Plato and Hegel. His early writings implicitly reject "philosophy" both as an elite activity dispensed to and shaping an acquiescent polity and as a merely mental appropriation of the historical totality.[12] For Marx, all true philosophy is autodidactic: laboring, producing, and thinking men are their own educators through their own praxis. This is foreshadowed in Fichte's notion of self-activity and in Hegel's notions of self-activity and immanent critique. Even the linkage between the self-activity of human labor and the formulation of immanent critiques is foreshadowed in Hegel's early discussion of "tools" and in his depiction of the slave's self-tutelage in the famous dialectic of "lordship and bondage."[13] But Marx developed a much more concrete and thorough description of this process and added the notion that the rational self-awareness of Hegel's slave is tantamount to a revolutionary consciousness.

At the same time, Marx shared with Hegel the view that individual praxis is in a dialectical relationship with history: through praxis, men collectively create their own history, which then limits and conditions their praxis. Marx, of course, could not accept Hegel's distinctive version of this dialectic. As he argued in the *Holy Family*:

> Already with Hegel, the absolute spirit of history has its material in the masses, but only finds adequate expression in philosophy. But the philosopher appears merely as the instrument by which absolute spirit, which makes history, arrives at self-consciousness after the historical movement has been completed. The philosopher's role in history is thus limited to this subsequent consciousness, for the real movement is executed unconsciously by the absolute spirit.[14]

Yet, after rejecting the "absolute spirit which makes history," Marx had difficulty deciding on the precise character and philosophical status of his own historical dialectic. As Helmut Fleischer has recently suggested, Marx approached the problem in three quite different ways at various points in his intellectual development.[15] The dialectic that he put forward in the *Economic and Philosophical Manuscripts* of 1844 is "anthropological," in the sense that history is conceived idealistically as the humanization of the species. The nature of the human "essence" or

Gattungswesen ("species being") can be discovered and portrayed as the subject in a dialectical unfolding where the emerging totality is invested with universal meaning. Just a year later, however, in the sixth *Thesis on Feuerbach*, Marx dismissed any such anthropological essence as a mystification. The resulting "pragmatological" dialectic found here and in the *German Ideology* treated human nature not as an "essence" but as the "ensemble of social relations" in a particular cultural-temporal setting. This conception remained teleological only in the weaker sense that collectively organized and situated individuals were seen as pursuing concrete aims to satisfy felt needs. In some of the later writings, such as the 1859 preface to the *Critique of Political Economy*, we encounter still a third, "nomological" conception of history, which, in contrast to the two earlier formulations, takes history to be a natural process unfolding through objective laws without regard to human subjectivity.

In each case, however, any conception of philosophy as a form of political tutelage by an elite over a passive citizenry seems to be rejected as firmly as it was by Hegel. Only the "nomological" conception can logically accommodate such a view, but it makes philosophy and education superfluous. In the two dialectical conceptions, philosophy and education are grounded in the self-activity of social labor, a move which effectively solves the riddle of "who shall educate the educator."

Though these two dialectics differ in the way such self-active praxis is incorporated into the larger historical framework, both assent to an internal dynamic of power and need as portrayed in the following passage:

> Immediately, *man* is a *natural being*. As a living natural being he is, in one aspect, endowed with the natural *capacities* and *vital powers* of an *active* natural being. These capacities exist in him as tendencies and capabilities, as *drives*. In another aspect as a natural, living, sentient and objective being man is a *suffering*, conditioned, and limited creature like an animal or plant. The *objects* of his drives, that is to say, exist outside him as independent, yet they are *objects* of his *need*, essential and indispensable to the exercise and confirmation of his *essential capacities*. . . .
>
> A being which does not have its nature outside itself is not a *natural* one and has no part in the system of nature.[16]

In this view, human qualities appear to be divided into two sorts: "powers" (or capacities) and "needs" (or drives).[17] People act because they have felt certain desires demanding satisfaction which are expressed as needs. Through these needs they learn of or develop certain powers which are then utilized in transforming objects to satisfy the needs. There is, however, no final satisfaction of needs, since the satisfaction of one set only produces another, which in turn encourages the development of new powers that transform new sets of objects. The interaction of human powers and needs with the natural environment is a thoroughly historical process. As new needs arise, old ones are discarded. Formerly active powers atrophy, and formerly dormant ones bloom. The dialectical otherness of nature is continually transforming in response.

In a well-known passage in the *German Ideology*, Marx connected this dynamic interplay of powers and needs with the formation of ideas:

> The production of ideas, of conceptions, of consciousness is directly interwoven with the material activity and the material relationships of men; it is the language of actual life. Conceiving, thinking, and the intellectual relationships of men appear here as the direct result of their material behavior. The same applies to intellectual production as manifested in a people's language of politics, law, morality, religion, metaphysics, etc. Men are the producers of their conceptions, ideas, etc., but these are real, active men, as they are conditioned by a definite development of their productive forces and of the relationships corresponding to these up to their highest forms. Consciousness can never be anything else except concious existence, and the existence of men is their actual life-process.[18]

However, when this conception is applied to the formation of consciousness in the capitalist mode of production, an important paradox emerges. For while capitalism does not stifle, indeed may even stimulate, the "need" for philosophical knowledge, Marx's descriptions of capitalist workers suggest that they lack the necessary "powers"—of logical inference; moral, aesthetic, and political judgment; even perception—necessary to satisfy that need. Capitalist labor "produces intelligence, but for the worker it produces imbecility and cretinism."[19] The paradox, however, is *not* that the pedagogy of what Marx once called the "hard but hardening school of labor"[20] is counterproductive simply because its pupils emerge from it so ill-equipped. As Hegel had suggested in the master/slave dialectic, the slave (worker) needs to be stripped of every human determination in order to achieve a consciousness of himself as pure humanity, and therefore a breakthrough to self-consciousness. The paradox is that once this breakthrough has been achieved, it is unclear how the worker in capitalist society (as opposed to the slave in Hegel's metaphysical and only vaguely historical account) can then build a personality complete with "powers" necessary for revolution in a labor process which continues to deprive him of embodied subjectivity.

Marx never offered a systematic discussion aimed at overcoming this perplexity, and the omission represents a crucial shortcoming in his account of the nature and role of philosophy. Though he always remained committed to the goal of philosophy realized in society, he was, as the famous eleventh *Thesis on Feuerbach* suggests, too impatiently revolutionary to specify exactly how this integration could begin. Instead, he seems to have retreated to a narrowly pragmatic concern with how the proletariat could gain class consciousness despite its enfeebled condition. The problems of philosophy and education were sometimes reduced to instrumental questions soluble through technical and organizational rationality,[21] and the "school of labor" was supplemented with conceptions of proletarian pedagogy that relied to some degree on "outside educators," in defiance of the third *Thesis on Feuerbach*. Especially in his letters and his more informal and occasional writings on politics, Marx worked with at least two such conceptions.

The first of these might be termed the "therapeutic image," since the role of the educator here, to speak somewhat anachronistically, is to act as a kind of nondirective therapist who, in wakening the world from its own dreams, only facilitates but does not impose a new and more correct praxis.[22] Such a role is perhaps still reconcilable with the third *Thesis on Feuerbach*. But sometimes Marx went even further. For instance, in his "Circular Letter" written in 1879 to the German Social Democrats, he advocated a "directive image" in which bourgeois intellectuals would play an active, educative role in bringing the proletariat to critical consciousness.[23] Such educators would "*join* the militant proletariat"; yet, in supplying the proletariat with "educative elements," they would come painfully close to dividing the proletariat "into two parts—one of which towers above."

The Second International and Its Critics

These ambiguities did not merely undermine the philosophical coherence of Marx's work, they provided an indispensable precondition for the major ideological disputes of the Second International, which pitted "orthodox Marxists" like Kautsky and Plekhanov, who proclaimed the inevitability of proletarian revolution, against the very diverse tendencies—from Bernstein's revisionism to Lenin's radical voluntarism—that were based on doubts in this inevitability. These disputes have been well analysed elsewhere, and we may simply highlight their main features here.[24]

What the orthodox and their critics tended to share was a view of Marxism as a "science of history." Most of them had cut their intellectual eyeteeth on Marx's later "economic" writings such as the famous description of the "Historical Tendency of Capitalist Accumulation" in *Capital*, and were heavily influenced by the late Engels's positivistic popularizations of Marx's work. Theirs was the "nomological" Marx for whom "philosophy" had been transcended by "political economy." Consequently, as Karl Korsch quipped in his famous polemic against this generation, "it was not regarded as impossible, for example, for a leading Marxist theoretician to be a follower of Arthur Schopenhauer in his private philosophical life."[25] When philosophy was taken seriously, as in Lenin's *Materialism and Empirio-criticism*, it tended to fall back into pre-Marxian and even precritical positions like eighteenth-century materialism and its "copy theory of perception."[26]

In such a Marxism, the cherished "unity of theory and practice" either ceased to exist or became a caricature of Marx's intention—a theory *for* practice rather than a theory *of* practice. Theory became a kind of technical instrument which anyone could wield, rather than a dialectical reflection of the experience of the working class as it matured toward revolution. In Lenin's case the result was blatant contradiction: the radical voluntarism that he advocated in *What Is to Be Done?* was logically incompatible with the materialist and determinist assumptions he took from Engels. But the great monument to the division of theory and practice in this period was the Erfurt Program around which the German Social Democrats united in 1891.[27] Drafted mainly by Karl Kautsky, the program came in two entirely unrelated sections. The first was a "theoretical" section modeled on the *Communist Manifesto*, which offered an analysis of the capitalist crisis and its slowly approaching but inevitable demise; the second outlined a series of short-run political objectives based entirely on the material interests of workers within the existing order.

Where the orthodox and their critics parted company was over the question of whether Marx's "science" and its "predictions," as they understood them, remained valid. This division led in turn to a radically different estimation of the nature and role of political education. If, like Kautsky or Luxemburg, one accepted these "predictions" or sought to revise them within the deterministic framework of capitalism's inevitable demise, political education did not have to be theorized at all; history would simply take care of itself. Of course, this did not necessarily mean that political education was ignored in practice. Indeed, Kautsky's Social Democrats built such an intricate network of educational facilities that it was often referred to as a "state within a state." But like the later *Università popolare* in Italy, these facilities were more like shelters to protect workers from the cold winds of capitalism than outposts on the road to revolution and socialized humanity. This prompted Luxemburg's argument that such institutions were counterproductive and that the most genuinely radical form of political education was to leave the worker free to be tossed about in the capitalist storm.[28]

But if, on the other hand, one came to doubt either the continuing applicability of Marx's economic analysis or the inevitability of revolution from economic conditions alone, then political education became much more significant in precisely an instrumentalist sense. The first doubt led to the reformism of Eduard Bernstein and the need to educate the worker to take full advantage of the existing parliamentary system.[29] The second doubt led to Lenin's voluntarism, the belief that the "school of labor" produced only "trade union consciousness" and that true consciousness would have to be imposed on the worker from outside.[30]

The major exception to this schematization of Second International Marxism was the Italian philosopher Antonio Labriola.[31] Though a relatively minor figure in terms of his general influence, Labriola was deeply admired by Gramsci and merits some attention here. As a university professor rather than a party militant, he had turned to Marxism only in his late forties, after a long stint as an Hegelian.[32] His major writings in the 1890s articulated a "philosophy of praxis"—Gramsci later borrowed the phrase—which was staunchly anti-positivist and which retained many Hegelian features. What Gramsci admired in Labriola was the intellectual revolution contained in "his affirmation (not always, admittedly, unequivocal) that the philosophy of praxis is an independent and original philosophy which contains in itself the elements of a further development, so as to become, from an interpretation of history, a general philosophy."[33]

Labriola's principal interest was in how men make history, and he leaned heavily on the dynamic category of praxis and on a "genetic method" rather than on the rigid social statics of then-influential positivists like Achille Loria. Loria had maintained the crude thesis that politics, culture, and other "superstructural" aspects of society were determined by the economic base in a direct and unmediated fashion.[34] For Labriola, historical prediction should be based not on a causal but on a dialectical (or "genetic") necessity, one which grasped a complexly mediated totality of constantly shifting structural and superstructural cleavages which rendered capitalism prone to crisis and incapable of forever deferring its collapse. History was to be studied as a succession of social "formations" governed in their transitions as much by ideology as by economic forces.[35] And Labriola grounded this view in a conception of subjective human will through which all knowledge, including that of the most exact sciences, was constituted in response to human needs.[36]

Yet, for all his dialectical dexterity, Labriola occasionally lapsed into a mechanicism that set him apart from the more thoroughgoing Hegelian Marxism of the postwar era.[37] And despite his recognition of the historically active role of human subjectivity, he dismissed as "utopian" those political theories incorporating a "subjective pedagogy."[38] Moreover, though extremely critical of Loria, he failed to perceive the positivist incrustations already present in Marx. While he occasionally hinted at reservations concerning the rampant positivism in the later Engels, he did not press the matter in their correspondence and was sufficiently admiring of Engels to recommend his chapter on "The Negation of the Negation" as an introduction to the Marxist dialectic.[39] Labriola then proceeded to use Engels's well-known reference to the decisiveness of the economy "in the last analysis"[40] as the grounding for a structural determinism which, as Gramsci later pointed out, was sharply at odds with his dialectical formulations.[41]

How is this tension to be explained? A close reading of the *Essays on the Materialistic Conception of History* suggests that Labriola was squaring off against two quite different antagonists. While he clearly hoped to rescue Marxism from its vulgarizers by stressing human activity and subjectivity, he was also acutely aware of the tendency of subjectively grounded philosophy to fall into an idealism which loses its integral connections with material reality. He therefore attacked those who believe that "ideas fall from heaven" at least as sharply as those who reduce ideas to their "economic determinations."[42] The acid test for resolving this ambiguity would seem to be his position on the nature and function of "historical laws," yet we do not encounter any explicit argument on this point in the *Essays*. While he ridiculed Darwinian conceptions of Marxism, he also spoke of "laws of movement" and "historical-social laws" without clarifying their logical and epistemological status.[43] Labriola certainly understood the poverty of philosophy in the Second International, but his own transcending of its conceptual coordinates was at best ambiguous.

In later years, perhaps under Croce's influence, Labriola began to think more systematically about the philosophy of history, and he seems to have become aware of the tension in his thought between subjectivity and mechanicism. Thus the bold, confident tone of the *Essays* gave way to much greater caution in *Socialism and Philosophy*, where, for example, he maintained that Marxism was still only at a "stage of first formation."[44] The decisive turn, however, came only in the last, posthumously published essays. Here he emphasized the "dangers of facile schematization" in historical inquiry;[45] ridiculed any philosophy of history which is "teleological";[46] claimed that his own historical understanding could be represented only as "fragments";[47] and even went so far as to dismiss the very notion of a "scientific" historical narrative.[48] The phrase "historical materialism" was retained, but its definition was drastically reduced to these two propositions: (1) that human organization is "always proportional to the relative state of economic articulation," and (2) that religious, mythological, and moral conceptions are "responses to a determinant social condition."[49] One is reminded of nothing so much as Croce's conception of Marxism as a canon of historical interpretation. Yet there is no evidence that Labriola was abandoning Marxism or socialism.[50] What did remain unclear, because of his death in 1904, was how he would have elaborated a new "philosophy of praxis" in the light of his revised, and more modest, conception of history.

The conceptual coordinates of Second International Marxism were also not transcended by those activists at the far left of the social democratic parties like Rosa Luxemburg, the Hungarian Erwin Szabó, the Dutch "Tribunists," and syndicalists like Georges Sorel. However, their Marxisms, though less philosophically trenchant than Labriola's, were often linked more explicitly to political education. Of particular importance here were the Dutch "Tribunists," particularly Anton Pannekoek, Henriette Roland Holst, and Herman Gorter. The best known among them was probably Gorter, who replied to Lenin's *Left-Wing Communism —An Infantile Disorder* immediately after it appeared in 1920. Gorter's point was to remind Lenin of a cause of revolution "which when inoperative makes the revolution fail to appear or misfire. . . . This cause is the *Geist* ['spirit'] of the masses."[51] Much like Gramsci's, Gorter's emphasis was on the need for overcoming the deleterious effects of bourgeois ideology through autonomous organizations of proletarian education. He and the other "Tribunists" had been making this point in polemics with Kautsky since 1912. "Why had the working class," asked Pannekoek, "still not been able to seize power despite its superiority to the bourgeoisie both in numbers and as producers?" His answer was the "*geistige* superiority of the present ruling class. As a class which lives from surplus value and controls the means of production, it reigns over all educational development."[52] Pannekoek saw clearly how Kautsky was paralyzed by "actionless waiting" which tried to "let the great mass actions occur passively like a natural event."[53] But very little was done with these insights to reconstruct a revolutionary and philosophically viable Marxism.[54]

This remained true in the 1920s even of such devastating critiques of Second International Marxism as Karl Korsch's 1923 essay, *Marxism and Philosophy*. Yet the 1920s also saw the first bold step toward a full reconstitution of Marxism in Georg Lukács's *History and Class Consciousness*, a collection of essays written from 1919 to 1922 and published in the same year as Korsch's book. With well over a decade of study of the greatest exemplars of "bourgeois" philosophy and literature behind him, Lukács struck out on a brilliantly charted and highly original path which nonetheless can be seen as a kind of thematic intersection of Labriola, Luxemburg, and Lenin.[55] Like Labriola, whose work he did not actually know, Lukács conceived of Marxist orthodoxy not in terms of an adherence to "this or that thesis" but to the dialectical method and "the point of view of totality."[56] But Lukács also went well beyond Labriola in the clarity and rigor with which he portrayed this totality. Without benefit from Marx's 1844 *Manuscripts*, which were not published in Germany for another decade, Lukács conceived totality not merely as the determining domination of the whole over the parts—a conception which could as easily lead to a romanticism or vitalist irrationalism as to Marxism—but as a "concrete" unity of historically interacting contradictions linked together by the all-important category of "mediation."

Against "bourgeois" empiricism, Lukács argued that in order to define some specific "thing" concretely, one had to grasp all the "mediations" between its "immediate" givenness and the whole.[57] Such mediations were "concrete" when conceived in terms of practico-critical activity rather than in terms of Hegelian categories, which, according to Lukács, floated above the historical process and so became frozen into new immediacies. But like Hegel and like the "anthropological dialectic" of the young Marx, Lukács stressed the dialectical necessity of the historical movement toward totality. History was the immanent realization of the human "essence";[58] and it was in this sense fated to have a happy ending.[59] Thus, Lukács could go very far with Luxemburg's economistic conception of ideas flowing directly from objective historical development even as he sought to comprehend the historically creative role of a self-conscious praxis.

Again like Luxemburg before him, Lukács viewed the revolutionary crisis situation itself as the key historical moment in which subjectivity and objectivity flowed together. To explain the mode of this fusion, however, Lukács formulated a novel conception of "class consciousness" grounded in the "identical subject-object" of history.[60] In stripping the worker of objectifications, capitalism deprives him of every human power except that of perceiving subjectivity itself. But the worker achieves a self-recognition of his pure humanity, Lukács argued, precisely because of this deprivation. "While the man reified in the bureaucracy, for instance, is turned into a commodity, mechanized and reified in the only faculties that might enable him to rebel against reification," the worker is able "to objectify himself *completely* against his existence."[61] Such a pure self-recognition is fertile soil for the nurturing of those powers of concentration, perception, and understanding necessary for revolutionary praxis. Though latent because inactive, these powers may become manifest during an economic crisis or even simply when the worker *qua* objective commodity is reunited on the market with his embodied subjectivity. In this sense, "the rise and evolution of its [the proletariat's] knowledge and its actual rise and evolution in the course of history are just two different sides of the same real process."[62]

Precisely how such a "school of labor" will be experienced concretely, however, is never convincingly elaborated. In this respect, Lukács's later self-criticism of his 1923 position seems justified:

But is the identical subject-object here anything more in truth than a purely metaphysical construct? Can a genuinely identical subject-object be created by self-knowledge, however adequate, and however truly based on an adequate knowledge of society, i.e., however perfect that self-knowledge is? We need only formulate the question precisely to see that it must be answered in the negative.[63]

At the time, the most obvious problem for Lukács arising from such a formulation was how to explain the proletariat's failure to achieve class consciousness sufficient for attaining political power during the European crisis of 1914-21. It is interesting that he developed the concept of reification only in 1922, after the waning of revolutionary prospects in Europe was widely perceived. By reification Lukács meant the power of capitalism to mystify the social totality and thus to prevent recognition of "things" as the human products of social labor rather than as given phenomena controlling social relations. Deficiencies in working-class consciousness might seem explicable in terms of an interference by reification in the transition from "pure humanity" to "revolutionary praxis"; but as we have just seen, the worker's complete objectification is precisely what is supposed to prevent such an interference. We can only conclude that Lukács's dialectic—while incorporating German Idealism's key insight of a subject, not yet fully extant, which knows its object only because it creates it—has been stated only formally and abstractly, which is to say that it does not transcend its idealistic origins.

Two further considerations reinforce this conclusion. In the final essay in *History and Class Consciousness*, Lukács tackled the problem of political organization. Though here he explicitly committed himself to the view that "organization is the form of mediation between theory and practice," he made no detailed account of this mediation as connected to his dialectic.[64] Instead, he simply adopted the external and therefore abstract solution available to him as the Leninist party.[65] As previous students of Lukács have noticed, he wound up with a philosophical construct deprived of organizational mediations and a theory of political organization without a philosophical grounding.[66]

Perhaps even a more serious problem for Lukács, however, was his failure to embed his dialectic within the natural world. In attacking Engels's claim for a "dialectic of nature," conceived as a set of natural laws which human beings can only contemplate, Lukács had been driven to the opposite extreme of a dialectic connected only to the "second nature" of human history. As Gramsci remarked:

If his [Lukács's] assertion presupposes a dualism between nature and man he is wrong because he is falling into a conception of nature proper to religion and to Graeco-Christian philosophy and also to idealism which does not in reality succeed in unifying and relating man and nature to each other except verbally. But if human history should be conceived also as the history of nature (also by means of the history of science) how can the dialectic be separated from nature? Perhaps Lukács, in reaction to the baroque theories of the *Popular Manual*, has fallen into the opposite error, into a form of idealism.[67]

To Gramsci, Lukács was certainly right as against Engels or Bukharin. What Lukács failed to see, however, was that nature is also "dialectical," for it too is a human creation. Since the history of nature is a part of human history—and not the other way around, as Engels would have it—there is every reason to study both history and nature dialectically.

Bukharin, Croce, and Gramsci

Though acute, Gramsci's criticism of Lukács was stated tentatively, for he knew very little of his work.[68] Apparently, he knew even less of Korsch.[69] But he shared with both of them a driving desire to rediscover the "genuine Marx," the Marx whose work represented an *Aufhebung* of the bourgeoisie in its highest achievements: the French Revolution and German Idealism.[70] Indeed, of the three men, Gramsci was probably the first to take up the project. Well before he knew much concretely about the Russian Revolution, he had recognized its significance as a "metaphysical event" and a "revolution against *Capital*," i.e., against the sterile economism of the Second International.[71] By the time he was helping to draft the Lyons Theses late in 1925, he had developed a sociological explanation for the "degeneration" of Marxism during the Second International.[72] Marxism, he thought, had won control of the European labor movement with the expulsion of the Bakuninists from the First International. But the rapid pace of capitalist expansion in the following decades had compromised that victory and prepared fertile ground for the growth of economism and reformism. In their zest for higher wages and benefits, workers turned their attention away from politics and the state. In Germany, where the new "labor aristocracy" was particularly strong, forms of "democratic utopianism" became plausible among erstwhile Marxists for the first time. Moreover, as the industrial sector of production grew, increasing numbers of the petty bourgeoisie and the peasantry were driven into the proletarian ranks, causing "a new diffusion . . . of national ideological currents as opposed to Marxist ones."[73]

This explanation for the Second International was characteristically Gramscian in the way it linked concrete economic developments and ideological trends into a practical political assessment. As Gramsci's interest in ideology became more concretely focused on the formation of intellectuals, this explanatory pattern was deepened. In the *Notebooks*, he drew an historical parallel between the formation and leadership of Second International intellectuals and those of the Protestant Reformation.[74] He argued that the Renaissance, for all its profound innovations in the arts and sciences, had been a reactionary movement that had ignored the plight of the popular classes. By addressing some of their concerns, the Reformation had swung the pendulum of counter-medievalism back in a more progressive direction. Unfortunately, this movement was flawed in its leadership. Reformation intellectuals were generally drawn from the traditional cultural elite, who, even in their most idealistic moments, could not make a full commitment to a popular cause. Gramsci thought that Erasmus symbolized the resulting "desertion of the intellectual . . . in the face of persecution and the stake."[75]

Something similar had happened to Marxism during the years of the Second International. While dynamics inherent in capitalist expansion were producing some proletarian intellectuals, the leadership of the European labor movement had still fallen to the "great intellectuals" of the "traditional intermediary classes." Perhaps unwittingly, these intellectuals had tended to subject the original Marxist "philosophy of praxis" to a "systematic revision rather than to advance its autonomous development."[76] The resulting practical failure only reinforced their attraction toward "economic determinism" or "fatalism" and away from an activist philosophy conceived of as political education. Second International theorists had donned "the clothing of the real and active will when in a weak position." The "mechanicist conception," Gramsci thought, had always been the natural "religion of the subaltern."[77]

In the decade before World War I, Gramsci found some evidence of a new proletarian activism reacting against the dominant orthodoxy.[78] In many cases, however, this was led by theorists like Sorel whose commitments to Marxism were tenuous at best. Moreover, no thinker of the period possessed the imagination to make a full reformulation of Marxism either theoretically or in practice.[79] Instead, the tendency was to restrict political vision to the search for a new proletarian institution upon which to fix one's attention. The syndicates represented such a fixation for Sorel, just as the tight-knit, elitist political party later did for Bordiga.

This was the condition of Marxism which Gramsci believed he had inherited. His philosophical response in the *Notebooks* was the Hegelian Marxism portrayed briefly in the Introduction and to be elaborated below. Yet this philosophy is not merely expounded. It rests on a double polemic: against Bukharin's *Popular Manual*,[80] the latest and most advanced successor to Second International mechanicism, which Gramsci took as representative of post-Leninist stagnation and deviation; and against Croce, whose speculative philosophy of "immanentism" and the "ethical-political moment" was to be dialectically surpassed just as Marx had surpassed Hegel.[81]

The critique of Bukharin goes back at least to 1925. In the climate of Bolshevization then prevailing, Gramsci chose to publish two chapters of the *Manual* as a didactic device for the party school. Yet this was far from being a mere parroting of orthodoxy. As Leonardo Paggi has recently shown, Gramsci made several highly significant interpolations in the text which undercut Bukharin's view of Marxism as a sociology in favor of viewing it as a "general philosophy."[82] In the *Notebooks*, this seed would sprout into a sustained elaboration of the connections between "sociology," "vulgar evolutionism," and political passivity on the one hand, and "philosophy," dialectics, and political activism on the other.[83] Though almost completely unknown outside Italy at the time, Gramsci can be seen in retrospect as a major participant in the Europe-wide debate on these issues involving Bukharin, Deborin, Zinoviev, Lukács, Korsch, and Marcuse.[84]

Bukharin's evolutionist misinterpretation of Marxism was mirrored in the logical order of his exposition. Since evolutionism ignored the active role that men take in creating history, it was only natural that Bukharin's starting point should be Marxism's relation "to the great systems of traditional philosophy and the religion of the leaders of the clergy, i.e., the conception of the world of the intellectuals and of high culture."[85] A dialectical approach, on the other hand, would have recognized that

> A work like the *Popular Manual*, which is essentially destined for a community of readers who are not professional intellectuals, should have taken as its starting point a critical analysis of the philosophy of common sense, which is the "philosophy of non-philosopher," or in other words the conception of the world which is uncritically absorbed by the various social and cultural environments in which the moral individuality of the average man is developed. Common sense is not a single unique conception, identical in time and space. It is the "folklore" of philosophy.[86]

Having begun with common sense, the author could then have invited the reader to join in a journey toward reason through which a critical awareness of his presuppositions and their relatedness to those of his language, class, and epoch could perhaps be realized.[87] Only as a medium of political education can philosophy become a material force.

Yet, Bukharin's error was not only to have forgotten that philosophy is a "cultural battle to transform the popular 'mentality'";[88] it was also to have failed to understand that philosophy itself is a form of collective activity. Gramsci never denied the existence of the "professional or technical philosopher,"[89] but he did argue that philosophy's practitioners are "much more similar to the rest of mankind than are other specialists." While "there can be specialists in entomology without everybody else having to be an empirical entomologist. . . , it is not possible to conceive of any man who is not also a philosopher, who does not think, because thought is proper to man as such, or at least to any man who is not a pathological cretin."[90] Philosophy is intrinsically a social activity because it is carried on by all people in everyday life. We think, we decide, we act, our actions affect others, we are affected by the results, and we think again. In this circularity, it is the social interaction that is important. Even the most traditional philosopher, who believed himself to be engaged in a pure and solitary contemplation, was intimately bound to the social order in his use of language, a totality of culturally produced notions, and in his practical intention, whether consciously or unconsciously expressed.[91] At bottom, philosophical claims about men and the world have always represented attempts "by a specific class of people to change, correct or perfect the conceptions of the world that exist in any particular age and thus to change the norms of conduct that go with them—in other words, to change practical activity as a whole."[92]

From this perspective Marxism could be understood as a becoming conscious of the full implications of philosophical activity and as a commitment by the new organic intellectuals of the proletariat to philosophy's full realization.[93] Such a commitment, however, would be subverted from the start so long as Marxism is conceived "objectively" as a positive science seeking the "laws" of historical development. Bukharin's concept of science presupposed "an extra-historical and extra-human objectivity" which entirely overlooked "the concepts of historical movement, of becoming and, therefore, of the dialectic itself."[94] This objectivity is "a hangover of the concept of God" transformed into a fetishism of science. An immanent alternative, however, is not a naive subjectivism; rather it entails recognizing that "objective always means 'humanly objective' which can be held to correspond exactly to 'historically subjective': in other words, objective would mean 'universal subjective.'"[95] Of course, any particular historical actor confronts a set of previously constituted social and political conditions which may thus be thought of as objective in an external way. In part for this reason,

Gramsci constantly quoted the passage from the preface to the *Critique of Political Economy* to the effect that "society does not pose for itself tasks the conditions for whose resolution do not already exist."[96] Yet, from the point of view of totality, the "objective" world is constantly created.[97] History records a "struggle for objectivity . . . and this struggle is the same as the struggle for the cultural unification of the human race. What the idealists call 'spirit' is not a point of departure but a point of arrival, it is the ensemble of the superstructures moving towards concrete and objectively universal unification and it is not a unitary presupposition."[98]

Contrary to Bukharin, then, history is lawlike only in a highly restricted sense. There can be no "question of 'discovering' a metaphysical law of 'determinism,' or even of establishing a 'general' law of causality." The most that can be hoped for is that the study of history will depict how "relatively permanent forces are constituted which operate with a certain regularity and automatism."[99] Conceivably, certain general statistical laws ("laws of tendency") might be developed from close empirical observations of society, and Gramsci conceded that such laws have some "practical utility," indeed that they may even represent one component in the process of "creating a collective will."[100] As practical instruments their truth value lies in their efficacy, which, however, is unlikely ever to be absolute. Paradoxically, such laws are absolutely accurate only to the extent that "the great masses of the population remain essentially passive."[101] Because history records the unfolding of human activity and creativity, the most that one can "foresee" in future history is its general character as a struggle for objectivity, "not the concrete moments of the struggle."[102]

One senses the proximity of Hegel's owl of Minerva to these formulations, and a strong case can also be made for Sorel's influence, especially in the notion of history as a struggle for objectivity.[103] Yet the figure who casts the longest shadow over this discussion is surely Croce, even if his influence is rather convoluted. When Gramsci wrote that "just as Hegelianism was the premise of the philosophy of praxis in the nineteenth century . . . so Crocean philosophy ought to be the premise of a revival of the philosophy of praxis in our own day," he was brandishing his major weapon in the struggle against the degeneration of Marxism that Bukharin represented.[104] Unconsciously and from a bourgeois perspective, Croce had taken over the development of the philosophy of praxis, and consequently he was indispensable to anyone who would further this reconstitution. At the same time, he was the political incarnation of a bourgeois anti-Marxism which, like Dühring, had to be openly confronted and repudiated.

The discussion of "laws of tendency" and prediction illustrates this nicely. As a staunch anti-positivist, Croce could be enlisted in the battle against Bukharin-style Marxism; yet he had gone to the opposite extreme of denying the possibility of historical prediction in any sense. We have seen that Gramsci had critically confronted this position already in 1919, and the point is reargued in the *Notebooks*.[105] Gramsci's pragmatological approach to prediction was an effort to mediate between the stark alternatives of Bukharin and Croce. Croce was right to deny the viability of prediction as a matter of pure theory, but he overlooked the possibility that prediction could be forged in the crucible of theory and practice, that it could acquire its only true objectivity when linked to a program whose realization would offer the verifying test.[106] Without a concept of prediction, Croce found direction in history only by smuggling in a concept of providence beneath the cover of a speculative retranslation of Vico.[107] In Gramsci's framework, "necessity" would be understood not as a logical or scientific category but as "an efficient and active *premise*, consciousness of which in people's mind has become operative, proposing concrete goals to the collective consciousness and constituting a complex of convictions and beliefs which acts powerfully in the form of 'popular beliefs.'"[108] When this relatively weak sense of necessity is applied to historical praxis, Croce's reduction of political practice to arbitrariness can be overcome while at the same time avoiding all transcendental incrustations.

Croce's object, as Gramsci had recognized since his university days, was to locate some common ground underlying mind and matter that would unite them as separate functions of a single process.[109] Croce believed that he had found such a grounding in the concept of history; for Croce, as for Hegel, history was an unfolding totality whose meaning was both the sum of our knowledge and the methodological premise of every partial science. Yet Croce, like Marx, repudiated Hegel's "world spirit" as a metaphysical construction: the only real history was human history; the only real spirit was the spirit of man. History was a stage constructed by men upon which they played out a drama which could be grasped as the reciprocal action of four moments: the aesthetic, the ethical, the true, and the useful. For Croce, however, these moments were not higher forces but heuristic aids, not component parts of a pan-logism but fully concrete representation of all of reality under each of its aspects. Not only Hegel's but all grand doctrines of philosophical history were discarded by Croce in favor of an "absolute historicism" which identified philosophy with history but which saw history as nothing more than the sum of human actions. Like the philosophies of the French Enlightenment, Croce's was not an "esprit de système" but an "esprit systématique."

For Gramsci this posture was wholly admirable; Croce's "greatest quality," he thought, "has always been the ability to disseminate his ideas about the world in a series of brief, unpedantic writings, which the public reality absorbs as 'good sense' and 'common sense.'"[110] Gramsci also admired Croce's "unshakeable belief . . . that history is rational."[111] Yet, for all his pretenses to having abandoned every trace of transcendentalism, Croce was no more able than the classical idealists to go beyond the concept of an abstract human essence (Croce's "spirit of man") and to conceive of man in the terms of the sixth *Thesis on Feuerbach*: as the "ensemble of social relations."[112] Indeed, in some ways Croce's dialectic was even more abstract than that of his classical precursors.[113] Not only did his "dialectic of distincts" suppress entirely the moment of antithesis, but it was conceived as a "pure conceptual dialectic," a mere tool of thought serenely unconnected with any concrete historical unfolding.[114] The category of "becoming" in Crocean philosophy is therefore nothing but the "concept of becoming," and his "history as the story of liberty" can rest only on some "utopistic basis" or upon the implicit determinism of a "hidden god."[115] The "philosophy of praxis" can resolve these contradictions, Gramsci argued, because it "continues the philosophy of immanence but purifies it of all its metaphysical apparatus and brings it onto the concrete terrain of history."[116]

Croce's inadequate understanding even of the idealist dialectic was reflected for Gramsci in his mechanistic interpretation of Marxism which reduced it ultimately to a mere "canon of interpretation."[117] Yet Croce's subsequent philosophizing had produced several formulations of decisive importance for a recomposition of the dialectical foundations of historical materialism. First among these, perhaps, was his theorization of the "ethical-political moment," which Gramsci credited, along with Lenin's concept of hegemony, as the chief inspiration for his own concept of hegemony. We will put off discussing this connection, however, until Chapter 6. Among the most important of Croce's other formulations were "absolute historicism," "the contemporaneity of history," and "immanentism."

Croce's affirmation of an "absolute historicism" identified history with human creation and philosophical truth, but this history was not a string of events wending its way forward from the infinite recesses of the past. All history was contemporary not merely because we inevitably introduce our presumptions and sensibilities as we relate it, but in the sense that we actively construct it. There exist no events "out there" to be related; there are only documents and monuments of a past which for us are present realities, just as our own memories of a personal past are encompassed by and not separated from the present.[118] Gramsci did not abandon this notion of a contemporaneous history; he radicalized its double identity of history and philosophy into a triple identity of history, philosophy, and politics. "In the investigation of past deficiencies and errors (of certain parties or currents), the interpretations of that past are not 'history' but actual politics in the making."[119] The active construction of history necessarily entails filtering it through present political needs; any effort to avoid this confrontation will only reduce history to the "external and mechanical."[120] Croce could not concede this point, since for him it would be tantamount to saying that history is only ideology. Philosophy was a universal or "high" value in Croce's view, politics was not. For Gramsci the distinction was artificial; "a man of politics writes about philosophy: it could be that his 'true' philosophy should be looked for rather in his writings on politics."[121] Likewise any historical judgment must always be understood in terms of the political source for which it serves as a mediation.

Several consequences that follow from this triple identity are crucial in grasping Gramsci's effort to theorize a radically open dialectic. Since history is an as yet uncompleted totality, all philosophy, including the philosophy of praxis, is necessarily "non-definitive."[122]

> If the philosophy of praxis affirms theoretically that every "truth" believed to be eternal and absolute has had practical origins and has represented a "provisional" value (historicity of every conception of the world and life), it is still very difficult to make people grasp "practically" that such an interpretation is valid also for the philosophy of praxis itself, without in so doing shaking the convictions that are necessary for action.[123]

Most Marxist-inspired political movements have therefore chosen to absolutize their principles into dogmatic ideologies which pretend to unlock history's secrets. In seeking to overcome this tendency, Gramsci revealed what was most revolutionary in his "absolute historicism" or "absolute secularization and earthliness of thought,"[124] namely, that whatever political innovations may occur in future history will be entirely the products of flesh and blood individuals joined together as a collective will engaged in collective action.

In reducing Marxist philosophy to ideological dogma, proletarian movements have tended to identify "historical materialism" with "traditional metaphysical materialism" in order to gain "an achieved and perfected system."[125] Though the opposition of metaphysical idealism and materialism had already been fully overcome in Hegel, "Hegel's successors destroyed this unity and there was a return to materialist systems on the one side and spiritualist on the other."[126] The philosophical enemy of the proletariat is not "idealism" but "metaphysics" in all its "reciprocally one-sided" forms.[127] Croce's concept of immanentism confronts this enemy directly and thus is far more valuable to the proletariat than theorizations of materialism.[128] The chief problem with immanentist philosophies is practical: though they have been readily absorbed as common sense and even good sense, "they have not been able to create an ideological unity between the bottom and the top, between the 'simple' and the intellectuals."[129] Thus, though privately committed to atheism, immanentism allows "the teaching of religion on the grounds that religion is the philosophy of the infancy of mankind renewed in every non-metaphysical infancy."[130] Nonetheless, the philosophy of praxis is best thought of as a form of "immanentism," indeed "the only consistent 'immanentist' conception."[131]

The Pragmatological Dialectic

If Gramsci unabashedly accepted "immanentism" rather than "materialism" as his starting point, the full shape of his dialectic and its implicit tensions can only be appreciated after we have seen how he reappropriated Marx. Attentive readers of Gramsci have always recognized how highly selective he was in this reappropriation. In part this was inevitable: he never knew of important early Marx texts like *The German Ideology* and the *Paris Manuscripts*, which were published in the West only in 1932. Though he certainly read a large number of Marx's other works, including *Capital*, his references nonetheless concentrate heavily on the *Theses on Feuerbach* and the 1859 preface to the *Critique of Political Economy*—a dozen or so pages from a lifetime of Marx's writing. Marx's "basic innovation" is thus presented as "the demonstration that there is no abstract 'human nature,' fixed and immutable (a concept which certainly derives from religious and transcendentalist thought), but that human nature is the totality of historically determined social relations,"[132] a proposition certainly derived from the sixth *Thesis on Feuerbach*. And the 1859 preface is referred to as the "most important authentic source for a reconstruction of the philosophy of praxis."[133]

This latter assessment is perhaps surprising in view of the wide currency given to the "Preface" in positivist accounts of Marxism. Yet in Gramsci's reading no special attention is given to the famous remark that "It is not the consciousness of men that determines their existence, but, on the contrary, their social existence determines their consciousness."[134] He concentrated instead on two other passages, one portraying the "period of social revolution," the other the material limits of human creativity:

> [a.] With the change of the economic foundation the entire immense superstructure is more or less rapidly transformed. In considering such transformations the distinction should always be made between the material transformations of the economic conditions of production, which can be determined with the precision of natural science, and the legal, political, religious, aesthetic or philosophic—in short, ideological—forms in which men become conscious of this conflict and fight it out. . . .
>
> [b.] No social order ever perishes before all the productive forces for which there is room in it have been developed; and new, higher relations of production never appear before the material conditions of their existence have matured in the womb of the old society itself. Therefore mankind always sets itself only such tasks as it can solve; since, looking at the matter more closely, it will always be found that the task itself arises only when the material conditions for its solution already exist or are at least in the process of formation.[135]

The first passage offers a clear rationale for a subjectivist starting point: Marx is shown to have recognized the significance of consciousness and ideology in revolutionary struggle and, even more importantly, to have identified these factors with social relations generally and not merely with the economic structure. The second passage, however, seems to set limits to human creativity in history, not through a one-sided determinism but rather by suggesting how previous human objectifications structure collective choices and how real concrete choices are necessarily grounded in material preconditions. Taken together, the two passages represent a dialectical view of history and freedom which not only does not clash with, but even reinforces, the philosophical outlook of the *Theses on Feuerbach*.

Has Gramsci, then, rejected a positivist Marxism in favor of the "pragmatological" dialectic that Marx began to develop in 1845? Such a conclusion seems to follow from the Marxian texts to which he most often referred, and it is further suggested by his reference to Marxism as a "philosophy of the act (praxis, development), but not of the 'pure' act, but rather of the real 'impure' act, in the most profane and worldly sense of the word."[136] The alternative is that Gramsci embraced some form of Marx's earlier "anthropological" dialectic. Yet, not only did Gramsci never use the language of "alienation," "species being," "human essence," etc., but he almost entirely lacked the reification problematic that Marx developed on the basis of these concepts. It is striking that in the "Americanism and Fordism" sections of the *Notebooks*, where Gramsci discussed the increasing rationalization of the worker in contemporary capitalism, he did not oppose this rationalization itself but only some aspects of its capitalist form. Americanism and Fordism "derive from an inherent necessity to achieve the organization of a planned economy";[137] Italian workers have championed rationalization, and their American counterparts have accepted even Prohibition in its name;[138] regulation of the sex habits of workers to improve output is "necessary";[139] and if Fordism "smashes" the "humanity" and "spirit" of the worker, this is only a repudiation of a particular form of rationalization, which nonetheless remains a revolutionary force.[140] We need not question the depth of Gramsci's insight into the nature of capitalism or the degree of proletarian oppression it involves; he had his own way of theorizing the overcoming of proletarian oppression, which we will come to shortly. But as it is posed in the anthropological dialectic, the problematic of reification simply does not lie within the purview of Gramsci's Marxism. Were it not for Lukács's brilliant reconstruction of a theory of capitalist reification upon such slender reeds as *Capital's* discussion of the "fetishism of commodities," one might be tempted to say that Gramsci *could not* have had such a problematic.

What exactly was entailed for him, then, in the pragmatological dialectic that he took over from Marx? We have already alluded to many of its elements: the grounding in subjectivity and intersubjectivity; the pragmatic conception of prediction; the concept of necessity as need made conscious; the repudiation of all transcendental and speculative notions, including traditional metaphysical materialism; and the concepts of history's contemporaneity, of the non-definitiveness of philosophy, and of philosophy as a collective activity pursued for practical, historical ends. Gramsci's philosophical outlook resulted from his taking the radical assertions of the *Theses on Feuerbach* with the utmost seriousness: circumstances are changed by men; men are the ensemble of their social relationships; truth is neither abstract nor timeless and must be proved in practice. His position entailed a categorical denial of the separation of subject and object, of being and thought; one cannot know reality independently of man. Gramsci would have agreed wholeheartedly with Sartre that what is needed "is a theory which *situates* knowing *in the world* . . . and which determines it in its *negativity*. . . . Only then will it be understood that knowing is not a knowing of ideas but a practical knowing *of things*."[141]

The three key concepts here are man, knowing, and the world; let us begin with the first. To say that "man" is "the ensemble of social relations" is not to suppress the category of the concrete subject or individual person. The point is to conceive of the concrete subject who "knows, wishes, admires, creates" through "active relationships" with other concrete subjects and the world.[142] And Gramsci insisted that, among these relationships, individuality is "perhaps the most important."[143] This provided him with the ontological basis for a view of human freedom as dependent both on "individuality" and on a properly constituted collectivity. At the same time, the individual is always situated in a particular present, however much he may believe that his individual thoughts express "the unity of the human spirit."[144] And his self-consciousness is necessarily intersubjective, since he "does not enter into relations with other men by juxtaposition, but organically, inasmuch, that is, as he belongs to organic entities which range from the simplest to the most complex."[145] Finally:

> It is not enough to know the *ensemble* of relations as they exist at any given time as a given system. They must be known genetically, in the movement of their formation. For each individual is the synthesis not only of existing relations, but of the history of these relations. He is a précis of all the past.[146]

Human beings also "enter into relations with the natural world . . . actively, by means of work and technique."[147] Yet this world is not "objectively real"—a misconception of "religious origin"—but actively constituted by human subjects.[148] At the same time, the category of "world" is not simply identical with that of human objectification; Gramsci nowhere denied the existence of an independent material reality, or what Marx called the "natural substratum."[149] Human objectification, after all, presupposes a "stuff" to be worked on; it would be sheer nonsense, to use Gramsci's example, to suppose that one creates news by opening a newspaper.[150] Rather, the appropriation of the world in human objectification is a complexly mediated process guided above all by particular human needs and interests.[151]

A person comes to know phenomena not through arbitrary choice or caprice but as "qualities" which he "has isolated in consequence of his practical interests (the construction of his economic life) and his scientific interests (the necessity to discover an order in the world and to describe and classify things, a necessity which is itself connected to mediated and future practical interests)."[152] This highly suggestive sentence posits two sorts of "interests" as underlying the search for knowledge: a "practical interest" (which seems to parallel what Jürgen Habermas calls a "technical interest"), and a "scientific interest" (roughly Habermas's "practical interest").[153] Interestingly, however, Gramsci portrayed these interests not as the analytically separate entities found in Habermas but as interpenetrating aspects of the unified nexus of subject and world.

Thus the general picture of human life which emerges in Gramsci's reappropriation of Marx is that of concrete individuals actively transforming the natural world in a collective process of social labor guided by shared practical and scientific interests. This praxis is not entirely open in the sense of a radical voluntarism; in Gramsci's dialectical view, men are both shaped by and shapers of their world. Yet there is an implied openness in the historical results of this praxis which, at the very least, seems to preclude any notion that history will necessarily turn out in a particular way. Gramsci's estimation of the philosophy of praxis itself—a "non-definitive philosophy" situated in a particular historical epoch—is entirely consistent with this view. A dialectical openness is also consistent with the philosophical mode that he extracted from Croce: the anti-positivism and the critique of scientistic fetishism which led him to deal so gingerly with the question of historical prediction, and the absolute historicism which seemed to rule out transcendental subjects altogether.

Yet whether it was because he sought to escape the threat of relativism or because he could not escape certain assumptions at the roots of the Marxist world view, Gramsci remained committed to certain teleological elements which strained and ultimately burst through the fetters set up by his pragmatological dialectic. The central such element, never critically examined in his entire corpus, is the view that the proletariat is a universal class whose inner meaning and historical mission are to achieve a breakthrough into the realm of "freedom" from that of "necessity." To be sure, Gramsci sometimes discussed this topic as if the transition were merely a possibility,[154] and he always treated it as something which would be produced by concrete human action.[155] Yet, in a passage we have already cited, he referred to Croce's "spirit" not "as a point of departure but as a point of arrival," one that *is* manifesting itself as "a concrete and objectively universal unification" of the human race.[156] In other passages as well, this unification is depicted not as something that *may* but as something that *will* happen.[157] The result appears paradoxical. The concept of a proletariat whose praxis holds the promise of an emerging "realm of freedom" seems to have led Gramsci to assert a quasi-essentialist image of the future he could not "predict."

Gramsci was not entirely unaware of this problem; indeed, he was sharply critical of Bukharin for his "unconscious teleology" presented in its "most infantile manifestations."[158] He argued, however, that an entirely immanent, Kantian form of teleology could be "maintained and justified by the philosophy of praxis."[159] The following is perhaps his most developed account of how this was possible:

> Accepting the affirmation that our knowledge of things is nothing other than ourselves, our needs and interests, that is, that our knowledge is superstructure (or non-definitive philosophy), it is difficult not to think in terms of something real beyond this knowledge—not in the metaphysical sense of a "noumenon," an "unknown God" or an "unknowable," but in

the concrete sense of a "relative" ignorance of reality, of something still unknown, which will however be known one day when the "physical" and intellectual instruments of mankind are more perfect, when, that is, the technical and social conditions of mankind have been changed in a progressive direction. We are then making an historical prediction which consists simply in an act of thought that projects into the future a process of development similar to that which has taken place from the past until today.[160]

An historical teleology seems to be implicit in the search for knowledge itself. Practical and scientific interests are a ground upon which the collective-historical and individual-subjective poles of the dialectic unite. For as human beings seek beyond the known to the unknown, they necessarily become implicated in the building of ever more powerful instruments for this pursuit. This telos is described modestly as a prediction, and Gramsci is perfectly justified in doing this. The problem is that he has no logical move from this limited prediction with its "progressive direction" to the grander one he wants to make: the coming of a realm of freedom as a "new intellectual and moral order."[161]

The same problem arises in the several other ways that Gramsci sought to ground a telos: in human nature generally, "which changes continuously with the changing of social relations" and thus "becomes";[162] or in the category of "rational will," which he self-consciously placed "at the base of [his] philosophy."[163] Knowledge is founded upon a rational will "in so far as it corresponds to objective historical necessity," which is to say, when and if it should "come to be accepted by the many, and accepted permanently . . . by becoming a culture, a form of 'good sense,' a conception of the world with an ethic that conforms to its structure."[164] Action ordinarily implies a multiplicity of "various wills with a varying degree of intensity and awareness and of homogeneity with the entire complex of the collective will."[165] Through collective action, men can learn to transcend their givenness as products of nature and history, to become aware of their knowledge-gaining capacities, and thus to act with consciousness and will. In this sense, the concept of "human" is not a "starting point" but a "point of arrival."[166] But once again, the leap from this to a new cultural totality is a leap of faith presented as a logical entailment.

To grasp the source of this difficulty, it may be helpful to follow the recent suggestions that Gramsci's critique of scientism, his immanentist and intersubjective philosophical starting point, and his conceptual apparatus of telos and the intentionality of consciousness amount to an incipient phenomenology.[167] For if what we have been calling his pragmatological dialectic can be viewed at bottom as a phenomenology, then a parallel between Gramsci and phenomenological Marxists like Merleau-Ponty would seem to be suggested.[168] As others have pointed out, phenomenology and Marxism are an explosive mixture.[169] Even one of its contemporary advocates concedes that "the forced synthesis of the two mechanically juxtaposed frameworks is bound to fail from the very beginning; either phenomenology dissolves in the dialectic, in which case it ceases to be phenomenology, or the dialectic is frozen in the phenomenological foundation and loses its dynamism, thus ceasing to be dialectical."[170] In Merleau-Ponty's case, the effort to reconcile phenomenology with a proletarian telos toward a final resolution of history's contradictions resulted in what one student has called the "muddled little tract," *Humanism and Terror*.[171] Unlike Gramsci, however, Merleau-Ponty eventually overcame this tension by disavowing all essentialist attributions to the proletariat in his *Adventures of the Dialectic*. It seems almost gratuitous to add that Merleau-Ponty's insight was very likely promoted by Stalinism's self-presentation in the events of the Cold War, hardly an inspiring image for a Marxist millenarianism.

If Gramsci's effort at a full philosophical reconstitution of Marxism seems in retrospect to have been doomed by the ingredients he selected, it nonetheless remains a powerful attempt. To round out our perspective on it, we will conclude this chapter with a brief glance back at Labriola and Lukács.

Unlike Labriola's, Gramsci's philosophical formulations were entirely devoid of all forms of economic determinism. Though both men sought to use Engels as an ally against vulgar Marxism, Gramsci made clear, as Labriola had not, how *Anti-Dühring* had provided the essential inspiration for Bukharin's and other versions of economism.[172] Given these divergencies, some writers have suggested that Gramsci's Marxism owes at least as much to Sorel's concept of "myth" and his emphasis on subjectivity as a factor in historical outcomes as to anything in Labriola.[173] In Chapter 6, we will see how Gramsci drew on Sorel's notion of an historical "bloc" in theorizing the practical political dimension of this problem. Yet it was Labriola, not Sorel, whom Gramsci referred to as "the only man who has attempted to build up the philosophy of praxis scientifically."[174] And an inventory of Gramsci's conceptual commitments reveals the persistent presence of such Labriolaisms as the elevation of praxis to a central position in Marxism,[175] the notion that Marxism is a "general philosophy,"[176] a commitment to an absolute historicism,[177] and an acknowledgment of the nonobjective nature of science and its grounding in human need.[178] Both efforts, moreover, were fraught with tension. If Labriola sometimes drifted toward economic determinism because of a desire to negate the idealist proclivities of the Italian philosophical tradition, Gramsci drifted toward a teleology of the proletariat as history's culmination because of a desire to sustain Marxist hope in a period of war, political crisis, and fascist repression.

From this perspective, the difference between Gramsci and Lukács is that while Lukács's anthropological dialectic implied a sense of historical closure even as it emphasized the category of praxis, Gramsci's pragmatological dialectic seemed to deny the necessity of an historical movement toward totality but then reintroduced this idea subterraneously in the concept of the proletariat itself. Lukács's "identity theory" may have been more coherent, but it was insufficiently concrete—it lacked crucial intersubjective and organizational mediations—while Gramsci's was so concrete that its broad historical contours were posited at the expense of logical coherence.[179] Lukács, one might say, suffered from a lack of patience characteristic of the armchair pundit, while Gramsci, whose long years as a PCI militant had taught him the virtues of patience and will, used theory in part to reach out for the hope and inspiration denied him by practice. In both cases, we find that the unmitigated rejection of positivist determinism led—whether as an escape from relativism or as a search for the absolute—to the reintroduction of deterministic elements of a more historicist sort, which flew in the face of the theorists' general intentions. Yet what Gramsci never accepted was the idealist supposition, ultimately shared by Lenin and Lukács, that knowledge of totality could only be brought to the proletariat from outside. Rather, as we will now see, Gramsci attempted to work out the concrete mediations in the dialectical movement from "common sense" to full proletarian self-understanding, mediations grounded in the "school of labor" but incorporating as well a political education conceived of as the "intellectual/moral bloc" of workers and their "organic intellectuals."

CHAPTER FIVE

Political Education as the Overcoming of Common Sense

The popular element "feels" but does not always know or understand; the intellectual element "knows" but does not always understand and in particular does not always feel.

(1932-33)

GRAMSCI was not just quibbling when he attacked Bukharin for the order of exposition in the *Popular Manual.* He was drawing upon his own sustained reflections concerning the way individuals gain consciousness of their life situations and the way philosophy could influence this process were it reconceived as a mode of political education. In this chapter we will explore how he understood the phenomenological pattern intrinsic to this process, how he theorized it at a collective level, and what he perceived to be its most general political implications.

Gramsci approached the issues of class consciousness and political education from a background rich in practical experience. While Marx had already suggested various means for stimulating class consciousness—a "school of labor," "continual agitation," the building of trade unions, and so forth—he had not done much to explain the process itself. With the workers' councils, Gramsci had updated and improved the conception of appropriate institutions while taking a decisive step toward understanding the process. That step was his insight that consciousness could only develop in a setting where the self-construction of the world through labor was organically combined with political self-governance and agitation against the existing state. Moreover, while Marx in the third *Thesis on Feuerbach* had raised the idea that political education prior to revolution was intrinsically connected to the possibility of a future society guided wholly through the self-activity of its citizens, Gramsci expanded and clarified this idea and gave it an institutional form. The factory council gave life to the belief that the present proletarian education, the relations of economic production, the coming revolution, and the future socialist society were all related aspects of one historical process.

In the *Notebooks* these insights became parts of a larger theory of political education, grounded by a pragmatological dialectic and incorporating both individual and collective perspectives. On the individual level, Gramsci's starting point was the concrete subject situated in a particular historical environment. This formulation implied a complex interaction of "subjective" and "objective" historical factors. It was "subjective" in the sense that it conceded history's ineffability apart from a knowledge of the people who make it; it was "objective" in that it began from the concrete circumstances in which people are situated. Thus, while Gramsci always set out from objective conditions in analyzing revolutionary movements, he also placed little emphasis on objective conditions as sources of proletarian action.[1] He was never impressed, for instance, by the radicalizing potential of economic crises, even when they reached depression levels.[2] The best that such events could do was to "create a terrain more favorable to the dissemination of certain modes of thought."[3] They became critical for the ruling class only when they provoked a "crisis of authority" which threatened its "hegemony," that is, its consensual basis within civil society.[4] This is why it was so crucial to attack existing "hegemony" and to create an alternative, proletarian source for it within present civil society. Both these tasks were matters of political education because:

> Mass ideological factors always lag behind mass economic factors and therefore, at certain moments the automatic thrust due to the economic factor can be slowed down, obstructed or even temporarily broken by traditional ideological elements. This means that there must be a conscious, planned struggle to insure that the exigencies of the economic position of the masses, which may conflict with the traditional leadership's policies, are understood. An appropriate political initiative is *always* necessary to liberate the economic thrust from the dead weight of traditional policies.[5]

This passage represents Gramsci's collective perspective on political education. The perspective may have been controversial, but it could be at least vaguely understood in conventional terms.

When he offered a first version of it in the Turin of the *biennio rosso*, most of his Marxist contemporaries either admired its implicit activism or questioned it as "reformism." No one saw the conceptual revolution behind the idea, since this revolution could not be grasped in the available "orthodox" terms. Gramsci's claim then and in the *Notebooks* was that all of society had to be understood as a vast "school" and acted upon from that point of view:

> The educational relationship should not be restricted to the field of the strictly "scholastic" relationships by means of which the new generation comes into contact with the old and absorbs its experiences and its historically necessary values and "matures" and develops a personality of its own which is historically and culturally superior. *This form of relationship exists throughout society as a whole* and for every individual relative to other individuals. It exists between intellectual and non-intellectual sections of the population, between the rulers and the ruled, elites and their followers, leaders and led, the vanguard and the body of the army. Every relationship of "hegemony" is necessarily an educational relationship.[6]

This formulation is based on a functional definition of education which escapes the narrow institutional context of the school and gives education a general sociological relevance. *School* comes to mean nothing less than the manner in which intellectuals are "elaborated" at each level within the social structure.[7]

The advantage of conceiving all societies, including existing bourgeois societies, as "schools" is that we become alerted to the multiple contexts in which legitimation processes occur and, conversely, in which alternative political outlooks can be prepared. Moreover, it allows such lofty socialist goals as an "autonomous and superior culture"[8] or a "total integral civilization"[9] to be concretely mediated by present educational programs. And such programs are themselves complexly mediated. Just as Gramsci had turned against "cultural messianism" in 1918, an early passage in the *Notebooks* critically confronts the "Enlightenment error" of "professional intellectuals" that "a 'clear idea' opportunely propagated will be internalized with the same 'ordering' effects" regardless of the social class involved.[10] Genuine political education depends both on the "elaboration" of intellectuals tied to the working class to provide it with "organic" leadership, and on the creation of institutional settings in which workers can raise themselves to a "philosophical" (as opposed to a mere "commonsense") view of the world.[11]

To see how Gramsci conceived the former task, we must introduce his concept of the intellectual and, in particular, his distinction between "traditional" and "organic" intellectuals. As a new class develops within the world of economic production, it tends to create "organically, one or more strata of intellectuals which give it homogeneity and an awareness of its own function not only in the economic but also in the social and political fields."[12] These are "organic" intellectuals. It is important to recognize how much broader this definition of *intellectual* is than the one in current everyday usage. For while Gramsci certainly meant to include the scholar, the writer, and other men of letters, he was referring generally to anyone whose social function is to serve as a transmitter of ideas within civil society and between government and civil society. Thus the organic intellectuals of the aristocracy in European feudal societies would include not only soldiers and other specialists in "technico-military capacity," but also priests in all their many functions. Under capitalism, the organic intellectuals are not just the specialists in management and industrial organization, the economists, the doctors, and the lawyers, but also the journalists, publishers, television personnel, and everyone else associated with what is now sometimes called the "culture industry." In the case of the proletariat under capitalism, one would include as organic intellectuals all those striving to create a new proletarian culture as well as production functionaries in a narrower sense, such as shop foremen, machine technicians, and trade union economists.

In the case of a subaltern class like the proletariat, organic intellectuals seek to inspire its self-confidence as an historical actor and to provide it with social, cultural, and political leadership. Until this process reaches an advanced stage, however, "traditional intellectuals" are likely to fill the leadership vacuum. Gramsci characterized such intellectuals as a relatively "autonomous and independent social group" which "experiences through an '*esprit de corps*' their uninterrupted historical continuity and their special qualification."[13] They have no single class or caste origin. Some of those serving the proletariat are likely to be former "organic" bourgeois intellectuals who defected. Others might be survivors of decadent or vanishing estates like the Church or the military aristocracy. Each of the latter groups was an important source of traditional intellectuals in Italy, where they were especially numerous and influential in Gramsci's era. Many remained closely attached to the Church; others, like their modern prototype Croce, were associated with idealist philosophy and, more ambiguously, with the bourgeoisie and fascism.

If this portrait of the traditional intellectual applied especially well to Italy, the alliance of at least some traditional intellectuals with a rising class is natural in any society, since such intellectuals already exist fully "elaborated" from the time this class begins to form. The problem is that, not being organically tied to the rising class, they tend at best to be aloof from, and at worst antagonistic toward, its interests. Therefore, as a class matures into a position where it can begin to assert its power politically, it becomes increasingly important to supplant traditional with organic intellectuals.[14]

The second task in the political education of a class is to ensure that this process of maturation proceeds smoothly. The development of a dedicated citizen body is never simply a function of the natural course of economic evolution. It depends on the active self-dedication of a class to its own self-education. For the proletariat, this means the mastery of techniques whereby "unskilled workers become skilled," and more broadly, a self-transformation which allows "every citizen to govern," or at the very least, places him or her "in a general condition to achieve this [capacity]."[15] As we have seen, Gramsci sought to develop institutions appropriate to this task throughout his practical political life. One new point that he made in the *Notebooks* was that since most proletarians would never be leaders, their collective development needed to be regulated according to "a well-studied and consciously established plan" that creates clear expectations of what any citizen must do to achieve public recognition and advancement.[16]

For Gramsci these two functional processes of creating leaders and citizens were linked in a dialectical fashion. Proletarian education depends on the active leadership of organic intellectuals:

> A human mass does not "distinguish" itself, does not become independent in its own right without, in the widest sense, organizing itself; and there is no organization without intellectuals, that is, without organizers and leaders, in other words, without the theoretical aspect of the theory-practice nexus being distinguished concretely by the existence of a group of people "specialized" in conceptual and philosophical elaboration of ideas.[17]

But organic leadership cannot be understood apart from the self-education of the masses:

> The process of development [of organic intellectuals] is tied to a dialectic between the intellectuals and the masses. The intellectual stratum develops both quantitatively and qualitatively, but every leap forward towards a new breadth and complexity of the intellectual stratum is tied to an analogous movement on the part of the mass of the "simple," who raise themselves to higher levels of culture and at the same time extend their circle of influence towards the stratum of specialized intellectuals, producing outstanding individuals and groups of greater or lesser importance.[18]

As the dialectic unfolds over time, the distance between intellectuals and masses tends to narrow and the two elements can coalesce into what Gramsci called an "intellectual/moral bloc."[19] This is a crucial concept for Gramsci, one which allowed him to overcome the central tensions in Marx's view of political education. As Gramsci conceived it, such a bloc always forms within a concrete institutional context such as a party, trade union, or factory council. Different organizational forms will have advantages and disadvantages, depending on specific historical circumstances; but regardless of which is chosen, the intellectual/moral bloc will be the embryo of future socialist society and the basis of a "potential state." Gramsci's insistence on this linkage raised him above the instrumentalism at times implicit in Marx, while also solving the problem of a power/need imbalance and of "outside educators." For the education built into the bloc provides the proletariat with the "powers" which the capitalist order denies them while at the same time producing many new organic intellectuals to replace traditional ones and narrowing the gap between organic intellectuals and the rest of the class.

One might, of course, still question whether there is not a necessary implication within such a dialectic that the "organic intellectuals" are superior to the rank and file being educated. Gramsci would not have hesitated in answering *yes*, but he would have vigorously denied any elitism. Organic intellectuals do not "tower above" in this conception, since they are continually being drawn from the ranks of the proletariat being educated. Moreover, the dialogue implicit in a dialectical model of education makes continuous self-correction possible. As Habermas has written of his own very similar conception of political education: "The vindicating superiority of those who do the enlightening over those who are to be enlightened is theoretically unavoidable but at the same time it is *fictive* and requires *self-correction*: in a process of enlightenment there can only be participants."[20] Gramsci would have concurred in this sentiment, but he would also have placed it in a phenomenological perspective notably absent in Habermas.[21] Workers and organic intellectuals are like complementary parts of a living person: "the popular element 'feels' but does not always know or understand; the intellectual element 'knows' but does not always understand and in particular does not always feel."[22]

With this dialectical view of political education, Gramsci made his most profound advance over all forms of voluntarism, spontaneism, and idealism. Perhaps because of his outrage at the alliance he saw between Italian fascism and traditional idealist intellectuals, he was most vehement in emphasizing his advance over the latter.[23] The idealist vision was fixated on a static separation of "philosophy" and "common sense" or "faith." Like the Catholic Church, which Gramsci thought had always offered one religion for the intellectuals and another for the masses,[24] the idealists assumed that the gap was rooted in a fixed inequality of human nature. Gramsci conceded that "in the masses *as such*, philosophy can only be experienced as faith."[25] But his pedagogical principle was "the antithesis of the Catholic. The philosophy of praxis does not tend to leave the 'simple' in their primitive philosophy of common sense, but rather to lead them to a higher conception of life."[26] The difficulty was to articulate the phenomenological movement underlying this principle in a manner convincing enough to overcome idealist and Catholic objections.

The Psychological Foundation

We have referred several times to Gramsci's essential indifference to the new fascination with psychology which captured the European intellectual world after 1900. The reasons for this indifference are unclear. They may reflect his intellectual isolation until just before the war, a faith in lower-class rectitude and rationality that he brought from his rural background and Turin experience, the peripheral blindness induced by his single-minded pursuit of a revolutionary praxis, or some combination of these factors. What is clear is that neither World War I nor the rise of Italian fascism shocked him out of the view that human beings act on the basis of rational calculations concerning their needs and interests. That he could continue to hold such a view in these circumstances is quite remarkable, and we need to reflect further on this point before considering what he thought about the phenomenological movement within genuine political education.

Gramsci displayed his psychological rationalism in a strikingly cavalier fashion, almost as if he thought it faced no significant challenge.[27] Unlike the later Lukács, who aggressively defended his view of proletarian rationality against almost the entire European philosophical world,[28] Gramsci did little to counter and nothing to avoid those writers who posited or sought a deeper understanding of the irrational forces of human life. He read at least one of Freud's book in prison,[29] and his letters reveal a personal interest in "Freudianism" because of his wife Giulia's bouts with nervous depression. Though he once suggested that Freud's theory of the Oedipal complex had had an "incalculable" influence on German literature and represented a "new revolutionary ethic,"[30] his usual estimate of it was very much lower. "Freudianism" was "an attempt to create a general philosophy on the basis of a few empirical observations, which is of very little import."[31] One notebook entry suggests that Freud's value lay in his insistence "on studying the morbid reverberations [*contraccolpi morbosi*] involved in every construction of 'collective man,' in every 'social conformism,' in every level of civilization. . . ."[32]

Yet the passage goes on to imply that this limited the theory's explanatory power to the crisis of the "ruling classes" at "the conclusion of the liberal period."[33]

Though his contact with Freud was fleeting and superficial, there were other writers engaged in pursuing the frontiers of psychology into the irrational whom he knew much better. One was the Italian playwright Luigi Pirandello.[34] "Did you know," Gramsci once wrote to his wife's sister, "that I discovered and helped Pirandello's theatre to success. . . ? I wrote enough about Pirandello from 1915 to 1920 to make a book of 200 pages, and in those days what I said was really novel and original: Pirandello used to be either graciously tolerated or openly derided."[35] Yet his comments in the *Notebooks* reveal a deep ambivalence toward the Sicilian. On the one hand, Gramsci's essentially classical literary taste led him to criticize Pirandello's comic nihilism, "pseudo-philosophical verbalism," and lack of real tragic personalities. On the other hand, he welcomed what he took to be the progressive political consequences of Pirandello's cultural and literary impact. In creating a "modern, 'critical' attitude as opposed to the traditional eighteenth-century 'melodramatic' attitude," Pirandello was undermining the aristocratic and Catholic presuppositions of mainstream Italian thought, just as Gramsci's own work was undermining its idealism.[36] As with Freud, Gramsci conceded Pirandello's merit only insofar as Pirandello's insights and cultural impact remained within the confines of Gramsci's own rationalist premises. That the psychological underpinnings of Pirandello's development of character might constitute an effective challenge to these premises as well as to Gramsci's rather traditional aesthetics was a possibility that he was unable or unwilling to consider.

It is therefore not surprising that Gramsci's view of human nature was little more than a restatement of the argument that Marx had put forward almost a century earlier in the *Theses on Feuerbach*. There is no *condition humaine*; human nature is but "the totality of historically determined social relations."[37] Thus, Gramsci argued at one point, for instance, that the apparent need which the masses expressed in the comforts of religion was only a "residue of the pre-capitalist world."[38] Human needs are always the self-creation of the personality through activity in specific circumstances. Probably Gramsci's best and fullest elaboration on this point is the following:

> Men create their own personality, (1) by giving a specific and concrete ("rational") direction to their own vital impulse or will; (2) by identifying the means which will make this will concrete and specific and not arbitrary; (3) by contributing to modify the *ensemble* of the concrete conditions for realising this will to the extent of one's own limits and capacities and in the most fruitful form. Man is to be conceived as an historical bloc of purely individual and subjective elements and of mass and objective or material elements with which the individual is in active relationship.[39]

Psychology is always primarily social psychology. The individual can never be fully understood in isolation because he becomes himself in his intercourse with his fellows as they collectively transform the natural world. Even more importantly, his personality develops amid concrete social, cultural, and political circumstances which he not only does not choose but which embody assumptions about the world which he cannot initially even identify.

This leads us directly into Gramsci's assumptions about the character of the situation from which political education must begin. Individuals are born into a world already shaped by previous class struggle. Out of that struggle some class or alliance of classes has emerged in a dominant and very often a "hegemonic" position. As we will see more fully in the next chapter, such a class will always attempt to secure a hegemonic position, i.e., to gain political legitimacy by weaving its own cultural outlook deeply into the social fabric. For this purpose it will place its own organic intellectuals at strategic points within the cultural and ideological "apparatus" and will make alliances with the most influential traditional intellectuals.[40] Over the long run, the world view articulated by its philosophers in the realm of high culture will trickle down and solidify into "common sense," the "folklore of philosophy."[41]

This notion of common sense is crucially important for Gramsci, since it represents the place from which any genuine political education must depart. He held that its "most fundamental characteristic is that it is a conception which, even in the brain of one individual, is fragmentary, incoherent and inconsequential. . . ."[42] Despite its connotation in English, then, "common sense" is ordinarily very far removed from the real needs and interests of the masses of ordinary people who hold it; thought that satisfies real needs and interests is referred to by Gramsci as "good sense." Yet, at the same time, common sense is never simply identical with ruling class ideology; this ideology at best only "limit[s] the original thought of the popular masses in a negative direction."[43] Common sense is a complex and disjointed amalgam influenced by all previous philosophical currents. "It contains Stone Age elements and principles of a more advanced science, prejudices from all phases of history at the local level and intuitions of a future philosophy which will be that of a human race united the world over."[44] Common sense must be understood as a series of "stratified deposits," an "infinity of traces without . . . an inventory."[45] And just as "every religion . . . is in reality a multiplicity of distinct and often contradictory religions," perceptions of these "deposits" and "traces" will vary along class lines.[46] Finally, common sense "is not something rigid and immobile, but is continually transforming itself, enriching itself with scientific ideas and with philosophical opinions which have entered ordinary life."[47]

The complexity of common sense is matched only by its seeming intractability. Because of its stratified character and because it is anchored to the interests of the present ruling class, common sense is more likely to incorporate philosophical challenges as new sedimentations within an ever-shifting whole than it is to be exposed and overthrown by them. This intractability is compounded by the embeddedness of common sense within language itself. From his university studies in linguistics to his 1918 polemic against Esperanto, to the interest in Italian folklore that he expressed in prison, Gramsci remained forever sensitive to the way in which language can be "at the same time a living thing and a museum of fossils of life and civilization."[48] In a striking anticipation of the recent linguistic turn in social theory, he conceived language as "a totality of determined notions and concepts and not just of words grammatically devoid of content."[49]

Languages are hegemonic instruments which can reinforce the values of common sense or potentially transmit new ones; national languages can exercise hegemony over other national languages.[50] Moreover, the overcoming of the limitations of common sense is more likely in some languages than in others. Reflecting perhaps on his native Sardinia, Gramsci argued that:

> Someone who only speaks dialect, or understands the standard language incompletely, necessarily has an intuition of the world which is more or less limited and provincial, which is fossilized and anachronistic in relation to the major currents of thought which dominate world history. His interests will be limited, more or less corporate or economistic, not universal.[51]

Thus, in order to break away from common sense, it may be necessary to learn a new language, just as it is surely necessary for a subaltern class challenging an incumbent hegemony to attempt to build a new common sense by attacking the assumptions embedded in existing language.[52]

The nature of common sense is further illuminated when one studies it as a form of ideology. For Gramsci, an historically organic ideology—as opposed to the idiosyncratic ruminations of a particular individual—is not a naked conceptual system but a class *Weltanschauung* clothed in the language, mores, and "ways of life" of a particular culture.[53] Like all ideologies, common sense may have "true" elements but is never a confirmation of truth;[54] its relation to truth is wholly subordinate to its function as the cultural cement smoothing relations between state and civil society. Yet ideologies do vary in their social roles: some are merely systems of mystification, while others are also potentially the media through which "men become conscious of fundamental conflicts and fight them out." Gramsci sometimes referred to common sense as an ideology of the latter kind, but he more often pictured it as a way of thinking which would have to be transcended by a self-conscious and coherent philosophical outlook for the proletarian telos of a "regulated society" to be realized.[55]

From the point of view of political education, then, common sense is not only its necessary starting point but also its most formidable obstacle. To supersede common sense, the "man-in-the-mass" must somehow be led to a "series of negations,"

negations which expose and repudiate the prevailing common sense.[56] How can this occur? From Gramsci's discussion of the intellectual/mass dialectic, one would expect such negations to be conceived of as part of a more formal and directed political education than the worker gains from the "school of labor" alone. Yet, remarkably, Gramsci discussed this problem directly only for the case of the worker outside such a setting:

> The active man-in-the-mass has a practical activity, but has no clear theoretical consciousness of his practical activity, which nonetheless involves understanding the world in so far as he transforms it. His theoretical consciousness can indeed be historically in opposition to his activity. One might almost say that he has two theoretical consciousnesses (or one contradictory consciousness): one which is implicit in his activity and which in reality unites him with all his fellow-workers in the practical transformation of the real world; and one, superficially explicit or verbal, which he has inherited from the past and uncritically absorbed.[57]

The man of common sense who comes under the influence of a coherent ideology is thus, at least for a time, a divided personality, a man whose conception of the world is at best an implicit "first glimmer" still clouded by his former outlook and manifested only "occasionally and in flashes" when he is able to act as part of an "organic totality."[58]

The most specific illustrations of this transformation of consciousness found in the *Prison Notebooks* do not involve the industrial worker but rather the "semi-feudal" Italian peasant.[59] For as long as the peasant has been conscious of living in a larger society, he has understood his own class position only as a generic hatred for an enemy he defines as "the *signore*." In this one figure, whom he rarely sees and thus negatively idealizes, he places a wide variety of fears and prejudices: for the "town" generally, for the way "they" dress and act, and for the civil servant (the only form in which he perceives the state). In other words, he defines himself socially in opposition to a single, diffuse "other." This peasant can reconstitute his world only through organized collective action in which specific antagonists are identified and confronted. When he undertakes such action, the various parts of his social world become concrete and he is gradually able to understand his own position with respect to the highly differentiated class structure that actually exists. This understanding is his "class consciousness."

Gramsci sometimes described this transition as a "catharsis"[60] which alleviates primordially understood doubts, fears, and contradictions. "Catharsis" alters the perception of "structure" from "an external force which crushes man, assimilates him to itself and makes him passive . . . into a means of freedom."[61] It develops the "power" of rationality as an ability to perceive "objective" class interests and to formulate a course of action corresponding to them. As political struggle becomes a way of life for a class, this "power" will become stronger and more habitual. But it is important to recognize that this catharsis by itself will not produce the "single and coherent conception of the world"[62] that Gramsci thought people needed in order to create a self-governing, democratic society. Political struggle differentiates the world and furnishes the actor with a collective identity and an "instinctive feeling of independence,"[63] but it does not itself guarantee growth in the capacity for individual self-reflection.

Though crucially important, the cathartic episode is only a "first stage towards a further progressive self-consciousness in which theory and practice will finally be one."[64] The second stage, in which independence is grounded in a self-reflecting rationality, seems to involve the acquisition of two further capacities. One is self-autonomy, which Gramsci described in a rather Kantian way as "being one's own guide, refusing to accept passively and supinely from outside the moulding of one's own personality."[65] The other is the historical consciousness which comes from the experience of having comprehended the rational self-conceptions of other classes and other epochs. "One cannot . . . have a critical and coherent conception of the world without having a consciousness of its historicity," without "'knowing thyself' as a product of the historical process to date which has deposited in you an infinity of traces, without leaving an inventory."[66] Neither of these capacities is held to be beyond the reach of the average man. Gramsci did not justify this assumption except to suggest that since "catharsis" can be universally experienced, the rational world view that it discloses should also be universally attainable, "if only within narrow limits."[67] As qualifying phrases such as this one indicate, he probably recognized the "optimism of the will" in his forecast.

The real difficulty, however, is not that these transitions are implausible but rather that Gramsci has neither described the phenomenological movement underlying them very precisely nor linked them organically to his political education dialectic. The first transition is described only in a quasi-natural version despite the fact that it seems more likely to occur as part of an intellectual/moral bloc in an organized political movement. How might one stimulate this particular process? Apparently the answer lies in the creative use of political agitation, but Gramsci did not elaborate the point. Moreover, it is unclear whether all such cathartic moments will lead to class consciousness. Might there not be circumstances in which cathartic experiences would only serve to fuel an irrational mass movement? Had Gramsci considered such a question, he might have deepened his understanding of the appeal of Italian fascism. As it was, he was powerless to explain the sudden surge in this appeal among workers and peasants as anything other than the failure of the PSI/PCI to be sufficiently aggressive.

The transition to philosophical reason seems necessarily connected to an intellectual/mass dialectic; few people, after all, can be expected to become genuinely self-autonomous and historically self-conscious on their own. But what concrete form could this dialectic take? Gramsci's conception of a telos based on a "rational will" suggests that, if catharsis can be achieved through *political struggle* against an antagonist, a "higher" view of life would be supported best by collective *political action*, i.e., action of a positive, constructive sort which develops new, self-governing institutions. Yet nowhere did he elaborate this connection. Moreover, even if he had, the problem of explaining successes and failures would once again be acute. His formulation of the transition seems to imply that if the worker movement fails to achieve philosophical reason, this is necessarily because of inadequate effort. This conclusion is reinforced by his prior analysis of the tremendous obstacles to the overturning of common sense. Together these positions allowed him to avoid coming to terms with the sources of irrationality in mass movements and the problem of human irrationality in general.

The Social and Historical Context

Perhaps Gramsci was simply too impatiently political to delve at all deeply into the psychological character of the transitions he portrayed. Certainly he concentrated his efforts on questions of a more political and social-structural type. We will take up three of these in the present chapter. First, how is an intellectual/moral bloc to be situated within relevant institutional settings already established in society? Secondly, how can the transitions be conceptualized on the level of collective action and thus connected with an unfurling historical telos? And finally, how is one to know whether a genuinely philosophical outlook has been realized on the level of a whole society?

While Gramsci defined political education functionally within society as a whole, he always conceived of its operation within concrete institutional settings. He did not analyze operations in detail for each one that he considered relevant, however, since his list would have included at least schools, churches, the press, political parties, trade unions, the courts, medical centers, and the army.[68] In addition, there were institutions like the worker councils constructed by the proletariat especially for educational purposes. Reflecting on the councils in the *Notebooks*, Gramsci recalled that they had been simultaneously accused of "spontaneism" and "voluntarism," a "contradictory accusation which, if one analyzes it, only testifies to the fact that the leadership given to the movement was both creative and correct."[69] The councils had shown how an intellectual/moral bloc was concretely possible. Other institutions relevant to political education would have to be reconstructed along the same general lines. The ones that Gramsci analyzed were the party, the "common school," and, to a lesser extent, the legal system. Since we will consider the party in Chapter 7 and the legal system in connection with Gramsci's conception of a "regulated society," we may center our attention here on the "common school."

Gramsci's essays on the "common school"[70] can only be understood against the background of the reforms of the Italian school system which Mussolini had enacted in 1923. Drafted by Gentile and inspired also by Croce, the reforms overhauled the traditional school system that had existed unaltered since the Casati Act of 1859. Ostensibly, their objective was to substitute "education," which teaches the student how to engage "actively" in thought, for mere "instruction," which only imparts a collection of facts and techniques. One purpose of Gramsci's notes was to expose this claim as fraudulent. In the first place, he argued, the new system could hardly promote "activity," since Gentile's understanding of the word remained the romantic one first defined by Rousseau. In this sense, *activity* above all meant "spontaneity"—the idea that "the child's brain is like a ball of thread the teacher simply helps to unwind."[71] This undialectical understanding was no truer in pedagogy than in politics. The only students who might be educated in such a system were those who, like the Emile of Rousseau's romance, were exposed to an environment so rich that it was itself almost a dialectical counterpart.

Gramsci sensed that this exclusiveness was quite intentional. Far from providing all students with the expanded mental and spiritual horizons formerly available only to those in "classical" schools, the new reform had perpetuated class divisions. Indeed, the emphasis on "vocational" schools had been expanded, and the impact of the "activist" reforms was therefore restricted to an ever-shrinking elite "who do not have to worry about assuring themselves of a future career."[72] Moreover, the reforms treated all students only as abstract "individuals," without roots in a family, neighborhood, or town.[73] They had failed to recognize that school represents "only a fraction of the life of the student who is part of human society . . . and who forms much stronger judgments on this 'extra-curricular' basis than is commonly believed."[74] As Gramsci had argued since 1916, the division between school and life implicit in the reformers' views would deaden education. When the teacher pays no heed to "the contrast between the type of culture and society which he represents and the type of culture and society represented by his pupils,"[75] his work becomes nothing more than the dissemination of rhetoric. Far from having made the creative advance on Plato for which they prided themselves, the Italian idealists had constructed merely "rhetorical schools"[76] in the service of a corrupt political order.

In outlining his alternative, Gramsci referred continually to the "idealist" model of education. His aim was to invert its misconceptions through a synthesis of its best aspects with some of those from the traditional system. The most general problem in the "idealist" view was that its

> active school was still in the romantic phase, in which the elements of struggle against the mechanical and Jesuitical school have become unhealthily exaggerated. . . . It was necessary to enter the "classical," rational phase, and to find in the ends to be attained the natural source for developing appropriate methods and forms.[77]

Gramsci's effort to theorize this transition involved three specific syntheses.[78]

First, he argued that there ought to be one common school for everyone which would combine "classical" and "vocational" approaches in an attempt to "strike the right balance" between the capacities fostered in each. The common school would offer a nine- or ten-year program which, as the total formal education for many citizens, would be designed to "impart a general, humanistic, formative culture," broader even than the one associated with the traditional school.[79] Yet Gramsci thought that it would be a mistake to ignore technical and vocational training even for the students most gifted in classical, intellectual work. In an industrial world, even political leaders "must have that minimum of general technical culture which will permit them, if not to 'create' autonomously the correct solution, at least to know how to adjudicate between the solutions put forward by the experts."[80]

Secondly, Gramsci aimed at a synthesis of "instruction" and "education." The "idealists" had been right to argue that the traditional emphasis on the former was too heavy but wrong to think that "education" could ignore it entirely. The common school must be "instructive," he thought, at least in the sense that its curriculum is "rich in concrete facts." These are of natural interest to the child and much more accessible to him than abstract concepts. "Instruction" also has the advantage of providing the child with an early sense of discipline for "diligence, precision, poise (even physical poise), [and] the ability to concentrate on specific subjects which cannot be acquired without a mechanical repetition of disciplined and methodical acts."[81] To all those "educators" captivated by Rousseau's experiment with Emile, Gramsci asked:

> Would a scholar at the age of forty be able to sit for sixteen hours on end at his work-table if he had not, as a child, compulsorily, through mechanical coercion, acquired the appropriate psycho-physical habits?[82]

He recognized a distinction between "imposed discipline" and "self-discipline" but argued that the latter could only be built on a foundation laid by the former. Gradually, as the transition to the professional world neared, he thought that the common school could become more "open" and "progressive" in the sense that the student would be free to pursue his own interests. In the last two years, the child could be given almost absolute free reign. Gramsci hoped that these years might represent a "decisive phase" in which the child could begin to make the transition from a rich basis in "common sense" to a more unified and coherent conception of the world.[83]

Finally, Gramsci sought a synthesis between school and life. As long as one followed the familiar pattern of bourgeois education—the child living at home, traveling to school, staying there a few hours, and then returning home—one could not hope to give all children an equal education or to stimulate their "collective sense." Gramsci therefore proposed a common school that would be "organized like a college, with a collective life by day and by night," and with "studies carried on collectively with the assistance of the teachers and the best pupils, even during the periods of so-called individual study."[84] Such a school would recognize that a child "breathes in" a vast quantity of notions and attitudes from his everyday life in society. It would actively seek to create as rich an environment as the one that had previously been available only to children of the wealthy and powerful. Together with the new sense of collective destiny that the students would also acquire, this richness would aid in all the specific learning programs of the common school.

One suspects, of course, that Gramsci intended these prescriptions mostly as suggestive anticipations of education in a socialist society. To the extent that current policy could be pushed in these directions, the conditions for an intellectual-mass dialectic would naturally be enhanced, but Gramsci did not attempt to portray the political education transitions in this particular setting. Rather, he thought of them only in the more general terms of collective political action.

This leads us to the second question posed above: how might such transitions be conceptualized at the level of collective action? To answer this question, we will need to turn again to Gramsci's analysis of "objective and subjective" factors in revolution.

Three "moments" in the development of a revolution are distinguished: the fulfillment of the objective factor in the "relation of social forces"; the fulfillment of the subjective factor in the "relation of political forces"; and the final test of each in the "relation of military forces."[85] Within his analysis of the second, political moment, Gramsci portrayed the shift from "common sense" to "catharsis" and suggested implicitly that it might extend as far as "philosophical reason." However, he dealt with the last transition only speculatively in connection with the "regulated society" anticipated by proletarian politics. We will therefore consider it only in the final section of this chapter; the present discussion of this moment is restricted to the attainment of "catharsis."

To gauge revolutionary potential, one first assesses the economic moment or the "relation of social forces." This is the product of factors "closely linked to the [economic] structure, objective, independent of human will . . . which can be measured with the systems of the exact or physical sciences."[86] Unless this relation is favorable to a rising class, revolution is inconceivable.[87] Despite his philosophical emphasis on subjectivity, Gramsci always argued that the idea of a "purely educative" movement operating without regard to the level and character of socioeconomic development was an "anarchist" fallacy.[88] In unfavorable circumstances, one could seek to manipulate objective conditions, but one could not ignore them. Ordinarily, however, activist intervention in history is concentrated directly on the political moment. By this, Gramsci meant "an evaluation of the degree of homogeneity, self-awareness, and organization attained by the various classes."[89] As the relation of political forces gradually becomes more favorable to the proletariat, the military moment or "relation of military forces" becomes central. Here Gramsci was referring not just to a comparison of forces in a "technical military sense" but also in a "politico-military sense."[90] Long before the proletariat has the capacity to confront the state's armies directly, it will have the ability to pursue

> political action which has the virtue of provoking repercussions of a military character in the sense: (1) that it has the capacity to destroy the war potential of the dominant nation from within; (2) that it compels the dominant military force to thin out and disperse itself over a large territory, thus nullifying a great part of its war potential.[91]

As in later theories of guerrilla war, Gramsci's point was that the relation between military forces of incumbents and insurgents will go through several stages before the proletariat can become as dominant militarily as its purely political power would suggest it should be.

In order to analyze the development of revolutionary consciousness within this schema, Gramsci broke down the political moment into three levels. Each is considered from the perspective of the rising class. At the lowest "economic-corporative" level, the individual producer may feel solidarity with other members of his profession or trade but not with his entire class. Gradually, as he gains a sense for his class interest in purely economic terms, he achieves a second level. Both of these levels involve a "common-sense" consciousness in which the individual undertakes political action only as an individual or, at most, as part of his class's attempt to win "politico-juridical equality" with the ruling elite. Even then the emphasis is less on challenging "existing fundamental structures" than on securing the right of the individual to participate in legislation and administration. Nonetheless, the shift from the first to the second level is important. As Marx had long before suggested, what begins as a struggle over narrowly defined issues always has the latent potential to evolve into an open struggle which pits antagonistic class interests.[92] When this happens, existing working-class ideologies will come into open conflict and compete until one of them ("or at least a single combination of them") predominates. Gramsci conceived of this struggle and the resulting unity as a third level which "marks the decisive passage from the structure to the sphere of the complex superstructure."[93] In this sense, it is analogous to the shift from "common sense" to "catharsis" on the individual, psychological level.

In a kind of analytical shorthand, Gramsci often referred to this transition as the emergence of a class's "hegemony" out of its "economic-corporative" formation. By *hegemony* he meant (in this context) the historical phase in which the proletariat unites ideologically and politically. The third level within the political moment can be characterized as "hegemony" because it "brings about not only a unison of economic and political aims, but also intellectual and moral unity, posing all the questions around which the struggle rages not on a corporate but on a 'universal' plane."[94] In his historical studies, which we will consider in the next chapter, Gramsci was centrally concerned with determining the conditions that have facilitated and retarded the unfolding of the political moment. His key assumption was that the level of hegemony is an empirical question, not a given as in the nearest Crocean analog to it, the "ethico-political moment." This assumption was especially crucial in studying Italian history, since Gramsci viewed this history as embodying a continual failure to supersede "economic-corporative" class formations.

The prime movers of any class through its political moment are the intellectuals. In studying the rise of the bourgeoisie in Italy, France, England, and Germany, Gramsci argued that three factors had been relevant to the ability of the intellectuals to play a significant historical role.[95] One was the alliance between traditional and organic intellectuals, with the gradual dominance of the latter. The second was an "organic" and "national," as opposed to a "diffuse" and "international," orientation of native intellectual groups. The third was their ability to play a significant role in both political and civil society. Only the French intellectuals in and after 1789 had combined all three factors. Their Italian counterparts, even in the Risorgimento, had always been too "diffuse" and "internationalist" to be effective in national development. The English had been "organic" and "national" enough but had confined their activity to the "economic-corporative" level, leaving the political arena largely under aristocratic control. Worst of all, German bourgeois intellectuals had tended to be "diffuse," "internationalist," *and* "economic-corporative," so that political power in the nineteenth century continued to be concentrated in the hands of the Junkers, who eventually became the "traditional intellectuals of the German industrialists."

Interesting as this analysis is, Gramsci never explicitly applied its methods to the proletarian case. Yet he used many of its elements to explain the failure of the postwar Italian revolutionary movement. In the first place, the proletariat of the *biennio rosso* had not sustained the institutions which produced its best organic intellectuals. Secondly, it had not developed "national-popular" strategies[96] centered on issues like the Southern Question. Thirdly, its fixation on the conquest of state power had distracted it from fashioning a significant role for itself within civil society. With a more effective policy in any of these respects, it might have achieved a national hegemony over the subaltern classes. Yet, though it failed in the postwar years, Gramsci thought that its development in the 1920s had illustrated a phenomenon which often accompanies the transitions toward "catharsis" on the individual level and "hegemony" on the social and political levels. This was the transition from a posture of "intransigence" to one of "class alliance."[97] Historically, subaltern classes have tended to define themselves initially through their autonomy within the dominant political system, just as individuals take their first steps beyond common sense "via a series of negations."[98] Should "catharsis" and "hegemony" be attained under an "intransigent" posture, the class's new sense of ideological unity and political integration would encourage it to look beyond its own autonomy and to strengthen itself through class alliance. "Catharsis," "hegemony," and class alliance are historical correlates.

The Coming of a Regulated Society

Parallels of this sort between psychological, sociological, and historical manifestations of class consciousness continually interested Gramsci. A similar one was implicit in his account of the historical evolution of Marxism. Since the Protestant Reformation, Western Europe had been undergoing a profound "intellectual and moral reformation, made dialectical in the contrast between popular culture and high culture."[99] "Renaissance and Reformation, German philosophy and the French Revolution, Calvinism and English classical economics, secular liberalism and . . . historicism"—these had marked the reformation's successive phases. Marxism was the latest one, the "crowning point of this entire movement."[100] The Second International had shown, however, that Marxism was still in its "populist phase" and was thus unable to establish a "real exercise of hegemony over the whole of society."[101] Marxism was the "crowning point" less for its achievements than because it understood the telos through which a higher level of society might be reached. Marxism was "a new culture in incubation which will develop with the development of social relations."[102] One could prepare the way for that new culture, even partially bring it about, through the organization of a proletarian "potential state." But Gramsci still suspected that "only after the creation of the new state does the cultural problem impose itself in all its complexity and tend towards a coherent solution."[103]

As we saw in the last chapter, Gramsci was unable to forge a coherent connection between his concept of necessity and the new culture that he foresaw as a telos. Yet there is no doubt that an "integrated" proletarian culture was his answer to the third question posed above, namely, how one might know whether a genuinely philosophical outlook had been collectively realized. In portraying the "potential state," Gramsci's imagery was reminiscent of the various education-states conceived by classical idealism.[104] Unlike the idealists, however, he sought to restrain utopian impulses and to conceive his vision as the extension of existing historical trends. One of the specific trends which most interested him in the modern popular reformation was the "unprecedented expansion" in the number of intellectuals in society.[105] Modern industrial production and the "democratic-bureaucratic" political system which often grew beside it had produced an enormous increase in the number of occupational positions in which a creative, problem-solving intelligence was constantly demanded. Western European societies had responded by organizing systems of mass education unprecedented in scale. Gramsci believed that these systems were "deepening and broadening the 'intellectuality' of each individual" while simultaneously attempting "to multiply and narrow the various specializations."[106] In this way, many of the basic conditions for democratic self-governance had finally been created. A new state could be built based on an "intellectual/moral bloc" of producers whose scope of decision would gradually be extended throughout political society. This prospect, in short, was Gramsci's idea of the "regulated society."[107]

While the "intellectualizing" of civil society was a necessary condition for regulated society, there were others as well. Gramsci thought that such a society certainly required a proletarian revolution. Moreover, this revolution would have to be "complete," not "passive." A complete revolution[108] occurs when a new class takes power after having attained each of the three levels of the second moment. In achieving "domination," it will therefore also possess "hegemony." As we will see in Gramsci's analysis of the Italian Risorgimento, this completeness does not necessarily characterize all revolutionary change. But it is indispensable for a regulated society, since, in achieving "catharsis" at the social level, it supplies a necessary though not sufficient condition for the "total" cultural reintegration of the proletarian class upon which the new state is predicated.

Gramsci's fascination with this new prospect for the state was strikingly original for a Marxist. Many Second International theorists, in their eager quest for the economic "laws" of history, had lost all sense of the importance of the political dimension in human affairs. Even those most critical of this tendency, like Luxemburg and Lenin, impoverished the concept of state by conceiving it as a mere epiphenomenon of class rule by the bourgeoisie. It was natural for them to have done so. Very few of the intellectual luminaries of the second half of the nineteenth century, including in some ways Marx himself, had succeeded in avoiding positivist and evolutionary influences. One result was the rise of "sociology" and the "decline of the concept of political science and the art of politics."[109] Only the idealists, with their roots still securely planted in the age of Hegel, had retained a serious concept of the state, though they tended to give it a more cultural and less political emphasis than Hegel had.

A central aim of Gramsci's Hegelian Marxism was to elevate

"politics" and "the state" to dominant positions within Marxist theory and practice. In this sense, Eric Hobsbawm is correct in arguing that, above all, Gramsci was a "political theorist, perhaps the only major Marxist thinker who can be so described."[110] Gramsci went well beyond Marx in ascribing to the state a universal "educative and formative role"[111] which transcended its instrumental function for the rule of any particular class. He also gave a political dimension to the dialectic between man and nature which Marx had first defined. For both Marx and Gramsci the end of human activity was to resolve the contradictions between man and nature. Economically, this would mean a harmony between the worker and the means of production. Philosophically, it would harmonize the "freedom" to be creative as a producer with the "necessities" of individual and group life. Gramsci's original contribution in this context was to seek a political resolution to the conflict between "activity" in civil society and "direction" by the state.

Contrary to Marx, he believed that the increasing complexity of civil society necessitated an increasing role for the state regardless of which class controlled it. The state was no longer only the "nightwatchman" over an autonomous civil society. It had penetrated society so deeply that it could now be equated with "the entire complex of practical and theoretical activities with which the ruling class not only justifies and maintains its dominance but manages to win the active consent of those over whom it rules."[112] This insight led Gramsci to redefine the state as

> the equilibrium between political society . . . (i.e., a dictatorship or some other coercive apparatus used to control the masses in conformity with a given type of production and economy) . . . and civil society (or the hegemony of a social group over the entire nation exercised through so-called private organizations such as the church, the unions, the schools, etc.).[113]

The corollary to this image of the state absorbing civil society is that the proletarian state could become integrated with, in effect absorbed by, a civil society based in the factory. The idea of the state as an extension of the factory was a motivating force behind the Turin worker councils, and the *Notebooks* reaffirm this, though with a certain vagueness and nostalgia.[114]

The other organizational features of the proletarian state foreseen by Gramsci can be divided according to their association with what he called, following Hegel, its "public warp" and its "private woof."[115] The core of the "public warp" is the legal system. Gramsci thought that the "juridical problem" for every state was how to "assimilate the entire grouping to its most advanced faction: it is a problem of educating the masses, of their 'adaptation' in accordance with the requirements of the goal to be achieved."[116] In this sense, the new state was no different from any other state. The uniqueness of its legal system would result from its rejection of "every residue of transcendentalism and of every absolute—in practice, of every moralistic fanaticism."[117] The legal system would act as an "educator" seeking "a new type or level of civilization."[118] Superstructural factors could not be "left to themselves, to develop spontaneously, to a haphazard and sporadic germination."[119] If the school system is a positive basis of political education within the education-state,

> the Law is the repressive and negative aspect of the entire positive, civilizing activity undertaken by the State. . . . It operates according to a plan, urges, incites, solicits and "punishes," for once the conditions are created in which a certain way of life is "possible," the "criminal action or omission" must have a punitive sanction, with moral implications, and and not merely be judged generically as "dangerous."[120]

Gramsci thought that the schools and the courts were the two most important political educators within the state, but he acknowledged that "a multitude of other so-called private initiatives and activities tend to the same end."[121] In a general way, this was a very old insight in Western political theory, particularly in the constitutionalist tradition. Yet, Gramsci argued that only with Hegel had a constitutional theorist thought to organize and educate the "private woof" so that consent would be institutionalized in civil society and not just expressed "generically and vaguely" in the instant of elections. German backwardness limited Hegel's concept of the private, however, and he "offered only one perfected example of organization—the 'corporative' (a politics grafted directly onto the economy)." Marx's experiences were only moderately richer in this respect. His journalistic and agitational activities did give him some sense for the trade union, the Jacobin club, and journalistic organization. But even he had virtually no understanding of the greatest modern innovation in this field: the political party.[122]

In Gramsci's view, only parties (and other affiliated mass organizations with which they might dialectically interact) were of sufficient scale and complexity to be the central "private" institutions for the formation and expression of consent within the new state. The very fact that mass political parties had emerged in so many contemporary political environments indicated, he thought, a common recognition that the modern state was too complex to have its consensual basis organized in any less rigorous fashion. The recognition was recent because new ruling classes like the nineteenth-century bourgeoisie always begin from a position of "economic-corporative primitivism" in which "super-structural elements will inevitably be few in number" and not yet "planned."[123] The "nightwatchman" state of the liberals was the first bourgeois political creation to go beyond the purely economic-corporative stage, but it still rested on the myopic identification of state with government. As industrial development had proceeded into the age of imperialism, the "minimal state" had become increasingly untenable. Political demands had been created which could only be satisfied by state intervention in the economy. Government, almost in spite of itself, had become totally interwoven with the civil society it regulated. Parties had become integral to this process, and their future role could only increase as society became more complex.[124]

This idea of the increasing penetration of state and society in an industrial system was a major discovery for a Marxist, even if, as we will see more fully in Chapter 7, it raised questions that he was not prepared to answer. The great advantage of this idea was that it led Gramsci to a novel conception of the "withering away of the state" that was far more realistic than the expectations of classical Marxism. Far from "withering," the state's role was increasing, even if it was also changing in character. The only part of it that might still wither under proletarian rule would be its "coercive element."[125] This is one reason why Gramsci retheorized the state not as the equivalent of "political society" (government in the narrow sense) but as "political society and civil society, in other words hegemony protected by the armor of coercion."[126] More than most Marxists, Gramsci argued that legitimate consent as the predominant means of political control was "normal" within all societies.[127] Traditionally, however, states have had to use force to restrain class conflict, especially when their consensual basis was weak. Whatever easing of burdens that a proletarian state might enjoy in this respect would be more than balanced by its increased regulative activity. Law, for instance, would become increasingly complex and extensive, though it would be mostly "civil law" suited to the regulation of civil society. When Gramsci spoke of the "end of the state," he therefore meant the end of the "class state," of the "internal division of the ruled."[128] He discarded as utopian any idea of a pure civil society unregulated from above. He referred variously to what remained as "a state without a state," an "ethical state," or a "regulated society."[129]

CHAPTER SIX

Hegemony, Historical Bloc, and Italian History

An effective Jacobin force was always missing and could not be constituted; and it was precisely such a Jacobin force which in other nations awakened and organized the national-popular will and founded the modern states.

(1932)

IN CONCEIVING philosophy as political education, Gramsci sought to show that society is inherently educational, that philosophy is an intrinsic part of social activity, and that political change is most usefully depicted in terms of a dialectical interaction between organic intellectuals and ordinary people. This formulation implied a psychological level of analysis, even if his efforts to develop one were never fully adequate. It also involved analyses at several other levels which, as we have seen, he carried out much better: the institutionalization of an intellectual-moral bloc, the conceptualization of education as collective action, and the depiction of the new political and cultural order which this education should promote. These latter analyses led Gramsci to history, especially to Italian history. Knowledge of how the "political moment" had unfolded at key junctures in Italian history would, he believed, provide the clearest orientation for present proletarian politics. What this inquiry revealed is a central concern of this chapter. Initially, however, we must say something more about his general historical outlook and the conceptual apparatus he employed.

In the years before his arrest, Gramsci had already shown a strong interest in historical analysis, though he devoted little time to detailed studies and investigated only contemporary topics close to his political concerns. Foremost among these was the Southern Question. That Italy's development had been uneven on both North-South and urban-rural axes was, as we have seen, an intensely personal concern for him, and may even have been the original source of his interests in politics and history. He returned to the theme continually in his journalism and developed his analysis most fully in the Lyons Theses and in his essay "Some Aspects of the Southern Question," written just prior to his arrest.[1]

The *Notebooks* did not pursue this theme directly, though a 1927 reference to the Southern Question essay as "short" and "superficial" suggests that Gramsci thought he could have.[2] The *Notebooks* did, however, take up many related historical interests which seem to have represented an effort to deepen the earlier problematic.[3] One of these was the evolution of the Italian intelligentsia, an interest also evident prior to his arrest. Another was the peasant question: peasant attitudes toward intellectuals and vice versa, the organizational inadequacies typical of peasant parties, and the resulting tendency of peasants never to gain parliamentary power in proportion to their real strength. Together with the Southern Question, these and other similar interests were like so many springs feeding a single stream; for not only did they suggest the need for a general reappraisal of Italian political history, but they also pointed in a common direction concerning the conceptual enrichments necessary for Marxist historical analysis.

Hegemony and Historical Bloc

As we have been using it, Gramsci's concept of "hegemony" has two related definitions. First, it means the consensual basis of an existing political system within civil society. Here it is understood in contrast to the concept of "domination": the state's monopoly on the means of violence and its consequent role as the final arbiter of all disputes.[4] Gramsci contended, however, that only weak states need to rely very often on the threat or use of force implied in their domination. Strong states rule almost exclusively through hegemony. In this sense, the importance of the concept is that it points to the need for the proletariat to develop political strategies which undermine the consent of the present ruling class. A central foundation of such strategies is the attempt to build an alternative proletarian hegemony within existing civil society upon which a postrevolutionary dictatorship of the proletariat can be founded.

In its second sense, hegemony is an overcoming of the "economic-corporative." Here the reference is to a particular historical stage within the political moment. The hegemonic level represents the advance to a "class consciousness," where class is understood not only economically but also in terms of a common intellectual and moral awareness, a common culture. Gramsci did not deny that a revolution could be carried out at the economic-corporative level. On the contrary, as we will see, part of his interest in the Italian Risorgimento was that he saw it as just such an event. What he did argue was that the attainment of an alternative hegemony was necessary before one could even hope for a "complete" revolution—one that brings to power a coherent class formation united behind a single economic, political, and cultural conception of the world.[5]

When we reflect back on the pre-prison writings, it is evident that Gramsci did not develop these two concepts of hegemony simultaneously but that the former grew out of the latter. In the politics of *biennio rosso* Turin, he thought about hegemonic relations (though he did not actually use the word in this sense) entirely in terms of the proletariat and its self-constitution.[6] Only after 1923, when he came to appreciate the necessary differences between revolution in the East and the West—differences resulting precisely from what he would later call the hegemonic capacity of the advanced capitalist state—was he in a position to theorize hegemony as a mode of rule for the bourgeoisie and for the proletarian "potential state." Nonetheless, his first explicit uses of the concept, in 1924 and 1925, adhere closely to the earlier meaning.[7] Even in the 1926 essay on the Southern Question, where he is self-consciously theorizing the role of the intellectual as a crucial mediation in proletarian politics, he has not yet extended the concept in opposition to domination.[8] Only in his prison reflections on the failure of the Italian workers movement did he make this highly original move.

It might be argued that the order in which the two concepts were developed shows that Gramsci's theorization of hegemony owed little to Lenin. For though in 1924 he credited Lenin with originating the idea, Gramsci was still only using it in opposition to the economic-corporative, a usage which, in crude practical terms, might be viewed as simply a very precise way of calling attention to the need for developing worker class consciousness, hardly an earthshaking insight. Yet Gramsci himself would not have agreed with this assessment. For he later suggested that Lenin, by the end of his life, had come over to the view that Western revolution would have to be different, given that Western states were different: they had hegemonic capacities far in excess of any possessed by czarism in 1917.[9]

In Italy, a debate has raged for two decades over the question of whether or not the principal origins of Gramsci's concept of hegemony are Leninist.[10] More recently the debate has migrated to the English-speaking world.[11] In terms of the present discussion, these debates can be viewed as disputes about which of the concept's two senses is primary, though these senses are almost never clearly distinguished. The Leninists seek to elevate the earlier and repress the later usage; as Palmiro Togliatti put it in 1958, the distinction between hegemony and domination "exists, but it is not one of substance."[12] The anti-Leninists seek to do just the opposite. Their fear, apparently, is that to acknowledge a Leninist influence in Gramsci's view of proletarian education would be to assimilate it too closely to an image of a dictatorship of the proletariat, which now appears repressive and totalitarian.

We will come in a moment to the question of whether there are any real grounds for such a fear. What is more immediately relevant is that such political considerations can have nothing to do with a correct historical assessment of Gramsci. On the one hand, it is futile to argue that the concept owes nothing to Lenin, in view of Gramsci's direct assertions to the contrary;[13] on the other hand, it is also evident that the broadly cultural orientation implicit in hegemony as a form of rule, and the educational orientation implicit in it as an opposition to "economic-corporative," owe a considerable debt to Croce and very little, if anything, to Lenin. Gramsci himself seems to have been well aware of these twin origins when he wrote that

Croce's thought must therefore, at the very least, be appreciated as an instrumental value. Thus it can be said that he has drawn attention energetically to the importance of cultural and intellectual facts in historical development; to the function of great intellectuals in the organic life of civil society and the State; to the moment of hegemony and consent as the necessary form of a concrete historical bloc. . . . Contemporaneously with Croce, the greatest modern theorist of the philosophy of praxis [Lenin], on the terrain of political struggle and organization and with a political terminology, gave new weight—in opposition to the various "economistic" tendencies—to the doctrine of hegemony as the complement to the theory of the state-as-force.[14]

Whatever their origins, however, the two senses of the concept of hegemony are employed with considerable independence. For instance, we have seen that Gramsci correlated a subaltern class's transition from "economic-corporatism" to "hegemony" with its experience of "catharsis" in political action and therefore with its new potential for attaining a "philosophical" view of the world. Yet this hardly means that the hegemony of currently dominant classes is ever practiced over masses who have taken either of these steps beyond common sense. In general, the associations that Gramsci made between hegemony on the one hand and philosophical achievements and historical processes on the other apply readily only when the concept is understood as a stage in the evolution of a subaltern class.

Gramsci made many such associations in his historical discussions. In contrast, he offered few generalizations about hegemonic rule. The reason seems clear: he recognized that hegemonic rule (or the overwhelming predominance of hegemony over domination as the form of political control) is the "normal" form of government, at least in industrial societies, and therefore almost infinite in its variety.[15] He did, however, throw some light on hegemonic rule when he contrasted modern bourgeois states with ancient slaveholding states and pre-modern or feudal states which organized themselves into closed estates and reproduced a fixed, static, and "mechanical" separation of dominant and subaltern classes.[16] In the bourgeois state, which is the first to use an extensive hegemonic apparatus, the autonomous castes of the pre-modern state become transformed into voluntary associations—

parties, unions, cultural institutions, etc.—which serve as hegemonic instruments. Yet if all such hegemonic states are necessarily mass-based, at least in the sense that they actively disseminate a dominant ideology throughout society, they nonetheless vary considerably in the pervasiveness and systemization with which their hegemonic apparatuses operate and in the degree of participation they foster. Just as ancient republics like Athens could be participatory without being hegemonic, so modern bourgeois states like fascist Italy could stymie participation while still being hegemonic to an increasing degree. "In a hegemonic system," Gramsci suggested, "democracy between the ruling group and ruled groups exists to the extent that the development of the economy, and therefore of the legislation which expresses that development, holds open the channels for the ruled to enter the ruling group."[17]

Passages like this one suggest that fears of "totalitarianism" lurking in Gramsci's concept of hegemony are unfounded. Hegemonic rule—whether by the bourgeoisie or the proletariat—is never a closed, static empire of thought and culture. Lenin's justification of a dictatorship of the proletariat on the grounds that all states are dictatorships had no parallel in a Gramscian view that since all states seek to impose a hegemony, the proletariat may impose a particularly rigid one. For Gramsci's hegemony is not a static concept but a process of continuous creation which, given its massive scale, is bound to be uneven in the degree of legitimacy it commands and to leave some room for antagonistic cultural expressions to develop. Nonetheless, it is not difficult to understand how some writers have seen totalitarian implications in a Gramscian hegemony, for hegemony in its opposition to domination is certainly not as dynamic a concept as hegemony as a stage in the political moment; the one refers to what might be called hegemony-maintenance, while the other refers to hegemony-creation. And if Gramsci did ordinarily describe hegemony-maintenance as an active, unfolding process, some of his descriptions of cultural unification suggest a static "point of arrival" with little room for future unfolding.[18]

The difficulty here may be due in part to the rather superficial attention Gramsci gave to the description of hegemonic regimes.

In contrast, he was quite interested in nonhegemonic regimes and in the process through which a hegemonic regime can falter or collapse. At least three kinds of nonhegemonic systems were studied. One is class domination pure and simple—prerevolutionary Russia, for instance. A second is the practice of *trasformismo* characteristic of Italian politics, 1860-1914, which we will consider below. Roughly, *trasformismo* involves the predominance of political society over civil society in such a way that the subaltern classes are held in a passive position because their potential leadership is co-opted. A third and very interesting case is the pseudohegemonic situation in which the government in power, in order to gain a functional equivalent of hegemony, pretends to exercise its power in the name of a class which in reality it does not represent. The Napoleonic Empire is an example. In Gramsci's view, the initial triumph of the French Revolution was based largely on a class alliance between the bourgeoisie and the petty bourgeoisie. The Jacobins, who gradually came to represent the interests of the latter class, pushed the bourgeoisie "to a far more advanced position than the originally strongest bourgeois nuclei would have occupied spontaneously, and even far more advanced than its historical premises should have allowed: hence the various forms of backlash and the function of Napoleon I."[19] This apparent victory of the bourgeoisie did not, however, mean either its hegemony or its domination. Napoleon's rule was essentially independent of bourgeois interests; and while to some extent he exercised his power in their name, the basis of his control over both the bourgeoisie and the subaltern petty bourgeoisie was a combination of personal charisma and a diversionary foreign policy.[20]

The incompleteness of Gramsci's assessment of hegemonic rule should not, however, conceal the monumental theoretical breakthrough that the concept represented. Whatever its intentions, classical Marxism never gave sufficient weight to noneconomic factors like ideology and culture in the reproduction of social relations. For the most part, Marx and Engels treated ideology narrowly as a belief system without being sensitive to the full range of its cultural manifestations. And their treatment of culture, it seems safe to say, never approached the level of depth and insight previously achieved by idealists like Kant, Schiller, or Hegel. With the concept of hegemony, Gramsci was able to surpass classical Marxism in both these respects. Not only did the concept call attention to the wide variety of cultural manifestations in which ideology appears, but it also revived the idealistic concern with culture and then superseded it by analyzing the complex interconnections between culture and politics which the idealists had suppressed. Moreover, as these points help to illustrate, hegemony served Gramsci as a point of intersection where many of his other conceptual commitments—culture, ideology, language, totality, intellectual, revolution, and political education dialectic—could be brought into mutual rapport.[21]

One other important concept may also be located at this intersection, though its relationship to hegemony is especially complex; this is the concept of an "historical bloc." We have said that Gramsci referred to the social formation of an intellectual-mass dialectic as an "intellectual and moral bloc." When he looked beyond the process of political education itself to the larger social implications of such a bloc, to its capacity for creating history, he referred to it as an "historical bloc." Such a bloc will have two dimensions, which can be thought of in rough parallel to the two aspects of hegemony. Just as hegemony represents a higher stage within the political moment of the development of a class, so an historical bloc is in one sense an effort to infuse this hegemony throughout society, above all by means of class alliances. Once these horizontal linkages are achieved, an historical bloc, like hegemony-maintenance, can be understood on a vertical dimension as a relatively stable ("organic") relationship between structure and superstructure, between the productive, economic life of a society and its political and cultural awareness, between its being and its consciousness.[22]

This notion of a vertical fusion of structure and superstructure is really an elaboration of Gramsci's *Ordine Nuovo* insight that political education must be grounded in the economic institutions of the workplace, which will in turn be politicized as the intellectual-mass dialectic unfolds. What was only implicit there, however, and what is theorized much more fully in the *Notebooks*, is the idea that the central mediation between structure and superstructure is the intellectual—the intellectual defined not in terms of personal particularity but functionally and within concrete institutional settings which connect him or her to the whole hegemonic apparatus of the state.[23] In Chapter 7, we will see how Gramsci incorporated these same notions in the theory of the party that he put forward in the *Notebooks*.

The distinction between the horizontal and vertical dimensions of an historical bloc is, however, only analytical and only implicit in Gramsci; the concept must also be seen in a unified focus. In such a focus, its central thrust is the suggestion that a class, as it develops itself historically, becomes more or less politically powerful not only because of its position within the economic structure but also because it is the carrier of certain values which, though certainly expressions of its experience in the world of work and everyday life, become detached as images or projections of its political outlook. Depending on the attractiveness of such images, the class will be able to attach itself to other political groups as joint power-seekers, potential power-shapers, and the social forces behind new cultural expressions.

It is important to recognize that there is nothing inevitable about the growth of such an historical bloc and that this growth may be arrested at any point. Though Gramsci treated the Moderate Party during the Risorgimento as a viable historical bloc by virtue of its well-coordinated intraparty relations and its dedicated organic intellectuals, he also argued that its social basis was narrower even than a single class and that it was correspondingly never able to extend its internal hegemony very fully by means of class alliances.[24] Its policy of emphasizing internal organization and liaisons with rival intellectual groups was a wise starting point but inadequate as a final strategy.[25] For it allowed the party to avoid undertaking a political initiative among the masses which might have liberated them from the dead weight of traditional practices, reoriented their political direction, and absorbed them into a truly national and hegemonic historical bloc.[26] How the Moderates or their principal competitors, the Mazzinian Action Party, might have achieved this is the central problem in Gramsci's reflections on the Risorgimento.

In short, hegemonies always grow out of historical blocs, but not all historical blocs are hegemonic. A social group or class which establishes an "intellectual and moral bloc" will by definition be hegemonic vis-à-vis itself, but its political alliances with other such groups may or may not develop into a hegemonic relationship. This point has eluded many students of Gramsci. Some have erred in the direction of drawing a neat, one-to-one correspondence between hegemony and historical bloc.[27] There are certainly some texts which leave this impression; yet it must be false, since Gramsci's whole interpretation of the Risorgimento rests on his ability to analyze the discrepancies between the two concepts.[28] Other interpreters, especially those preoccupied with Gramsci's "Leninism," have made the much more serious error of reducing the notion of historical bloc to a class alliance.[29] This ignores the relationship of an historical to an intellectual and moral bloc; it ignores the way the latter is defined relative to political education; and it even ignores the notion of an intermeshing of structure and superstructure inherent in the definition of historical bloc itself. Moreover, when Gramsci did point to an intellectual ancestor for this concept, he mentioned not Lenin but Sorel.[30] In his debate with Antonio Labriola in the late 1890s, Sorel had insisted that an historic "rupture" had taken place between objective events and the development of a socialist consciousness in the working class; and though he did not elaborate on it, he had proposed the notion of a "bloc" between structure and superstructure as a way of conceiving the necessary historical reconstitution.[31]

Like hegemony, historical bloc is a concept whose thrust is to circumvent all sharp distinctions of base and superstructure which treat the latter as a mere epiphenomenon, as in many Second International Marxisms, or which assume that a new superstructure can be built independently of the base, as in Lenin's voluntarism. Yet, though this distinction lends itself to the vulgarization of Marxism, Gramsci chose not to abandon it but rather to attempt to show how Marx's own formulation of it in the 1859 "Preface" militated against such an economistic reading. Hence his fondness for quoting the passage about how "men acquire consciousness of structural conflicts on the level of ideology."[32] We will pursue Gramsci's retheorization of the base/superstructure distinction in Chapter 7. Suffice it to say here that Gramsci conceived of this distinction as a circular movement within an organic whole rather than as a linear, mechanical relationship between source and reflection or cause and effect. By stressing the integration of all the economic, political, or cultural expressions of a particular society, the concepts of hegemony and historical bloc suggested not how some of these spheres are reflected in others but rather how they are partial totalities of potentially equal significance which are knit together or drift apart in accordance with the political actions that people carry out in concrete historical circumstances.

These concepts also carried fresh implications for the conduct of proletarian politics. For if bourgeois domination in the West had become internalized by the masses through culture, as Gramsci had been arguing since 1924, political change would depend on the construction of an alternative hegemony which might bore from within and foment a new historical bloc. Yet this notion of an alternative hegemony raised an extremely critical problem which we can only suggest here but which we shall consider more fully when we discuss Gramsci's distinction between civil and political society. The possibility of an alternative hegemony seems to presuppose a social order in which the existing hegemonic apparatus is not so powerful and pervasive as to disrupt all organized, collective challenges and yet which is sufficiently dependent on that hegemonic apparatus for its stability so that an alternative hegemony would pose a serious threat. This would seem to be an unlikely combination and one, in any case, at odds with Gramsci's own suggestions about the nature of the advanced capitalist state.

The Polemic Against Croce

Whatever difficulties might be posed by the theorization of an alternative hegemony did not, however, have to be faced as practical questions by Gramsci in prison. The most that could be attempted there, in the short run, was to attack the present hegemonic influence of leading Italian traditional intellectuals. Over a longer term, the particular problems posed by Italian political tradition and institutions for the construction of a counterhegemony might perhaps be addressed on the basis of a systematic study of the Italian political experience. For Gramsci, both of these matters turned on his relationship to Croce. It will be recalled that Gramsci, in his essay on the Southern Question, had raised the problem of the current hegemony of certain "top intellectuals" over the rest of the Italian intelligentsia in the service of fascism, and had even labeled Croce, along with Giustino Fortunato, as "the two greatest figures of the Italian reaction."[33] But if Croce was a "kind of lay pope"[34] who had to be deposed, and if his stance as an historian was ultimately ideological and had to be exposed as such, his approach to history might also be investigated for clues about what a proper historical orientation might be.

Gramsci's assessment of Croce's relation to fascism was no doubt harsh; in part this may have been a reflection of the fact that his respect for Croce's intelligence was almost as great as his disdain for the use to which Croce had put it, viz., his effort "to reabsorb the philosophy of praxis and to incorporate it as the handmaid of traditional culture."[35] Croce was an effective hegemonic force for fascism precisely because he seemed to so many to be a dissenter or, at the very least, an Olympian figure far removed from fascism's excesses.[36] Yet, if he declined to lend explicit support to the regime, he nonetheless conferred a tacit legitimacy upon it by publishing his articles in the fascist press.[37] And even more disturbing, certain of the methodological premises behind his historical analysis—premises which very much affected its content—played directly into the hands of a repressive and violent regime like Mussolini's.

We earlier remarked on Gramsci's appropriation of certain aspects of Croce's historical outlook: Croce's doctrine of the contemporaneity of history and his absolute historicism. What disturbed Gramsci did not have to do with these matters but rather with the choices and judgments that Croce made as he actually wrote history. The organization of his two major works, *The History of Europe in the Nineteenth Century* and *The History of Italy, 1871-1915*, raised unsettling questions:

Is it possible to write (conceive of) a history of Europe in the nineteenth century without an organic treatment of the French Revolution and the Napoleonic Wars? And is it possible to write a history of Italy in modern times without a treatment of the struggles of the Risorgimento? In other words, is it fortuitous, or is it for a tendentious motive, that Croce begins his narratives from 1815 and 1871? That is, that he excludes the moment of struggle; the moment in which the conflicting forces are formed, are assembled and take up their positions; the moment in which one ethical-political system dissolves and another is formed. . . ? Is it fortuitous or not that he placidly takes as history the moment of cultural or ethical-political expansion?[38]

Evidently, political purposes loomed large in Croce's histories. This was not in itself improper, but Croce refused to acknowledge them and thus to admit that he sought "to create an ideological movement corresponding to that of the period with which he was dealing, i.e., the period of restoration-revolution, in which the demands which in France found a Jacobin-Napoleonic expression were satisfied by small doses, legally, in a reformist manner." When Croce had acted on this desire, the results had been ironic. The same writer who conceived of "history as the story of liberty" had also "contributed to a reinforcement of fascism—furnishing it indirectly with an intellectual justification, after having contributed to purging it of various secondary characteristics."[39]

Two key premises had allowed Crocean history to bypass the moment of struggle. One stemmed from his 1906 appraisal of the "living" and "dead" in Hegel, in which he claimed to have discovered a fundamental confusion between "opposites" and "distincts."[40] The richness of Hegel's own discovery of a "dialectic of opposites," Croce thought, had so intoxicated him that he had applied it everywhere in a panlogistic bacchanal. Yet this dialectic, "so far from being the whole of philosophy, is not even the whole of logic."[41] One could legitimately use it to analyze true "opposites" like beautiful/ugly or being/nothing, but not mere "distincts" such as fancy/intellect or art/philosophy. The former were not really concepts but mere abstractions made concrete only in their synthesis, as, for instance, in the synthesis of being and nothing in becoming. Distincts, however, involve two concepts, "the second of which would be abstract and arbitrary without the first, but which, in connection with the first, is as real and concrete as it is."[42] Distincts are therefore not to be grasped dialectically but in a more linear fashion, which Croce dubbed the "theory of degrees" of spirit.

Gramsci saw in the "theory of degrees" a fundamental philosophical underpinning of all Crocean thought, one which retreated from the full force of Hegelian negativity and which therefore represented a distinct "step backwards from Hegel."[43] Yet perhaps even more fundamental in Croce's failure to come to grips with history as class struggle was his refusal to acknowledge the philosophical seriousness of political expression. He defined politics in terms of individual and group conflicts over scarce resources and reduced it to a mere "passion" or "error," to "the moment which in the *Theses on Feuerbach* is called *schmutzig-jüdisch* [dirty Jewish]."[44] He therefore had thought it appropriate and legitimate to minimize politics as far as possible through centralized state administration. Whatever its consequences for justice and freedom, Gramsci argued that such a view of politics made no logical sense:

> Permanent passion is a condition of orgasm and of spasm which means operational incapacity. It excludes parties, and excludes every plan of action worked out in advance. However, parties exist and plans of action are worked out, put into practice, and are often successful to a remarkable extent. So there is a flaw in Croce's conception.[45]

Either party politics for Croce is not real politics, in which case his argument is trivial, or it is politics, in which case his argument is contradictory.

What, then, had Croce meant by "ethical-political" history? This phrase is not, as one might suspect, a conjunction of opposites; it stands really just for the ethical moment in the life of states, where by *ethical* is meant the extent to which states will the "universal" and thus promote human liberty.[46] Though this moment is said to pervade state behavior at all times, it does not entirely dominate the historical stage. States also always act from a different and autonomous form of motivation, the "economic moment," i.e., what is "useful" for the state in the neutral sense of technical achievement. Thus state life for Croce is essentially contradictory: the state is forever grappling with the conflicting goals of being the educator concerned with the moral improvement of its citizenry and of ensuring ultimate survival at whatever cost.

Gramsci certainly perceived the difference between Croce's view that the ethical-political moment is an historical constant, even if it is also constantly rivaled, and his own formulation in which hegemony was sometimes the principal political mode, sometimes secondary, and sometimes supplanted entirely by domination.[47] This was precisely his criticism: by treating history as a smooth lake, Croce had eyes only for fair weather. While this had led him to demonstrate "the importance of cultural and intellectual facts in historical development,"[48] a great corrective to mechanical materialism, it had blinded him to history's darker clouds. In *Etica e politica*,[49] Croce had praised Machiavelli for having been the first to spell out the dualism of economic and ethical-political moments in history, and, as we will see more fully in the next chapter, Gramsci echoed this sentiment in his own terms. Yet he also perceived that Croce had entirely lost Machiavelli's "Jacobin" sense for what was involved in acts of large-scale political creativity.

From this polemical confrontation with Croce, then, Gramsci was able to define the uses of history: History was present politics in the making; to make an historical reconstruction was not only to grasp present political issues in the fullness of their historical development but to create an historical mediation which offered direction for present political struggles by analyzing similar efforts in the past, both successes and failures. Croce had inspired this outlook with his doctrine of history's contemporaneity and, unwittingly, with the implicit political orientation underlying his work. Moreover, his emphasis on "ethical-political" history, even if flawed in his own execution, remained appropriate, especially for the Italian case. Why had no class ever succeeded in becoming hegemonic over all of Italian national life? What were the specific shortcomings of the historically progressive forces in Italy which had prevented them from exercising the necessary role of popular political educators? These and similar questions were suggested by Croce's accounts, and they became the questions that Gramsci strove to answer in his own historical reconstructions. While it is therefore accurate to regard these reconstructions as political acts rather than as "pure" history, one must remember that Gramsci shared this general orientation with Croce and that, in both cases, their approaches were not arbitrary but followed from fundamental philosophical assumptions.[50] Thus, in the analysis of

Gramsci's historical writings to which we may now turn, we will not be particularly concerned to assess them as scholarship;[51] rather, we must judge them in terms of the political lessons they allowed him to draw, how he drew them, and how they related to his political outlook more generally.

Jacobinism and Its Absence

In principle, any political movement arising in civil society is capable of forming an historical bloc, allying with other subaltern classes, and creating an alternative hegemony. Yet Gramsci thought that historically the French Revolutionary Jacobins had been the first modern political movement to do this, and he made a practice of referring to all such movements before and since as "Jacobin." In applying this concept across European history, Gramsci took its essence to be a dialectical subordination of the countryside to the city, in which peasant consent was mobilized by an organized political party or other urban movement. Thus, Machiavelli was a "precocious Jacobin" because his "intention through the reform of the militia" was to allow "the great mass of peasant farmers to burst *simultaneously* into political life."[52] Moreover, his project showed that he had applied his "will to the creation of a new equilibrium among the forces which really exist and are operative." He had moved "on the terrain of effective reality . . . in order to dominate and transcend it."[53]

This enthusiastic portrait of Machiavelli the Jacobin is very far from the view of Jacobinism that Gramsci took in his early writings on the Russian Revolution.[54] There, in his concern to show that the Bolsheviks represented a new proletarian class and unprecedented historical possibilities, he had portrayed the French Jacobins as elitist, conspiratorial, narrowly bourgeois, and lacking a universal program. He had emphasized that their revolution was more than a century out of date and not to be confused with contemporary events, as some Western journalists were doing. In the *Notebooks*, Gramsci's far greater respect for Jacobinism was not, however, so much a change in this attitude as a deepening of it. He still saw the "historical" Jacobins as the left wing of the French bourgeoisie, driving it "forward with kicks in the backside" but also quite incapable of transcending this role.[55] What he now argued was that this meant that they were realists of the Machiavellian stamp and not abstract dreamers. They were convinced of the absolute truth of their slogans about equality, fraternity and liberty, and, what is more important, the great popular masses whom the Jacobins stirred up and drew into the struggle were also convinced of their truth. The Jacobins' language, their ideology, their methods of action reflected perfectly the exigencies of the epoch, even if "today," in a different situation and after more than a century of cultural evolution, they may appear "abstract" and "frenetic."[56]

What the French Revolution needed when the Jacobins arose was exactly what they had given it: the destruction of enemy forces to prevent counterrevolution and the expansion of bourgeois cadres capable of leading a national force against enemies in the Vendée and elsewhere.[57] Their success in blunting the Girondin attempt to manipulate federalist sentiment against Jacobin Paris was particularly remarkable. In a matter of months, they had done no less than to organize a hegemony for Paris over rural France. Even if their political dominance was short-lived, they still had to be credited with having "created the bourgeois state, made the bourgeoisie into the leading, hegemonic class of the nation—in other words, with having given the new State a permanent basis in a compact, modern French nation."[58]

Gramsci's fascination with this now much richer and fuller historical image of Jacobinism led him to universalize it as a political category. To do this he distinguished the "historical" Jacobins from "the particular methods of party and government activity which they displayed."[59] In part these were matters of character and style: Jacobins had "extreme energy, decisiveness and resolution."[60] In part they were matters of program: Jacobins built "national-popular" mass movements based on urban-rural alliances. In this sense, the Italian Communists were "modern Jacobins" who sought an historical bloc and eventually a national hegemony. They had a well-organized party, a determined program, an emphasis on worker-peasant alliances, roots in a specific class base, and a great deal of determination and energy. Although they had suffered temporary setbacks in the postwar era, they were significant just for having recognized the importance of these Jacobin aims. In Gramsci's view, the theme that had dominated Italian political development since the end of the Roman Empire was that "an effective Jacobin force was always missing."[61] This was why the fundamental political changes in

Italian history had always come in the form of "passive revolutions."

By a "passive revolution" or a "revolution without a revolution," Gramsci generally meant elite-engineered social and political reform.[62] He credited the phrase to Vincenzo Cuoco (1770-1823), a far-sighted Neapolitan conservative who had argued in 1799 that Italy could avert its own version of the French Revolution only by an active campaign of social and political reform. Passive revolution became attractive when a regime possessed domination but lacked hegemony and needed to curb a progressive force, preferably without any resort to violence, or at least without a protracted struggle. This could be accomplished by launching a minimally progressive political campaign designed to undercut the truly progressive classes—a tactic employed, for instance, by the Moderate Party of d'Azeglio and Cavour during the Risorgimento. However, the situations which prompted passive revolutions were not without opportunities for the truly progressive classes; if the regime's domination prevented their overt advance, its lack of hegemony gave them room for covert maneuver. Indeed, from their independent base they might be able to mount a "molecular" upsurge carrying them into power. Examples of such progressive undercurrents—which Gramsci also referred to as passive revolutions—were Christianity under the Roman Empire, the French bourgeoisie during the Restoration (1815-30), and Gandhiism in India.[63] In these cases, substantial hegemonic force existed without a capability for domination; in the more usual sense of passive revolution, a capability for domination had existed without substantial hegemonic force.

When Gramsci delved into Italian history for the source of the tendency toward non-Jacobin "passive revolutions," much of his interest focused on the evolution of the Italian medieval communes. Stimulated by the work of Henri Pirenne, whose book on the medieval city was among those he read in prison,[64] Gramsci argued that the Italian communal bourgeoisie was the first to have established itself as an "economic-corporative" power in medieval Europe, but that it had never succeeded in transcending this phase. In part, he traced this to the influence of the Catholic hierarchy, which opposed the "nascent capitalist economy" and sought to prevent it from gaining hegemony. However, the most important sources of the communes' failure were internal:

By 1400, the spirit of initiative of the Italian merchants had been broken. They preferred to make safe investments of their acquired riches and to have a secure income from agriculture rather than to risk them once again in travels and investments abroad. Yet how did this collapse come to pass? Several elements contributed: fierce class warfare within the communal cities, the insolvency of regal debtors . . . , the absence of a large state to protect the citizens from foreign threats. In short, the fundamental cause is to be found in the structure of the communal state which was incapable of developing itself into a large territorial state.[65]

The commune was only a "mechanical bloc" created by the common activity of commerce. As such it was entirely autonomous, independent both of other communes and similarly constituted blocs of "proletarians, serfs and peasants."[66] For centuries this isolation had been to the bourgeoisie's advantage, allowing its culture and class sense to incubate. But by the fifteenth century, this process was very far advanced, and the bourgeoisie's continued lack of integration in national life could only result in its stagnation. A basic need had emerged for a "modern state which would have substituted for the mechanical bloc of social groups, their subordination to the active hegemony of the directive and dominant group, hence abolishing certain autonomies which would nonetheless have been reborn in other forms, as parties, trade unions and cultural associations."[67]

One significant result of the failure to meet this need was a legacy of isolation and mutual distrust between the country and the city, which made future political alliances very difficult. Once fallen from their grandeur, the Italian communes had become "cities of silence" in which there existed and still exists:

among all social groups, an urban ideological unity against the countryside, a unity which even the most modern nuclei in terms of civil function do not escape. . . . There is hatred and scorn for the "peasant," an implicit common front against the demands of the countryside, which, if realized, would make impossible the existence of this type of city. Reciprocally, there exists an aversion . . . of the country for the city, for the whole city and all the groups which make it up.[68]

One later historical episode in which this city-country relationship was particularly visible was the Neapolitan Revolution and the resulting Parthenopean Republic of 1799. There the attempt at a "passive revolution" by an enlightened city elite was "crushed" by the neighboring peasantry, who had been organized by the local Cardinal.[69] Yet Gramsci argued that the peasants had rallied to the conservative elite, rather than to the enlightened one, not because their interests were better represented by the former but because the latter had completely ignored them. The aristocratic and bourgeois elements in the city had not been able to overcome their fear that a coalition with the peasants would eventually produce a political situation in which their own landed property would be expropriated.

This tension between the country and the city was further exacerbated later in the Risorgimento, when the spreading influence of Piedmont in the North appeared to be reproducing the split on overall North-South lines.[70] Even though the Risorgimento culminated in a unified Italy—substantially by 1861, completely by 1870—the traditional urban-rural and North-South rivalries were certainly an important source of the political arrangements which raised the Southern Question in subsequent years. Moreover, these rivalries made it that much more difficult for any subsequent effort to solve the problems of the South by organizing the subaltern classes for political action. Yet when Gramsci turned back to the earliest years of the Risorgimento, the late eighteenth and early nineteenth centuries, he could also see the social and cultural factors that had fueled the movement for national integration. Especially after the French Revolution, a "consciousness of national unity" had developed, first as the call for ridding the Italian peninsula of foreign influence, later as a "sensibility of certain ideal exigencies."[71] Moreover, the French Revolution had produced a new sense of hope and of the need for combat and political sacrifice among the peasantry in both the North and South of Italy.[72] Among elites there were unifying factors too. One very important one was the "literary rhetorical tradition which exalted the Roman past, the glory of the Communes and the Renaissance, and the universal function of the Italian Papacy."[73]

In short, Gramsci found in the early Risorgimento many of the major reasons why no class in modern Italian history had ever established a hegemony over the rest, but he also found certain new factors which had at least raised the possibility of achieving the unprecedented. For this reason, the great historical problem which the Risorgimento posed for him was double-edged: why did the Risorgimento evolve into a purely passive revolution, and under whose direction and in what ways might the subaltern classes have been educated and organized to produce a more complete transformation?

There is an important assumption in this way of posing the problem. Unlike many historians before and after him, Gramsci never viewed the Risorgimento as a regal conquest pure and simple. Cavour's machinations, whose cunning and brilliance he never for a moment doubted, were the major force behind the Austrian ouster from the peninsula, and in that sense, behind the unification of Italy. But both the political movement for which Cavour spoke, and the problems that his solutions provoked, had roots which descended much deeper into society. Gramsci saw that the political currents of the Risorgimento were directed as much against the South and the peasantry as against the old order of church, aristocracy, and the Austrian alliance. The Risorgimento had grown out of social and political unrest, much of it among the Southern peasantry.[74] That the forces producing this unrest remained in disarray may have been the period's tragedy; but precisely for that reason, they could not be ignored. "The Risorgimento," Gramsci argued, "is a complex and contradictory historical development which achieves wholeness from all its antithetical elements: its protagonists and antagonists, their struggles and the reciprocal modifications these struggles bring about, the function of latent and passive forces like the great peasant masses, and above all, naturally, the function of international relations."[75]

If, as these images suggest, Italian unification left as many of the Risorgimento's threads dangling as it knotted, then the answers to the questions that Gramsci posed would no doubt emerge from an analysis of the period's political actors—the way they had organized themselves, the opportunities they had taken advantage of, and those they had missed. This, at any rate, seems to have been Gramsci's basic working assumption, one that corresponded to his long-held belief that people can shape, if not control, their historical destiny through political organization and initiative. As he surveyed the political forces of the Risorgimento, he saw that the years 1848 and 1849 had marked an important watershed. With the defeats they had suffered then, both Carlo Cattaneo's federalist-republican idea of a United States of Italy within a United States of Europe and Vincenzo Gioberti's neo-Guelph design for an Italian confederation of states under Papal leadership had collapsed as visions commanding political respect. This had effectively narrowed the field of political actors to two: the Moderate Party, which Cavour ultimately commanded; and Mazzini's Action Party, whose control in the end was shared with Garibaldi.

The Moderate Party became a major actor in Risorgimento politics when it absorbed the remains of the neo-Guelph movement in 1849. Initially federalist like the neo-Guelphs, it soon became a political arm of the Kingdom of Sardinia. Guided first by d'Azeglio and then by Cavour, the party's political line became much more *realpolitik* and its organization became much more a "real, organic vanguard of the upper classes" sustaining a "national bloc."[76] Once unification was achieved, it became the political right within the Italian parliament and governed until 1876.

The Action Party, in contrast, was a loose aggregation of secular, mostly republican elements, linked almost wholly through a common devotion to Mazzini. Although not formally constituted until 1853, most of the factions within the Action Party had fought together in the struggles of the 1840s. In the decisive years that preceded unification, their role was extremely limited. Their only major efforts were the Sicilian Expedition of the "Thousand," led by Garibaldi in April 1860, and the subsequent takeover of Naples that September. Eventually they became the vital nucleus of the Italian parliamentary left and the source of much of the antagonism to the post-Risorgimento that we mentioned in earlier chapters.

For Gramsci, the twin issues of the Risorgimento's ultimate "passivity" and its inherent but unexplored possibilities for the hegemony of one class over the rest tended to center on the comparative analysis of these two political forces. Basically, his analysis revealed that the contest had been unevenly matched from the beginning. While never close to a national hegemony, the Moderates had always exercised more of a "spontaneous attraction" over the "whole mass of intellectuals" than had the Action Party.[77] Some of this attraction resulted from their genuinely progressive economic policies.[78] Moreover, once the tragic defeats of 1848-49 had shattered all utopian illusions, the market value of political "realism" had soared, and the Moderates had attracted many new cadres from former allies and even adversaries. In this atmosphere, they had been able to make an effective and virtually unchallenged use of "unity" slogans.[79] But perhaps their greatest asset was the passivity of their opponents. Far from challenging the Moderate claim to be leading a unified movement, the Action Party seemed to relish the role of being off center stage. Gramsci found it difficult to pinpoint the source of this tendency. Perhaps it lay in the atmosphere of intimidation created by 1848; perhaps in a simple failure of nerve on the part of the leadership.[80] Or was it perhaps even more a product of their lack of vision? This would be an ironic thesis in view of Mazzini's romantic obsession with political vision. Yet, as Gramsci looked back on post-1848 Italy, he saw that the Action Party's only hope for playing an effective leadership role would have been to develop a truly "organic" (as opposed to the Moderates' merely "empirical") program of mass-elite relations.[81]

In other words, it should have become a Jacobin party. But unlike the Moderates, who at least "represented a relatively homogeneous social group" and maintained a rough ideological consistency over time,[82] the Action Party had no specific class base; nor did it seem to feel the need for establishing one. In the last analysis, this meant that it represented the interests which the Moderates wanted it to represent. Moreover, it had no concrete program of governance, a fact that made its differences with the Moderates appear to be more a matter of "temperament" than of organic politics.[83] For their part, the Moderates were shrewd and calculating, and though they could be understood as an historical bloc, they remained strangely aloof. They never saw the need for building a mass movement out of the "nuclei of homogeneous leading classes" which they represented.

> These nuclei undoubtedly existed, but their tendency to unite was extremely problematic; also, more importantly, they—each in its own sphere—were not "leading" [*dirigente*]. The "leader" presupposes the "led," and who was "led" by these nuclei? These nuclei did not wish to "lead" anybody, i.e., they did not wish to concord their interests and aspirations with the interests and aspirations of other groups.[84]

While they remained dominant, the Moderates made no attempt to widen their influence through a hegemony. This, essentially, is why the Risorgimento stagnated as a passive revolution in which "what was involved was not a social group which 'led' other groups, but a state which, even though it had limitations as a power, 'led' the group which should have been 'leading.'"[85]

Was there a viable alternative outcome that had been at least conceivable at the time? Gramsci seems to have regarded this question as one of the most important to be faced in any effort to assay the Risorgimento experience.[86] His answer was complex. It was negative in the sense that no leader within the Action Party had seen the need for Jacobinism, a fact for which there was a solid explanation based on objective historical developments. Insofar as the Italian bourgeoisie had any intellectual leadership after 1815, it was energized almost wholly from abroad, mostly from France. The only Italian who even came close to seeing "that what was lacking in the Risorgimento was a 'Jacobin' ferment" and to having "a strategic conception" was Carlo Pisacane.[87] He had understood part of what Mazzini had missed: that the presence of Austrian troops on Italian soil was a potent fact around which to do political organizing. He had further argued that such organizing should be at least democratic enough to provide the basis for a national army recruited by compulsory conscription.[88] Yet, however acute his military sense, he had been no more successful than Mazzini in perceiving the political imperative of establishing a strong mass-based party with a solid program and an articulate strategy. In temperament too, Pisacane was no more the Jacobin realist than Mazzini. For instance,

Gramsci found "inexplicable" his "aversion for Garibaldi's strategy and his mistrust of Garibaldi."[89]

Whatever his insights, Pisacane's ultimate shortcomings seem to have convinced Gramsci that no Risorgimento leader had the elements of a Jacobin vision. Yet he was also convinced that the objective conditions for a Jacobin movement had always existed just below the surface. "Agrarian reform had been a strongly felt exigency,"[90] he thought, and "action directed at the peasantry was certainly always possible."[91] Moreover, the actual course that the movement had taken in the climactic years of 1859-61 showed the feasibility of a North-South alliance which, presumably, could have been fashioned for much more radical ends.[92] At long last, the "Northern urban force" had proven capable of smoothing over intercity tensions and organizing itself as a unified movement under the direction of the Piedmontese state. From this position it had established contact with the "Southern urban force," which, unlike its Northern counterpart, had never been strong enough to establish a hegemony over the rural forces in its sector. Through self-assertion, the Northern forces had succeeded in persuading the South of this fact and of what they took to be the logical consequence, namely, that the South's "directive function should be limited to insuring the leadership of North over South in a general relation of city to countryside."[93] The eventual result was a series of mechanical alliances which allowed

> the North to initiate the struggle, the Center to adhere more or less peacefully and the Bourbon state in the South to collapse under Garibaldi's attack, a relatively weak one. This happened because the Action Party (Garibaldi) intervened at the right time, after the Moderates (Cavour) had organized the North and Center; i.e., it was not the same politico-military leadership (Moderates or Action Party) which organized the relative simultaneity, but the (mechanical) collaboration of the two leaderships which were successfully integrated.[94]

If a true Jacobin party had been leading this alliance, a much more formidable result might have been achieved.

All of these considerations entered into Gramsci's positive answer to the question of a viable alternative to the historical course of the Risorgimento. Largely to substantiate his answer, he made what often seems like an unceasing inventory of Action Party "mistakes." These can be grouped roughly into three categories. The first is by now the most obvious: the Action Party had paid insufficient attention to the Italian peasantry, both Northern and Southern. Gramsci thought that this negligence stemmed less from a lack of awareness of the agrarian question than from a fear that a genuine mass movement might eventually produce "a terror like that of 1793" or like "the events in France of 1848-49."[95] This fear also made them hesitate to organize the "intellectuals of the middle and lower strata."[96] Thus they overlooked the "dialectical" alliance which could have been forged from these intellectuals and the peasantry to serve as the core of a new "liberal-national formation."[97]

The second set of mistakes concerned the internal organization of the Action Party. Gramsci never clarified whether he thought the existing leadership was hopelessly inadequate and in need of replacement, or whether it would have been enough for them to have overcome their more obvious irrationalities. In any case, the problem was serious. Garibaldi was "desultory" and accepted "personal subordination to the Moderate leaders" without a challenge.[98] Mazzini, for all his worldly pretensions, had a rather silly Francophobia which blinded him to the merits of Jacobinism.[99] Neither man had thought to organize the party according to a plan or to develop a concrete program of government.[100] Neither possessed any real knowledge of the cultural basis of the peninsula, nor had either sought it. Instead, they persisted in confusing the cultural unity of "a very thin stratum of the population, and polluted by the Vatican's cosmopolitanism, with the political and territorial unity of the great popular masses who were foreign to that cultural tradition and who, even supposing that they know of its existence, couldn't care less about it."[101] This undermined the popular appeal of the Action Party, particularly since Mazzini insisted on the necessity of religious reform. As Gramsci pointed out, such reform "is not only of no interest to the great rural masses, it on the contrary rendered them susceptible to being incited against the new heretics."[102]

Perhaps the biggest single mistake that the Action Party had made, however, was its failure to challenge the Moderate slogan of "independence and unity."[103] Indeed, far from challenging it, Mazzini had promoted it. This policy had destroyed his power to lead, and it showed Gramsci that Mazzini understood neither his own historical role nor Cavour's:

> If . . . Mazzini had possessed such awareness—in other words, if he had been a realistic politician and not a visionary apostle (i.e., if he had not been Mazzini)—then the equilibrium which would have resulted from the convergence of the two men's activities would have been different, would have been more favorable to Mazzinianism.[104]

Mazzini's apparent willingness to allow the Moderates to lead helped to obscure the real sources of conflict in Risorgimento politics. Ultimately, this had disastrous consequences for Italy. Not only did it help to ensure that the Risorgimento would remain a passive revolution, but it also sowed the seeds for the false-consensus politics of *trasformismo* in the post-Risorgimento era. At that point, cries of dissatisfaction from Mazzini and his followers burst forth like a spring flood, but this was too little too late. *Trasformismo* was not a post-Risorgimento imposition; it was rooted in the Risorgimento itself.[105] By the 1870s, former devotees of the Action Party were reduced to the uncomfortable alternative of siding with the Tweedledums of the parliamentary left or opting out of mainstream party politics altogether.

To sum up: Gramsci's reflections on Italian history could only have confirmed him in the wisdom of the premises which had underlaid his PCI chairmanship. Two things, specifically, could be perceived as necessary for a progressive reorientation of Italian politics: an effective organizational machinery capable of coordinating political activity on a national scale, and a truly "national-popular" program of political education aimed at developing enthusiasm for such a reorientation. As Gramsci had already recognized in 1924, the Turin worker council movement had achieved the latter but evidently at the expense of the former. What the historical inquiry had demonstrated more fully was how deeply rooted the Italian urban-rural divisions were. Moreover, the experience of the communes had shown that the incubation of an alternative hegemony—even if carefully nourished over a long period—would still come to naught in the absence of a Jacobin force. Gramsci's reflections on political organization in the

Notebooks therefore understandably emphasized the need for national organization through a Jacobin political party. We will take this up in the next chapter after we have explored how he understood the immediate historical context of *trasformismo* and fascism.

Transformism and Crisis of Authority

Since he saw it as the result of a prior failure, the era of *trasformismo* (1860-1914) never interested Gramsci as much as the Risorgimento, but he nonetheless recognized its importance for a full understanding of fascism.[106] If the Risorgimento had failed to move the subaltern classes beyond an economic-corporative stage to a hegemonic one, *trasformismo* had been a "molecular" process in which their common sense itself had increasingly degenerated. Unlike genuine antagonists, the Action Party and the Moderates in the Risorgimento had quarreled and flirted like unmarried lovers; no wonder they had

> produced a bastard. . . . The wretched political life of 1870-1900, the elemental and endemic rebelliousness of the Italian popular classes, the narrow and stunted existence of a skeptical and cowardly ruling class, these are all the consequences of that failure. . . . In reality, furthermore, the rightists of the Risorgimento were great demagogues: they made the people-nation into an instrument, into an object, they degraded it. In this consisted its greatest and most despicable demagoguery.[107]

These were the brute facts: the Cavourian right ruled for six more years after the addition of Rome in 1870 finally completed Italian unification; the next four and a half decades saw the left in power, first under the rather pallid former Action Party functionary Agostino Depretis, then under the fiery demagogue Francesco Crispi, and finally under the coldly analytical power broker Giovanni Giolitti. The word *trasformismo*, which in its most restricted sense referred to the practice of filling cabinet posts from both sides of the parliamentary aisle, was first coined to characterize the Depretis years. But as one historian has maintained:

> Depretis was exploiting a trend which already existed, and the word *trasformismo* was coined merely to express that absence of party coherence and organization which had itself brought about the fall of the

Right. Transformism was only the rationalization of Cavour's practice. None of the prime ministers since 1852 had been strictly party men, and all of them had been willing to accept support from anywhere except the two extremes.[108]

Transformism was not any single technique but a comprehensive style, and a remarkably durable one at that. Gramsci located only one significant shift in the way it had operated from 1860 to the onset of the First World War.[109] This had more or less coincided with Giolitti's ascendancy around 1900. Before then, transformism was "molecular" in the sense that the political recruitment for the "conservative-moderate 'political class'" operated by co-opting individual members of the parliamentary opposition. This process was "characterized by its aversion to any intervention of the masses in state life, to any organic reform which would substitute a 'hegemony' for crude, dictatorial 'domination.'"[110] After 1900, the recruitment function tended to operate on "entire groups of leftists who pass over to the moderate camp."[111] Gramsci was thinking here, for instance, of the formation of the Nationalist Party out of former syndicalists and anarchists. In a smaller way (with a larger consequence), the shift of Mussolini and his immediate followers from socialism to fascism was another instance of this kind.

Gramsci probed the peculiar psychology of this sort of politics through his critical estimates of Crispi and Giolitti. Crispi held a certain fascination for him. "In his program, Crispi was a Moderate pure and simple; his most noble Jacobin 'obsession' was the politico-territorial unity of the country." Yet, as "a man of strong passions, he hated the Moderates as individuals: he saw in them the latecomers, the heroes of the eleventh hour, the people who would have made peace with the old regimes if these had become constitutional."[112] Crispi's public oratory was filled with intimations of this fact, and his imperialist policies converged with the desires of the peasantry for gaining more land, even across the Mediterranean in Africa. But his imperialism was only a ploy to gain national unity, and the building of a mass movement with large peasant representation was the farthest thing from the mind of this "true man of the new bourgeoisie."[113]

Giolitti may also have been plagued by similar conflicts

between private emotional and public political needs, but he showed them less. The hypocrisy of his transformism still provoked deep cynicism among opposition intellectuals, but his greater calmness of manner and purpose gave him greater success in achieving political stability, however shallowly it was rooted. "For Crispi's Jacobin temperament, Giolitti substituted industriousness and bureaucratic continuity."[114] Giolitti also had the greater sense of vision. His was the first serious attempt to overcome Italy's greatest political liability: its huge dead weight of "social parasites" clinging to the body politic from their footholds in outdated "social sedimentations."[115] He did this by "breaking the retrograde and asphyxiating hold of landed property on the state by giving a larger role in it to the new bourgeoisie and putting the former under state direction."[116] His success was well beyond what one would expect, given the relatively small Italian bourgeoisie with which he had to work.

Gramsci was far from admiring Giolitti, but he did respect his political abilities, especially as they were displayed in the prewar era. Indeed, it was fitting that transformism, as the final example of Italy's historical failure to develop a Jacobin politics, had itself ended under the leadership of one of its most artful practitioners. For the tragedy of four centuries of Italian political history was too profound to be blamed on individuals, however much some of them might have made a difference at critical junctures. Certainly fascism was far more than a response to the failure of individual political leaders or even to the accumulation of their mistakes in and after World War I. Fascism was a frenetic surge of the "forgotten" classes, led at best uncertainly by a coterie of disaffected nationalists, who sought to free the political system from the inertia of half a century of transformism.

We saw in an earlier chapter how Gramsci had reacted to the growth and relative stabilization of fascism in the years prior to his imprisonment. Once incarcerated, of course, he was no longer able to write about fascism openly, but there are nonetheless many passages in the *Notebooks* which deal with it sub rosa and which connect it to the conceptual framework that he was developing for the analysis of politics in advanced capitalism. One of fascism's sources, Gramsci now proposed, was the detachment, in a moment of intense "hegemonic crisis," of all of the most important social classes from the political parties with which they had previously been associated.[117] In general, such a crisis will occur "either because the ruling class has failed in some major political undertaking for which it has requested, or forcibly extracted, the consent of the broad masses (war, for example), or because huge masses (especially of peasants and petit-bourgeois intellectuals) have passed suddenly from a state of political passivity to a certain activity, and put forward demands which taken together, albeit not organically formulated, add up to a revolution."[118]

One of two outcomes then becomes likely. An "organic solution" to the crisis may emerge in the form of a single party which marshals the troops of many previous parties and creates the political basis for a new hegemony. Had the PSI organized itself properly as a collective will in 1919, it might have produced such an outcome.[119] When such a party is missing or fails in its efforts, the political field becomes open to a second possibility, a violent solution led by "charismatic 'men of destiny.'"[120] Such a solution has the effect of restoring a "static equilibrium," which means only that no other group, progressive or traditionalist, can muster a viable challenge. As an outcome of this type, fascism nonetheless did not "solve" the Italian crisis; a "static equilibrium" never involves a true hegemony. Yet, through its ruthless domination and its partial but unstable consensual basis in civil society, fascism was generally able to contain that crisis.

This is the essential point that Gramsci made about fascism in the *Notebooks*. Yet the richness and complexity of his understanding of it can only be appreciated in the light of the three more general concepts he developed in conjunction with this analysis: "Caesarism," "war of position," and "passive revolution."

If fascism is a species, Caesarism is its genus.[121] Caesarism refers to a political intervention by some previously dormant or even previously unknown political force capable of asserting domination and thus of restoring a static equilibrium during a hegemonic crisis. As such it has progressive (Julius Caesar and Napoleon I) and reactionary (Napoleon III and Bismarck) variants. It may be the sudden creation of a single heroic figure, or it may be the gradual and institutionalized outcome of a coalition government.[122] But whatever its specific nature and source in a particular instance, Caesarism always seeks to strengthen itself by building up the level of its hegemony to match that of its domination, thus rendering the latter less evident and less necessary. Likewise, the efforts of rival political forces to weaken it are best waged amidst the complex superstructures of civil society, where Caesarism's fragile hegemony can be further eroded and challenged by a counterhegemony. Though its intensity may vary considerably, Caesarism always involves a struggle for popular support which is more intense than that associated with processes of legitimation in noncrisis politics.

Gramsci referred to such a struggle as a "war of position."[123] Fascism was a particularly fierce, institutionalized waging of this war, which, however, it was unlikely ever to win, given its apparently insuperable antagonism toward the working classes (and of them toward it). Yet in this respect fascism was only one manifestation of the sort of politics which, for Gramsci, had become characteristic of Western societies. War of position was his metaphor in the *Notebooks* for the form taken by the class struggle in the complex superstructures which had become characteristic of the West and which he had noted at least as early as his February 1924 letter to Togliatti. As such it is to be contrasted with a "war of movement," the seizure of power through military confrontation, as in the Bolshevik coup of November 1917. Such politics, as fascism had helped to show, were now outmoded. In the current "culminating phase" of a "political-historical situation," Gramsci believed that the war of position "once won"—whether by incumbents or insurgents—would by itself be "decisive definitively."[124] We will deal with this concept more fully in Chapter 7.

Gramsci's analysis of fascism also introduced the concept of passive revolution, which, in a sense, comprehended the other two. If fascism was a Caesarism because of its imbalance between domination and hegemony, and if it was a war of position because of the perpetual struggle this imbalance touched off, it was a passive revolution because, despite the constraints of imbalance and perpetual struggle, it managed to play an historically progressive role.[125] And like many, though not all, passive revolutions, fascism was progressive in a defensive fashion, since it was designed to curb a still more progressive political force. Its peculiar feat was to have promoted the development of industrialism without the radical cataclysm of a proletarian revolution.

Together, the various modes through which Gramsci analyzed fascism in the *Notebooks* provided him with a reasonably clear understanding of its source, nature, and developmental tendencies, as well as with a coherent answer to a most vexing problem: how had Italian capitalism been able to survive despite an unresolved and apparently permanent crisis? An answer to this question could not fail to have implications for Gramsci's philosophy of praxis in general. The central implication, to which we may now turn, concerns the relation between politics and economics as "moments" or partial totalities within a larger cultural whole.

CHAPTER SEVEN

The Autonomy of Politics

In politics, the "war of position," once won, is decisive definitively.

(1931)

AS EARLY AS 1926, Gramsci had maintained that "in advanced capitalist countries the dominant class possesses political and organizational reserves which were not found, for instance, in Russia. This means that even the gravest economic crises do not have immediate repercussions in the political sphere. Politics always lags, and lags far behind, economics."[1] By 1930, when Gramsci had fully absorbed the impact of the Sixth Comintern Congress's adoption of a "social fascism" line and its "turn" away from the politics of a united front and toward the politics of a proletarian offensive, his earlier conviction could only have been strengthened. In stooping to the basest of economisms, Stalin's Comintern was not only disastrously wrong in its analysis of a concrete situation but wholly insensitive to the theoretical considerations which require that politics be considered an "autonomous science."[2]

This view of politics distinguished Gramsci's position from those of other dissidents in the Third International such as Trotsky and August Thalheimer.[3] Though their reaction to fascism was similar in stressing the distance between its political and economic elites, they implied that this made fascism an exceptional state. For neither of them had gone beyond the view long ago articulated by Engels that most states were merely executive committees of ruling classes.[4] If fascism was a "Bonapartism" because, as a form of politics based on class compromise, it was relatively autonomous from the class struggle, it was also for this very reason an exceptional state and not one capable of being used as a model for all contemporary politics. Gramsci's analysis was necessarily more radical than this, for when he combined his analysis of fascism with his comparative analysis of superstructures in Russia and the West, he was led to see fascism as the clearest single example of the politics of hegemonic struggle that had become characteristic of postwar bourgeois society in the West.

Thus it is perhaps not surprising that one encounters in the *Notebooks* generalizations like the following:

> Politics becomes permanent action and gives birth to permanent organizations precisely in so far as it identifies itself with economics. But it is also distinct from it, which is why one may speak separately of economics and politics, and speak of "political passion" as of an immediate impulse to action which is born on the "permanent and organic" terrain of economic life but which transcends it, bringing into play emotions and aspirations in whose incandescent atmosphere even calculations involving the individual human life itself obey different laws from those of individual profit.[5]

This is an extraordinary statement for a Marxist and Communist revolutionary to have made in 1932. Its inspiration derives less from Marx than from a reading of Machiavelli, whose theme of the autonomy of politics complemented the influence of Croce (who denigrated and feared politics) in Gramsci's recasting of Marxism as a philosophy of praxis adequate to the new age of monopoly capital, imperialism, and fascism. Politics, Gramsci was saying, is autonomous because it has its own principles and laws of tendency distinct from those of economics as well as morality and religion; it is, as Machiavelli had fully understood, human activity par excellence.

If one looks back at the way Gramsci constructed Italian history, it is evident that his whole analysis reflected a conception of politics as an autonomous sphere. He employed the historical category of Jacobinism without regard to any economic considerations even if, in principle, he always set out from the "economic moment" and even if the concept of an historical bloc presupposed the unity of structure and superstructure. Whether this implies a "voluntarist" position is an important question that we shall shortly consider. Our main purpose in this chapter, however, will be to take up Gramsci's arguments on how to structure a fully adequate party organization for the proletariat and how to comprehend relations between politics and society in a theory broad enough to aid in analyzing every concrete situation that might confront a Jacobin party. We will also consider Gramsci's analysis of the future of Jacobin revolution in the West. But first we must pay still closer attention to his notion of the autonomy of politics, which underlies each of these matters.

In Machiavelli, Gramsci saw a political theorist who, while appreciating the extent to which men were motivated by riches, had also appreciated how they responded to the purely political desire for "glory." Moreover, Machiavelli had been among the first political theorists to base his political calculations on the "effective reality" of the social and economic world. He had conceived that world not statically but dynamically, as a "relation of forces in continuous motion" which could be shaped into a "new equilibrium" by a creative political will. And he had the great virtue of having written about politics "neither in the form of a cold utopia nor as learned theorizing, but rather as a creation of concrete fantasy which acts on a dispersed and shattered people to arouse and organize its collective will."[6]

For all of these reasons, Machiavelli was an inspiration to Gramsci, and most of the assumptions in Gramsci's "autonomous science" of politics were rooted in Machiavelli's outlook. One of these assumptions was Gramsci's stoical insistence that "there really do exist rulers and ruled, leaders and led," and that any attempt to base the "science and art of politics" on something other than this "primordial fact" was doomed to failure.[7] Another was his suspicion that one could conceivably specify a set of universally necessary conditions for the formation of a "collective will."[8] Still another was his assumption that even if the development of the modern world "is in the direction of internationalism. . . , the point of departure is 'national' and it is from here that one must take off."[9] Gramsci's hope was to collect these and other insights into a systematic treatise on politics, a work he planned to call *The Modern Prince*.

This project bore affinities as well with Machiavelli's successors in the Italian political tradition, especially the "elite theorists" of the prewar generation, Mosca, Michels, and Pareto. Though usually critical of their work, Gramsci was aware of the ways in which they had already explored his territory. He was sufficiently intrigued with Michels to devote a section of the *Notebooks* to a critique of *Political Parties*.[10] As might be expected, Gramsci recoiled from its conception of an "iron law of oligarchy"; Michels had simply reified the oligarchic tendencies of capitalism into a timeless proposition. Yet Gramsci appreciated the way Michels had drawn attention to the need for "ethical embellishments" in the successful management of power and to the "organization of a collective will" as a prerequisite for effective political action.[11] Michels had even recognized the pivotal importance of organic intellectuals ("labor leaders of proletarian origin")[12] in political education, though he had found them no less oligarchically inclined than any other elite.

Gramsci saw Mosca's work as "an enormous hodgepodge of a sociological and positivistic character," yet Mosca had "understood the political technique of the subaltern classes better in 1883 than the representatives of those same classes . . . several decades later."[13] Moreover, some of Mosca's major concepts in *The Ruling Class* had rather Gramscian resonances. The concept of a "political formula" was not unlike Gramsci's descriptive notion of hegemonic rule in its stress on the moral and cultural basis of legitimation, even if it was closer to a Sorelian "myth" in its concern with the irrational appeals often made to the dominant social type. Similarly, Mosca's concept of "juridical defense" called attention to an effective way of organizing morality and consent, even if its liberal concern with an institutional "balance of social forces" was foreign to Gramsci's vision of an ethical state. Mosca even had a concept of "hegemony," though, like the other elite theorists, he did not elaborate it beyond its common meaning of political control.

What principally distinguished Gramsci from the elite theorists was that while they could pursue insights about the autonomy or even primacy of politics without fear of internal contradiction, Gramsci was writing in a Marxist tradition which had always insisted on the decisiveness of the "economic factor." How, then, could he reconcile his apparently heterodox views with this commitment?

It must be recognized, first of all, that Gramsci conceived of political activity as only *relatively* autonomous, in the sense that the political moment is connected to the economic moment, though by a long and complex chain of mediations. Among these mediations are an evolving human nature, moral norms and rules, ideological systems, and language itself; together with politics and economics, these moments form a rapidly shifting and interpenetrating cultural totality. Politics and the state are therefore not determined, even distantly, by the economic moment, but neither are they neutral mediators over it. Politics is autonomous in the sense that its practitioners have margins of maneuver, given the multiple and complex mediations between economic and political elites and given that political relations have their own independent logic.

Yet if such formulations serve to clarify Gramsci's intentions, they are hardly sufficient to resolve the issue. One might well ask, for instance: How relative is the relative autonomy of politics? Are there historical cases in which a Jacobin movement would actually have been precluded from the start by purely economic considerations? Are there cases in which government elites function with complete independence from business pressure in capitalist society? Gramsci never dealt with such questions directly, but his writings do provide clues to his answers, above all to the last question. Full governmental autonomy, he would likely have argued, depends on a whole host of contingent factors. His 1926 typology of European states suggests that one such factor is the regime's position—advanced, transitional, or peripheral—within the structure of international capitalism. His essay on the Southern Question suggests a parallel factor operating at the national level. Both factors set limits upon, and encourage certain directions of, governmental action. Other obvious contingent factors include the level of a regime's hegemony and domination; as these increase, one would expect the regime to be relatively more powerful and, roughly speaking, to have the capacity for a greater exercise of autonomy.

Fewer clues exist in answer to the question about the relative autonomy of politics. While Gramsci, in principle, condemned the failure to consider the economic bases of politics as an anarchist illusion, his own historical inquiries, as we have seen, paid those bases little or no account. This anomaly was never confronted; he moved instead to the formulation of a theory of praxis based narrowly on an implicit "optimism of the will." The question of economic obstacles to the formulation of a collective will was bypassed in favor of the practical question of how to maximize the effectiveness of counterhegemonic political organization. This is certainly a major theoretical weakness and one to which he may well have been led by his desire to maintain faith in proletarian politics in the midst of fascist rule. We will return to this point in connection with his view of civil society.

The Modern Prince

In developing a theory of proletarian political organization in the *Notebooks*, Gramsci took the Machiavellian theme of political leadership as a starting point. Unlike Machiavelli, however, he rejected any revival of the classical image of the "great legislator." In the modern world, "an historical act can only be performed by 'collective man.'" The modern prince

> cannot be a real person, a concrete individual. It can only be an organism, a complex element in society in which a collective will, which has already been recognized and has to some extent asserted itself in action, begins to take concrete form. History has already provided this organism, and it is the political party—the first cell in which there come together germs of a collective will tending to become universal and total.[14]

The political party is an ideal institutional vehicle of a counterhegemony because it is capable of functioning both as a political educator and as an umbrella organization coordinating a national movement. As already suggested, Gramsci thought that a great many civic institutions could be restructured to aid in the process of transforming "common sense" through "catharsis" into "philosophical reason," but a party would always be necessary to spearhead a revolutionary challenge. The highly defensive circumstances in which the Italian proletariat found itself after 1921 further encouraged Gramsci to think of counterhegemonic organization solely in terms of the PCI.

What, then, was the insight and guidance to be gained from previous Marxist discussion on the subject of political parties?

The main texts in this discussion were Lenin's writings on Bolshevism, much of which Gramsci seems to have read while he was in Russia in 1922-23.[15] Like Lenin, he was extremely critical of the "economistic" view that the "organic" foundation of politics (the mode of production) could be assumed to be the mechanical producer of all operative causes.[16] In that case, the party would be understood only as a support structure for a movement that it could not fundamentally shape. Yet, far more than Lenin, Gramsci was also critical of the "ideologist" position which reduced political analysis entirely to a consideration of purely "conjunctural" elements—political ideas, strategies, leaders, and so forth.[17] If his own thought moved dangerously close to this, its voluntarism could nonetheless be distinguished, he thought, from the vulgarized versions usually found in Second International and prewar anarcho-syndicalist debates:

> A distinction must be made between two kinds of voluntarism or Garibaldism. On the one hand there is that which theorizes itself as an organic form of historico-political activity, and celebrates itself in terms which are purely and simply a transposition of an ensemble of "supermen" (celebration of active minorities as such, etc.). On the other hand there is voluntarism or Garibaldism conceived as the initial moment of an organic period in which the organic collectivity, as a social bloc, will participate fully.[18]

Gramsci could never accept the first undialectical sort of voluntarism in which praxis is conceived as entirely open to human will. He did seem to accept the second sort, however, because it understands itself only as an "initial moment" in a dialectic of political education which will hopefully stimulate the formation of a well-integrated historical bloc. Some initial force is necessary, Gramsci seemed to suggest, in order for this process to begin. If even such a qualified voluntarism appears partially at odds with his analysis of revolution, it does conform to the subjectivism of his epistemological starting point. And, on the level of political realism, the necessity of such a voluntarism could be perceived as another instance of a "primordial fact." Indeed, it was the pretended absence of a vanguard and not its open dominance that Gramsci feared. There are always leaders and led; invisible leaders tend to exist in pseudo-mass parties where masses have no other political function than a generic loyalty, of a military kind, to a visible or invisible political center. (Often the visible center is the mechanism of command of forces which are unwilling to show themselves in the open, but only operate indirectly, through proxies and a "proxy ideology"). The mass following is simply for "maneuver," and is kept happy by means of moralizing sermons, emotional stimuli, and messianic myths of an awaited golden age, in which all present contradictions and miseries will be automatically resolved and made well.[19]

To establish a genuine mass base engaged in self-education, one needs visible leadership in the context of a democratic social movement. In a highly revolutionary situation which permits the organization of alternative worker institutions, this may mean retaining a vanguard party. In more defensive circumstances, the need will be for internal party democracy presided over by an active central committee and coupled perhaps with class alliances in the Jacobin manner. In theorizing the latter possibility in the *Notebooks*, Gramsci addressed two related questions: what is internal party democracy, and how can it be operationalized, especially in order to eliminate the problem of bureaucracy?

Gramsci operated with at least two different working definitions of political democracy. In one, which we have already quoted, he pointed to the need for high social mobility in elite recruitment.[20] This definition presupposes a relatively stable division of labor between elites and masses, leaders and led. Yet he also left no doubt that the truest democracy would be found where this "primordial fact" was breaking down—not through the false method of making leadership invisible, but in reality. In this sense, a democratic political organization is one in which the fundamental premise of operation is not "that there should always be rulers and ruled" but that "the conditions in which this division is no longer necessary" ought to be created.[21] Presumably, this definition becomes practically relevant only under the fairly special conditions of an advanced prerevolutionary party or, especially, of a party in postrevolutionary socialist society. Yet Gramsci made the point boldly:

Since every party is only the nomenclature for a class, it is obvious that the party which proposes to put an end to class divisions will only achieve complete self-fulfillment when it ceases to exist because classes, and therefore their expressions, no longer exist.[22]

The degree to which a party seeks to overcome its internal divisions through political education is a good index of its internal democracy. If and when it ever finally achieves this, the achievement will have been one of creative destruction.

The postulation of such an evolutionary criterion raises hard questions about the conditions under which the evolution is to be made. In particular, one might ask: is genuine internal democracy for Gramsci in any sense "liberal"? Views on the proper answer to this are sharply divided, particularly among Gramsci's interpreters in the Anglo-American community, where it has received the most attention.[23] But any answer worthy of serious attention must discriminate among several senses of the word *liberal.* Certainly if one takes it to refer to the fear of political power and therefore to the practice of minimizing political intervention in civil society and of checking and balancing political power, then Gramsci's democracy was not liberal. The answer is less straightforward if one takes liberal to mean the concern with "individuals," "individual rights," and freedom that is "negative" in the sense that the goal is the protection of the individual and his or her property from interference by political authority or other citizens. We saw in Chapter 4 that, unlike some Marxists, Gramsci did recognize the importance of "individuality" for human freedom, and he provided it with a clear ontological basis. Yet he was at least equally concerned with a more "positive" freedom which aims at maximizing the participation of all citizens in the political decisions that affect them.[24] His hope was to dissolve the split between citizen and private individual characteristic of life in bourgeois democracies.[25]

If, however, one takes the essence of liberalism to be absolute freedom of inquiry and discussion, then Gramsci's notion of democracy in the *Notebooks* was definitely liberal, at least in principle:

> Who is to fix the "rights of knowledge" and the limits of the pursuit of knowledge? And can these rights and limits indeed be fixed? It seems necessary to leave the task of researching after new truths and better, more coherent, clearer formulations of the truths themselves to the free initiative of individual specialists, even though they may continually question the very principles that seem most essential.[26]

One may, of course, contrast this statement with some of those cited in Chapter 3, which Gramsci made in 1923 and 1926 when he had a direct interest in silencing Bordiga and consolidating his own hold on the Party.[27] Yet, as was argued in the earlier chapter, Gramsci relaxed his assumption of a need for "ideological unity" in the wake of the Comintern's Sixth Congress. Thus the *Notebooks* echo his earlier attitudes only in their general adherence to a Jacobin conception of the party through which the national hegemony that had always eluded the progressive classes in Italy might finally be organized. As the above passage illustrates, where his concern is with articulating a dialectic of political education, he showed full awareness of the sterility of a pedagogical setting in which access to information is controlled and the free confrontation of all rival views is not permitted. Since the essence of Gramscian democracy is educational, it must accept the liberal principle of the free pursuit of truth.

Nonetheless, to be convinced that Gramsci held this principle with real conviction, we need to know how it was operationalized to overcome, in particular, the dangers of bureaucratization. Certainly he was concerned with these dangers: if he viewed a certain level of bureaucratization as inevitable within all advanced societies,[28] he sought nonetheless to define a form of party organization and style that would avoid it as much as possible. We see this in his contrast of "bureaucratic" and "democratic" centralism.[29] He was uncompromising in his castigation of the former, which "fetishizes" itself into "a phantasmagorical being, the abstraction of the collective organism, a kind of autonomous divinity."[30] His portrait of the latter is as a "centralism in movement . . . , a matching of thrusts from below with orders from above, a continuous insertion of elements thrown up from the depths of the rank and file into the solid framework of the leadership apparatus which ensures continuity and a regular accumulation of experience."[31] But what this actually means in terms of concrete organization can be grasped with confidence only when we consider his detailed description of a democratic party.

In a well-known passage, Gramsci offered a proposal for such an organization based on a three-level structure. At its core is a central committee whose function is to exercise "great cohesive, centralizing, and disciplinary powers" as well as to make basic innovations when and where necessary.[32] Gramsci avoided the term "elite," yet his account leaves us no reason to think that he meant something other than the Bolshevik organ that Lenin headed or what he himself had formed for the PCI in 1924. Below the central committee, and led by it, is a second, "mass element, composed of ordinary, average men whose participation takes the form of discipline and loyalty, rather than any creative spirit or organizational ability."[33] Gramsci left unclear whether he thought this mass base might include other classes besides the proletariat or whether he saw intersubaltern relationships best handled through class alliances. But his description makes it obvious that he intended to cast the net very wide, probably much more so than in Lenin's practice, where the emphasis on political education was much more secondary. Still, if these had been the only two elements in the party structure, one might well conclude that Gramsci's "democratic centralism" was essentially Leninist.

His innovation was in postulating a third or "intermediate element which articulates the first element with the second and maintains contact between them, not only physically but also morally and intellectually."[34] These middle-level cadres were to be organic intellectuals of the proletariat, leading the dialectic of political education. Why Gramsci theorized this new element rather than simply relying on a political education through central committee/mass interaction has been the subject of some speculation. It has been suggested, for instance, that the middle-level cadres are a means for ensuring the predominance of organic over traditional intellectuals.[35] This is certainly plausible, since, given Marx's expectations and Second International political practice, one might well expect traditional intellectuals to predominate within the central committee. This would be especially likely in a young party or in a society with a relatively low level of industrialization, where a large group of organic intellectuals would not have been formed. By situating the dialectic of political education at a lower level, one is ensured that it will take place between elements of the same class. Moreover, Gramsci had written in his 1926 essay on the Southern Question that an apparatus was needed for organizing the "democratic intellectuals" of the rural North and South. To the extent that they could be attracted to Marxism, middle-level cadre positions would offer them a creative role to play.

Yet Gramsci may well have had even more fundamental reasons for theorizing this third level. He had begun with a conception of the party which emphasized its role as a "school of state life."[36] From his own lengthy practical experience, however, he knew that the central committee of a major Communist party is continually preoccupied with coordinating national strategy and international diplomacy from a "political-military" point of view. As early as 1919, he was referring to the party vanguard in terms of military metaphors.[37] To reemphasize the importance of a vanguard for his view of the party in the *Notebooks*, he wrote: "One speaks of generals without an army, but in reality it is easier to form an army than to form generals."[38] He seems to have perceived that if one left the elite side of the political education dialectic to the central committee, there might be very little political education at all. More likely, one would see a sharp polarization in which internal party democracy would be reduced to ritual without consent. Internal party democracy and the political education which supports its growth require mutual rapport between "elements" and the close, continual interaction which can alone foster that rapport. This, no doubt, is why he chose to describe "democratic centralism" with motion imagery. It is also why middle-level cadres would remain crucial, even supposing that the central committee could be composed entirely of organic intellectuals.

To put the point in still another way: it is Gramsci's introduction of middle-level cadres as the key organizational mediation in the political education dialectic that allowed him to incorporate the notion of a vertical fusion of structure and superstructure directly into the party. The party is an historical bloc in the making; through class alliances it will seek to extend itself on the horizontal plane and to become hegemonic throughout society.

Given these close connections between the party and Gramsci's political theory in general, one must conclude that his organizational conception was not Leninist despite obvious terminological similarities. This conclusion is strengthened when one reflects on how much the tripartite structure of Gramsci's party appears to be the product of the *Ordine Nuovo* mind. The reader will recall that the essential features of Gramsci's organizational strategy in the *Ordine Nuovo* years were also tripartite. Of primary importance were the factory councils in which the workers educated themselves politically within the context of their daily productive lives. In electing their own representatives, they legitimized a set of organic intellectuals who might then inspire a deepening of the class's consciousness and culture. Outside this nexus stood the party, which Gramsci conceived as a vanguard directing the overall regional and national "political-military" strategy. We have noted also how, in the defensive circumstances of his party chairmanship, Gramsci retained these functional elements while assembling them all under one organizational roof. The theory of the party in the *Notebooks* seems best understood as a continuation of this strategy; central committee, middle-level cadres, and mass base are simply the reorganized counterparts of vanguard party, factory council organic intellectuals, and workers.

Yet one may well doubt whether, in this translation, the democratic ethos of the Turin movement is not inevitably negated by the new, all-encompassing structure of the party. In this design, perhaps, he *was* flirting with Leninist consequences. For if, even in the earlier politics, there had been a tension between the military function of the vanguard party and the educative function of the intellectual/moral bloc, this tension could now only be exacerbated. The new central committee is invested with an ultimate authority which the party was never to have had in 1920. The party has been elevated to a pedestal from which it not only oversees but controls the entire range of significant political practice, and its organizational boundaries in effect become congruent with those of the "potential state." Clearly, Gramsci intended a party of workers rather than of bureaucratic functionaries seeking worker support. Yet even if the organization is democratic in the sense of open channels of elite recruitment—and there is no guarantee of this openness—it certainly embodies a very different sort of democracy from that practiced by self-governing worker councils.[39]

A larger and somewhat tragic element also seems to be implicated in this comparison. Were we to compare the *Ordine Nuovo* and the later conceptions only in terms of their institutional relationships, we might well conclude from the absence of worker councils in the latter that the prefigurative dimension of Gramsci's counterhegemonic politics had undergone a marked decline. Yet, paradoxically, after 1923 this dimension is understood by Gramsci to be *the* crucial element for a strategy of revolution in the West, where the power of the state is so closely connected with the complex superstructures of civil society. The decline of the worker councils is not a reflection of any waning of his interest in prefigurative structures but rather of an historical tragedy which has forced the "modern prince" to uphold the entire struggle at a time when any other such expression would be ignominiously crushed.

State and Society

Implicit in Gramsci's conception of an autonomous political party as the centerpiece of an emerging counterhegemony is a particular conception of the relation between state and civil society. On the one hand, civil society must be somehow distinguishable from the state so that it can be independently conquered; otherwise the tactic of creating an alternative hegemony would make little sense. But, on the other hand, civil society must be linked to the state at least to the degree that its conquest will be guaranteed to have political ramifications. Gramsci's problem, then, was to make conceptually clear how the state and civil society could be both separate and linked in the required senses.

Had he pursued this issue in terms of a reconceptualization of the structure/superstructure distinction, he also could not have avoided confronting the autonomy-of-politics problem more directly. For if, as in Marx, civil society is conceived as the economic structure and the state is conceived as one aspect of the superstructure, then Gramsci's strategic problem could have been restated as the conceptual issue of how "economics" could be both separate from and linked to "politics." Yet Gramsci made no such restatement because for him the structure was narrowly conceived as the material and technical instruments of production; civil society was placed not here but in the domain of the superstructure.[40]

How may one account for this rather startling departure from Marxist convention? The best answer seems to be that it followed from Gramsci's conception of political education. For if Marx treated civil society within the structure because of his profound interest in analyzing the dynamics of capitalist production, Gramsci seems likely to have shifted it to the superstructure in order to clarify his notion that the political education necessary for revolution is a broadly social process. Marx could explain political actions as something like the epiphenomena of a more basic structure because he was primarily concerned with explaining mainstream political maneuverings within an ongoing capitalist society. Where this was less the case, as in some of the historical essays like *The Eighteenth Brumaire of Louis Bonaparte* or *The Civil War in France*, one finds a much richer treatment of the superstructure. For Gramsci, however, explanations of political life could pause briefly at the level of the structure in order to establish broad contextual limits and then pass on to the superstructure because his concern was less with the internal workings of capitalism than with the prospects of revolution by the subaltern classes. And, as Marx himself had suggested, it was at the level of ideology, i.e., within the superstructure, that men become conscious of class conflicts and fight them out.

By situating civil society within the superstructure, Gramsci transformed the problem of relating state and civil society into the problem of clarifying the relationships internal to the superstructure. That this superstructural orientation served as conceptual support for his own particular brand of voluntarism seems clear, yet it is important to recognize its consonance with political developments in the postwar era. If in Gramsci's early writings the state could still be pictured as a dictatorship pure and simple,[41] fascism had dramatized the degree to which popular consent could be used to gain political power and how political power in turn could be consolidated through consensual appeals. The failure of Western revolution had also dramatized the degree to which incumbent elites could mobilize existing common sense in antiprogressive directions. Moreover, Gramsci's study of the

Southern Question had alerted him to the crucial role of intellectuals as a mediation within the hegemonic process. Consequently, he was led in the *Notebooks* to a very broad functional conception of the intellectual, who operates within a society conceived in essentially educational terms.

From these considerations it followed that any distinction between civil and political society could only be analytical. This is why Gramsci abandoned the commonsense, and unduly restricted, understanding of the state as "political society" in favor of one which grasped it as the "equilibrium between political society and civil society," that is, as the totality of superstructures.[42]

There is an anomaly in this reorientation, however. For while Gramsci ordinarily spoke of the state in the new expanded sense, he sometimes still spoke of political society as "the state proper."[43] It has been suggested that this represents an equivocation in Gramsci's theory, one which arises from his not having fully abandoned conventional category definitions even though his analysis of state/society relations in the West would seem to have led him beyond them.[44] Yet, given that his insight into the peculiarities of Western social systems goes back to 1924, the notion that he harbored contradictory images of state/society relations in the *Notebooks* is not very convincing.[45] A more plausible explanation emerges when one recognizes that the two senses of hegemony—its opposition to domination and its opposition to the economic-corporative—correspond to two possible images of the state/society relation. To the extent that Gramsci was thinking of hegemony as a supersession of the economic-corporative, he was thinking of an isolated civil society and of the state as an object to be gained by a rising class; he could thus slip easily into referring to political society as "the state proper." To the extent, however, that he was thinking of hegemony in contrast to domination, he had in mind how existing bourgeois states actually function, viz., as linkages of political and civil society.[46]

The more important and interesting question, already raised above, concerns the manner in which political and civil society could be conceived as both separate and linked within the superstructure. Perhaps the place to begin in answering this question is with the intellectual influences that may have underlaid Gramsci's relocating of civil society, and his expanding of the concept of the state to subsume it. He himself several times pointed to Croce as the essential inspiration for these moves;[47] yet Norberto Bobbio seems entirely justified in suggesting that both Croce and Gramsci owed considerable debts on these points to Hegel.[48] Even more than Croce, and far more than his other Italian contemporaries and near-contemporaries who had studied Hegel (Labriola, Gentile, Mondolfo), Gramsci had read and pondered Hegel's description of civil society. As Bobbio points out, Gramsci acknowledged this debt explicitly:

> One must distinguish civil society, as Hegel understood it, and as it has frequently been used in these notes (that is, in the sense of the cultural and political hegemony of a social group within the whole of society as the ethical content of the state) from the sense which the Catholics give it where civil society is instead political society or the state, confronting the society of family and Church.[49]

Gramsci was at one with Hegel in including within civil society not only the economic division of labor but also the corporations, the administration of justice, and the police. And Gramsci's notion of the state subsuming both civil and political society resembles nothing so much as Hegel's conception of the state as the historical moment of civil society canceled and preserved.

We must note in passing, however, that Bobbio goes too far when he asserts that by embracing Hegel on these matters, Gramsci was reversing the Marxian "primacy" of structure over superstructure, making the latter "primary" and the former "secondary."[50] While Marx's very choice of the term *superstructure*, with its attendant image of a base and a rise, may have implied secondariness, the reverse was not necessarily the case with Gramsci. For the concepts of "primary" and "secondary" imply a reductive relationship in which one level determines the other. Gramsci, however, rejected deterministic, mechanistic, and causal forms of explanation in favor of an organicist conception of mediations within a totality. In this circular rather than linear image, the concepts of "primary" and "secondary" make little sense. It is thus not surprising that Bobbio is unable to point to a single passage in which Gramsci affirms a "primacy" of superstructure.[51]

Even in adopting an essentially Hegelian view of civil society,

Gramsci was not uncritical in his embrace of Hegel. He was well aware that Hegel's view had been developed in a particular socio-historical context and that it could not be applied mechanically to new circumstances. Indeed, his central criticism of the liberal conception of civil society/political society relations was on just this point.[52] The liberals claimed to be able to separate the institutions of each domain into neat subsets almost as if these actually corresponded to territorial divisions. Yet if this had been problematic even under the nineteenth-century "nightwatchman state," it was completely untenable under the more comprehensive state regulation of advanced capitalism.

Instead, Gramsci's strategy was to make the distinction on a functional basis relevant to a particular society at a particular time. Institutions which supported the state's claim to monopolize the means of violence and through which it exercised force would be conceived as parts of political society. Some of these institutions—the army, the bureaucracy, the penal system—were almost by necessity parts of political society in all states. But the same, certainly, would not be true for the institutions of civil society. The Church, for instance, had been part of political society in one era, civil society in another. A functional answer would include in civil society those institutions which, in a given society at a given time, were involved in the creation of organized consent over their members or potential members through some combination of cultural, spiritual, and intellectual means. So, for instance, one such institution in Gramsci's Italy might be a major newspaper like *La Stampa*. To the extent that a particular government had some control over or was able to manipulate this newspaper, however subtly, in order to legitimate its own consensual position, one could say that political society was manipulating an institution of civil society. The difficulty which Gramsci sensed was that political society was becoming increasingly involved in this activity in the contemporary world, and in ways which made it difficult to distinguish between the effort to gain legitimate consent and the subtle use of force.

Consider, for instance, Gramsci's notes on "public opinion":

What is called "public opinion" is closely connected with political hegemony, namely with the point at which civil society makes contact with political society, and consent with force. The state, when it wants to undertake an unpopular action, creates adequate public opinion to protect itself; in other words, it organizes and centralizes certain elements within civil society. The history of "public opinion": naturally, elements of public opinion have always existed, even in Asiatic satrapies. But public opinion as we understand it today was born on the eve of the fall of the absolute state, i.e., in the period in which the new bourgeois class was struggling for political hegemony and for the conquest of power.[53]

The state, through its manipulation of public opinion, is now able to force its point of view over a reluctant populace in a way that is hardly distinguishable functionally from more traditional and openly forceful means like intimidating threats to life or livelihood. In what sense, then, do the institutions of public opinion remain part of civil society and not political society?

Gramsci was able to answer this question only by injecting an historical element into the analysis. To say that what is "organized" and "centralized" during public opinion formation are "elements within civil society" is to say something about their origin. "Public opinion" as a set of institutions rose with a particular class, the bourgeoisie. During that rise, the newspapers, parties, associations, etc., that the bourgeoisie controlled were purely institutions of civil society. (Similarly, all the proletarian institutions of political education that Gramsci helped to create were pure elements of civil society.) But once the bourgeoisie seized power and eventually became dominant, the status of these institutions became much more ambiguous. As far as I can discover, Gramsci made no real effort to reclarify his distinction for these circumstances.

The upshot of this is that a sharp, analytical distinction between civil society and political society is possible for Gramsci only as the contrast between the institutions of a subaltern class and those of the dominant classes. The former are necessarily in civil society; the latter, though parts of an interpenetrating civil and political society in advanced capitalism, are ultimately under the control of political society. This particular alignment, of course, will not characterize all social formations, and Gramsci's inability to make the civil society/political society distinction for other cases is undoubtedly a theoretical weakness. But this case is the crucial one for his strategic analysis and political theory in general. And one can see how, in Gramsci's understanding of this case, civil and political society could be grasped as separate and linked in the required senses. For if, as in the political ascendance of the French and English bourgeoisies after 1700, a hegemony was built over large sections of civil society prior to the direct exercise of political power, one might well conclude that civil society was independently conquered. And in the modern state, where politically dominant elites need hegemony to stabilize their rule over the long term, such an independent conquest could not, presumably, be ignored forever.

The difficulty here is that this formulation seems to depend on social features characteristic of a particular historical period and one which, as Gramsci himself recognized, had already been superseded. The ability of the French and English bourgeoisies to gain an ascendancy within civil society may simply reflect the weakness of civil society/political society linkages in an earlier capitalism. Unfortunately for Gramsci's political and cultural theory, there is no guarantee that the proletariat will have anything close to the same freedom of maneuver within contemporary civil society. Indeed, experiences like that of the Turin worker councils in 1920 would seem to suggest the opposite. That Gramsci was apparently unable to see this, or in any case incapable of coming to terms with it, leaves his theory of Western superstructures in a rather paradoxical state. On the one hand, he recognized that in advanced Western societies the key to political power lay in the hegemonic control of civil society; the image of a proletarian seizure of power in a 1917-style coup had become mere fantasy. Yet, on the other hand, the ability of those controlling Western political societies to block the formation of an alternative hegemony was unprecedentedly high. Thus the discovery of the political importance of civil society seems to be largely negated by the obstacles to institutional innovation within it.

We shall pursue this problem in the Conclusion, but before passing on to other matters, we should probably remind ourselves that, whatever its difficulties, Gramsci's conception of the state also undoubtedly had advantages for a Marxian political theory. As was suggested in Chapter 5, Gramsci was able to conceptualize the "withering away of the state" under communism far more realistically than had either Marx or Engels. By including both civil and political society as subordinate moments of the state, he could recognize that the state would remain necessary as a coordinating mechanism even if its coercive element were to be displaced. Moreover, this insight is symptomatic of a still more general reorientation that Gramsci sought to provide for Marxism. He wanted to restore a certain dignity to the concept of the state by giving it a positive identification with education, culture, and the hopeful prospect of a rising level of civilization. In particular, the image of the "regulated society," with which he sought to encapsulate his teleological point of arrival, suggests both the absence of coercion and the active and productive public life that would and should continue to flourish.

Revolution as "War of Position"

Gramsci's inquiry into the structural contours of the postwar European situation utilized a series of theoretical couplets—structure/superstructure, civil society/political society, domination/hegemony, East/West, passive revolution/complete revolution—that were designed to serve in the end as a guide to a revamped proletarian praxis. Taken together with his analysis of the Italian political past, he was led to conceive this revamping in terms of the formation of a Jacobin force which, through increasingly potent vertical and horizontal linkages, could establish itself as a viable historical bloc exercising hegemonic influence in large sections of Italian civil society. We have already referred to the paradoxical conception of civil society upon which this strategy was dependent. But whether and to what extent Gramsci was himself conscious of the tensions within his formulation and the correspondingly diminished chances of its success is difficult to ascertain. His theoretical resolve seems never to have been seriously dampened, but the continuous failure of postwar European revolutions and the apparent triumphs of fascism in Italy and of Nazism in Germany did chasten his political outlook considerably, even over what it had been in the three years prior to his arrest.

Well before Hitler's open triumph in 1933, the European proletariat was everywhere divided, defensive, disheartened, and suppressed. Gramsci's fate was not unusual, but it was certainly more extreme than that of most Communists. It is noteworthy, then, that he never once took refuge behind the facile "history-is-on-our-side" slogans that attracted many of his comrades in arms. Like other Communists, he was unlikely to turn his "pessimism of the intelligence" into despair so long as the Soviet Union stood secure, as it did throughout the period. Yet, at the same time, we know from reports of conversations that Gramsci had with his fellow prisoners in 1930 that he found the international leadership coming forth from Moscow to be anything but reassuring.[54]

In 1926, just before being sent to prison, he had expressed certain polite reservations about Stalin's leadership in a letter to the Comintern.[55] But according to numerous prison reports, these objections intensified dramatically once Stalin began leading the International through the "left turn" of 1929. In the intervening years, Stalin had consolidated his leadership into a virtual dictatorship over international communism. The "turn" was only one expression of this, even if a particularly ironic one. Arguing that the predicted economic crisis of capitalism would encourage a rapid leftward movement of the European masses, Stalin had drawn tactical consequences very similar to the ones Trotsky and Bordiga had advocated half a decade earlier and which Lenin had then decisively rejected. His contention, in short, was that workers were to join in a "frontal attack" against their oppressors and to reject all "class alliances" and "social-democratic" compromise. Gramsci reportedly saw this as the resurfacing of an old "maximalism" now a decade out of date.[56] In the face of some vicious verbal attacks from other Communist inmates, he reaffirmed his 1924 prescription for proletarian action in defensive circumstances: the undermining of incumbent hegemony through class alliance, mass political education, and a "constituent assembly" as a transition stage toward the "regulated society" of the proletariat.

In the *Notebooks*, Gramsci referred collectively to these measures as the waging of a "war of position," a phrase he employed as a capsule description of his entire strategic argument. The "war of movement" or "frontal attack" strategy to which "war of position" was contrasted had been perfectly appropriate in Western Europe before 1870 and in Russia in 1917. It still was appropriate in developing nations, indeed anywhere that

> society was still, so to speak, in a state of fluidity from many points of view: greater backwardness of the countryside and almost complete monopoly of political and state power by a few cities or even by a single one (Paris in the case of France); a relatively rudimentary state apparatus, *and greater autonomy of civil society from state activity*; a specific system of military forces and of national armed services; greater autonomy of the national economies from the economic relations of the world market, etc.[57]

These conditions were, however, increasingly rare in Western Europe. With their colonial and industrial expansion after 1870, these nation-states had become increasingly

> complex and massive, and the Forty-Eightist formula of the "permanent revolution" became expanded and transcended in political science by the formula of "civil hegemony." The same thing happens in military art: war of movement increasingly becomes war of position, and it can be said that a state will win a war in so far as it prepares for it minutely and technically in peacetime. The massive structures of the modern democracies, both as state organizations and as complexes of associations in civil society, constitute for the art of politics as it were the "trenches" and the permanent fortifications of the front in the war of position; they render merely "partial" the element of movement which before used to be the "whole" of war, etc.[58]

The Leninist revolution, which had been theorized and waged as a war of movement, entailed seizure of the organized political power of the state. This was made possible by the proper organization of a professional vanguard and a breakdown in the economic viability of capitalism. Power was conceived instrumentally; the proletariat was to gain control of the means of collective violence as the foundation for its political dominance. Once this foundation had been secured, and only then, the proletariat could proceed toward its final goal of a socialist and communist transformation. Such a view of political power was related to a theory of the state as a mere exploitative instrument of the dominant classes. In this sense, all states were essentially dictatorships despite their varying constitutional forms. The dictatorship of the proletariat was no different from any other state except for its preparatory role in human emancipation.

By articulating the concept of a "war of position," Gramsci sought to put forward a fundamentally new theory of revolution, one which would be better suited to the intricate civil societies and superior state strength possessed by the more advanced Western nations.[59] Such a revolution would be an extended campaign for hegemonic influence among the population at large; once this was attained, political power would be essentially at hand and many of the conditions of the socialism would already have been realized. In this sense, the trajectory of a war of position can be plotted as a single unified movement spanning pre-domination, domination, and post-domination stages. Power, however, is never conceived merely as domination; on the contrary, it is self-justificatory, anchored in popular consent, and expressed through collective dialogue toward concerted decision.[60] Proletarian revolution *is* the establishment of this sort of power; the proletarian state, as an embodiment of Hegelian *Sittlichkeit*, is an expanding counterhegemony which has burst the boundaries of civil society to encompass political society as well. One important consequence of this is that the dictatorship of the proletariat loses its Leninist connotations and arrives instead only in a majoritarian form, as an ascending historical bloc which is becoming a state.[61]

Such a revolution can be expected to occur not so much because of the classically formulated contradiction between productive forces and relations of production—an incumbent class with hegemony should be able to defuse such a crisis rather easily—but because civil society and political society enter into contradiction. This crisis reaches its most acute stage when the ruling classes, though still dominant, are no longer hegemonic, and when the insurgent classes exercise considerable hegemony but without domination.

Can one expect such a crisis to be resolved without the violence and bloodshed inherent in a "war of movement"? Or did Gramsci think of the seizure stage itself as a momentary lapse toward "war of movement" within a more general "war of position"? Given Gramsci's revolutionary activism and his acid critique of Croce, who had reduced history merely to an "ethical/political moment," one might guess that the latter was the case. And the final sentence of the long passage we have just quoted does lend this view some support. Yet the central thrust of Gramsci's writing on

Western revolution is to suggest the opposite; the problem of "consent" and "hegemony" is his primary concern. Political society is a mere "outer ditch" which falls easily in comparison with the "powerful system of fortresses and earthworks" of civil society which lie "behind."[62] Gramsci believed that the West had

> entered a culminating phase in the political-historical situation, *since in politics the "war of position," once won, is decisive definitively.* In politics, in other words, the war of movement subsists so long as it is a question of winning positions which are not decisive, so that all the resources of the state's hegemony cannot be mobilized. But when, for one reason or another, these positions have lost their value and only the decisive positions are at stake, then one passes over to siege warfare. . . .[63]

If the war of movement is still relevant at all, it is somehow preliminary; the only decisive battles are those in the war of position. Perhaps this is why Gramsci saw war of position as "the most important question of political theory that the postwar period has posed, and the most difficult to solve correctly."[64]

Ultimately, however, the fairest judgment would seem to be that Gramsci's prison writings leave the question of revolutionary violence ambiguous. Certainly his divergence from Leninist strategy is marked, if not total. Yet there is no warrant for including Gramsci under a social-democratic rubric, even if his "revolution" is entirely a matter of creating a new "historical bloc" by an apparently "peaceful road."[65] For, as we have seen, Gramsci held fast to a goal of social transformation which involved nothing less than recomposition of society as a culturally integrated totality. Though faithful to the value of total transformation beyond capitalism, Gramscian revolution also offered a gradualist approach consistent with the cultural and political complexity of the West and which seemed—by virtue of its unified character—to be devoid of the means-ends paradoxes that had plagued classical Leninism.

What then, more exactly, was entailed in the actual conduct of a war of position? In one of his more detailed discussions, Gramsci suggested that "Gandhi's passive resistance is a war of position, which at certain moments becomes a war of movement," that "boycotts are a form of war of position," but that strikes are a form of "war of movement."[66] Though helpful, such examples do not add up to a clear distinction. We do better simply to recognize that, in the Italian context especially, "war of position" is characterized by a close association with "passive revolution."[67] When a class becomes "dominant but not hegemonic" through passive revolution, the way is usually open for a "molecular" and "covert" advance of the more progressive subaltern classes. The tactics of alternative hegemony to which these adjectives refer—essentially boycotts, propaganda campaigns, countercultural education, nonviolent demonstrations, and the like—are the methods of "war of position." In 1923-24, when Gramsci recognized that the fascists had in effect staged a passive revolution, these were generally the sorts of tactics he considered. Because of the "complexity and massiveness" of Italy in the entire postwar era, Gramsci began to see then that even his tactics of 1919-20 should have been more adapted than they were to a war of position.

With their much expanded capacity to shape and control the forces of civil society for political ends, the ruling classes all over postwar Western Europe had increased their power immensely. Hegemonic rule had always made for the most secure exercise of power, but the interweaving of civil and political society had very much increased the feasibility of such rule. Later Western Marxists, particularly the theorists of the Frankfurt School, would explore this observation through a detailed critique of the politicization and "one-dimensional" denigration of cultural life under advanced industrial capitalism. Gramsci, however, was the first to recognize this situation, and, just as significantly, to respond to it with a new strategic idea for proletarian revolution. Certainly he was correct to argue that Trotsky had failed to make such a response. "Bronstein," he wrote, though "apparently 'Western' was in fact a cosmopolitan" who theorized "frontal attack in a period in which it only leads to defeats."[68] Gramsci's judgment that Lenin had adopted an incipient "war of position" mentality with his tactic of "united front" in the early 1920s, but had simply "not had time to expand his formula," was more questionable.[69] In any case, neither Russian had even begun to move toward an identification of "the superstructures of civil society" with "the trench-systems of modern warfare."[70]

Gramsci was the first to concede that this development had

considerably complicated the proletariat's task. Yet, since he coupled a dialectical understanding of history with a conception of human rationality and educability, he also saw what later Western Marxists would increasingly ignore, namely, that the incumbent regime's increasing need for hegemony could also decisively increase its vulnerability. When a regime recognized this need and was generally successful in meeting it, the proletariat was pushed to the defensive and forced to engage in a protracted war of position in which the prospects for victory were indeed discouraging. When, however, the incumbent powers failed to forge their own hegemony or to recognize fully the imperative for it, their vulnerability to an alternative hegemony was very great. In such situations especially, a Jacobin revolution could certainly be conceived. The more difficult practical problem was to organize the collective will that would make it an historical reality.

Conclusion: Gramsci's Political Theory in Historical Perspective

GRAMSCI began his *Notebooks* in February 1929. Most of their major themes were developed between 1930 and 1933 in the prison compound at Turi. They were partly revised and amplified while he was confined to a clinic at Formia in 1934 and 1935. He died on April 27, 1937, having devoted very little of his energy in the previous year and a half to anything besides personal correspondence. The work he intended to write "*für ewig*" is therefore incomplete and tentative. No doubt, as he more than once suggested, publication would have required additional revisions that would have "radically altered" the work; indeed, "the very opposite of what is now asserted may well turn out to be the case."[1] Moreover, a close chronological reading of the notes reveals some very basic shifts in his thematic focus, if not in his arguments themselves.

As one might expect, the earliest notes are generally preoccupied with the political, tactical, and historical questions that were raised by the triumph of fascism in Italy, with Gramsci's East-West reassessment of 1923-24, and with the politics of his chairmanship. In these notes he was centrally concerned, for instance, with the "national-popular" functioning of intellectuals in recent French and Italian history. By 1931, however, and especially by 1932-33, such relatively practical concerns appear to give way to more sustained philosophical reflection, which, if not a retreat from open political confrontation, at least places it within a much larger theoretical compass. Still another shift appears to occur between 1933 and 1935; by the latter date, Gramsci's emphasis was neither political nor philosophical but on the particularities of Italian national culture, in its literature, folklore, journalism, etc. In the final notebook, he seemed to be returning to what had been a major interest of his at the University of Turin: the general theory of grammar. Thus it is not implausible to believe that his "pessimism of the intelligence" led him ultimately beyond politics in a manner not unlike that which occurred in the intellectual development of some earlier political philosophers such as Rousseau. In any case, it is very difficult to surmise how Gramsci would have reshaped his material had he lived to publish it.

Yet, as I have tried to show throughout these pages, Gramsci's political understanding did develop with substantial continuity from a thematic basis already well established in 1918. The problems and the intellectual influences which weighed on him then remained predominant throughout his later life. However widely his mind roamed through the social, political, and intellectual history of European civilization, his concerns were always those of his day and his people. Even his practical predispositions, which, as we have seen, did alter continually in dialectical interplay with circumstances, forever bear the marks of his earliest allegiances to anti-positivism, to the peasant and Southern causes, and to a Mazzinian faith in the capacity of the downtrodden for political education. What prison did, with its enforced idleness, was only to permit a time for broad reading and reflection that was previously unavailable to him and that allowed him to develop a far more comprehensive political and cultural theory than he had previously possessed.

In discussing the many aspects of this theory in the last four chapters, I have tried to suggest the ways in which Gramsci was particularly original and penetrating as well as to offer criticisms where they seemed appropriate. What remains to be done is to collect these points into a critical summation which, understood in its proper historical context in the fading twilight of optimism about Soviet Russia, but also at the dawning of an era of unprecedented social and technological complexity, ought to permit some judgments about Gramsci and throw some light on the still more recent political outlook and climate of the Western European left.

From the perspective of the evolution of the PCI and other "Eurocommunist" parties in the last three decades, one might identify two diverging strands within Gramsci's Marxism. On the one hand, his strong counterhegemonic thrust suggests the need to build prefigurative institutions—worker councils, cooperatives, cultural associations, etc.—where new cultural modes and allegiances can be spawned and nurtured. Such base-building remains the essential program of many on the extra-parliamentary left in Italy, as well as of some of the PCI left itself, a grouping that we might think of as representing the contemporary "Gramscians of the Left." To ignore counterhegemonic structures in favor of building broad-based electoral coalitions is, they claim, to incorporate the left into the existing hegemony and to impair perception of what is distinctive about a socialist alternative. On the other hand, Gramsci's emphasis on the intertwining of civil and political society, and the encompassing of both by the advanced capitalist state, suggests that a counterhegemony may well not be feasible, at least initially; that some significant strength within the existing parliamentary system may be necessary as a precondition for any construction of alternative institutions. When this point is taken together with Gramsci's emphasis on the importance of class alliances—and with the assumption that, on the current scene, electoral competition is likely to be the most effective means to foment such alliances—one arrives at a rough sketch of the contemporary "Gramscians of the Right."

No doubt, many other facets of Gramsci's theory could be brought into play in depicting this quite fundamental division. Yet this division is, by itself, only a signpost indicating the vast domain of Marxian political theory that is at stake in a full reassessment of Gramsci's prison writings. To understand what the *Prison Notebooks* mean for the politics of the present, we must view them against the still broader background of classical Marxism's reflections on politics. Only then will we be in a position to assess Gramsci's contributions in their largest context as well as to set out the agenda which the tensions and deficiencies in his formulation left for posterity.

For the purposes of this discussion, we will treat the works of Marx, Engels, and their nineteenth-century epigoni together under the common category of "classical Marxism." With respect to the traditional problems of political theory, their assumptions and formulations are sufficiently similar to allow us to pay only marginal attention to internal variations. Classical Marxism as a whole, I would suggest, stands at a curious intersection in modern European intellectual history. It is, first of all, both a product of and a main exhibit in the sociologizing of the human understanding which, as an outgrowth of historicism, sent nineteenth-century thinkers scurrying for the "underlying social and economic basis" of human action. While eminent precursors like Montesquieu can be found in the pre-French Revolutionary era, the first full exemplars of this tradition—de Tocqueville, Saint-Simon, Lorenz von Stein—came only in its wake. Marx himself came to it, in large part, through his Feuerbachian critique of Hegel, in which the logic of the "transformative method" suggested that society, and not state, must be taken as "subject," and state, not society, as "predicate." The emancipation of the species could not be merely "political," as the liberals would have it, but social and "human." In the later Marx, this sociological predisposition was reinforced by his enthusiasm (generally characteristic of the 1860s and 1870s) for a model of knowledge based on the natural sciences. Their success led him away from the concrete individual subject, and the political praxis that such a subject may choose, to the evolutionary patterns of collective subjects and the more sociological, and even deterministic, modes of analysis that such a focus tends to provoke.

Yet Marx's work was also part of a chapter in the great ethical state tradition of Western political theory. In this tradition, moral and political education is theorized not merely as a means but as a modus vivendi in the good or just society. Thus, as was suggested in Chapter 4, the classical quest for the good city is reconceived as the historical pathway to communism. Marx's contribution to this tradition, however, compromised its premises in one crucial respect. Where Greek political theory had posited the indivisibility of politics and ethics, Marxism dialectically postponed it. The union of politics and ethics came to be viewed as a point of arrival, as the end of an historical telos. If this move is anticipated in Kant and Fichte, Marx stretched it still further by invoking the most anti-ethical of political traditions—the Machiavellian—as the means by which the desired end-state is to be secured. Not only are means judged exclusively in terms of their efficiency, but they are not, in the classical sense, those of politics but of violent anti-politics. As Hannah Arendt has written, "Marx's theory of ideological superstructures ultimately rests on this anti-traditional hostility to speech and the concomitant glorification of violence."[2]

In short, even as the capstone of the ethical state tradition—a tradition very much devalued in the modern West, given liberalism's generally hegemonic position—Marxism participated simultaneously in a debunking of the traditional enterprise of political theory. Its premises about the nature of the social world acted as a set of impediments to a fully articulated political outlook. Five such impediments may be cited here. There was, first of all, the sociological bias and the concomitant tendency to avoid the concrete individual subject as a philosophical starting point, to which we have already alluded. Even though Marx himself rotated his philosophy around the Aristotelian category of praxis, this philosophy's location amidst other, more historicist concepts tended to dissipate its political thrust. This was even more the case in later variants of classical Marxism.

A second and related impediment, also more prevalent in late classical Marxism, was the tendency to rely single-mindedly on the "economic factor" in sociological explanation—or at the very least, to explain social change not as it is actually made in the world through human praxis but more schematically as, for instance, the conflict of the forces and relations of production. This was reinforced by a mechanistic model of the structure-superstructure relationship which tended to move directly from economic cause to political, ideological, or cultural effect.

Because classical Marxism thought of class struggle as the central, if not exclusive, mode of social life, it tended, thirdly, to adopt the very limiting notion of politics as a "sphere of domination," one which will be *aufgehoben* ("canceled, preserved, overcome") in the future proletarian society. Consequently, conceptions of public space were denigrated as mere ideological constructs, and the formulation of public policy was viewed narrowly as a matter of technical administration. This led directly to a fourth impediment: the inability to entertain, even in principle, the possibility that there might exist autonomous features of politics (e.g., a constitutionalist tradition) except as the imperatives of organization. Indeed, political theory itself was grasped as an epiphenomenon of social relations, which is to say, as mere ideology.

Finally, because classical Marxism sought to distinguish itself very sharply from "utopian socialism," it claimed to have "no ideals to realize" and proceeded only very gingerly to describe the nature of the good and just society. For this reason, its theory of the state could be reduced, essentially, to the theory of the capitalist state, which would, in turn, be dismissed as little more than the "executive committee of the bourgeoisie."

Thus, even to the extent that classical Marxism engaged in political theory, it did not always do it well, for reasons internal to its general outlook. Its tendency to fixate on social relations as class relations commonly resulted in schematizations which attended inadequately to the complexity of social forces and ideologies behind the state. Its metaphysical investment in a conception of the proletariat as the final carrier of history's telos could act as much as an obstacle to, as a source of, careful and thoughtful political analysis. The same is true of its narrow focus on ideology as a belief system rather than as a whole universe of cultural norms and values shared as common sense. Thus the creation of a mass movement could be conceived in a rather mechanistic and rationalistic fashion as a matter of rebutting "false consciousness" rather than as the construction of an alternative culture. Finally, even in the domain of political strategy, classical Marxism foundered on the horns of a dilemma it could not transcend. On the one hand, "reformism" was usually dismissed as a capitulation to the bourgeoisie, and, even by its proponents, it was regarded as a denial that the present class struggle could be dialectically transcended. On the other hand, violent revolution not only flew in the face of the ethical impulse behind the communist society, but also seemed to be unpredictable in its political consequences, and just as disturbingly, suffered defeat after defeat throughout the century. A generation later, it was clear that a revolutionary seizure of power was appropriate only to relatively weak—and this meant non-developed and often non-capitalist—states. Thus, no successful European revolutions followed the Bolshevik triumph, and their prospects became dimmer with each passing year.

Now, while these problems certainly apply more to some exemplars of classical Marxism than to others—and my purpose is not to glorify Gramsci as against a straw man—there is no doubt that his is an unusually well-developed example of an "open" and pragmatological Marxism which overcomes many of the impediments to a Marxist political theory, though by no means all of them. One of Gramsci's great merits, I have suggested, was that he never succumbed to the temptation to seek the "general laws" of historical development, but that he moved instead to a view which linked theory and practice by identifying how individuals come to constitute—and can therefore conceivably *re*constitute—their worlds. The world is not objectively given; what is objective is only what is universally subjective; all metaphysical constructs are to be rejected in favor of an absolute immanentism and historicism; all truths must be proved in practice. These and related premises undergird a theory of political education that is uncompromisingly based in the ethical state tradition and attuned to constructivist philosophical assumptions. In this theory, philosophy is conceived as a cultural battle to transform the popular mentality. Yet philosophy is not to be pursued abstractly; it is mediated on a conceptual level by an intellectual/moral bloc and institutionally by the *Ordine Nuovo* vision or the tripartite structure of the modern prince. In this sense, Gramsci's voluntarism overcomes the ambiguity of spontaneist determinism and unmediated voluntarism inherent in Marx, which later produced many of the ideological conflicts within the Second International.

From a grounding in concrete subjectivity and political education, Gramsci was able to incorporate further conceptual refinements and insights into a general political and cultural theory of Marxism. Its bracing pillars are the concepts of hegemony, historical bloc, and revolution as war of position. Hegemony portrays the larger social framework in which praxis and education fit. It transcends the standpoint of ideology by incorporating culture; at the same time, it does not isolate culture idealistically but remains sensitive to its political underpinnings. In insisting on the importance of "political culture" as a means of legitimation and of political change, it retreats from the mechanicism of structure/superstructure and the quasi-determinism of "forces versus relations of production" and upholds instead the concrete relations of civil and political society. Moreover, from the point of view of hegemony, politics is no mere "sphere of domination" under the sovereign control of a ruling class; it is infused in various forms throughout civil and political society. These in turn are not isolated spheres but interpenetrating totalities encompassed by the state.

Insofar as hegemony refers to counterhegemony or the overcoming of the economic-corporative, its ideal political constellation is an historical bloc. The vertical and horizontal dimensions of such a bloc suggest the intricate complex of forces and values behind both the incumbent and the potential state. Not only does this take us beyond schematizations of the world in terms of class relations, it also suggests that mass movements cohere because of the cultural associations they symbolize and because they are carriers of certain values. If class struggle remains on history's center stage, its resolutions are not determined merely by the structural placements of the actors but also by their political astuteness and cultural awareness.

The concepts of hegemony and historical bloc lead naturally into the image of revolution as "war of position," by which they were in part inspired. To conduct such a war is to participate in a dialectic of political education from which an historical bloc may emerge. Such a bloc may in turn produce a counterhegemony; though as Gramsci's historical analysis of the Risorgimento showed, this is not always the case. As a theory of political change, such a war resolves, in principle, the problems of "outside educators," the imbalance between the "powers" and "needs" of the proletariat, and the radical disjunction of violent means and ethical ends which had plagued classical Marxism. For the concept of an intellectual/moral bloc not only explains the role of organic intellectuals and the development of proletarian powers, it also represents the new society in embryo and plots the realization of the good as an uninterrupted trajectory from past into future. Nothing, of course, prevents violence from wending its way into this design. Gramsci knew as well as anyone that real, lived history does not chronicle some pristine "ethical-political moment." But the way in which he conceived the revolution and institutionalized its counterhegemonic dynamics in a theory of the party is in deliberate contrast to a violent and minoritarian seizure of power.

Innovative as it is, however, Gramsci's political theory remains encumbered by structural gaps and tensions which call into question the stability of its very foundations. To recognize what these are, we need only restate some of the classical questions of political theory. What precisely is the nature of the good and just state? How is it to avoid being corrupted even in the process of its creation? What is to prevent a later devolution into tyranny? Is moral and political education sufficient to curb the irrationalities of human nature? Many of these questions, though posed differently, have already been addressed above, and the following critical summation can therefore be relatively brief. To facilitate the discussion, we will divide the issues into three categories: those pertaining to Gramsci's general philosophical position; those pertaining to the transition to a socialist "regulated society"; and those pertaining to the nature of that society.

The major problems in the first category concern Gramsci's commitments to historical teleology and psychological rationalism. We saw earlier that Gramsci's positing of a certain teleology in historical development was not entirely consistent with his commitment to the non-definitiveness of all philosophy and to a conception of prediction limited to "laws of tendency." We further suggested that the source of this tension lay in his desire to retain the notion of the modern industrial proletariat as the universal class which grounds the final resolution of the dialectic of freedom and necessity. Yet Gramsci perceived many of the historical factors which have rendered this notion far more problematic in our own time than in that of classical Marxism. He recognized that the increasing complexity of industrial organization, and of the division of labor generally, which the monopolization of capital had brought on, was not only increasing the size of the working class but fragmenting it into many different strata with diverse outlooks and expectations. Moreover, he saw revealed in the political history of the postwar era a bourgeoisie that was far from dead, a proletariat whose material conditions were improving, sometimes dramatically, and a fascist state to which significant segments of the proletariat had willingly capitulated. The world of the "two great hostile camps" imaged by *The Communist Manifesto* had passed into history. Yet Gramsci himself could not concede this conclusion. From the tenacity with which he clung to the image of the universal class, one suspects that this concession would have meant for him the loss of all hope.

One might be led to a similar suspicion in the case of his psychological rationalism, had the weakness of this position been more apparent from the historical evidence and intellectual climate that confronted him. As it was, however, the success of fascism's irrational appeal could be passed off as a temporary aberration produced by the war. Even as late as 1932, Gramsci explained D'Annunzio's popularity largely in terms of a postwar situation which had made the masses "morally and socially vagabond" and which had raised "sexual questions," especially for women, who, after all, had been somewhat deprived during the war years.[3] Moreover, he could contend quite justifiably that "spirit" was not the beginning but the goal of his political program and that full, self-autonomous individuality would be possible only in the context of a realized spirituality. The difficulty, however, was that the transition to such spirituality was neither immanently necessary nor even fully explicable so long as the phenomenological movement within the political education of the person was not adequately portrayed. In the absence of such an account, nonrational diversions from his prescribed course could be understood only as the incomplete institutionalization of a proletarian pedagogy.

Gramsci's understanding of the transition to socialism raised other problems as well. We have referred already to the paradox of civil society: while the key to political power in the advanced Western nations lies in the hegemonic control of civil society, the capacity of the incumbent state to block counterhegemonic developments is also unprecedentedly high. This paradox, which explains the more recent division of Italian communism into Gramscians of the left and right, may itself be explained by the incorporation in the *Notebooks* of conceptual insights drawn from very different periods in Gramsci's thought. For while the notion of a counterhegemonic struggle is already developed in everything but name by 1919, and is thus not dependent on a recognition of the differences between politics East and West, the notion of civil and political societies as interpenetrating partial totalities within the state is dependent both on his 1924 reassessment and on his conception of the functional role of intellectuals, which takes firm root only in 1926. Yet, whatever the source of this paradox, it places a great deal of Gramsci's political theory at stake, more perhaps than is immediately evident.

The most obvious consequence is to call into question the conception of revolution as war of position, given the dependence of this conception on a relatively autonomous civil society. Once this is acknowledged, however, many other Gramscian conceptions are simultaneously cast into doubt: the organic intellectual, the autonomous political party, even "class consciousness" itself. One might argue that Gramsci's notion of the organic intellectual is itself the intellectual product of a particular stage in the development of the industrial working class, a stage in which that class's internal fragmentation by skill had begun but was not yet far along. Yet what is finally problematic about the organic intellectual is not his datedness but the very possibility of his relatively autonomous outlook. Similarly, the political party, which, according to Gramsci, "carries out in civil society the same function as the State carries out . . . in political society,"[4] may not in fact be permitted to operate so independently.

Gramsci seems to have grasped this difficulty on a practical level when he insisted upon the need for the "cohesive, centralizing, and disciplinary powers" of a Jacobin central committee within the tripartite structure of the party.[5] An intellectual/moral bloc unshielded from external counterinfluences and unguided by an exemplary vanguard might well splinter and collapse. Yet, as suggested earlier, this hardly resolved the difficulty. For if a dialectic of political education required an organizational commitment to the free pursuit of truth, the even greater need for victory might well make "criticism" into a "luxury" at certain points.[6] Thus, in 1923-25, when confronted with this conflict in practice, Gramsci put forward some rather monolithic images of the party in which minority dissent was viewed as "extremely dangerous."[7] Once this concession is made, we seem to have entered, or at least to have come perilously close to, the world of Machiavellian means-ends paradoxes which had plagued classical Marxism but which seemed to have been overcome by Gramsci.

Thus it appears that because of the shadow thrown over many of his concepts by the paradox of civil society, Gramsci was led to defend his war of position strategy with means that contradicted the unified design implied by his conception of revolution. Recognizing this, some of his interpreters have gone on to assert that his thought was intrinsically totalitarian.[8] Gramsci himself did use the word to characterize his position, though, situated as he was on the far side of Stalinism, his usage was politically innocent and had more in common with the philosophical notion of totality than with practical matters of organization and control. Nonetheless, the questioning of his design in light of the word's later connotations is not completely groundless. Consider once again his description of objectivity:

> Man knows objectively insofar as knowledge is real for the whole human race *historically* unified in a single unitary cultural system. But this process of historical unification takes place through the disappearance of the internal contradictions which tear apart human society.[9]

As in the German Idealist tradition, Gramsci tended philosophically toward a unitarist rather than a pluralist position; he seemed to believe in a kind of anthropological impetus immanent in history which supports political movements and forms of political organization tending toward uniformity and against diversity. While Kant's politics led him in the same direction, he shied away in *Perpetual Peace* from the idea of a world state because he feared its tyrannical tendencies. Though Gramsci did not speak explicitly of a world state, there is nothing in his writing to suggest a fear of this or other "totalitarian" conceptions. Given the influence of Hegel on him, one suspects that the culturally integrated totality that he foresaw would have been complexly mediated. Yet his failure to be fully explicit about the character of these mediations, coupled with other indications such as his treatment of language (e.g., the need to educate people away from regional dialects), casts doubt on this suspicion, especially when it is brought into conjunction with the politics of the "modern prince." For rather than a knitting together of partial communities into a larger whole, Gramsci sometimes portrayed a "totalitarian" politics in which party members find in this allegiance "all the satisfaction they formerly found in a multiplicity of organizations," and which ought to "destroy all other organizations or incorporate them in a system of which the party is the sole governor."[10] Gramsci avoided the rampant substitutionalism of Lenin's or Lukács's politics—proletariat for humanity, party for proletariat, and central committee for party—but he was just as uncompromisingly fixed on the ultimate goal of proletarian internationalism.

These observations, however, do not in my opinion justify the conclusion that the "totalitarianism" that Gramsci himself acknowledged had implications of political repression and control which the word has more recently acquired. Not only are these observations but a few isolated fragments from a very large corpus, but the interpretation of them as totalitarian relies on drawing out their implications in ways that Gramsci himself did not do. Moreover, as was argued earlier, his ontological suppositions show a clear awareness of the importance of "individuality" for human freedom. This is concretely reinforced by his concept of hegemony with its suggestion of a dynamic democratic movement from below at odds with any static image of totalitarian control from above. As is clear from his lifelong anti-sectarianism and his castigation of bureaucratic centralism in the *Notebooks*, he favored an activist movement of real workers, not of professional politicians and bureaucrats manipulating a passive working class.

However, the totalitarian charge should at least alert us to what

I take to be the central problem area in Gramsci's political theory: his failure to go much beyond general phrases in depicting the nature of the future society. As we saw in Chapter 5, Gramsci did offer a number of suggestions from which a sketch of his "regulated society" can be pieced together. Yet this sketch—and it is no more than that—is restrained by the same anti-utopianism that is characteristic of classical Marxism. Thus, for example, the central issue raised by his *Ordine Nuovo* experience and by his reflections on "Americanism and Fordism" in the *Notebooks* is never confronted at all. This, of course, is the issue of how industrial society is to be organized and how, in particular, this organization is to be integrated with democratic political expression. Gramsci might have been led to clarify this to some degree had he taken up the theme of capitalist reification. Since he did not, and since on the contrary he embraced an only moderately qualified Taylorism, many unanswered and perhaps unanswerable questions are raised. To cite just the most obvious one: is the worker who spends his day enmeshed in a mechanical process of preprogramed or, at any rate, depersonalized operations really likely to be a creative citizen or to soar into philosophical consciousness in his nonworking hours?

There is also the still larger question of the nature of hegemonic rule. We have already suggested that Gramsci had no well-developed analysis of this process, yet the problem seems to be deeper than a mere matter of omission. In deploying the concept of hegemony to characterize the wielding of state power, he seems to use it in two different senses. It is used, first of all, in a morally neutral and instrumental sense to characterize those bourgeois regimes that have proved capable of organizing mass consent effectively. But it is also used in an essentially ethical sense to characterize the functioning of a proletarian regulated society. Here is another instance in which the attempt to incorporate Machiavellian and ethical state traditions raises perplexing and unresolved questions. Is the sort of consent being obtained the same in both cases? Or is consent in a bourgeois hegemony somehow passive and noncritical, while under proletarian auspices it would be active, participatory, and philosophical? If so, what more fully is the institutional basis of this latter sort of control?

The theoretical difficulty here, however, is not only a matter of specifying different forms of consent. As Perry Anderson has suggested,[11] Gramsci's dichotomy of force and consent is itself far too simple to comprehend the diversity and complexity of motives and behavior actually encountered in the politics of everyday life. To come to terms with the nature of hegemonic rule, one would need to develop a much fuller and more systematic analysis of the forms of political legitimation. Presumably, force and consent are only the endpoints of a continuum that includes such intermediate positions as constraint (e.g., fear of unemployment), co-optation, and perhaps even Arendt's category of authority.[12]

Still another difficulty in Gramsci's analysis of a socialist future is the now familiar "new class" or bureaucratic ossification problem. To be sure, he did show some awareness of this problem in his attack on bureaucratic centralism. Yet one does not have to peer very deeply into his proposed party organization to detect the rather facile and un-Gramscian "optimism of the intelligence" that it presupposes. In the intensity of a counterhegemonic struggle, one might well expect the revolution's middle-level cadres to avoid bureaucratic ossification through their educative and coordinating functions. Yet, in the more placid period after political power has been consolidated, these cadres might just as easily subvert Gramsci's values as support them. No doubt, he would answer this by advocating still further politicization of the masses, which is why those who draw parallels between Gramsci and Mao are not entirely wrong, even if they overlook the all-important difference that Gramsci's theory is essentially focused on Europe while Mao's is focused on Asia.[13] In any case, I find little encouragement in a solution which appears to depend on the periodic destruction of revolutionary organizations in order to prevent the formation of a counterrevolutionary coalition of dissatisfied intelligentsia and masses longing more for political slumber than for justice.

Many problems, then, are raised by Gramsci's discussions of a future socialist society. While he succeeded in meeting many of the challenges to a Marxian political theory posed by classical Marxism, he did not overcome this one nor did he escape a teleological notion of the proletariat and the difficulty of conceiving even a relative autonomy of politics within this perspective. Yet I would suggest that his political theory does succeed in raising the essential, still unresolved issues for anyone interested in the possibility of a coherent, democratic, and historically serviceable political theory within the Marxist tradition. Certainly the difficulties just discussed—those of industrial organization, hegemonic rule, and bureaucratic ossification—are critical items on this tradition's agenda. I would like, by way of conclusion, to suggest three others.

First, and perhaps of most pressing immediate consequence today, there is the need to overcome what I have called the "paradox of civil society." If a Marxian political theory is to have any meaning at all, it must not only be capable of conceiving the broad outlines of a progressive future, but it must also be able to plot the trajectory along which this future can be reached from the concrete historical circumstances of the contemporary West. What is needed is a theory of the advanced capitalist state that grasps its complex internal cleavages as a dialectical movement of the political, economic, and cultural spheres. And in addressing itself to the relation of these spheres, the theory must confront the problem of "relative autonomy" with far more persistence and clarity than Gramsci did. While several promising partial studies of these topics have recently appeared, no one has yet offered a fully adequate or even comprehensive one.[14] Moreover, such a theory must transcend Gramsci's preoccupation with the political party as the principal linking agency between civil and political society. Contemporary social science has shown quite clearly, especially for the case of "third world" politics, how classes and groups articulate themselves in a broad array of military, bureaucratic, and special interest organizations.

Secondly, while I have contended that Gramsci's category of hegemony is one of his most original and suggestive, much remains to be done to flesh out the perspective it opens up. Certainly it was not his intention to argue that a society's culture is very often, if ever, the perfect, totalized expression of its hegemonic apparatus. His suggestion was that states seek to defuse a hegemonic outlook as best they can, and that major works of art and literature are therefore likely to reflect, and perhaps also to influence and shape, this hegemony. Such a qualification, however, considerably increases the difficulty of operationalizing the concept as an analytical guide to grasping the politics of cultural and intellectual history. How does one explain the differential influence of the prevailing hegemony in the world of culture? Are there complementary processes of "mimesis" which operate upwards from subordinate to ruling classes?[15] How exactly does hegemony function as a set of concrete linkages between the political and cultural spheres? Are there patterns in these linkages which seem to lead predictably to the formation of counterhegemonies? Moreover, if counterhegemonies cohere because of the symbols they evoke and manipulate and because of the values they carry, how might one adequately comprehend this process at the level of a political psychology?

Finally, and perhaps of most crucial long-term consequence, there is the need to clarify the epistemological status of Marxian political theory. One of the basic antinomies here, as has been suggested, is that between the concrete pragmatological analysis of class struggle and the concept of a universal proletariat as historical actor. The study of Gramsci's political theory leads me to conclude that the latter must be abandoned in the name of the former. Such a radicalization of Gramsci's pragmatological dialectic would emphasize the need for close empirical analysis of class fragmentation and recomposition as an ongoing process within all advanced industrial societies. Any political movement that expressed an impulse toward a liberating form of practice would be analyzed, however inchoate or seemingly misdirected that impulse might be. A commitment to the industrial proletariat of classical Marxism could still be preserved—not, however, in historical-teleological terms but only in the essentially ethical terms by which Marxism is committed to all other oppressed groups and classes.

Yet this move is not without costs and dangers. In rejecting the notion of historical reconciliation through the proletariat, it is all too easy to fall into an essentially apolitical and impotent theoretical position such as Adorno's "negative dialectics."[16] Pledges not to surrender an interest in class analysis and in the search for historical actors are difficult to maintain when one is no longer guided by a coherent vision of historical movement.

And efforts to do so just the same inevitably run into a whole host of difficult questions concerning connections between theory and practice, conflicts between practices at different levels (local, national, international), and conflicts regarding priorities among diverse political issues.[17] In comparison, Gramsci's was a far simpler world—one which led to a "pessimism of the intelligence" but which still promoted an "optimism of the will." Though his is no longer our world, his experience remains a critical moment in the development of Western Marxism from which we can all continue to learn.

Notes

Whenever possible, quotations from Gramsci's works have been taken from existing English translations, though I have not hesitated to revise where I thought I could make them more accurate or more readable. In the remaining cases, translations have been made from the Italian original. In citing sources, I have given preference to English versions where they are available, except in the case of the *Prison Notebooks*, where reference is given to both English and Italian editions in order to allow the reader to make use of the extensive critical apparatus of the recent Gerratana edition. Each citation is accompanied by a date: the exact date of publication in the case of published works, the best estimate available in the case of unpublished ones. In the case of the *Prison Notebooks*, I have used Gerratana's research as the basis for estimating dates of composition, which are restricted to the year of writing.

Citations from Gramsci's writings are given by (abbreviated) volume title, followed by page number(s), followed by date of publication or composition in parentheses. Hence "S.P.W., II, 67 (August 21, 1921)" refers to a passage from an article published on that date and reprinted on page 67 of the second volume of *Selections from Political Writings*, translated and edited by Q. Hoare. The abbreviations used for the volumes are as follows:

C.P.C. *La Costruzione del Partito Comunista* (1923-1926).
H.P.C. *History, Philosophy, and Culture in the Young Gramsci*, trans. and ed. P. Cavalcanti and P. Piccone.
L.C. *Lettere dal Carcere*, ed. S. Caprioglio and E. Fubini.
L.F.P. *Letters from Prison*, trans. L. Lawner.

M.P.	*The Modern Prince and Other Writings*, ed. L. Marks.
O.N.	*L'Ordine Nuovo* (1919-1920).
P.V.	*Per la Verità* (1913-1926), ed. R. Martinelli.
Q.C.	*Quaderni del Carcere*, ed. V. Gerratana.
S.	*Scritti 1915-1921*, ed. S. Caprioglio.
S.F.	*Socialismo e fascismo* (1921-1922).
S.G.	*Scritti Giovanili* (1914-1918).
S.M.	*Sotto la Mole* (1916-1920).
S.P.N.	*Selections from the Prison Notebooks*, trans. and ed. Q. Hoare and G. Nowell Smith.
S.P.W., I	*Selections from Political Writings, 1910-1920*, trans. and ed. Q. Hoare.
S.P.W., II	*Selections from Political Writings, 1921-1926*, trans. and ed. Q. Hoare.

Introduction

1. Benedetto Croce, *Quaderni della Critica*, 3:8 (July 1947), 86.

2. John Cammett, *Antonio Gramsci and the Origins of Italian Communism* (Stanford, Calif.: Stanford University Press, 1967).

3. Martin Clark, *Antonio Gramsci and the Revolution that Failed* (New Haven, Conn.: Yale University Press, 1977).

4. Gwyn Williams, *Proletarian Order* (London: Pluto Press, 1975).

5. Giuseppe Fiori, *Antonio Gramsci: Life of a Revolutionary*, trans. T. Nairn (New York: Schocken, 1970); and A. B. Davidson, *Antonio Gramsci: Towards an Intellectual Biography* (London: Merlin Press, 1977).

6. The major volumes, listed above, are those edited by Q. Hoare and G. Nowell Smith, by P. Cavalcanti and P. Piccone, and by Q. Hoare.

7. Eric Hobsbawm, "The Great Gramsci," *New York Review of Books* (April 4, 1974), 41.

8. Cf. Paul Piccone, "Gramsci's Hegelian Marxism," *Political Theory*, 2:1 (February 1974), 32-45.

9. However, I do find Karl Korsch's correlation between periods of revolutionary activism and non-positivist Marxist theory to be a promising lead in this regard. Cf. Karl Korsch, *Marxism and Philosophy*, trans. F. Halliday (New York: Monthly Review Press, 1970).

10. L. D. Easton and K. H. Guddat, eds., *Writings of the Young Marx on Philosophy and Society* (Garden City, N.Y.: Doubleday, 1967), p. 368.

11. See Zinoviev's introductory speech at the Fifth Comintern Congress, in *Fifth Congress of the Communist International: Abridged Report of Meetings held at Moscow June 17th to July 8th, 1924* (London: Communist Party of Great Britain, n.d.), p. 17. Whether or not these accusations were fair is not here in question; for the view that, in Korsch's case, they were not, see Douglas Kellner, ed., *Karl Korsch: Revolutionary Theory* (Austin: University of Texas Press, 1977), pp. 44-45. In view of Lukács's very sympathetic study of Lenin, published in 1924, one could probably make a similar case for him; see Chapter 4, note 65, below.

12. The first side has been taken by many of the contributors to the journal *Telos*, edited by Paul Piccone, while the second has been assumed in many quarters but especially by Perry Anderson, editor of *New Left Review*. See Piccone, "Gramsci's Hegelian Marxism" and "From Spaventa to Gramsci," *Telos*, 31 (Spring 1977), 35-65; and Perry Anderson, "The Antinomies of Antonio

Gramsci," *New Left Review*, 100 (November 1976-January 1977), 5-78. The classic argument in favor of Gramsci the Leninist is contained in the works of Palmiro Togliatti (see Bibliography).

13. The phrase is Nicola Auciello's; see his *Socialismo ed egemonia in Gramsci e Togliatti* (Bari: De Donato, 1974), p. 70.

14. For studies emphasizing the "Croceanism" in Gramsci's outlook, see Nicola Matteucci, *Antonio Gramsci e la filosofia della prassi* (Milan: Guiffre, 1951); and Guido Morpurgo-Tagliabue, "Gramsci tra Croce e Marx," *Il Ponte*, 4:5 (May 1948), 429-438. On the question of Gramsci's "Bordiganism," especially in 1920-22, see Williams, *Proletarian Order*, pp. 177, 184, 191, and 233-234, and Davidson, *Antonio Gramsci*, pp. xiii, 171-180, and 196-223.

15. Gwyn A. Williams, "The Concept of 'Egemonia' in the Thought of Antonio Gramsci: Some Notes on Interpretation," *Journal of the History of Ideas*, 21:4 (October-December 1960), 586-587.

16. S.P.N. 385; or Q.C. 1843 (1933).

17. See especially Davidson, *Antonio Gramsci.*

18. S.P.N. 383; or Q.C. 1841 (1933).

19. S.P.N. 383-384; or Q.C. 1841-42 (1933).

Chapter 1

1. The PSI was an anomaly within the Second International on at least three other grounds, though their relationship to the Party's neutralism is not precisely clear: (1) it was founded only in 1892 and in a milieu which had always been more receptive to anarchism than to Marxism; (2) its founding preceded the development of a large and active trade union movement, and it retained a much more intellectualist cast than did other European socialist parties; and (3) it had much stronger neo-Hegelian and anti-positivist leanings even in the 1890s and especially after 1900 than did the other European parties. On the intellectual background of Italian socialism, see Giacomo Marramao, *Marxismo e revisionismo in Italia* (Bari: De Donato, 1971).

2. For an incisive analysis of the events leading up to this shift, see Richard A. Webster, "From Insurrection to Intervention: the Italian Crisis of 1914," *Italian Quarterly*, 5:20-6:21 (Winter 1961-Spring 1962), 27-50.

3. H.P.C. 120 (October 31, 1914).

4. Ibid., 118.

5. Ibid.

6. For a later denial of this charge, see S.F. 12-13 (January 2, 1921).

7. See Chapters 4 and 7, below.

8. See Gaetano Salvemini, *Scritti sulla questione meridionale, 1896-1955* (Turin: Einaudi, 1955). Interesting also in this connection is A. W. Salomone's observation in his *Italy in the Giolittian Era* (Philadelphia: University of Pennsylvania Press, 1960), p. 15: "From Mazzini to Salvemini the problem of Italian democracy had been considered as inherently one of moral education and of the uplifting of the masses to a consciousness of their human and political dignity."

9. H.P.C. 117 (October 31, 1914).

10. Ibid., 119.

11. Ernst Nolte, *Three Faces of Fascism*, trans. L. Vennewitz (New York: Holt, Rinehart and Winston, 1966), p. 150. For more detailed treatments of Italian intellectual life, 1900-14, see Peter M. Riccio, *On the Threshold of Fascism* (New York: Casa Italiana, Columbia University, 1929); and Emilio Gentile, *"La Voce" e L'età giolittiana* (Milan: Pan, 1972).

12. See especially Mosca's *Teorica dei governi e governo parlamentare*, 2nd ed. (Milan: Soc. Anon. Istituto Editoriale Scientifico, 1925), pp. 133-298. The first edition appeared in 1884.

13. Modern Italian historiography tends to split along the same lines. For a

view emphasizing the weaknesses of the Risorgimento solution, see Denis Mack Smith, *Italy: A Modern History* (Ann Arbor: University of Michigan Press, 1959). For a defense of the post-Risorgimento period and an attack on the cultural output of those who would not accept it, see Benedetto Croce, *A History of Italy, 1871-1915* (Oxford: Clarendon Press, 1929); and John Thayer, *Italy and the Great War: Politics and Culture, 1870-1915* (Madison: University of Wisconsin Press, 1964).

14. The now classic study of this theme is H. Stuart Hughes, *Consciousness and Society* (New York: Alfred A. Knopf, 1961).

15. Croce, *A History of Italy*, p. 240.

16. Ibid., p. 241.

17. On Hegelianism in Italy, see Sergio Landucci, "L'Hegelismo in Italia nell'Età del Risorgimento," *Studi storici*, 6:4 (October-December 1965), 597-628; and Guido Oldrini, ed., *Il Primo Hegelismo Italiano* (Florence: Vallechi, 1969) and *Gli Hegeliani di Napoli: Augusto Vera e la corrente ortodossa* (Milan: Feltrinelli, 1964).

18. See Piccone, "From Spaventa to Gramsci."

19. Quoted in Thayer, *Italy*, p. 193. For discussions of Corradini, see Thayer, chap. 7; and Monique de Taeye-Henen, *Le Nationalisme d'Enrico Corradini et les origines du fascisme dans la revue florentine Il Regno, 1903-1906* (Paris: Didier, 1973).

20. Riccio, *Fascism*, pp. 12 and 15.

21. It should be noted, however, that in the "neutralist/interventionist" cleavage of 1914-15, the socialists were the only group predominantly on the neutralist side, and they had always been the weakest link in the "rejuvenation movement."

22. For a portrait of the conditions that Franchetti and Sonnino found, see Gaetano Salvemini, *The Origins of Fascism in Italy*, ed. R. Vivarelli (New York: Harper and Row, 1973), pp. 1-10; Mack Smith, *Italy*, pp. 230-242; and Shepherd B. Clough, *The Economic History of Modern Italy* (New York: Columbia University Press, 1964). Recently, both the degree and the meaning of Southern "underdevelopment" have been the subjects of hot debate. See Antonio Carlo and Edmondo Capecelatro, *Contro la questione meridionale* (Rome: La nuova sinistra, 1972); Rosario Villari, "L'interdipendenza tra nord e sud," *Studi storici*, 18:2 (April-June 1977), 3-20; and the entire issue of the *International Journal of Sociology*, 4:2/3 (Summer-Fall 1974).

23. See Salvemini's speech to the Milan Congress of the PSI in 1910, his final PSI speech: *Resoconto stenografico del XI Congresso Nazionale del PSI* (Milan, October 21-25, 1910), pp. 59-70. Also: Salvemini, "Dopo la vittoria giolittiana," *La Voce* (March 10, 1910).

24. Salvemini, "Il discorso del 1 maggio," reprinted in *La Voce* (May 11, 1911).

25. For an investigation of Italian anarchism and early socialism with many useful bibliographical references, see Gian Mario Bravo, "A un Secolo della Fondazione della Prima Internazionale. Stato degli studi e delle ricerche," *Rivista storica del socialismo*, 8:24 (January-April 1965), 3-51. For more recent studies, see Marramao, *Marxismo*, pp. 3-19; and Franco Damiani, *Carlo Cafiero nella storia del primo socialismo italiano* (Milan: Jaca, 1974).

26. Cf. Richard Hostetter, *The Italian Socialist Movement: Origins, 1860-1882* (Princeton, N.J.: Van Nostrand, 1958), pp. 418-425 and 429.

27. Croce, *A History of Italy*, p. 39.

28. Ibid., p. 146.

29. See Marramao, *Marxismo*, pp. 19-30.

30. See Mario Spinella et al., eds., *Critica Sociale*, 2 vols. (Milan: Feltrinelli, 1959), vol. II, pp. 363-420. Antonio Labriola, for instance, wrote frequently for *Critica Sociale* in the 1890s, and they returned him the favor by publishing

posthumously his "fourth essay" on Marxism, "From One Century to the Next," in 1925.

31. Ibid., pp. 677-757 and passim.

32. See, for example, the discussion of commodity fetishism in *Studio su Marx*, 2nd ed. (Naples: Morano, 1926), pp. 109 ff. The first edition appeared in 1908. See also the brief discussion of the "essence of capitalism" in *Economia, Socialismo, Sindicalismo* (Naples: Società Editrice Partenopea, 1911), pp. 174-177. Gramsci, however, never perceived Labriola's originality and dismissed him in 1926 as a kind of neo-liberal; cf. M.P. 38; or S.P.W., II, 450 (1926).

33. According to Salomone, *Giolittian Era*, p. 80, PSI membership increased from about 20,000 on the eve of the Reggio Emilia Congress to 49,148 just two years later.

34. Croce, *A History of Italy*, p. 247.

35. On this point, see Enzo Tagliacozzo, *Gaetano Salvemini nel Cinquantennio Liberale* (Florence: La Nuova Italia, 1959), pp. 137-174.

36. Letter to Giulia, 1923, in Ferrata and Gallo, eds., *2000 Pagine di Gramsci*, 2 vols. (Milan: Il Saggiatore, 1964), vol. II, p. 24.

37. Letter to Tatiana, October 3, 1932, in L.C. 682.

38. Letter to Grazietta, October 31, 1932, in ibid., p. 696 and note.

39. Letter to Tatiana, October 3, 1932, in ibid., p. 682.

40. Letter to Giulia, March 6, 1924, in Ferrata and Gallo, *2000 Pagine*, vol. II, p. 33.

41. Ibid., vol. I, p. 174.

42. Ibid., vol. II, p. 33.

43. See Davidson, *Antonio Gramsci*, p. 50.

44. See Fiori, *Antonio Gramsci*, p. 56. Cf. also S.G. 28 (March 4, 1916).

45. H.P.C. 158 (November 1910).

46. See, for instance, Salvemini's *La Voce* essays: "Cocò all'Università di Napoli a la scuola della mala vita" (January 3, 1909); and "La riforma della scuola media" (May 27, 1909). Salvemini broke with the PSI in 1910.

47. See Q.C. 2022 and 2484 (1934).

48. See Fiori, *Antonio Gramsci*, pp. 77-78. Gramsci also later wrote that in 1911 he had favored the "national independence of the [Sardinian] region." See the letter to Giulia, March 6, 1924, in Ferrata and Gallo, *2000 Pagine*, vol. II, p. 33.

49. Quoted in Fiori, *Antonio Gramsci*, p. 77.

50. See ibid., p. 56.

51. M.P. 31; or S.P.W., II, 444 (1926).

52. P.V. 3-8 (February 5 and May 20, 1913). For the argument that these articles should be attributed to Gramsci, see Renzo Martinelli, "Gramsci e il 'Corriere Universitario' di Torino," *Studi storici*, 14:4 (October-December 1973), 906-910.

53. Even after joining the PSI in 1913, he participated rather little until he left the university; cf. Davidson, *Antonio Gramsci*, p. 64.

54. Quoted in Fiori, *Antonio Gramsci*, p. 83.

55. Ibid., p. 85.

56. Ibid., pp. 87-88.

57. Ibid., p. 85.

58. Ibid., p. 88.

59. See M.P. 32 (or S.P.W., II, 444), which shows that Gramsci was a socialist by 1914. We do not know exactly when he acquired a party card. Togliatti wrote in an April 1964 letter to Alfonso Leonetti that when he (Togliatti) did so in 1914, Gramsci already had one. This is confirmed by Leonetti's own subsequent investigations; see his *Note su Gramsci* (Argalia: Urbino, 1970), pp. 165-166 and 170.

60. M.P. 32; or S.P.W., II, 445.

61. See the letters to Tatiana of 23 February 1931 (L.C. 410-413) and 17 August 1931 (L.C. 464-467) as well as the letter of Umberto Cosmo, his close former teacher at Turin, to Gramsci, dated 10 August 1931, and reprinted in L.C. 467-468. See also Domenico Zucàro, "Antonio Gramsci all'Università di Torino 1911-1915," *Società* 13:6 (December 1957), 1091-1111.

62. Zucàro, "Antonio Gramsci," p. 1109.

63. See Davidson, *Antonio Gramsci*, pp. 69-70; P.V. 18-29 (December 21, 1915-February 26, 1916); and S. 3-5 (November 27, 1915-January 7, 1916).

64. See Battista Santhià, *Con Gramsci all'Ordine Nuovo* (Rome: Riuniti, 1956), p. 43.

65. See, for instance, Davidson, *Antonio Gramsci*, p. 72. Davidson, however, does not seem clear in his own mind about the nature of Gramsci's political allegiances in 1916-17. Thus he claims both that Gramsci subscribed to the ideas of *La Voce* between 1915 and 1917 (p. 81) and encouraged workers to read it even late in 1917 (pp. 76 and 79); and that he "could no longer see eye to eye with the journal after 1915" (p. 99).

66. H.P.C. 21 (January 29, 1916).

67. For an argument that Gramsci was substantially influenced by Vico, see Eugene Kamenka, "Vico and Marxism," in Giorgio Tagliacozzo and Hayden V. White, eds., *Giambattista Vico, An International Symposium* (Baltimore: Johns Hopkins University Press, 1969), p. 141.

68. H.P.C. 75 (February 11, 1917). Original emphasis.

69. Q.C. 1233 (1932).

70. The four parts are: *Aesthetics* (1902), *Logic* (1905), *Practice* (1908), and *Historiography* (1916). We may suspect that Gramsci had done the additional reading, since, according to a letter he wrote in 1918, he used to assign selections from it to the young militants he was tutoring. See the letter to Giuseppe Lombardo Radice, reprinted in *Rinascita*, 21:10 (March 7, 1964), 32; or in Giancarlo Bergami, *Il Giovane Gramsci e il Marxismo, 1911-1918* (Milan: Feltrinelli, 1977), pp. 154-155.

71. Croce, *A History of Italy*, p. 243.

72. Though our information is less direct and detailed than one might like, there is no doubt that Gramsci read Labriola in this period. On January 5, 1918, he published a short excerpt from the *Essays on the Materialistic Conception of History* in *Il Grido del popolo*, and he referred to Labriola approvingly in an article of January 29, 1918 (S.G. 163). Even earlier, Gramsci's writings revealed a markedly similar argument against positivism (e.g., S.G. 74), and, according to Togliatti's later testimony, Gramsci read several books by Labriola as a student (see Marcella and Maurizio Ferrara, eds., *Conversando con Togliatti* [Milan: Cultura Sociale, 1953], p. 29). This last point is supported by Annibale Pastore, Gramsci's teacher at the University of Turin in 1914-15, who claims to have attempted in his classes "to save from oblivion Antonio Labriola's doctrine of causation mediated by the state of consciousness." See Pastore's *Il Problema della causalità con particolare riguardo alla teoria del metodo sperimentale*, 2 vols. (Turin: Bocca, 1921), vol. II, p. 3. Moreover, Attilio Carena, a young worker whom Gramsci tutored in 1918, wrote a detailed essay on Labriola's *Del Materialismo storico* (the second of the *Essays*) in *Il Grido del popolo* (August 31, 1918). This text has been reproduced by Bergami, *Giovane Gramsci*, pp. 164-168. Further evidence that Gramsci had read Labriola in this period is that Carena's library, now in the possession of Alfonso Leonetti, included both the second and third *Essays*; see Bergami, *Giovane Gramsci*, p. 188.

73. Croce, *A History of Italy*, p. 240.

74. Ibid., p. 243.

75. For Gramsci's admiration of De Sanctis, see H.P.C. 26 (November 20,

1915), where he calls De Sanctis "the greatest critic Europe has ever produced." For Croce's assessment, see *A History of Italy*, pp. 243 and 248.

76. See, for instance, H.P.C. 41 (February 11, 1917) and 45 (December 24, 1917).

77. S.G. 117 (June 19, 1917).

78. Q.C. 2188-89 (1934).

79. Carena's library (see note 72, above) contained numerous philosophical books by Croce, Labriola, and Bertrando Spaventa, as well as one by Bergson (*Philosophy of Intuition*), one by Sorel (*Contemporary Religion*), one by Pisacane (*Essays on the Revolution*), and representative texts of German philosophy (Kant, Fichte, Schelling, and Schopenhauer). See Leonardo Paggi, *Gramsci e il moderno principe* (Rome: Riuniiti, 1970), p. 39; and Bergami, *Giovane Gramsci*, pp. 175-193.

80. For Rolland's influence, see S.M. 10-11 (January 11, 1916); S.G. 33 (May 6, 1916), 185 (March 2, 1918), and 194 (March 16, 1918); H.P.C. 21 (January 29, 1916); and Alfonso Leonetti's recollections in "Romain Rolland e Gramsci," *Rinascita*, 26:25 (June 20, 1969), 19-20. For Péguy, see S.M. 118 (April 19, 1916); and S.G. 33-34 (May 6, 1916). From Gramsci's later praise of Barbusse (O.N. 493-494; December 11-18, 1920) and his journal *Clarté*, which was one of the models for *Ordine Nuovo*, we may assume that he was already reading *Clarté* in this period; see also G. Amoretti, "Con Gramsci sotto la Mole," in *Gramsci Scritti di Palmiro Togliatti ed altri* (Rome: Unità, 1945), p. 44, who claims that Gramsci met Barbusse in 1917. In Sorel's case, though Gramsci did not cite him until September 1920 (O.N. 154), he would certainly have known of him much earlier, given Sorel's immense popularity in Italy, and probably read his early articles in *La Voce* (February 10 and April 14, 1910). Moreover, there are early references to Sorelian concepts such as "social myths" (H.P.C. 37; August 18, 1917), and Carena's library had a volume of Sorel in it (see note 79, above).

81. According to Leonetti, *Note su Gramsci*, p. 70, Gramsci had read the following works by Marx and Engels by 1918: *The Communist Manifesto*, *Revolution and Counterrevolution in Germany*, *The Holy Family*, *The Poverty of Philosophy*, and the preface to the *Critique of Political Economy*. Labriola had much more influence on Gramsci in the *Prison Notebooks* than in Gramsci's early writings; but see note 72, above. For some evidence that Gramsci had contact with Mondolfo before 1917, see Mondolfo's letter to Norberto Bobbio (May 6, 1967), republished in part in Rodolfo Mondolfo, *Umanismo di Marx* (Turin: Einaudi, 1968), p. xlv, note 2. See also H.P.C. 39 (January 12, 1918).

82. H.P.C. 71 (February 11, 1917).

83. Ibid.

84. S.P.W., I, 75-76; cf. O.N. 16 (July 12, 1919).

85. H.P.C. 39 (January 12, 1918).

86. For this reason there is much validity in the views of those critics who assert that Gramsci's debts to Croce in this period have been overestimated. Nonetheless, it seems pointless to contend that he was not Crocean at all. See Paggi, *Gramsci*, pp. 15-16; and Eugenio Garin, "Gramsci nella cultura italiana," in *Studi Gramsciani* (Rome: Riuniti, 1958), pp. 398-399.

87. Letter to Galetto, reprinted in *L'Unità*, June 25, 1967.

88. H.P.C. 72 (February 11, 1917).

89. S.M. 365 (February 5, 1918).

90. S.G. 117 (June 19, 1917).

91. H.P.C. 101-104 (April 1, 1916).

92. S.G. 41 (July 7, 1916).

93. In July 1917, Gramsci attended the Florence Conference that revived the "intransigent revolutionary" faction of the PSI. See below, page 38.

94. Quoted in Paggi, *Gramsci*, pp. 52-53.

95. O.N. 52 (November 25, 1919).
96. S.G. 269-275 (June 29, 1918).
97. H.P.C. 100 (September 14, 1918).
98. Ibid.
99. S.G. 259 (June 15, 1918).
100. Quoted in Paggi, *Gramsci*, p. 131, this was originally stated in *Il Grido del popolo*, September 15, 1917.
101. H.P.C. 58 (December 8, 1917).
102. Roberto Michels's argument in *Political Parties*, which came out in 1911, was roughly that all parties and hence all governments tend to be under an elitist or "Bonapartist" control. This has sometimes been summarized as his "iron law of oligarchy." Gramsci did not explicitly confront this view in the early writings, but he seemed to be doing so implicitly at many points. See, for instance, H.P.C. 50-51 (August 31, 1918), where he argued that the education, autonomous culture, and organization of knowledge and experience which the proletariat should and could create would have the effect of providing them with independence from an intellectual elite, however much intellectuals might have to furnish the initial impetus for these developments.
103. H.P.C. 33-35 (December 24, 1917).
104. S.G. 61-64 (December 29, 1916).
105. Ibid.
106. Quoted in Paggi, *Gramsci*, p. 139; H.P.C. 98 (December 18, 1917).
107. Letter to Giuseppe Lombardo-Radice, reprinted in *Rinascita*, 21:10 (March 7, 1964), 32.
108. H.P.C. 43-45 (December 24, 1917).
109. H.P.C. 144 (June 22, 1918).
110. Ibid.; and S.G. 268.
111. H.P.C. 22 (January 29, 1916).
112. S.G. 36-37 (May 17, 1916). See also H.P.C. 22 for Gramsci's analysis of the cultural function performed by the Enlightenment for the French Revolution.

Chapter 2

1. For an interesting, recent study of the interplay between the end of the war, events in Russia, and the impact on Europe, see Albert S. Lindemann, *The Red Years: European Socialism versus Bolshevism, 1919-1921* (Berkeley: University of California Press, 1974).
2. Oskar Jászi, *Revolution and Counter-Revolution in Hungary* (New York: Howard Fertig, 1969), p. 66.
3. Quoted in A.J. Ryder, *The German Revolution of 1918* (Cambridge, England: Cambridge University Press, 1967), p. 85.
4. Ibid.
5. O.N. 180 (July 1920).
6. S. 58 (September 29, 1917). Reports in *Avanti!*, for instance, relied on the Russian émigré Vassily Suchomlin, who had been a Social Revolutionary. This, perhaps, is where Gramsci gained the erroneous impression about Chernov.
7. S.P.W., I, 28-30; or H.P.C. 126-128 (April 29, 1917).
8. Ibid.
9. S.P.W., I, 34-37; or H.P.C. 123-126 (November 24, 1917).
10. H.P.C. 39 (January 12, 1918).
11. H.P.C. 123-124; or S.P.W., I, 34-35 (November 24, 1917).
12. H.P.C. 144 (June 22, 1918).
13. S.M. 352 (January 3, 1918).
14. The most important descriptions were probably the articles from Russia by John Reed, which were widely disseminated in the Western European press in 1918 and appeared in nearly every issue of *The Liberator*, an I.W.W. journal

edited from New York by Max Eastman. In his memoirs, Eastman claims that Gramsci later told him that he had gotten his "first inkling of what was really going on in Russia" through a translation from *The Liberator* of Eastman's essay on Lenin. See Eastman, *Love and Revolution: My Journey through an Epoch* (New York: Random House, 1964), p. 138. Reed's essays were reprinted in *L'Ordine Nuovo* on May 1 (p. 3), May 15 (p. 11), May 24 (pp. 22-23), and June 7, 1919 (pp. 33-34). Reed's articles on "How a Soviet Works" were also reprinted in the June 21 (pp. 49-50), June 28 (pp. 57-58), July 12 (pp. 65-66), and October 25, 1919 (p. 177) issues. In addition, *Ordine Nuovo* printed many other articles on Russia and the soviets, all of which suggested that the soviets were the basic organ of governance. See *L'Ordine Nuovo* (1919-20 and 1924), reprint (Milan: Feltrinelli, 1966).

15. O.N. 374 (May 15, 1919). The validity of this judgment is not here in question; suffice it to say that it was common to most of the reports in the Western left-wing press that Gramsci read. Note also that while he often used the words *soviet* and *council* interchangeably, he recognized, when being precise, that the latter, grounded in the workplace, was only the incipient basis for the former, organized territorially.

16. S.P.W., I, 53-54; or H.P.C. 154-155 (July 25, 1918).

17. Ibid.

18. Ibid.

19. See *Il Grido del popolo*, October 19, 1918, quoted in Paggi, *Gramsci*, pp. 74-75. For Gramsci's later theory of intellectuals, see Chapters 3 and 6, below.

20. For Gramsci's reading in Labriola and Marx, see Chapter 1, notes 72 and 81, above. We know that he was reading Gentile in 1917 (see S.M. 296; March 8, 1917), and that he paid him some considerable tribute as a philosopher early in 1918 (*Il Grido del popolo*, January 19, 1918, as quoted in Paggi, *Gramsci*, p. 21). The reference to Marxism as a philosophy of the impure act comes in 1932 or early 1933 (S.P.N. 372; or Q.C. 1492).

21. H.P.C. 11 (May 4, 1918).

22. H.P.C. 9.

23. Piero Gobetti, *La Rivoluzione liberale* (Turin: Einaudi, 1964), p. 107.

24. Articles by Lenin appeared in the following issues of *Ordine Nuovo*: June 14, 1919, pp. 41-42 (an extract from *The Proletarian Revolution and the Renegade Kautsky*); July 12, 1919, p. 66 (on soviets); July 26, 1919, p. 84 (a report on the Socialist Youth International meeting in Switzerland in 1915); August 23, 1919, pp. 113-115 (his speech to the First Comintern Congress, March 1919, on "Bourgeois and Proletarian Democracy," full of references to the Paris Commune and the soviets); October 4, 1919, p. 155 (article from the March 6, 1919 issue of *Pravda*, captioned by Gramsci "Revolutionary Preparation: The Victory of the Soviet"); October 11, 1919, p. 161 ("Democracy and Dictatorship in Germany"); November 1, 1919, p. 187 (interview with an American Red Cross official in the USSR, entitled "The Future of the Soviet"); December 27, 1919, pp. 245-246 ("The Third International"); January 17, 1920, p. 271 ("The Emancipation of Women"); February 21, 1920, p. 299 ("Voluntary and Compulsory Work"); May 29, 1920, pp. 20-22 ("Economics and Politics during the Dictatorship of the Proletariat," again emphasizing soviets); and December 4, 1920, p. 162 ("Revolutionary Tactics," with the first references to "conscious vanguards"). In addition, Gramsci printed a five-part article by Zinoviev on Lenin's life (June 5-July 10, 1920); a two-part "Conversation with Lenin" by Arthur Ransome (September 13 and December 27, 1919, the latter with an accompanying article by Radek on soviets); and an article by Radek on Lenin (December 4, 1920).

These articles, some of which appeared slightly earlier in *The Liberator* or in French left periodicals like *Nouvelle Internationale*, are among the very few Italian translations of Lenin's work in this period. Gramsci's reading of the French press would have introduced him to a few other articles of the same genre; see Alastair

Davidson, "Gramsci and Lenin 1917-1922," *The Socialist Register, 1974* (London: Merlin Press, 1974), pp. 130-131. From *The Liberator*, Gramsci probably read in addition: "A Letter to American Workingmen" (August 1918), which stressed the soviets; "Brest-Litovsk: A Brigade's Peace" (October 1918); a selection from the Eighth Conference of the Russian Communist Party, March 1919, on the "Self-Determination of Nations" (reprinted June 1920); and an article by Maxim Gorky on Lenin (November 1920).

25. In a major statement which Gramsci probably read (see Paggi, *Gramsci*, p. 225), Lenin's only reference to the party portrayed it as a genuine and therefore somewhat disorganized expression of the masses:

> Of course, not weeks, but long months and years are required for a new social class, especially a class which up to now has been oppressed and crushed by poverty and ignorance, to get used to its new position, look around, organize its work and promote its own organizers. It is understandable that the Party which leads the revolutionary proletariat has not been able to acquire the experience and habits of large organizational undertakings embracing millions and tens of millions of citizens.

(See "The Immediate Tasks of the Soviet Government," in V.I. Lenin, *Selected Works*, 3 vols. [New York: International Publishers, 1967], vol. II, pp. 666-667.) This statement is consistent with the concept of the party that Lenin advocated in these years. At the First Congress of the Third International in 1919, Lenin did not insist on Bolshevik-style party organizations in other European nations. Only at the Second Congress in 1920 did he put forward the Bolsheviks as a model for international emulation; and even then, in the Italian case, he insisted only on the attempt to gain a communist majority within the PSI.

26. O.N. 387 (December 20, 1919). Though this article does not make explicit reference to *What Is to Be Done?*, a review of the book by Carlo Rappoport appeared in *Ordine Nuovo* three weeks later and referred to its thesis, in terms identical to Gramsci's, as that of the "qualified revolutionary"; see *Ordine Nuovo*, January 10, 1920, p. 263.

27. S.P.W., I, 194 (May 8, 1920).

28. In his interview with Arthur Ransome (see note 24, above), Lenin referred approvingly to Daniel De Leon, the American socialist whom Gramsci and Togliatti had also studied by 1917 and to whom Gramsci also referred approvingly in this connection (S.P.W., I, 296; August 28, 1920). See Ferrara and Ferrara, *Conversando*, p. 44.

29. See "Letters on Tactics," in V.I. Lenin, *Collected Works*, 45 vols. (Moscow: Foreign Language Publishing House, 1963), vol. XX, p. 107; and "Draft Resolution for the Fifth Congress of the Russian Social Democratic Party," in *Collected Works*, vol. X, p. 388.

30. See "On Slogans," in Lenin, *Selected Works*, vol. II, pp. 179-180. Lenin's misgivings were well-founded, since at the national congress of soviets held in June, only 105 of 777 delegates had been Bolshevik; see W.H. Chamberlin, *The Russian Revolution, 1917-1921*, 2 vols. (New York: MacMillan, 1935), vol. I, p. 114.

31. On the latter link, see Ryder, *German Revolution*, pp. 165-187.

32. The best book in English is Clark, *Antonio Gramsci.*

33. See Enzo Rutigliano, "The Ideology of Labor and Capitalist Rationality in Gramsci," *Telos*, 31 (Spring 1977), 91-99.

34. For an interesting critique of Gramsci which casts considerable doubt on the viability of his strategy, irrespective of the nature of the PSI, see Franklin Adler, "Factory Councils, Gramsci, and the Industrialists," *Telos*, 31 (Spring 1977), 67-90.

35. See Davidson, *Antonio Gramsci*, p. 77.

36. M.P. 22; or S.P.W., I, 291 (August 14, 1920).

37. M.P. 23; or S.P.W., I, 293 (August 14, 1920).

38. See O.N. 493 (December 11-18, 1920). *Clarté*'s inspiration is apparent from the article about it in the second issue (May 15, 1919). Articles by Barbusse appeared in the August 9 and 23, October 25, 1919, and May 8 and July 3, 1920 issues.

39. O.N. 494. Articles concerning *Proletkult* appeared in the June 12 and August 28, 1920 issues.

40. See Paolo Spriano, *Gramsci e "L'Ordine Nuovo"* (Rome: Riuniti, 1965), p. 149; and, more generally, Paggi, *Gramsci*, pp. 207-229.

41. V. I. Lenin, "Theses on the Fundamental Tasks of the Second Congress of the Communist International," in *Collected Works*, vol. XXXI, p. 199.

42. M.P. 23; or S.P.W., I, 293 (August 14, 1920).

43. M.P. 24; or S.P.W., I, 293-294.

44. On De Leon, see note 28, above; on Eastman, see note 14, above. Gramsci wrote a major article on the English shop-steward committees for *Il Grido del popolo* on April 27, 1918.

45. S.P.W., I, 65-68 (June 21, 1919).

46. Ibid., p. 67.

47. S.P.W., I, 295 (August 28, 1920).

48. S.P.W., I, 100 (October 11, 1919).

49. "Commissars" were elected from each "labor squad" and served only as long as they enjoyed its confidence. A multi-tiered system of elections produced an executive committee of three to nine members within each factory. Voting was open to all workers, union members or not, though only the former were allowed to become commissars.

50. For the list of lecture topics for the first monthly sessions, see *Ordine Nuovo*, November 29, 1919, p. 216. All of the lecturers were *Ordine Nuovo* affiliates and included the four original editors and Zino Zini. Gramsci's topics were syndicalism, the Russian Revolution, unions and soviets, the dictatorship of the proletariat, and religion.

51. See Davidson, "Gramsci and Lenin 1917-1922," p. 132; and "Gramsci and the Factory Councils," *Australian Left Review*, 45 (October 1974), 45-46.

52. O.N. 4 (June 1, 1919).

53. See Clark, *Antonio Gramsci*, pp. 9, 17, 69-70.

54. Ibid., pp. 69-70.

55. See Chapter 4, below, for Gramsci's lack of a reification problematic in the *Notebooks*.

56. The articles were by Carlo Petri (Pietro Mossi) and were entitled "The Taylor System and Producer Councils." They appeared in the October 25 (p. 178), November 1 (pp. 188-189), November 8 (pp. 197-198), November 15 (pp. 205-206), and November 22, 1919 (pp. 209-210) issues.

57. S.P.N. 279; or Q.C. 2139 (1934).

58. Thus, in defining Taylorism, Clark (*Antonio Gramsci*, p. 17) includes as a part of it that the "class war" is perceived as "obsolete." Certainly this was very far from Gramsci's view, even though Clark claims that Gramsci was a Taylorist.

59. S.P.W., I, 67 (June 21, 1919).

60. S.P.W., I, 265-268 (June 12, 1920).

61. S.P.W., I, 191 (May 8, 1920).

62. S.P.W., I, 66 (June 21, 1919).

63. S.P.W., I, 260 (June 5, 1920).

64. Ibid.

65. Ibid., p. 263.

66. S.P.W., I, 191 (May 8, 1920) and 307 (July 3, 1920).

67. S.P.W., I, 143 (December 27, 1919).

68. Ibid.

69. S.P.W., I, 134 (November 29, 1919).
70. S.P.W., I, 143 (December 27, 1919).
71. S.P.W., I, 309 (July 3, 1920).
72. S.P.W., I, 99 (October 11, 1919).
73. S.P.W., I, 267 (June 12, 1920).
74. S.P.W., I, 103-104 (October 25, 1919).
75. S.P.W., I, 110 (November 8, 1919).
76. S.P.W., I, 265 (June 20, 1920).
77. S.P.W., I, 99 (October 11, 1919).
78. S.P.W., I, 266 (June 20, 1920).
79. S.P.W., I, 101 (October 11, 1919).
80. Ibid.
81. S.P.W., I, 267 (June 12, 1920).
82. Williams, *Proletarian Order*, p. 155. Original emphasis.
83. S.P.W., I, 67-68 (June 21, 1919).
84. S.P.W., I, 92 (September 13, 1919).
85. S.P.W., I, 306 (July 3, 1920).
86. S.P.W., I, 89 (September 13, 1919). See also S.P.W., I, 85 (August 2, 1919).
87. S.P.W., I, 348 (September 24, 1920).
88. See his letter to Togliatti et al., February 9, 1924, reprinted in Palmiro Togliatti, *La formazione del gruppo dirigente del partito comunista italiano* (Rome: Riuniti, 1962), pp. 196-197, and now available in S.P.W., II, 199-200. See also Chapter 3, below.
89. See S.P.W., I, 83-87 (August 2, 1919) and 147-149 (January 3, 1920).
90. See Andrea Viglongo, "Primi contatti tra contadini e operai," *Ordine Nuovo* (May 8, 1920), p. 7, as well as Viglongo's retrospective view, "Momenti della lotta di classe nella prima metà del 1920," in *Il Ponte*, 26:10 (October 1970), 1323.
91. Amadeo Bordiga, "Per la costituzione dei consigli operai," *Il Soviet*, 3:1 (January 4, 1920), 2, reprinted by the Istituto Feltrinelli (Milan, 1966). The passage is translated at S.P.W., I, 214. Bordiga followed this with a series of attacks on the *ordinovisti* which appeared in the January 11 and February 1, 8, and 22 issues of *Il Soviet*. Most of this material is also available in Amadeo Bordiga, *Scritti scelti*, ed. F. Livorsi (Milan: Feltrinelli, 1975), pp. 85-94. For discussions of Bordiga's attitudes toward the councils, see Andreina De Clementi, *Amadeo Bordiga* (Turin: Einaudi, 1971), pp. 102-132; and Franco Livorsi, *Amadeo Bordiga, Il pensiero e l'azione politica 1912-1970* (Rome: Riuniti, 1976), pp. 115-135.
92. See Filippo Turati, *Le Vie Maestre del Socialismo*, ed. R. Mondolfo and G. Arfé (Naples: Morano, 1966), pp. 313-346 and especially pp. 317-318, where Turati refers to "the substitution of the 'soviet' for Parliament" as a rejection "of all the principles, methods, and organisms which we have worked to affirm, conquer, and perfect for thirty years."
93. Giacinto M. Serrati, "I Comitati di fabbrica," in *Comunismo*, 1:6 (December 15, 1919), 77-91.
94. Serrati, "Documentazione unitaria," in *Comunismo*, 2:10 (February 15-28, 1921), 536-550 and 2:11 (March 1-15, 1921), 598-604.
95. The best general study of these controversies is Franco De Felice, *Serrati, Bordiga, Gramsci* (Bari: De Donato, 1971).
96. S.P.W., I, 220 ("Per la costituzione dei consigli operai," *Il Soviet*, 3:2 [January 11, 1920], 3).
97. S.G. 33-34 (May 6, 1916).
98. Eduard Bernstein, *Evolutionary Socialism*, trans. E. Harvey (New York: Schocken Books, 1961), p. 187.
99. Ibid., p. 125.

100. Serrati, "Documentazione unitaria," 541.

101. O.N. 460 (October 11, 1919). The statement appeared originally in *Resto del Carlino* (October 5, 1919).

102. Ibid.

103. S.P.W., II, 450; or M.P. 37-38 (1926). Original emphasis.

104. Ibid.

105. Ibid.

106. The PSI won 156 of 508 seats in the Chamber of Deputies and received 32.2 percent of the national vote; see Clark, *Antonio Gramsci*, p. 78.

107. O.N. 387-389 (December 20, 1919) and S.P.W., I, 142 (December 27, 1919).

108. S.P.W., I, 142-146 (December 27, 1919).

109. Ibid., p. 144.

110. S.P.W., I, 154 (January 24, 1920).

111. Ibid., p. 157.

112. S.P.W., I, 192-193 (May 8, 1920).

113. Ibid., pp. 193-194.

114. Ibid., p. 195.

115. S.P.W., I, 305-309 (July 3, 1920).

116. Ibid., pp. 309, 307. Hoare's translation of the latter passage takes the sting out of it by omitting the word *hallucination*; compare O.N. 137.

117. Ibid., p. 307.

118. Ibid., p. 308.

119. See O.N. 483, where Gramsci cites Lenin's explicit agreement with Gramsci's May 8 article, "Towards a Renewal of the Socialist Party."

120. See Paolo Spriano, *Storia del Partito Comunista Italiano*, 5 vols. (Turin: Einaudi, 1967-75), vol. I, pp. 72-73. When informed by the PSI maximalists that *Ordine Nuovo* was considered "syndicalist," Lenin retracted any implied endorsement of the group and simply reaffirmed his support for the position set forth in the article. See *Il Soviet*, 3:24 (October 3, 1920), 4.

121. See Lenin, *Selected Works*, vol. III, pp. 335-430. The pamphlet was originally published in Russia on June 8, 1920, and was immediately translated into German, French, and English. Translated copies were circulated at the Second Congress.

122. See F. Bellini and G. Galli, *Storia del partito comunista italiano* (Milan: Schwarz, 1953), who report that Bordiga claimed his renunciation had been based only on "a tactical difference which in no way involved questions of theory and principle" (p. 41).

123. S.P.W., I, 338 (September 4, 1920).

124. That this was in fact his intention is clear from Gramsci's correspondence of 1923-24. In May 1923, he wrote to Togliatti that he had decided not to enter his faction after the Congress so as to improve relations with the Bordigans. In January 1924, he told a friend, Mauro Scoccimarro, that he had tried in August 1920 to establish good relations with the PSI left while the other *ordinovisti* had been more concerned with the PSI right. See S.P.W., II, 138-139 and 175.

125. For the details of this dispute as well as for the general political picture within the Turin section in 1920, see Franco Ferri, "La Situazione interna della sezione socialista torinese nell'estate del 1920," in *Rinascita*, 14:4 (April 1958), 259-265. Briefly, the issue was whether or not the Turin section should take a formal stand on "abstentionism," thus almost guaranteeing a major organizational split.

126. See "The Tasca Report and the Congress of the Turin Chamber of Labour," S.P.W., I, 255-259 (June 5, 1920); and "On the *L'Ordine Nuovo* Program," S.P.W., I, 291-298, or M.P. 22-27.

127. See his letter to Scoccimarro (January 5, 1924), S.P.W., II, 175.

128. The PSI had opportunities to assert itself at two points during the crisis. Early on, the Confederation of Labor leaders, who wanted no part in any of this,

offered their resignations if the PSI wished to take over direct control of the unions for revolutionary purposes. The PSI refused. Then, under pressure to act, the PSI turned to the Turin factory council representatives and asked them to lead an insurrectionary bid for state power. Cognizant of the fact that no single local nucleus could lead a national revolution, the Turin leaders probably saw this as an attempt to blame revolutionary defeat on someone else, and they rejected it outright. The best account of these events is Paolo Spriano's *L'Occupazione delle fabbriche, Settembre 1920* (Turin: Einaudi, 1964).

129. See Cammett, *Antonio Gramsci*, chaps. 5-6, but especially pp. 110-111 and 122-123. See also Giorgio Bonomi, *Partito e rivoluzione in Gramsci* (Milan: Feltrinelli, 1973), p. 149.

130. O.N. 421 (October 24, 1920). Gramsci had said much the same a week before; see S.P.W., I, 352 (October 17, 1920).

131. S.P.W., I, 363-365 (December 18, 1920).

132. Cammett, *Antonio Gramsci*, p. 110.

133. See Williams, *Proletarian Order*, pp. 177, 184, 188, 191, and 290, who seems to want to push the date back to the spring of 1920, at least as regards "an infusion of Bordiga's style." See also Davidson, *Antonio Gramsci*, p. 134, though he partially contradicts this statement on p. 137.

134. On the defeat of the councils, see Clark, *Antonio Gramsci*, p. 194. On Gramsci's continued support for the councils in 1922 (and the general theory of organization for which they were the centerpiece), see S.F. 57, 83, 91, and 499-519, especially 512. For his support of councils in the 1924-26 period and the prison period, see Chapter 3, below. Of course, the PCI, in contrast to the PSI, had not arisen "in the sphere of bourgeois democracy and political liberty" (S.P.W., I, 260; June 5, 1920), but was a fully proletarian party born of revolutionary struggle. It therefore did not need to be strictly subordinate to the councils, as the PSI was supposed to have been in 1919-20 (S.P.W., II, 33; April 12, 1921). But the accent in both periods was on the dialectical interplay of party and councils.

135. S.P.W., II, 189 (January 28, 1924).

Chapter 3

1. S.P.W., I, 191 (May 8, 1920).

2. S.F. 172-175 (May 28, 1921), 217-222 (June 30, 1921), and 240-241 (July 16, 1921).

3. In his article, "The Elections," for *Il Soviet*, 4:7 (April 17, 1921), 1, Bordiga said that the PCI would participate only because the Second Congress decisions required them to do so. Should the issue arise at the Third Congress in June-July 1921, he vowed to vote once again with the abstentionists.

4. S.F. 137 (April 13, 1921), 125 (April 5, 1921), and 56 (January 31, 1921).

5. S.F. 137-138. Gramsci's criticism here of PSI "socialist" culture was exactly the same as the one he had leveled against Salvemini, the *Università popolare*, and Tasca in earlier days—namely, that it failed to integrate culture with economic life, or as he put it here, that it failed "to arise out of the spiritual expansion of the proletariat liberated from oppression and capitalist chains."

6. S.P.W., I, 376 (January 13, 1921).

7. S.F. 52-55 (January 29, 1921), 71-73 (February 16, 1921), and S.P.W., II, 57 (July 15, 1921).

8. Though arranged for the lakeside resort of Gardone, the meeting never took place, because D'Annunzio failed to appear. Two months earlier, Gramsci had written of a possible schism in the fascist ranks between D'Annunzio's legionnaires and Mussolini (S.F. 76-79; February 19, 1921). For a complete accounting of the "failed encounter," see Sergio Caprioglio, "Un mancato incontro

Gramsci-D'Annunzio a Gardone nell'aprile 1921 (con una testimonianza di Palmiro Togliatti)," *Rivista storica del socialismo*, 5:15-16 (January-August 1962), 263-273.

9. S.P.W., II, 18 (March 4, 1921).

10. There is some indication that these setbacks may have led him to some doubts about Bordiga's leadership. Thus, Nino Danieli (the link between Gramsci and D'Annunzio in April 1921) remembers him as being "not so much optimistic as critical with regard to his Party." See Caprioglio, "Mancato incontro," p. 271.

11. See Lenin's statement of August 14, 1921 that Bordiga "had a trifle exaggerated the fight against centrism, had gone a trifle over the limit beyond which this fight becomes a kind of sport." Quoted in Fiori, *Antonio Gramsci*, p. 153.

12. S.P.W., II, 380 (February 24, 1926), cited in ibid.

13. See Togliatti's statement quoted by Fiori, ibid., p. 154, and by Ferrara and Ferrara, *Conversando*, p. 103.

14. S.F. 441 (January 14, 1922).

15. S.P.W., II, 120-122, as reported by *Ordine Nuovo*, March 28, 1922. The 1921-22 volumes of *Ordine Nuovo* were reprinted by Editori Riuniti (Rome, 1972).

16. S.F. 512 (January 29, 1922); or *Ordine Nuovo*, February 7, 1922, p. 2.

17. See Bordiga's statement, reprinted in *Ordine Nuovo* (March 28, 1922), p. 3, in which he justifies "syndical unity" only for its presumed utility "after the revolution" and not for any specific advantages which might accrue in the short term. This has apparently led some observers to conclude that the trade union theses were not discussed at the Congress; see the note on S.F. 499. However, a short article in *Ordine Nuovo* (March 26, 1922), p. 1, indicates they did pass unanimously "after brief debate."

18. See his letter to Togliatti et al., S.P.W., II, 196 (February 9, 1924). However, it should be borne in mind that this recollection is somewhat self-serving, since Gramsci was very anxious to distance himself from Bordiga in 1924.

19. See Togliatti, *Formazione*, p. 25. Gramsci's later writing lends support to this view. See S.P.W., II, 303-304 (July 3, 1925), where he links the "right-wing danger" with Bordiga's extremist, anti-Comintern politics, "especially after the Rome Congress."

20. The PSI decision followed by only slightly more than a year their decision to sign a pacification pact with the fascists.

21. For Gramsci's account of this incident, see Togliatti, *Formazione*, pp. 228-229 (March 1, 1924).

22. A transcript of the Congress which takes note of these events is available in *Lo Stato Operaio*, 2:7 (March 13, 1924).

23. Jules Humbert-Droz, *Il contrasto tra l'Internazionale e il PCI 1922-1928* (Milan: Feltrinelli, 1969), pp. 38-39.

24. For Bordiga's view of fascism, see *Il Soviet*, April 10, 1921 (reprints from a speech made at a Turin provincial PCI congress); *Il Comunista*, May 29, 1921 and November 17, 1921; *Ordine Nuovo*, November 17, November 30, and December 3, 1921; Gramsci's statement in S.P.W., II, 201-202 (February 9, 1924); and Bordiga's 1923 statement, "La difesa dei comunisti in un memoriale di Bordiga," now reprinted in Bordiga, *Scritti scelti*, pp. 163-171. Bordiga also addressed both the Fourth and Fifth Congresses of the International on fascism. The text of the latter is available in *Fifth Congress of the Communist International*, pp. 212-214. See also Livorsi, *Amadeo Bordiga*, pp. 198-224.

25. S.P.W., II, 481n.*114*.

26. S.P.W., I, 372 (January 2, 1921).

27. S.F. 76-79 (February 19, 1921).

28. S.P.W., II, 63-65 (August 25, 1921).

29. I follow here the interpretation of Alastair Davidson, *Antonio Gramsci*, p. 189.

30. S.P.W., II, 38 (April 26, 1921).

31. S.P.W., II, 39; see also S.F. 168 (May 25, 1921).

32. S.P.W., II, 45 (June 11, 1921); also S.P.W., II, 59 (July 21, 1921), and 257-259 (July 27, 1921).

33. S.P.W., II, 63-65 (August 25, 1921). See also S.F. 544-546 (August 9, 1921) for an argument about the political repercussions of the past.

34. Quoted in S.F. 301 (August 26, 1921). Gramsci's early perception of the division within fascism between its largely petty bourgeois mass base and its financial backing by big business is confirmed by the recent study of Roland Sarti, *Fascism and the Industrial Leadership in Italy, 1919-1940* (Berkeley: University of California Press, 1971), p. 113.

35. S.F. 301.

36. Ibid.

37. S.F. 494 (May 23, 1922). For Gramsci's perception of fascism that spring, see also S.F. 465-467 (March 4, 1922), and S.P.W., II, 87 (May 5, 1922).

38. S.P.W., II, 129-131 (November 20, 1922).

39. S.P.W., II, 340-375 (January 1926), 441-462 (late 1926); the prison discussions are most extensively reported in Athos Lisa, *Memorie: In carcere con Gramsci* (Milan: Feltrinelli, 1973), pp. 81-103. In the *Prison Notebooks*, Gramsci goes back even further and connects fascism with the larger groups of petty bourgeoisie formed by the disintegration in the early modern era of those smaller cities of the Northern Italian interior dubbed by D'Annunzio the "cities of silence"; see S.P.N. 131, or Q.C. 1560 (1932).

40. S.P.W., II, 129-130.

41. See Martin Kitchen, "Thalheimer's Theory of Fascism," *Journal of the History of Ideas*, 34:1 (January-March 1973), 67-78. For a later statement clearly linking fascism's victory in 1922 with the proletariat's defeat in 1920, see S.P.W., II, 349 (January 1926).

42. He was exploring this parallel as late as February 19, 1922; see S.F. 497.

43. The textual evidence for this, however, comes only in the form of Gramsci's 1924 reflections on his earlier views; C.P.C. 163 (March 1, 1924).

44. For an illustration of this in the *Notebooks*, see Q.C. 1200-02 (1932).

45. Spriano, *Storia*, vol. I, p. 260.

46. Quoted in Fiori, *Antonio Gramsci*, p. 162.

47. The speech was reprinted in *Lo Stato Operaio*, 2:13 (April 24, 1924).

48. The manifesto is reprinted in "Nuovo documentazione sulla 'svolta' nella direzione del PCI nel 1923-1924," *Rivista storica del socialismo*, 7:23 (September-December 1964), 515-521. An English translation is available in Helmut Gruber, ed., *International Communism in the Era of Lenin* (Garden City, N.Y.: Doubleday, 1972), pp. 327-335.

49. S.P.W., II, 132-137 (May 1, 1923) and 138-142 (May 18, 1923).

50. This is clear from the "Lettera inedita per la fondazione de 'L'Unità,'" written September 12, 1923 and reprinted in *Rivista storica del socialismo*, 6:18 (January-April 1963), pp. 115-123 and in *Rinascita*, 21:6 (February 8, 1964), 25. See also S.P.W., II, 154-156 (June 1923).

51. "Lettera inedita per la fondazione de 'L'Unità,'" ibid.

52. S.P.W., II, 174 (January 5, 1924).

53. Quoted in Fiori, *Antonio Gramsci*, p. 167.

54. S.P.W., II, 154 (June 1923).

55. See *Rinascita*, 21:17 (April 25, 1964), 32. Gramsci's affection for Russia is also clear from his letters written to his wife after leaving Moscow for Vienna at the end of 1923. He noted, for instance, that "one experiences great distaste when

leaving proletarian for bourgeois territory." See Ferrata and Gallo, *2000 Pagine*, vol. II, p. 26 (December 16, 1923).

56. See Davidson, *Antonio Gramsci*, p. 227; and S.P.W., II, 408-411 (August 2-3, 1926).

57. S.P.W., I, 260 (June 5, 1920).

58. S.P.W., I, 305-309 (July 3, 1920).

59. S.P.W., I, 76 (July 12, 1919).

60. S.P.W., I, 336 (September 4, 1920).

61. See S.G. 230 (May 18, 1918); O.N. 379-380 (June 28, 1919); and S.P.W., I, 263 (June 5, 1920).

62. As Gramsci wrote in August 1926: "This means that even the gravest economic crises do not have immediate repercussions in the political sphere. Politics always lags, and lags far behind, economics" (S.P.W., II, 408-409).

63. S.P.W., II, 199-200 (February 9, 1924).

64. See Mario Garuglieri, "Ricordo di Gramsci," *Società*, 2:7-8 (July-December 1946), 692-693.

65. See *Ordine Nuovo*, March 1, 1924, p. 3.

66. See Chapter 7, below.

67. C.P.C. 25-28 (July 2, 1924); and S.P.W., II, 255-256 (September 1, 1924).

68. S.P.W., II, 275 (November 15, 1924).

69. See S.P.W., II, 409 (August 2-3, 1926), and especially Lisa, *Memorie*, p. 89.

70. S.P.W., II, 409-410.

71. Ibid.

72. Ibid.

73. Ibid.

74. S.P.W., II, 225 (April 1; 1924).

75. S.P.W., II, 314, 360, and 361 (January 1926). For an earlier statement, see *Lo Stato Operaio*, I:8 (October 18, 1923).

76. C.P.C. 299-301 (December 5, 1925); and S.P.W., II, 360.

77. S.P.W., II, 364, 367-368 (January 1926); 298 (May 11-12, 1925); and 387 (February 24, 1926).

78. C.P.C. 271-273 (August 15, 1925); and S.P.W., II, 315 and 363-364 (January 1926).

79. S.P.W., II, 363 (January 1926). Unfortunately this translation contains a crucial error. The sentence, "It is certain that the Communist Party can be solely a party of workers," should read "*cannot* be solely a party of workers." See C.P.C. 504.

80. S.P.W., II, 198 (February 9, 1924). For the operation of the party's new internal political education function, see C.P.C. 48-62 (April 1, 1925); and S.P.W., II, 391-392, 358, and 362 (January 1926).

81. This is no doubt largely responsible for Gramsci's persistent harping against "fractionalism" in this period. See S.P.W., II, 334, 364 (January 1926); and C.P.C. 238-306 (June 1925-January 1926), passim.

82. Cited in Salvadori, "Questione meridionale," p. 421; see also the citations in Spriano, *Storia*, vol. I, pp. 412 ff.; and *Lo Stato Operaio*, 1:8 (October 18, 1923), and 2:3 (March 1928), 82-88.

83. See Salvadori, "Questione meridionale," p. 419.

84. See his letter to Giulia (September 18, 1924), in Ferrata and Gallo, *2000 Pagine*, vol. II, p. 58.

85. C.P.C. 464-465 (October 21, 1924), and 206-207 (November 12, 1924).

86. C.P.C. 48-62 (April 1, 1925).

87. S.P.W., I, 375 (January 13, 1921).

88. S.P.W., II, 203 (February 9, 1924).

89. C.P.C. 478 (November 9-10, 1925).

90. For the text of the Lyons Theses, see S.P.W., II, 340-375. For a good discussion of how they were drafted and of their overall character, see Cammett, *Antonio Gramsci*, pp. 171-180.

91. S.P.W., II, 316 (January 1926).

92. S.P.W., II, 462; or M.P. 51 (1926).

93. S.P.W., II, 454; or M.P. 42 (1926).

94. Ibid.

95. S.P.W., II, 456; or M.P. 45.

96. S.P.W., II, 454; or M.P. 43.

97. S.P.W., II, 455; or M.P. 43.

98. S.P.W., II, 455-456; or M.P. 44.

99. S.P.W., II, 456; or M.P. 44-45.

100. S.P.W., II, 459; or M.P. 47.

101. S.P.W., II, 460; or M.P. 48.

102. See Chapter 7, below.

103. S.P.W., II, 290 (April 1925).

104. A good example is Gramsci's translation of the Comintern slogan "worker and peasant government" into the strategy of worker-peasant committees and class alliance aimed at a "federal republic of workers and peasants." See also Davidson, *Antonio Gramsci*, pp. 220 and 236.

105. See S.P.N. 341, or Q.C. 1393 (1932); and Chapter 7, below.

106. C.P.C. 456 (June 1923). The passage is quite clearly directed against Bordiga.

107. S.P.W., II, 358 (January 1926).

108. S.P.W., II, 426-432 (October 1926).

109. Ibid., pp. 427-428.

110. Lisa, *Memorie*. See also Giovanni Lay, "Colloqui con Gramsci nel carcere de Turi," *Rinascita*, 22:8 (February 20, 1965), 21-22; Gustavo Trombetti, "'Piantone' di Gramsci nel carcere di Turi," *Rinascita*, 22:18 (May 1, 1965), 31-32; and Mario Garuglieri, "Ricordo," pp. 692-693. For critical discussions of these reports, see Cammett, *Antonio Gramsci*, pp. 182-186; Fiori, *Antonio Gramsci*, pp. 253-258; Lucio Colletti, "Antonio Gramsci and the Italian Revolution," *New Left Review*, 65 (January 1971), 87-94; and M.A. Macchiocchi, *Pour Gramsci* (Paris: Editions du Seuil, 1974), chaps. 1-3.

111. On this history, see Spriano, *Storia*, vol. II, pp. 3-307. For an interesting recent analysis of the Comintern in this period, see Fernando Claudín, *The Communist Movement: From Comintern to Cominform*, trans. B. Pierce and F. MacDonagh (London: Peregrine, 1975), pp. 46-293.

112. Lisa, *Memorie*, pp. 85-86.

113. S.P.N. 341; or Q.C. 1393 (1932).

114. Spriano, *Storia*, vol. II, p. 41.

115. S.P.N. 145; or Q.C. 1753 (1933).

116. See Fiori, *Antonio Gransci*, pp. 252-253.

117. Paolo Spriano, *Gramsci in carcere e il partito* (Rome: Riuniti, 1977), pp. 48-51 and passim. The key documents upon which Spriano relies are the recent testimony of Luigi Longo (in M.P. Quercioli, ed., *Gramsci vivo* [Milan: Feltrinelli, 1977], p. 76), Bruno Tosin (in Bruno Tosin, *Con Gramsci* [Rome: Riuniti, 1976], p. 95), and Togliatti's letter of August 27, 1930 to Giuseppe Berti (quoted at length by Spriano on pp. 49-50).

118. S.P.W., II, 252-253 (May 29, 1924). See also S.P.W., II, 284 (February 6, 1925). For a full discussion of Gramsci's relation to Trotsky, see Giancarlo Bergami, "Sui rapporti tra Gramsci e Trotsky," *Rivista di storia contemporanea*, 7:4 (October 1978), 559-585.

119. See the resolution against Trotskyism approved by the PCI Central

Committee on February 6, 1925, and now reprinted in Silverio Corvisieri, *Trotskij e il comunismo italiano* (Rome: Samona e Savelli, 1969), pp. 185-191.

120. C.P.C. 211-212 (November 19, 1924).

121. S.P.W., II, 432 (October 1926).

122. Some of those who would accuse Gramsci of "totalitarianism" have concentrated too heavily on the 1923-26 years and have failed to explore his response to the "turn." See, for instance, Thomas R. Bates, "Antonio Gramsci and the Bolshevization of the PCI," *Journal of Contemporary History*, 11:2/3 (1976), 115-131. See also Chapter 7, below.

123. The key analysis is by Alfonso Leonetti, who, though perhaps overly sympathetic to Trotsky, did know Gramsci well in this period. See his *Note su Gramsci*, pp. 181-208. See also M.A. Macchiocchi, *Pour Gramsci*, pp. 94-97, 100n.*2*, and 106n.*6*; and Spriano, *Storia*, vol. II, pp. 267-279.

124. S.P.N. 240; or Q.C. 1729 (1933).

125. S.P.N. 238; or Q.C. 801-802 (1931).

126. S.P.N. 237; or Q.C. 866 (1931).

127. Leonetti, *Note su Gramsci*, pp. 183-184.

128. See Lenin's obituary in *L'Ordine Nuovo*, March 1, 1924, p. 3.

129. See Chapter 4, below. Given the sharp opposition between the philosophical views of Lenin and Gramsci, it would be interesting to know what Gramsci knew of Lenin's philosophical writings. While there is no evidence that he knew of *Materialism and Empirio-criticism* (the bibliography on Lenin in the March 1, 1924 *Ordine Nuovo* lists it as *Marxism and Empirio-criticism*), he may have known something of the *Philosophical Notebooks*. For in March 1925, during a meeting of the EKKI that Gramsci attended, the first issue of the theoretical journal *Bolshevik* was published containing the crucial chapter "On the Question of Dialectics."

130. S.P.W., II, 298 (May 11-12, 1925). The fourth of these is the only one which, in the words of Alastair Davidson, is "capable of being understood as 'Leninist' in the sense applied to the word by the post-Leninist communist world." Yet, as Davidson convincingly argues, Gramsci's method of obtaining discipline depended on suasion rather than expulsion or coercion. See Davidson, *Antonio Gramsci*, pp. 235-236.

131. Quoted in Fiori, *Antonio Gramsci*, p. 230.

Chapter 4

1. Letter to Tania, L.F.P. 79 (March 19, 1927). The German phrase means "for eternity."

2. S.P.N. 462; or Q.C. 1434 (1932).

3. S.P.N. 462-463; or Q.C. 1434-35 (1932).

4. See S.P.N. 327; or Q.C. 1379 (1932).

5. See Lisa, *Memorie*, and Christine Buci-Glucksmann, *Gramsci et L'État* (Paris: Fayard, 1975), pp. 250-312.

6. See S.P.N. 199, or Q.C. 331 (1930); also S.P.N. 323-325, 327, or Q.C. 1375-79; S.P.N. 330-332, or Q.C. 1383-84 (1932); and the various linkages of "gnoseology" and "hegemony" (S.P.N. 357, or Q.C. 886; S.P.N. 365, or Q.C. 1249-50; all 1932).

7. See Nicholas Lobkowicz, *Theory and Practice* (South Bend, Ind.: University of Notre Dame Press, 1967), pp. 3-57.

8. G. W. F. Hegel, *The Phenomenology of Mind*, trans. J. B. Baillie (London: George Allen and Unwin, 1931). See the section entitled "The Spirit in Self-Estrangement: The Discipline of Culture," especially pp. 519-536.

9. Ibid., pp. 533-536.

10. Ibid.

11. See G.W.F. Hegel, *Hegel's Philosophy of Right*, trans. T.M. Knox (London: Oxford University Press, 1967), p. 11.

12. Although directed explicitly against eighteenth-century materialism, the third *Thesis on Feuerbach* is incompatible with any view advocating the use of outside "educators." The critique of Hegel's view of philosophy is developed above all in *The Holy Family*. Consider the following passage cited by Georg Lukács, *History and Class Consciousness*, trans. R. Livingstone (Cambridge, Mass.: MIT Press, 1971), p. 16:

> For, as absolute spirit does not appear in the mind of the philosopher in the shape of the creative world-spirit until after the event, it follows that it makes history only in the consciousness, the opinions, the ideas of the philosophers, only in the speculative imagination.

13. On the former, see the discussion in Georg Lukács, *The Young Hegel*, trans. R. Livingstone (Cambridge, Mass.: MIT Press, 1976), pp. 319-337. For a good discussion of the latter, see George A. Kelly, *Hegel's Retreat from Eleusis* (Princeton, N.J.: Princeton University Press, 1978), chap. 2.

14. Cited in Lukács, *History and Class Consciousness*, p. 16.

15. Helmut Fleischer, *Marxism and History*, trans. E. Mosbacher (New York: Harper and Row, 1973), pp. 11-37. Fleischer, however, goes too far when he suggests (pp. 16-17, 23-24) that these approaches to history can be treated as separate phases in Marx's intellectual development. For there is some temporal overlap even though the first is dominant in the pre-1845 period, the second is dominant in 1845-46 and recurrent thereafter, and the last becomes pronounced only in 1859 and after.

16. See L.D. Easton and K.H. Guddat, eds., *Writings of the Young Marx on Philosophy and Society* (Garden City, N.Y.: Doubleday, 1967), pp. 325-326. This book will henceforth be cited as Y.M.

17. See Shlomo Avineri, *The Social and Political Thought of Karl Marx* (London: Cambridge University Press, 1968), chap. 3; and Bertell Ollman, *Alienation* (London: Cambridge University Press, 1971), chap. 7.

18. Y.M. 414.

19. Y.M. 291.

20. Y.M. 368.

21. See the discussion in Jürgen Habermas, *Knowledge and Human Interests*, trans. J. Schapiro (Boston: Beacon Press, 1971), pp. 25-42.

22. For a clear statement embodying this image, see Y.M. 214. I discuss this image more fully in my "Marx and Political Education," *The Review of Politics*, 39:3 (July 1977), 363-385.

23. Robert Tucker, ed., *The Marx-Engels Reader* (New York: Norton, 1972), pp. 399 ff.

24. See, for instance, Lewis A. Coser, "Marxist Thought in the First Quarter of the 20th Century," *American Journal of Sociology*, 78 (July 1972), 173-201; Andrew Arato, "The Second International: A Reexamination," *Telos*, 18 (Winter 1973-74), 2-52; Lucio Colletti, "The Marxism of the Second International," *Telos*, 8 (Summer 1971), 84-91, and his "Bernstein and the Marxism of the Second International," in *From Rousseau to Lenin* (New York: Monthly Review Press, 1972), pp. 45-108; Peter Gay, *The Dilemma of Democratic Socialism* (New York: Columbia University Press, 1952); James Joll, *The Second International* (New York: Harper and Row, 1966); and Carl E. Schorske, *German Social Democracy, 1905-1917* (Cambridge, Mass.: Harvard University Press, 1955).

25. Karl Korsch, *Marxism and Philosophy*, trans. F. Halliday (New York: Monthly Review Press, 1970), p. 33.

26. V.I. Lenin, *Materialism and Empirio-criticism* (Moscow: Foreign Languages Press, 1962), especially chap. 1. The major exception was Antonio

Labriola, a professor of philosophy and an Hegelian well before turning to Marxism; see below.

27. For the document itself, see Felix Salomon, *Die deutschen Parteiprogramme* (Leipzig: B. G. Teubner, 1907). For a good discussion of the program, see Schorske, *German Social Democracy*, pp. 4-8.

28. In schematizing this history I do not mean to assimilate Luxemburg's Marxism, with its not inconsiderable dialectical propensity, to the mechanicism of mainline Social Democratic theoreticians like Kautsky. Nonetheless, as nearly all her interpreters have suggested, there is considerable tension between her simultaneous stresses on economic determinism and proletarian subjectivity. See J. P. Nettl, *Rosa Luxemburg*, 2 vols. (London: Oxford University Press, 1966), vol. I, p. 217; Dick Howard, "Rereading Luxemburg," *Telos*, 18 (Winter 1973-74), 98; and Arato, "The Second International," p. 15.

29. For Bernstein's treatment of political education, see his *Evolutionary Socialism* (New York: Schocken Books, 1971), pp. 125, 161, and 187. A good secondary treatment of Bernstein, especially of the influence on him by English Fabianism, can be found in Gay, *Dilemma of Democratic Socialism.*

30. V.I. Lenin, *What Is to Be Done?* (New York: International Publishers, 1969).

31. Labriola's main works of interest here are contained in the *Saggi sul materialismo storico*, ed. V. Gerratana and A. Guerra (Rome: Riuniti, 1964). The essays are: *In memoria del Manifesto dei Comunisti* (1895); *Del materialismo storico. Delucidazione preliminare* (1896); *Discorrendo di socialismo e di filosofia* (1898-99); *Storia, filosofia della storia, sociologia e materialismo storico* (based on University of Rome lectures, 1902-03, completed just before Labriola's death in 1904, and published posthumously); and *Da un secolo all'altro* (based on lectures, 1901-02, but never completed). The first two of these have been translated as *Essays on the Materialistic Conception of History*, trans. C. H. Kerr (Chicago: Charles H. Kerr, 1908); the third is translated as *Socialism and Philosophy*, trans. E. Untermann (Chicago: Charles H. Kerr, 1918). For fuller discussions of Labriola, see Francesco de Aloysio, *Studi sul pensiero di Antonio Labriola* (Rome: Carucci, 1976); Valentino Gerratana, "Marxismo ortodosso e marxismo aperto in Antonio Labriola," in *Annali Feltrinelli 1973*, vol. 15 (Milan, 1974), pp. 554-580; and Paul Piccone, "Labriola and the Roots of Eurocommunism," *Berkeley Journal of Sociology*, 22 (1977-78), 3-43.

32. Labriola, *Socialism and Philosophy*, p. 95.

33. S.P.N. 390; or Q.C. 1855 (1933).

34. Labriola, *Socialism and Philosophy*, pp. 42-43 and 59-62; for the criticism of Loria, see Labriola, *Essays*, pp. 69-70; for Loria's own view, see his *Carlo Marx* (Genoa: A.F. Formiggini, 1916).

35. Labriola, *Essays*, p. 25; see also Nicola Badaloni, *Il Marxismo di Gramsci* (Turin: Einaudi, 1975), chap. 1.

36. Labriola, *Socialism and Philosophy*, pp. 65-66; see also Enzo Paci, *The Function of the Sciences and the Meaning of Man*, trans. P. Piccone and J.E. Hanson (Evanston, Ill.: Northwestern University Press, 1972), pp. 305-310. Gramsci followed Labriola in this assumption; see S.P.N. 446, or Q.C. 1416 and 1457 (1932).

37. See especially Labriola, *Essays*, pp. 113-114, 201-202. Tronti puts the point well when he writes: "Labriola is not on positivist terrain, but neither is he on terrain directly opposite to positivism, as Croce and Gentile will be from the start" (Mario Tronti, "Tra materialismo dialettico e filosofia della prassi: Gramsci e Labriola," in *La Città Futura*, ed. A. Caracciolo and G. Scalia [Milan: Feltrinelli, 1959], p. 148).

38. Labriola, *Essays*, p. 208. Labriola's attitude toward "political education"

was entirely typical of the Second International. He appreciated its virtues in building socialist organization, but he denied any link between "philosophy" and "political education," in part on the grounds that not everyone was fit for philosophy. This contrasts sharply with Gramsci's thesis of philosophy as political education, as Gramsci himself later recognized (Q.C. 1366-68; 1932). See Labriola, *Socialism and Philosophy*, p. 14; and his letter to Pasquale Villari of November 13, 1900, in Antonio Labriola, *Scritti Politici 1886-1904*, ed. V. Gerratana (Bari: Laterza, 1970), pp. 463-464.

39. For the recommendation, see Labriola, *Socialism and Philosophy*, pp. 53 and 149. For the hesitations, see Labriola, *Socialism and Philosophy*, p. 49; and his letter to Engels of June 13, 1894, where he politely suggests replacing the word *dialectical* with *genetic* in order to indicate that the term has both a "formal-logical" meaning *and* embraces the real content of things which become" (*Lettere a Engels* [Rome: Rinascita, 1949], p. 147). This does suggest a very cautious criticism of Engels, who had reduced dialectic to something like a "formal-logical" method, but the overwhelming tone of Labriola's letters to Engels is one of immense respect bordering on reverence.

40. Labriola, *Socialism and Philosophy*, p. 124; Labriola, *Essays*, p. 201.

41. Q.C. 1366-68 (1932).

42. For Labriola's anti-idealist statements, see, for instance, Labriola, *Essays*, pp. 113, 124, 132, 153; for his anti-positivist statements, see pp. 114, 119, 120, 121, 140, 211, 217, 218, and 228 in the same volume.

43. Labriola, *Essays*, pp. 114, 156, and 160.

44. Labriola, *Socialism and Philosophy*, p. 13.

45. Labriola, *Saggi*, p. 358.

46. Ibid., pp. 321, 355, 368.

47. Ibid., p. 345.

48. Ibid., pp. 321, 324. However, Labriola took great pains to distinguish his view from Croce's notion of "history as art." Noting that the word *history* has two very different senses (as a series of events and as the narration of those events by the historian), Labriola argued that the first kind of history leaves traces (documents, monuments) which can be recovered through rigorous ("scientific") inquiry, but that the subsequent narration of results is necessarily more subjective and intuitive.

49. Ibid., p. 339.

50. Croce himself believed that Labriola had abandoned Marxism and socialism after 1900; see Croce's "Come nacque e come morì il marxismo teorico in Italia," in Antonio Labriola, *La Concezione materialistica della storia*, ed. E. Garin (Bari: Laterza, 1953), p. 312. However, more recent research into Labriola's political writings in this period has shown that this is not the case. See Giuliano Procacci, "Antonio Labriola e la revisione del marxismo attraverso l'epistolario con Bernstein e con Kautsky, 1895-1904," in *Annali Feltrinelli, 1960*, vol. 3 (Milan, 1961), pp. 274-275.

51. A. Pannekoek and H. Gorter, *Organisation und Taktik der Proletarischen Revolution*, ed. H. Bock (Frankfurt: Neue Kritik, 1969), p. 224.

52. A. Pannekoek, "Massenaktion und Revolution," in *Die Massenstreikdebatte*, ed. A. Grunenberg (Frankfurt: Eurpäische Verlagsanstalt, 1970), p. 266. For a recent selection of and commentary on Pannekoek's writings in English, see Serge Bricianer, *Pannekoek and the Workers' Councils*, trans. M. Carroll (St. Louis: Telos Press, 1978).

53. Pannekoek, "Massenaktion," p. 284.

54. Indeed, while he opposed Lenin's politics, Pannekoek's major philosophical statement, like Lenin's, flew in the face of his own conception of political education; see Pannekoek, *Marxism and Darwinism*, trans. N. Weiser (Chicago: Charles Kerr, 1912).

55. Our discussion of this highly complex work must necessarily be schematic; for fuller treatments, see István Mészáros, *Lukács' Concept of Dialectic* (London: Merlin Press, 1972); and George Lichtheim, *Georg Lukács* (New York: Viking Press, 1970).

56. Lukács, *History and Class Consciousness*, pp. 1 and 27. For the same point in Labriola, see his *Socialism and Philosophy*, pp. 42-43.

57. Lukács's central illustration here was a passage drawn from Marx's *Wage Labor and Capital*:

> A negro is a negro. He only becomes a slave in certain circumstances. A cotton-spinning jenny is a machine for spinning cotton. Only in certain circumstances does it become capital. Torn from those circumstances it is no more capital than gold is money or sugar the price of sugar.

58. For this and other evidences that Lukács was recapturing Marx's anthropological dialectic, see *History and Class Consciousness*, pp. 8, 40, 99, and 177. Lukács did offer a strong criticism of Feuerbachian anthropology (pp. 186-187), and may not have been fully aware at the time of how his own concept of "reification" depended on an anthropological grounding.

59. For Lukács's concept of "objective necessity," see *History and Class Consciousness*, pp. 178 and 197-198.

60. Ibid., pp. 159-172.

61. Ibid., p. 172. Emphasis added.

62. Ibid., p. 21.

63. Ibid., p. xxiii.

64. Ibid., p. 299.

65. Ibid., pp. 304 and 326. One year later, in his *Lenin: A Study in the Unity of his Thought*, trans. N. Jacobs (London: New Left Books, 1970), Lukács opted openly for Bolshevism.

66. See Lichtheim, *Georg Lukács*, p. 45; and Paul Piccone, "The Problem of Consciousness," *Telos*, 5 (Fall 1970), 187.

67. S.P.N. 448; or Q.C. 1449 (1932). This same criticism of Lukács was developed later by Theodor Adorno, according to two of the latter's recent interpreters. See Susan Buck-Morss, *The Origin of Negative Dialectics* (New York: MacMillan Free Press, 1977), pp. 48-49 and 55-56; and Martin Jay, "The Concept of Totality in Lukács and Adorno," *Telos*, 32 (Summer 1977), 133. However, neither author cites any specific passages from Adorno to support the point.

68. It has sometimes been speculated that Gramsci met Lukács in Vienna in 1924, but this seems unlikely since Gramsci never even mentioned Lukács at that time and his only discussion of Lukács in the *Notebooks* is the brief passage just cited.

69. As Secretary-General of the PCI, Gramsci almost certainly knew of Korsch, who was a member of the KPD central committee in 1924 and a left-wing oppositionalist by late 1925. But we have no evidence that he knew anything of Korsch's theoretical writings. Bordiga corresponded with Korsch in the 1925-26 period concerning Soviet politics and left-opposition tactics, but questions of theory and philosophy were not raised. See Bordiga's letter of October 28, 1926, reprinted in Bordiga, *Scritti scelti*, pp. 197-200.

70. H.P.C. 123 (November 24, 1917); for Korsch on the "genuine Marx," see *Marxism and Philosophy*, p. 56; for Lukács, see *History and Class Consciousness*, pp. 77-78.

71. H.P.C. 123; see also S.P.W., I, 28-30 (April 29, 1917) and 48-55 (July 27, 1918).

72. S.P.W., II, 340-341 (January 1926).

73. S.P.W., II, 341.

74. S.P.N. 397; or Q.C. 1862 (1933).
75. Ibid.
76. Ibid.
77. S.P.N. 337; or Q.C. 1389 (1932).
78. S.P.N. 389; or Q.C. 1854-55 (1933).
79. Gramsci nonetheless admired many thinkers and activists in this period, especially Daniel DeLeon, the American socialist. See S.P.W., I, 296 (August 28, 1920).
80. Nicolai Bukharin, *Historical Materialism: A System of Sociology* (Ann Arbor: University of Michigan Press, 1969).
81. Q.C. 1233 (1932).
82. Leonardo Paggi, "Gramsci's General Theory of Marxism," *Telos*, 33 (Fall 1977), 41. For a contrasting interpretation of this text which misses the interpolations, see Buci-Glucksmann, *Gramsci et L'État*, p. 281.
83. S.P.N. 419, or Q.C. 1396; S.P.N. 426, or Q.C. 1432; S.P.N. 429, or Q.C. 1430 (all 1932).
84. See Karel Kosík's discussion of this point in "Gramsci et la Philosophie de la Praxis," *Praxis*, 3:3 (1967), 328-332.
85. S.P.N. 419; or Q.C. 1396 (1932).
86. Ibid.
87. S.P.N. 323-325; or Q.C. 1375-78 (1932). For a full discussion of this point, see Chapter 5, below.
88. S.P.N. 348; or Q.C. 1330 (1932).
89. S.P.N. 347; or Q.C. 1342 (1932).
90. Ibid.
91. For Gramsci's view of language, see S.P.N. 323, or Q.C. 1375; S.P.N. 327-328, or Q.C. 1379-80; and S.P.N. 450, or Q.C. 1438 (1932); see also his early article on Esperanto in H.P.C. 29-33 (February 16, 1918).
92. S.P.N. 344; or Q.C. 1255 (1932).
93. For the distinction between "traditional" and "organic" intellectuals, see Chapter 5, below.
94. S.P.N. 445, or Q.C. 1415; S.P.N. 436, or Q.C. 1401-02 (1932).
95. S.P.N. 445; or Q.C. 1415-16 (1932).
96. S.P.N. 409-410, or Q.C. 855 (1930). See also S.P.N. 106, or Q.C. 1774; S.P.N. 177, or Q.C. 1579 (1933); S.P.N. 367n., or Q.C. 1244; S.P.N. 432, or Q.C. 1422; and S.P.N. 459-460, or Q.C. 1440 (1932).
97. This view might seem to bring Gramsci close to a pragmatist position, yet he was critical of American pragmatism for its rather apolitical concept of practice. See Q.C. 1925-26 (1933).
98. S.P.N. 445-446; or Q.C. 1416 (1932).
99. S.P.N. 412; or Q.C. 1478 (1930).
100. S.P.N. 428, or Q.C. 1429; S.P.N. 438, or Q.C. 1404 (1932).
101. S.P.N. 428; or Q.C. 1429.
102. S.P.N. 438; or Q.C. 1403.
103. See Badaloni (*Il Marxismo di Gramsci*), who has made the strongest case for Sorel's influence on Gramsci's conception of Marxism; however, there is also no doubt that Gramsci's orientation toward Sorel was intensely critical (e.g., see Q.C. 447 [1930]; and S.P.N. 395, or Q.C. 1860 [1933]) and that he accorded him only a small fraction of the attention he accorded Croce.
104. Q.C. 1233 (1932).
105. S.P.W., I, 75-76 (July 12, 1919); S.P.N. 127n., or Q.C. 1557 (1932).
106. S.P.N. 171; or Q.C. 1810 (1933).
107. S.P.N. 413; or Q.C. 1480 (1930).
108. S.P.N. 412-413; or Q.C. 1479-80 (1930).

109. For critical studies of Croce's philosophy and its relation to Gramsci, see Emilio Agazzi, "Filosofia della prassi e filosofia dello spirito," in *La Città Futura*, ed. A. Caracciolo and G. Scalia (Milan: Feltrinelli, 1959), pp. 187-270; Giacinto Lentini, *Croce e Gramsci* (Rome: Mori, 1967); Emilio Agazzi, *Il Giovane Croce e il Marxismo* (Turin: Einaudi, 1962); and Carlo Carini, *Benedetto Croce e il Partito Politico* (Florence: Olschki, 1975). For studies in English of Croce's philosophy, see Hayden White, *Metahistory* (Baltimore: Johns Hopkins University Press, 1973), chap. 10; L.M. Palmer and H.S. Harris, eds., *Thought, Action and Intuition as a Symposium on the Philosophy of Benedetto Croce* (New York: Georg Olms, 1975); and H. Wildon Carr, *The Philosophy of Benedetto Croce* (London: MacMillan, 1927).

110. Letter to Tania, L.F.P. 233 (April 25, 1932).

111. Ibid.

112. Letter to Giulia, L.F.P. 162-163 (December 30, 1929). See also Gramsci's criticism of Croce's concept of "spirit": S.P.N. 371; or Q.C. 1250 (1932-33).

113. For Croce's dialectic, see especially his *What Is Living and What Is Dead of the Philosophy of Hegel*, trans. D. Ainslee (London: MacMillan, 1915).

114. S.P.N. 356; or Q.C. 886 (1932).

115. Q.C. 1240, 1229-30 and 1225; S.P.N. 356, or Q.C. 886 (1932).

116. S.P.N. 450; or Q.C. 1438 (1932).

117. Q.C. 1236 (1932); see also Q.C. 1282 (1932). Gramsci always credited Croce, rather than Bernstein, Sorel, or Loria, with having led the bourgeois assault on Marxism in the 1890s; see Q.C. 1207 (1932).

118. See Benedetto Croce, *Teoria e storia della storiografia* (Bari: Laterza, 1954).

119. Q.C. 1815 (1933).

120. Q.C. 1983 (1934).

121. S.P.N. 403; or Q.C. 1493 (1932-33).

122. S.P.N. 138; or Q.C. 1570 (1932).

123. S.P.N. 406; or Q.C. 1489 (1932-33).

124. S.P.N. 465; or Q.C. 1437 (1932).

125. S.P.N. 455; or Q.C. 1409 (1932).

126. S.P.N. 396; or Q.C. 1861 (1933).

127. S.P.N. 402; or Q.C. 1248 (1932).

128. S.P.N. 465; or Q.C. 1437 (1932).

129. S.P.N. 329; or Q.C. 1381 (1932).

130. Ibid.

131. S.P.N. 371; or Q.C. 1477 (1932-33).

132. S.P.N. 133; or Q.C. 1598-99 (1933).

133. S.P.N. 460; or Q.C. 1441 (1932).

134. Karl Marx and Friedrich Engels, *Basic Writings on Politics and Philosophy*, ed. L. Feuer (Garden City, N.Y.: Doubleday, 1959), p. 43.

135. Ibid., p. 44. For Gramsci's discussion of the first passage, see S.P.N. 138, or Q.C. 1570; S.P.N. 162, or Q.C. 1592; S.P.N. 365, or Q.C. 1249 (all 1932); and S.P.N. 371, or Q.C. 1492 (1932-33). For the second, see S.P.N. 106, or Q.C. 1774; S.P.N. 177, or Q.C. 1579 (all 1933); S.P.N. 367, or Q.C. 1274 (1932); S.P.N. 409-410, or Q.C. 855 (1930); and S.P.N. 432, or Q.C. 1422 (1932).

136. S.P.N. 372; or Q.C. 1492 (1932-33).

137. S.P.N. 279; or Q.C. 2139 (1934).

138. S.P.N. 292, or Q.C. 2156; S.P.N. 279, or Q.C. 2139 (1934).

139. S.P.N. 296; or Q.C. 2150 (1934).

140. S.P.N. 303, or Q.C. 2165; S.P.N. 317, or Q.C. 2179 (1934).

141. Jean-Paul Sartre, *Search for a Method*, trans. H. Barnes (New York: *Random House, 1963), p. 32n9.*

142. S.P.N. 354, or Q.C. 1346; S.P.N. 352, or Q.C. 1345 (1932).

143. S.P.N. 352; or Q.C. 1345 (1932).
144. S.P.N. 404; or Q.C. 1487 (1932-33).
145. S.P.N. 352; or Q.C. 1345 (1932).
146. S.P.N. 353; or Q.C. 1345-46 (1932). This discussion makes it apparent that Gramsci held a version of the philosophy of "internal relations" as described by Ollman, *Alienation*, pp. 12-42. Yet, unlike the ontology of pure relations which Ollman finds in Marx, Gramsci's version entails (1) the ontological independence of individuals, even as they are embedded in social relations; and (2) a view of the totality as *both* the structures of experience at any particular moment *and* the genetic development of those structures. This version, then, is much closer to the view of Marx held by Carol Gould in *Marx's Social Ontology* (Cambridge, Mass.: MIT Press, 1978).
147. S.P.N. 352; or Q.C. 1345.
148. S.P.N. 441; or Q.C. 1411-12 (1932).
149. See R.J. Bernstein, *Praxis and Action* (Philadelphia: University of Pennsylvania Press, 1971), p. 74.
150. S.P.N. 443; or Q.C. 1414 (1932).
151. While Gramsci spoke of "needs and interests" (S.P.N. 368, or Q.C. 1291), he made no effort to explore the relationship between the two concepts, and he elaborated his view mainly in terms of the category of "interest." Certainly, his discussion bears no consciousness of the more recent debate between partisans of phenomenology and those of Habermasian critical theory as to whether "need" or "interest" is the better grounding for a theory of knowledge. For a discussion of this issue in relation to Marx's work, see Agnes Heller, *The Theory of Need in Marx* (New York: St. Martin's Press, 1976), especially pp. 58-66. For a phenomenological critique of Habermas, see Pier Aldo Rovatti, "Critical Theory and Phenomenology," *Telos*, 15 (Spring 1973), 25-40.
152. S.P.N. 368; or Q.C. 1290-91 (1932).
153. Cf. Jürgen Habermas, *Knowledge and Human Interests*, trans. J.J. Schapiro (Boston: Beacon Press, 1968), p. 308 and passim.
154. S.P.N. 382, or Q.C. 882 (1933); S.P.N. 242, or Q.C. 1566 (1932); S.P.N. 317, or Q.C. 2178-79 (1934); and S.P.N. 388, or Q.C. 1509 (1933).
155. S.P.N. 407, or Q.C. 1490 (1932-33); also Q.C. 1233 (1932).
156. S.P.N. 445-446; or Q.C. 1416 (1932). See also the reference (S.P.N. 445) to "the process of historical unification" which "takes place" through the disappearance of the internal contradictions which tear apart human society.
157. S.P.N. 407, or Q.C. 1490 (1932-33); S.P.N. 462, or Q.C. 1434-35 (1932).
158. S.P.N. 470-471; or Q.C. 1450 (1932).
159. S.P.N. 471n.; or Q.C. 1426 (1932).
160. S.P.N. 368; or Q.C. 1291 (1932).
161. S.P.N. 388; or Q.C. 1509 (1933).
162. S.P.N. 355; or Q.C. 885 (1932).
163. S.P.N. 345; or Q.C. 1485 (1932).
164. S.P.N. 346; or Q.C. 1485 (1932).
165. S.P.N. 364-365; or Q.C. 1780 (1932).
166. S.P.N. 355; or Q.C. 884 (1932).
167. See Paci, *Function of Sciences*, pp. 311-316; and Paul Piccone, "Phenomenological Marxism," *Telos*, 9 (Fall 1971), 10n.*20*. Paci's account, provocative though it is, fails to persuade me that Gramsci held a concept of intentionality in Husserl's sense; rather, as we have seen, Gramsci dealt with the underlying structure of consciousness in terms of practical and scientific interests. Moreover, unlike Husserl, Gramsci did not conceive of subjectivity as itself constituting the object; rather, the process of constitution is mediated by action in the social world, i.e., by praxis.

168. In the next chapter, where we deal with Gramsci's understanding of the transition from "common sense" to "philosophy," this connection will become even more plausible. However, it will also become apparent that Gramsci did not pursue the phenomenological underpinnings of political education very deeply.

169. See Fred Dallmayr, "Phenomenology and Marxism: A Salute to Enzo Paci," in George Psathas, *Phenomenological Sociology* (New York: John Wiley, 1973), pp. 305-356; and James Miller, "Merleau-Ponty's Marxism: Between Phenomenology and the Hegelian Absolute," *History and Theory*, 15:2 (1976), 109-132.

170. Piccone, "Phenomenological Marxism," p. 11.

171. Miller, "Merleau-Ponty's Marxism," p. 118.

172. See Q.C. 1449 (1932).

173. See Badaloni, *Il Marxismo di Gramsci*, especially chaps. 3-6.

174. S.P.N. 387; or Q.C. 1507-08 (1932).

175. See Labriola, *Socialism and Philosophy*, pp. 42-43.

176. Ibid., pp. 62 and 74.

177. Ibid., pp. 60-61.

178. Ibid., p. 65.

179. Whatever one may think of the general merits of Althusser's theoretical project, his failure to recognize these distinctions—and thus to draw the conclusion that Gramsci had no theory of human nature in the "humanist" sense that Althusser is criticizing—considerably mars his interpretation of Gramsci; see Louis Althusser, "Marxism Is Not a Historicism," in L. Althusser and E. Balibar, *Reading Capital*, trans. B. Brewster (London: New Left Books, 1970), pp. 119-144.

Chapter 5

1. See Gramsci's discussion of the "three moments" in the development of revolution, in S.P.N. 180-183, or Q.C. 1583-86 (1932).

2. S.P.N. 313-316; or Q.C. 2175-78 (1934).

3. S.P.N. 184; or Q.C. 1587 (1932).

4. S.P.N. 210; or Q.C. 1603 (1932).

5. S.P.N. 168; or Q.C. 1612 (1932). Emphasis added.

6. S.P.N. 350; or Q.C. 1331 (1932). Emphasis added.

7. S.P.N. 10; or Q.C. 1517 (1932).

8. S.P.N. 388; or Q.C. 1509 (1933).

9. S.P.N. 462, or Q.C. 1434 (1932); see also S.P.N. 33, or Q.C. 1537-38 (1932).

10. Q.C. 33 (1929-30).

11. See S.P.N. 12, or Q.C. 1518-19 (1932); and S.P.N. 419, or Q.C. 1396 (1932).

12. S.P.N. 5; or Q.C. 1513 (1932).

13. S.P.N. 7; or Q.C. 1515 (1932).

14. This is by no means as simple a process as this summary statement might suggest. Rather, it is a complicated coordination "of the form and the quality of the relations between the various intellectually qualified strata" (S.P.N. 341), which may take several generations to be achieved.

The early *Notebooks* in particular reveal a great deal of reading about Western European intellectuals, e.g., Julien Benda. See, for instance, *Quaderno*, 3 (1930), 283-289, 295-296, 297-299, 304-307, 353-373, 396-400, and 402-411.

15. S.P.N. 40; or Q.C. 1547-48 (1932).

16. S.P.N. 26; or Q.C. 1531 (1932).

17. S.P.N. 334; or Q.C. 1386 (1932).

18. S.P.N. 334-335; or Q.C. 1386.

19. S.P.N. 332-333; or Q.C. 1385.

20. Jürgen Habermas, *Theory and Practice*, trans. J. Viertel (Bsoton: Beacon Press, 1971), p. 40. Emphasis added.

21. For an elaboration of this point, see my "Beyond Reform or Revolution: Notes on Political Education in Gramsci, Habermas, and Arendt," *Theory and Society*, 6:3 (November 1978), 429-460.

22. S.P.N. 418; or Q.C. 1505 (1932-33).

23. Even though Croce's support for fascism was very ambiguous, and was recognized as such by Gramsci, it was Croce that he had most in mind here because of the persuasive power that Croce could have exercised but did not.

24. S.P.N. 331; or Q.C. 1383 (1932).

25. S.P.N. 339; or Q.C. 1390 (1932). Some students of Gramsci have misinterpreted this passage as an embrace of the idealist or Catholic view; see, for instance, Mihaly Vajda's review of the *Prison Notebooks*, in *Telos*, 15 (Spring 1973), 156.

26. S.P.N. 332; or Q.C. 1384 (1932). This view also contrasts sharply with Leninist paternalism.

27. See, for instance, his statement, already quoted above, which applauds Croce for his "unshakeable belief that . . . history is rational" (L.F.P. 233; April 25, 1932) or his "invitation to people to reflect and to realize fully that whatever happens is basically rational and must be confronted as such . . ." (S.P.N. 328, or Q.C. 1380 [1932]). See also Q.C. 767 (1931). Of course, Gramsci's psychological rationalism entailed no commitment to any ontological or methodological rationalism. He held an absolute historicism quite consistent with his psychological rationalism. For while he held that human nature was continually changing, he could still conceive of the variations within the limits of rational (means/ends) behavior.

28. See, for instance, Georg Lukács, *Die Zerstorung der Vernunft* (Berlin: Aufbau, 1954).

29. See the letter to Tania, L.C. 428 (March 20, 1931). The book was *Introduction à la Psychanalyse*. Gerratana indicates, however (Q.C. 2467), that this book has not been found among those that Gramsci had in jail.

30. Q.C. 288 (1930).

31. Ibid.

32. Q.C. 1833 (1933).

33. Ibid.

34. For an interesting treatment of Gramsci's view of Pirandello, and a fuller one then I can venture here, see Nikśa Stipcević, *Gramsci e i problemi lettarari* (Milan: Mursia, 1968), chap. 5.

35. Letter to Tania, L.F.P. 80 (March 19, 1927). Gramsci's theater criticism was written for the Turinese edition of *Avanti!* and has not been republished. For his views of Pirandello in the *Notebooks*, see especially Q.C. 1195-97 (1932) and 1670-73 (1932-33).

36. Letter to Tania, L.F.P. 80 (March 19, 1927).

37. S.P.N. 133; or Q.C. 1599 (1933).

38. S.P.N. 392; or Q.C. 1857-58 (1933).

39. S.P.N. 360; or Q.C. 1338 (1932).

40. For the concept of "hegemonic apparatus," see S.P.N. 228, or Q.C. 912 (1931).

41. S.P.N. 419; or Q.C. 1396 (1932).

42. Ibid.

43. S.P.N. 420; or Q.C. 1396 (1932).

44. S.P.N. 324; or Q.C. 1376 (1932).

45. Ibid.

46. S.P.N. 420, or Q.C. 1397; S.P.N. 326, or Q.C. 1378 (1932).

47. S.P.N. 326n.5; or Q.C. 2271 (1934).

48. S.P.N. 450; or Q.C. 1438 (1932).

49. S.P.N. 323; or Q.C. 1375 (1932).
50. S.P.N. 451; or Q.C. 1428 (1932).
51. S.P.N. 325; or Q.C. 1377 (1932).
52. S.P.N. 453, or Q.C. 1407; S.P.N. 424, or Q.C. 1400-01 (1932).
53. S.P.N. 376-377; or Q.C. 868-869 (1931).
54. S.P.N. 423; or Q.C. 1399-1400 (1932).
55. S.P.N. 424, or Q.C. 1401; S.P.N. 330n., or Q.C. 1382-83; S.P.N. 323-324, or Q.C. 1375-76 (all 1932).
56. S.P.N. 333, or Q.C. 1385 (1932); S.P.N. 273, or Q.C. 324 (1930).
57. S.P.N. 333, or Q.C. 1385 (1932).
58. S.P.N. 273, or Q.C. 323 (1930); S.P.N. 327, or Q.C. 1379 (1932).
59. S.P.N. 272-273; or Q.C. 323-324 (1930).
60. S.P.N. 366; or Q.C. 1244 (1932). In an explanatory note on this page, editors Hoare and Nowell Smith argue that Gramsci's "highly original" use of the word *catharsis* in this context can probably be taken as just another example of the lengths to which he was driven in avoiding the prison censor. There may be something to this, though it is hard to see what more exact but objectionable word Gramsci was avoiding. What is more important is how good a choice the word was. Few observers of the peasantry in our time have been as aware as Gramsci was of the enormous power that primordial sentiments can exert within the world view of an historically repressed class.
61. S.P.N. 367; or Q.C. 1244 (1932).
62. S.P.N. 333; or Q.C. 1385 (1932).
63. Ibid.
64. Ibid.
65. S.P.N. 323-324; or Q.C. 1375-76 (1932).
66. S.P.N. 324; or Q.C. 1376 (1932).
67. S.P.N. 334; or Q.C. 1386 (1932).
68. See S.P.N. 342; or Q.C. 1394 (1932).
69. S.P.N. 198; or Q.C. 330 (1930).
70. S.P.N. 24-42, or Q.C. 1530-50 (1932); and Q.C. 245 (1930), 843-844 (1932), 1054-55 (1932), and 1183-87 (1932).
71. Q.C. 114 (1929-30).
72. S.P.N. 27; or Q.C. 1531 (1932).
73. S.P.N. 35; or Q.C. 1542 (1932).
74. Q.C. 114 (1929-30).
75. S.P.N. 35-36; or Q.C. 1542 (1932).
76. S.P.N. 36; or Q.C. 1542.
77. S.P.N. 32-33; or Q.C. 1537 (1932).
78. See S.P.N. 26-42, or Q.C. 1530-50 (1932).
79. One way in which Gramsci thought that it ought to be broadened was by a specifically political education which would introduce the idea of "rights and duties," and with it, "the first notions of the state and society as primordial elements of a new conception of the world which challenges the conceptions that are imparted by the various traditional social environments, i.e., those conceptions which can be termed folkloristic" (S.P.N. 30; or Q.C. 1535 [1932]).
80. S.P.N. 28; or Q.C. 1532 (1932).
81. S.P.N. 37; or Q.C. 1544 (1932).
82. Ibid. See also S.P.N. 42, or Q.C. 1549-50 (1932), where Gramsci points to the special need for early discipline among children from the lower classes.
83. It is interesting that Gramsci's phases—early discipline and late freedom—are precisely the opposite of Rousseau's in *Emile*. To the extent that Gramsci was "progressive" at all in this respect, he insisted that the later "creative phase" would be worthless unless the rudiments of self-discipline were already present. He was

interested, for instance, in the "Dalton Method" and other progressive spin-offs from pedagogical theorists like Maria Montessori, but he thought they had a "serious defect. The pupils generally postpone doing their work until the last days of the month, and this detracts from the seriousness of the education and represents a major difficulty for the teachers who are supposed to help them but are overwhelmed with work, whereas in the first weeks of the month they have little or nothing to do" (Q.C. 1184 [1932]).

84. S.P.N. 31; or Q.C. 1536 (1932).

85. S.P.N. 180-183; or Q.C. 1583-86 (1932).

86. S.P.N. 180; or Q.C. 1583.

87. Ibid.

88. S.P.N. 149; or Q.C. 1940 (1933).

89. S.P.N. 181; or Q.C. 1583.

90. S.P.N. 183; or Q.C. 1585-86.

91. Ibid.

92. See Karl Marx, *The Poverty of Philosophy* (London: Lawrence and Wishart, 1956), pp. 194-195.

93. S.P.N. 181; or Q.C. 1584 (1932).

94. Ibid.

95. S.P.N. 17-19; or Q.C. 1524-27 (1932).

96. For Gramsci's notion of the "national-popular," see S.P.N. 130-133, or Q.C. 1559-61; S.P.N. 421, or Q.C. 1398 (1932).

97. S.P.N. 53; or Q.C. 2289 (1934).

98. S.P.N. 273; or Q.C. 324 (1930).

99. S.P.N. 395; or Q.C. 1860 (1933).

100. Ibid.

101. S.P.N. 396; or Q.C. 1861 (1933).

102. S.P.N. 398; or Q.C. 1863 (1933).

103. Ibid.

104. For a study of this theme in Kant, Fichte, and Hegel, see George A. Kelly, *Idealism, Politics, and History* (London: Cambridge University Press, 1969).

105. S.P.N. 13; or Q.C. 1520 (1932). This insight, original in Gramsci, has become a commonplace on the contemporary European left. See, for instance, André Gorz, *Strategy for Labor*, trans. M. Nicolaus and V. Ortiz (Boston: Beacon Press, 1967).

106. S.P.N. 10; or Q.C. 1517 (1932).

107. S.P.N. 257-259, or Q.C. 693, 56-57 (1930), and 1049-50 (1932); S.P.N. 263, or Q.C. 763-764 (1931). The phrase seems to be derived from Marx's tenth *Thesis on Feuerbach.*

108. So far as I know, this term was not actually used by Gramsci, but it is logically required to complement his notion of "passive revolution," i.e., an "incomplete" revolution in which the class taking power has failed to win "hegemony."

109. S.P.N. 243; or Q.C. 1765 (1933).

110. Eric Hobsbawm, "The Great Gramsci," p. 41.

111. S.P.N. 242; or Q.C. 1565-66 (1932).

112. S.P.N. 244; or Q.C. 1765 (1933).

113. L.F.P. 204; or L.C. 481 (June 6, 1932).

114. See, for instance, Q.C. 863 (1931); and S.P.N. 198, or Q.C. 330 (1930).

115. See S.P.N. 258-261, or Q.C. 693, 1049-50, 56-57, 937, 801, and 1056 (1930-32).

116. S.P.N. 195; or Q.C. 757 (1931).

117. S.P.N. 246; or Q.C. 1570 (1932).

118. S.P.N. 247; or Q.C. 1570-71.

119. Ibid.

120. Ibid.

121. S.P.N. 258; or Q.C. 1049 (1930).
122. S.P.N. 259; or Q.C. 56-57 (1930).
123. S.P.N. 263; or Q.C. 1053 (1931).
124. S.P.N. 262-263; or Q.C. 763-764 (1931).
125. Ibid.
126. Ibid.
127. Q.C. 1638 (1933).
128. S.P.N. 259; or Q.C. 1050 (1930).
129. S.P.N. 263; or Q.C. 763-764 (1931).

Chapter 6

1. S.P.W., II, 340-375 (January 1926) and 441-462 (1926); M.P. 28-51 is another version of the latter.

2. L.F.P. 79 (March 19, 1927).

3. The main piece of evidence for this is Gramsci's March 19, 1927 letter to Tania, ibid.

4. For this discussion, see, for instance, S.P.N. 57, or Q.C. 2010 (1934); and S.P.N. 56n., or Q.C. 1235 (1932).

5. Ibid.

6. For anticipations of the concept of hegemony in this period, see S.P.W., I, 78 (July 12, 1919), 91 (September 13, 1919), and 146 (December 27, 1919); S.G. 339 (November 25, 1918); O.N. 79 (February 11, 1920) and 493 (December 18, 1920); and S. 127 (July 13, 1918). When Gramsci used the word *hegemony* in this period, he adhered to the ordinary language definition of preponderance or domination; see, for instance, O.N. 76 (February 11, 1920).

7. See *Ordine Nuovo*, March 1, 1924, p. 3; and *L'Unità*, September 1, 1925.

8. S.P.W., II, 443; or M.P. 30 (January 1926).

9. S.P.N. 237; or Q.C. 866 (1930).

10. For the "Gramsci as Leninist" view, see Luciano Gruppi, *Il Concetto di egemonia in Gramsci* (Rome: Riuniti, 1975); for the anti-Leninist position, see Gian Carlo Jocteau, "Sul Concetto di egemonia in Gramsci e Togliatti," *Rivista di storia contemporanea*, 1 (January 1973), 1-39.

11. For the Leninist view, see Anderson, "The Antinomies of Antonio Gramsci"; for the anti-Leninist reply, see Piccone, "From Spaventa to Gramsci."

12. Palmiro Togliatti, "Il Leninismo," p. 34.

13. S.P.N. 365, or Q.C. 1249-50 (1932); Q.C. 1235 (1932).

14. S.P.N. 55n.*5*; or Q.C. 1235 (1932).

15. S.P.N. 12, or Q.C. 1518-19 (1932); Q.C. 1638 (1932).

16. Q.C. 2287 (1934).

17. Q.C. 1056 (1932).

18. See S.P.N. 445-446, or Q.C. 1416 (1932); S.P.N. 407, or Q.C. 1490 (1932-33). There are also passages which convey the opposite impression; see, for instance, S.P.N. 242, or Q.C. 1565-66 (1932).

19. S.P.N. 77; or Q.C. 2027 (1934).

20. See S.P.N. 180, or Q.C. 1582 (1932); S.P.N. 219-222, or Q.C. 1619-22 (1933).

21. See the similar appraisal of hegemony in Raymond Williams, *Marxism and Literature* (New York: Oxford University Press, 1977), pp. 108-114.

22. S.P.N. 137, or Q.C. 1569; S.P.N. 366, or Q.C. 1050-51 (1932).

23. Gramsci sometimes refers to his "extension of the concept of intellectual" (S.P.N. 12, or Q.C. 1519 [1932]).

24. S.P.N. 60; or Q.C. 2012 (1934).

25. S.P.N. 75; or Q.C. 2024-25 (1934).

26. See S.P.N. 168, or Q.C. 1612 (1932).

27. Hugues Portelli, *Gramsci e le Bloc Historique* (Paris: Presses Universitaires de France, 1972), pp. 68-96.

28. See S.P.N. 55n.*5*, or Q.C. 1235 (1932); and S.P.N. 418, or Q.C. 1505 (1932-

33) for texts suggesting a one-to-one correspondence between hegemony and historical bloc. See S.P.N. 57-59, or Q.C. 2010-11; S.P.N. 76, or Q.C. 2026; S.P.N. 100, or Q.C. 2045; and S.P.N. 61, or Q.C. 2013 (1934) for the description of the Moderates as internally hegemonic leaders of a national bloc, yet lacking national hegemony.

29. See J.M. Piotte, *La Pensée Politique de Gramsci* (Paris: Anthropos, 1970), p. 155. Giorgio Bonomi also shows this tendency in his *Partito e rivoluzione in Gramsci* (Milan: Feltrinelli, 1973), pp. 33-35.

30. Q.C. 1321 (1932).

31. For Sorel's exact formulation, see the passage quoted in Badaloni, *Il Marxismo di Gramsci*, p. 60. The connections between Sorel's and Gramsci's concepts are nonetheless extremely obscure and uncertain. Gerratana points to an entirely different passage from Sorel as the probable source of this connection; cf. Q.C. 2632.

32. S.P.N. 365; or Q.C. 1249 (1932).

33. S.P.W., II, 454; or M.P. 42 (1926).

34. L.F.P. 204 (September 7, 1931).

35. S.P.N. 462; or Q.C. 1435 (1932).

36. L.F.P. 204; and S.P.N. 128n.*6* (June 6, 1932).

37. S.P.N. 128n.*6*.

38. S.P.N. 118-119; or Q.C. 1209 and 1226-27 (1935).

39. S.P.N. 119; or Q.C. 1228 (1935).

40. Croce, *What Is Living*, pp. 78-99.

41. Ibid., p. 33.

42. Ibid., p. 90.

43. Q.C. 1317 (1932).

44. S.P.N. 138; or Q.C. 1569 (1932).

45. S.P.N. 138-139; or Q.C. 1567 (1932).

46. For Croce on the "ethical-political," see his *Etica e politica* (Bari: Laterza, 1945). especially pp. 176-183 and 213-283.

47. For a contrasting view, see Thomas R. Bates, "Gramsci and the Theory of Hegemony," *Journal of the History of Ideas*, 36:2 (April-June 1975), 355.

48. S.P.N. 55n.*5*; or Q.C. 1235 (1932).

49. Croce, *Etica e politica*, pp. 250-256.

50. As Hayden White once wrote of Croce: "All of Croce's historical works are more properly designated as moral tracts than 'pure' scholarship" ("The Abiding Relevance of Croce's Idea of History," *Journal of Modern History*, 35:2 [June 1963], 121).

51. For critical assessments of this type which have stirred considerable debate in Italy, see Rosario Romeo, *Risorgimento e capitalismo* (Bari: Laterza, 1959); Giuseppe Galasso, "Gramsci e il problema della storia italiana," in *Gramsci e la cultura contemporanea* (Rome: Riuniti, 1969), vol. I, pp. 305-354; Alexander Gerschenkron, *Economic Backwardness in Historical Perspective* (New York: Holt, Rinehart and Winston, 1962), pp. 90-118; and Cammett, *Antonio Gramsci*, pp. 213-222.

52. S.P.N. 132; or Q.C. 1560 (1932). Original emphasis.

53. S.P.N. 172; or Q.C. 1578 (1932).

54. S.P.W., I, 32 (July 28, 1917).

55. S.P.N. 77 and 79; or Q.C. 2027 and 2029 (1934).

56. S.P.N. 78; or Q.C. 2028 (1934).

57. Ibid.

58. S.P.N. 79; or Q.C. 2029 (1934).

59. S.P.N. 65-66; or Q.C. 2017 (1934).

60. Ibid.

61. S.P.N. 131; or Q.C. 1559-60 (1932).

62. S.P.N. 59; or Q.C. 2011 (1934).
63. S.P.N. 107; or Q.C. 1775 (1933).
64. See Q.C. 641 (1931), where Pirenne is cited approvingly.
65. Q.C. 719 (1930).
66. Q.C. 2287 (1934).
67. Ibid.
68. S.P.N. 91; or Q.C. 2036 (1934).
69. S.P.N. 92; or Q.C. 2036-37 (1934).
70. Ibid.
71. Q.C. 745-746 (1931) and 1965 (1934).
72. Q.C. 1968 (1934).
73. Q.C. 1966 (1934).
74. S.P.N. 92; or Q.C. 2037 (1934).
75. Q.C. 961 (1931-32).
76. S.P.N. 60 and 76; or Q.C. 2012 and 2026 (1934).
77. Ibid.
78. Ibid.
79. S.P.N. 59 and 76; or Q.C. 2011 and 2026 (1934).
80. S.P.N. 61; or Q.C. 2012-13 (1934).
81. Ibid.
82. S.P.N. 57; or Q.C. 2010 (1934).
83. S.P.N. 62 and 65; or Q.C. 2014 and 2016-17 (1934).
84. S.P.N. 104-105; or Q.C. 1822 (1933).
85. S.P.N. 105; or Q.C. 1823.
86. The only other question of comparable importance concerned the consequences of the Risorgimento. See the discussion of this below.
87. Q.C. 2032 (1934); Q.C. 1931-32 (1933).
88. S.P.N. 65, or Q.C. 2016 (1934); see also S.P.W., I, 110-111 (November 8, 1919).
89. S.P.N. 65; or Q.C. 2016 (1934).
90. Q.C. 1986 (1934).
91. S.P.N. 82; or Q.C. 2032 (1934). More recent historians such as Galasso have cast much doubt on this conclusion: see "Gramsci e storia italiana," pp. 329-330. But see also Denis Mack Smith, "The Peasants' Revolt in Sicily, 1860," in his *Victor Emanuel, Cavour, and the Risorgimento* (London: Oxford University Press, 1971).
92. S.P.N. 97-100; or Q.C. 2041-45 (1934).
93. S.P.N. 99; or Q.C. 2043 (1934).
94. S.P.N. 98; or Q.C. 2042-43.
95. S.P.N. 61; or Q.C. 2012-13 (1934).
96. S.P.N. 74; or Q.C. 2024 (1934).
97. Ibid.
98. S.P.N. 61; or Q.C. 2013.
99. S.P.N. 64; or Q.C. 2015 (1934).
100. S.P.N. 62; or Q.C. 2014.
101. S.P.N. 63; or Q.C. 2014.
102. S.P.N. 102; or Q.C. 2046 (1934).
103. S.P.N. 76; or Q.C. 2026 (1934).
104. S.P.N. 108; or Q.C. 1767 (1933).
105. Q.C. 962 (1931-32).
106. Q.C. 962-964 (1931-32).
107. S.P.N. 90; or Q.C. 2053-54 (1934).
108. Denis Mack Smith, *Italy: A Modern History*, p. 110.
109. Q.C. 962-64 (1931-32).
110. Ibid.

111. Ibid.
112. S.P.N. 66; or Q.C. 2017 (1934).
113. S.P.N. 67; or Q.C. 2018 (1934).
114. S.P.N. 68; or Q.C. 2019 (1934).
115. Q.C. 1996 (1934).
116. Q.C. 997 (1931-32).
117. S.P.N. 210; or Q.C. 1602-03 (1932).
118. Ibid.
119. S.P.N. 228-229; or Q.C. 912-913 (1931).
120. S.P.N. 210; or Q.C. 1602-03 (1932).
121. S.P.N. 219-223; or Q.C. 1619-22 and 1680-81 (1933). It is quite likely that Gramsci invented the term Caesarism as a way of speaking indirectly about fascism; parallels between Caesar and Mussolini were quite common in the Italy of this era. See Q.C. 1924 (1933).

122. That Caesarism is not necessarily tied to the great heroic figure and sometimes uses the mass organizations of modern political life may have been one reason that Gramsci preferred it to the concept of Bonapartism. Another reason may have been that he saw fascism as having resulted not from an equilibrium of rival class forces, as in Marx's portrayal of Bonapartism, but from the defeat of one and the intrinsic weakness of the other.

123. See S.P.N. 229-243, or Q.C. 120-123, 801-802, 810-811, 865-866, 1613-16 (1929-33); and Q.C. 1088-89 (1932).
124. S.P.N. 239; or Q.C. 801-802 (1931).
125. Q.C. 1088-89; for an analysis of fascism's progressive role, see the discussion of "black parliamentarism" in S.P.N. 255-256, or Q.C. 1742-44 (1933).

Chapter 7

1. S.P.W., II, 408-409 (August 2-3, 1926).
2. S.P.N. 136-143; or Q.C. 1567-76 and 1022 (1932). For Gramsci's critique of the "left turn," see Lisa, *Memorie*, chap. 5.
3. For recent treatments of Thalheimer's and Trotsky's views of fascism, see Kitchen, "Thalheimer's Theory of Fascism"; and Robert S. Wistrich, "Leon Trotsky's Theory of Fascism," *Journal of Contemporary History*, 11:4 (October 1976), 157-184.
4. See Friedrich Engels, "On the Origin of the State," in Robert Tucker, ed., *The Marx-Engels Reader* (New York: Norton, 1972), pp. 653-654.
5. S.P.N. 139-140; or Q.C. 1022 (1932).
6. S.P.N. 172 and 126; or Q.C. 1578 and 1556 (1932).
7. S.P.N. 144; or Q.C. 1572 (1933).
8. S.P.N. 130 and 194; or Q.C. 1559 and 1057 (1932).
9. Q.C. 1729 (1933).
10. Q.C. 230-239 (1930).
11. Roberto Michels, *Political Parties* (Glencoe, Ill.: Free Press, 1958), pp. 55 and 61.
12. Ibid., p. 277.
13. S.P.N. 6 and 214, or Q.C. 956 and 1606 (1932); and Gaetano Mosca, *The Ruling Class*, trans. H. Kahn (New York: McGraw-Hill, 1939).
14. S.P.N. 129; or Q.C. 1558 (1932).
15. Evidence on this point, though less solid and plentiful than one would like, can be drawn from the obituary of Lenin published in *Ordine Nuovo*, March 1, 1924. The obituary includes an annotated list of Lenin's major works, including *What Is to Be Done?*; *Two Tactics*; *Imperialism*; *State and Revolution*; *The Proletarian Revolution and the Renegade Kautsky*, and *Left-Wing Communism—An Infantile Disorder*. See *Ordine Nuovo*, March 1, 1924, Feltrinelli reprint.

16. S.P.N. 178; or Q.C. 1580 (1932).
17. Ibid.
18. S.P.N. 204; or Q.C. 1675-76 (1933).
19. S.P.N. 150; or Q.C. 1940 (1933).
20. Q.C. 1056 (1932).
21. S.P.N. 144; or Q.C. 1752 (1933).
22. S.P.N. 152; or Q.C. 1732-33 (1933).
23. See, for instance, H. Stuart Hughes, *Consciousness and Society* (New York: Knopf, 1961), p. 101; George Lichtheim, *Marxism: An Historical and Critical Study* (New York: Praeger, 1961), p. 369; and Thomas R. Bates, "Antonio Gramsci and the Bolshevization of the PCI," pp. 116, 124-129.
24. On Gramsci's concern for "individuality," see S.P.N. 352, or Q.C. 1345 (1932). The distinction between "positive" and "negative" freedom was popularized by Isaiah Berlin in his essay *Two Concepts of Liberty* (Oxford: Clarendon, 1958). Ultimately, the distinction goes back at least as far as Benjamin Constant's "On the Liberty of the Ancients as Compared with that of the Moderns," in *Cours de Politique Constitutionelle*, 2 vols, ed. E. Laboulaye (Paris: Laboulaye, 1861). The essay appeared originally in 1819.
25. The distinction goes back at least to Rousseau's discussion in *Emile* and *The Social Contract*. For Marx's discussion of it, see his essay "On the Jewish Question," Y.M. 216-248.
26. S.P.N. 341; or Q.C. 1393 (1932).
27. See S.P.W., II, 154 (June 1923), 358 (January 1926), and Chapter 3, above.
28. S.P.N. 186; or Q.C. 1632 (1932).
29. S.P.N. 187-190, or Q.C. 1633-35 (1932); see also Q.C. 1706-07 (1933).
30. Q.C. 1770 (1933).
31. S.P.N. 188-189; or Q.C. 1634 (1932).
32. S.P.N. 152; or Q.C. 1733-34 (1933).
33. Ibid.
34. S.P.N. 153; or Q.C. 1734 (1933).
35. Sidney Tarrow, *Peasant Communism in Southern Italy* (New Haven, Conn.: Yale University Press, 1967), p. 121.
36. S.P.N. 268; or Q.C. 920 (1931).
37. S.P.W., I, 348 (September 24, 1920); see also S.P.W., I, 67-68 (June 21, 1919).
38. S.P.N. 152-153; or Q.C. 1733-34 (1933).
39. Q.C. 1056 (1932). The difference is analogous to the distinction in liberal discussions betweeen "participatory" and "elite" theories of democracy.
40. For evidence of this, see S.P.N. 208, or Q.C. 1253 (1932), where civil society is described as standing between the "state" and the economic structure; and S.P.N. 234-235, or Q.C. 1615 (1932), where the economy is described as making "incursions" into Western civil society.
41. See S.G. 230 (May 18, 1918); O.N. 380-381 (July 5, 1919).
42. L.F.P. 204; or L.C. 481, September 7, 1931.
43. See the citation by Merrington, "Theory and Practice," p. 153; and Anderson's analysis, "Antinomies of Antonio Gramsci," pp. 12-13.
44. See Anderson, ibid., pp. 26-33.
45. Anderson's article is marred, here and elsewhere, by a failure to locate the origins of Gramsci's concepts in the *Notebooks* within the context of his intellectual development.
46. This former orientation underlies all the major "war of position" passages—S.P.N. 229-243; or Q.C. 120-123, 801-802, 810-811, 865-866, 1613-16 (1929-33)—while at S.P.N. 263, or Q.C. 763-764 (1931), where Gramsci introduced the "state = civil society + political society" equation, he clearly had in mind the way existing bourgeois states function in order to contrast this with the way a future

"regulated society" might work. Similarly, Gramsci used the concept of hegemony as *direzione* when his concern was with the proletariat becoming hegemonic; it is in those few instances when he referred to the hegemonic rule of existing bourgeois states (e.g., S.P.N. 80n.) that he defined it as *direzione + dominio.*

47. Q.C. 858 (1930), and 1087, 1223-24, 1302 (1932).

48. Norberto Bobbio, "Gramsci e la concezione della società civile," in *Gramsci e la cultura contemporanea*, vol. I, pp. 75-100.

49. Q.C. 703 (1931).

50. Bobbio, "Gramsci e società civile," p. 88.

51. The only direct evidence from the *Notebooks* which Bobbio cites to support his claim is the passage in which "catharsis" is defined as movement

> from the purely economic . . . to the ethico-political moment, that is, the superior elaboration of the structure into superstructure in the minds of men. This means also the passage from "objective to subjective" and from "necessity to freedom" (S.P.N. 366-367; or Q.C. 1244 [1932]).

Because the "catharsis" shift is from a lower level of consciousness to a higher one, Bobbio contends that the "primacy" of the latter element in each of the subsequent pairings may be assumed. This is, to say the least, a rather oblique inference; and given the tentativeness of Gramsci's writings, it seems particularly unwarranted to base such a large point on just a single, short note. Yet, even if we grant the basis for the inference, Bobbio has gone too far. Gramsci's reference in this passage was to a particular historical transformation, not to structure-superstructure relations in all times and places. As we have already suggested, for Gramsci the relative importance of the structure as opposed to the superstructure was an empirical question. In ignoring this point and the historicism that underlies it, Bobbio's contention is simply the fallacy of economism in reverse.

52. S.P.N. 159-160; or Q.C. 1589-90 (1932).

53. Q.C. 914-915 (1931).

54. See Chapter 3, note 110, above.

55. S.P.W., II, 426-432 (October 1926).

56. Lisa, *Memorie*, p. 18. Given Gramsci's long-standing political dispositions, it is not likely that he would have found much food for thought in Stalin's argument about the coming economic crisis of capitalism. He always considered an exclusive preoccupation with the so-called "objective" conditions for revolution to be disastrously one-sided.

57. S.P.N. 243; or Q.C. 1566 (1933). My emphasis.

58. Ibid.

59. On this point, see Gramsci's comment to Mario Garuglieri as related by Ernesto Ragionieri, "Gramsci e il dibattito teorico nel movimento operaio internazionale," in *Gramsci e la cultura contemporanea*, vol. I, pp. 136-137.

60. For a recent treatment of the "communicative" concept of power in the sense I intend here, see Jürgen Habermas, "Hannah Arendt's Communications Concept of Power," *Social Research*, 44:1 (Spring 1977), 3-24.

61. Only in one note does Gramsci approach the Leninist concept of proletarian dictatorship; see his remarks on "statolotry" in S.P.N. 268, or Q.C. 1020 (1931). However, since revolution as "war of position" is for Gramsci the equivalent of gaining a "civil hegemony," he seems to be implying that the need for statolotry occurs only after a revolutionary "war of movement" such as that which occurred in 1917 in Russia.

62. S.P.N. 238; or Q.C. 866 (1931).

63. S.P.N. 239; or Q.C. 802 (1931). Emphasis added.

64. S.P.N. 238; or Q.C. 801 (1931).

65. This conclusion was first fully articulated by Giuseppe Tamburrano, himself a social democrat, in *Antonio Gramsci. la vita, il pensiero, l'azione* (Manduria:

Lacaita, 1963). Some members of the Italian extra-parliamentary left have also accused Gramsci of favoring a "revolution without a revolution"; see Tito Perlini, *Gramsci e il Gramscismo* (Milan: Celuc, 1974). Perry Anderson comes close to this view in his article "Antinomies of Antonio Gramsci," where he concludes that Gramsci was overtly contradictory on his most central theme: "Gramsci never relinquished the fundamental tenets of classical Marxism on the ultimate necessity for violent seizure of state power, but at the same time his strategic formula for the West fails to integrate them" (p. 69). More plausible, it seems to me, is the view that Gramsci's conception of revolution transcended those "fundamental [and outmoded] tenets."

66. S.P.N. 229; or Q.C. 122 (1931).
67. S.P.N. 108; or Q.C. 1766 (1933).
68. S.P.N. 237-238; or Q.C. 866 and 801-802 (1931).
69. S.P.N. 238; or Q.C. 866 (1931).
70. S.P.N. 235; or Q.C. 1655 (1931).

Conclusion

1. Q.C. 1365 (1932).
2. Hannah Arendt, *Between Past and Future* (New York: Viking, 1963), p. 23. Arendt, however, goes too far in denying Marx's place within the ethical state tradition, however idiosyncratic his own formulation may appear within it.
3. Q.C. 1201 (1932).
4. S.P.N. 15; or Q.C. 1522 (1932).
5. S.P.N. 152; or Q.C. 1733 (1933).
6. Letter to Terracini, March 27, 1924, in Togliatti, *Formazione*, p. 262.
7. S.P.W., II, 154 (June 1923).
8. See the literature cited in Chapter 7, note 23, above. I will use quotation marks around "totalitarian" to distinguish Gramsci's from contemporary usage.
9. S.P.N. 445; or Q.C. 1416 (1932). Original emphasis.
10. Q.C. 800 (1931).
11. Anderson, "Antinomies of Antonio Gramsci," p. 41n.*78*.
12. Anderson, ibid., suggests the first two; on the last, see Hannah Arendt, "What Is Authority?" in *Between Past and Future*, pp. 91-141.
13. See Macchiocchi, *Pour Gramsci*, especially pp. 234-239; Carl Boggs, "Gramsci's Prison Notebooks," *Socialist Revolution*, 12 (November-December 1972), 40-49; and Nigel Todd, "Ideological Superstructure in Gramsci and Mao Tse-tung," *Journal of the History of Ideas*, 35:1 (January-March 1974), 148-156.
14. See especially Jürgen Habermas, *Legitimation Crisis* (Boston: Beacon Press, 1975); James O'Connor, *The Fiscal Crisis of the State* (New York: St. Martin's Press, 1973); and Ralph Miliband, *The State in Capitalist Society* (New York: Basic Books, 1969), and *Marxism and Politics* (New York: Oxford University Press, 1977).
15. On this point, see Sharon Zukin, "Mimesis in the Origins of Bourgeois Culture," *Theory and Society*, 4 (1977), 333-358.
16. For a discussion of Adorno on this point, see Buck-Morss, *Origin of Negative Dialectics*, chap. 2.
17. For a good discussion of some of these problems in relation to Frankfurt School critical theory, see William Leiss, "Critical Theory and Its Future," *Political Theory*, 2:3 (August 1974), 330-349.

Selected Bibliography

I. Gramsci's Writings

Opere di Antonio Gramsci. Turin: Einaudi, 1947-.

[1] Lettere dal Carcere. Rev. edition, ed. S. Caprioglio and E. Fubini, (1965).
[2] Vol. VIII. Scritti giovanili, 1914-18 (1958).
[3] Vol. IX. L'Ordine Nuovo, 1919-20 (1954).
[4] Vol. X. Sotto la Mole, 1916-20 (1960).
[5] Vol. XI. Socialismo e fascismo, 1921-22 (1972).
[6] Vol. XII. La Costruzione del partito comunista, 1923-26 (1972).

The Modern Prince and Other Writings. Ed. L. Marks. London: Lawrence and Wishart, 1957.

"Lettera inedita per la fondazione de 'L'Unità,'" *Rivista storica del socialismo*, 6:18 (January-April 1963) 115-123. Also in *Rinascita*, 21:6 (February 8, 1964), 25.

2000 Pagine di Gramsci. Ed. G. Ferrata and N. Gallo. Milan: Il Saggiatore, 1964.

"Una Lettera inedita del 1918 a Giuseppe Lombardo Radice: Una iniziativa di Gramsci," *Rinascita*, 21:10 (March 7, 1964), 32.

Selections from the Prison Notebooks of Antonio Gramsci. Trans. and ed. Q. Hoare and G. Nowell Smith. New York: International Publishers, 1971.

Letters from Prison. Trans. L. Lawner. New York: Harper and Row, 1973.

Per la Verità, Scritti 1913-1926. Ed. R. Martinelli. Rome: Riuniti, 1974.

Quaderni del Carcere. 4 vols. Ed. V. Gerratana. Turin: Einaudi, 1975.

History, Philosophy, and Culture in the Young Gramsci. Trans. and ed. P. Cavalcanti and P. Piccone. St. Louis: Telos Press, 1975.

Scritti 1915-1921. Ed. S. Caprioglio. Milan: Moizzi, 1976.

Selections from Political Writings, 1910-1920. Trans. and ed. Q. Hoare. New York: International Publishers, 1977.

Selections from Political Writings, 1921-1926. Trans. and ed. Q. Hoare. New York: International Publishers, 1978.

II. Books and Articles on Gramsci

Agazzi, Emilio. "Filosofia della prassi e filosofia dello spirito," in *La Città futura*, ed. A. Caracciolo and G. Scalia. Milan: Feltrinelli, 1959, pp. 187-270.

Aimo, M. A. "Stato e rivoluzione negli scritti sulla questione meridionale," in *Gramsci e la cultura contemporanea*, 2 vols. Rome: Riuniti, 1969, vol. II, pp. 183-192.

Alicata, Mario. "Gramsci e l'Ordine Nuovo," *Società*, 11:2(1955), 197-204.

Anderson, Perry. "The Antinomies of Antonio Gramsci," *New Left Review*, 100 (November 1976-January 1977), 5-78.

Auciello, Nicola. *Socialismo ed egemonia in Gramsci e Togliatti.* Bari: De Donato, 1974.

Badaloni, Nicola. "Gramsci storicista de fronte al marxismo contemporaneo," *Prassi rivoluzionario e storicismo in Gramsci, Critica Marxista*, 3 (1967), 97-118.

———. "Il fondamento teorico della storicismo gramsciano," in *Gramsci e la cultura contemporanea*, 2 vols. Rome: Riuniti, 1969, vol. 2, pp. 73-80.

———. *Il Marxismo di Gramsci.* Turin: Einaudi, 1975.

Bates, Thomas R. "Antonio Gramsci and the Soviet Experiment in Italy," *Societas*, 4 (Winter 1974), 39-54.

———. "Gramsci and the Theory of Hegemony," *Journal of the History of Ideas*, 36 (April-June 1975), 351-366.

———. "Antonio Gramsci and the Bolshevization of the PCI," *Journal of Contemporary History*, 11 (July 1976), 115-133.

Bergami, Giancarlo. *Il giovane Gramsci e il Marxismo, 1911-1918.* Milan: Feltrinelli, 1977.

———. "Sui rapporti tra Gramsci e Trotsky," *Rivista di storia contemporanea*, 7:4 (October 1978), 559-585.

Bobbio, Norberto. "Nota sulla dialettica in Gramsci," in *Studi Gramsciani.* Rome: Riuniti, 1958, pp. 73-86.

———. "Gramsci e la concezione della società civile," in *Gramsci e la cultura contemporanea*, 2 vols. Rome: Riuniti, 1969, vol. I, pp. 75-101.

Boggs, Carl. "Gramsci's Prison Notebooks," *Socialist Revolution*, 11 (September-October 1972), 79-118, and 12 (November-December 1972), 29-56.

———. "Gramsci's Theory of the Factory Councils: Nucleus of the Socialist State," *Berkeley Journal of Sociology*, 19 (Winter 1974-75), 171-187.

———. *Gramsci's Marxism.* London: Pluto Press, 1976.

Bonomi, Giorgio. *Partito e rivoluzione in Gramsci.* Milan: Feltrinelli, 1973.

———. "La Teoria della rivoluzione in Gramsci," in *Annali Feltrinelli 1973.* Milan: Feltrinelli, 1974, pp. 1276-94.

Borghi, Lamberto. "Educazione e scuola in Gramsci," in *Gramsci e la cultura contemporanea*, 2 vols. Rome: Riuniti, 1969, vol. I, pp. 207-238.

Broccoli, Angelo. *Antonio Gramsci e l'educazione come egemonia.* Florence: La Nuova Italia, 1972.

Buci-Glucksmann, Christine. "Gramsci et l'état," *Dialectiques*, 4-5 (1974), 5-27.

______. *Gramsci et L'État.* Paris: Fayard, 1975.

______. "Eurocommunisme et problemes de l'état," *Dialectiques*, 18-19 (1977), 121-152.

Buzzi, A.R. *La Theorie Politique d'Antonio Gramsci.* Paris: Béatrice-Nauwelaerts, 1967.

Cammett, John M. *Antonio Gramsci and the Origins of Italian Communism.* Stanford, Calif.: Stanford University Press, 1967.

______. "Communist Theories of Fascism, 1920-1935," *Science and Society*, 31:2 (Spring 1967), 149-163.

Caprioglio, Sergio. "Un Mancato incontro Gramsci—D'Annunzio a Gardone nell'aprile 1921 (con una testimonianza di Palmiro Togliatti)," *Rivista storica del socialismo*, 5:15-16 (January-August 1962), 263-273.

Caracciolo, Alberto. "A Proposito di Gramsci, la Russia e il movimento bolscevico," in *Studi Gramsciani.* Rome: Riuniti, 1958.

______, and Gianni Scalia, eds. *La Città futura.* Milan: Feltrinelli, 1959.

Carbone, Giuseppe. "I libri del carcere di Antonio Gramsci," *Movimento operaio*, 4 (July-August 1952), 640-689.

Clark, Martin. *Antonio Gramsci and the Revolution that Failed.* New Haven, Conn.: Yale University Press, 1977.

Colletti, Lucio. "Antonio Gramsci and the Italian Revolution," *New Left Review*, 65 (January 1971), 87-94.

Croce, Benedetto. "De Sanctis—Gramsci," *Lo Spettatore italiano*, 5:7 (July 1952), 294-296.

Davidson, Alastair. *Gramsci, The Man and His Ideas.* Sydney: Australian Left Review Publications, 1968.

______. "The Varying Seasons of Gramscian Studies," *Political Studies*, 20:4 (December 1972), 448-461.

______. "Gramsci and Reading Machiavelli," *Science and Society*, 37:1 (Spring 1973), 56-80.

______. "Gramsci and Lenin, 1917-1922," in *The Socialist Register.* London: Merlin Press, 1974, pp. 125-150.

______."Gramsci and the Factory Councils," *Australian Left Review*, 45 (October 1974), 38-48; and 46 (March 1975), 35-44.

______. *Antonio Gramsci: Towards an Intellectual Biography.* London: Merlin Press, 1977.

De Felice, Franco. "Questione meridionale e problema dello stato in Gramsci," *Rivista storica del socialismo*, 9:27 (January-April 1966), 1189-1220.

______. *Serrati, Bordiga, Gramsci.* Bari: De Donato, 1971.

______. "Una chiave di lettura in 'Americanismo e fordismo,'" *Rinascita*, 29:42 (October 27, 1972), 33-35.

Femia, Joseph. "Hegemony and Consciousness in the Thought of Antonio Gramsci," *Political Studies*, 23 (March 1975), 29-48.

Ferreti, Giancarlo. "Gli *Scritti giovanile* nella formazione di Antonio Gramsci," *Società*, 15:2 (January-February 1959), 308-324.

Ferri, Franco. "Consiglio di fabbrica e partito nel pensiero di Gramsci," *Rinascita*, 14:9 (September 1957), 461-467.

Fiori, Giuseppe. *Antonio Gramsci: Life of a Revolutionary*. Trans. T. Nairn. New York: Schocken Books, 1970.

Galasso, Giuseppe. "Gramsci e il problema della storia italiana," in *Gramsci e la cultura contemporanea*, 2 vols. Rome: Riuniti, 1969, vol. II, pp. 305-354.

Galli, Giorgio. "Gramsci e le teorie delle 'élites,'" in *Gramsci e la cultura contemporanea*, 2 vols. Rome: Riuniti, 1969, vol. II, pp. 201-216.

Garin, Eugenio. "La formazione di Gramsci e Croce," *Prassi rivoluzionario e storicismo in Gramsci, Critica Marxista*, 3 (1967), 119-133.

Garuglieri, Mario. "Ricordo di Gramsci," *Società*, 2:7-8 (July-December 1946), 691-701.

Grisoni, Dominique, and Robert Maggiori. *Lire Gramsci*, Paris: Editions Universitaires, 1973.

Gruppi, Luciano. *Il Concetto di egemonia in Gramsci*. Rome: Riuniti, 1975.

______. *Storicità e Marxismo*. Rome: Riuniti, 1976.

Hobsbawm, E.J. "The Great Gramsci," *New York Review of Books*, April 4, 1974, pp. 39-44.

Jocteau, Gian Carlo. "Sul Concetto di egemonia in Gramsci e Togliatti," *Rivista di storia contemporanea*, 1 (January 1973), 1-39.

______. *Leggere Gramsci*. Milan: Feltrinelli, 1975.

Karabel, Jerome. "Revolutionary Contradictions: Antonio Gramsci and the Problem of Intellectuals," *Politics and Society*, 6 (Spring 1976), 123-172.

Kiernan, V.G. "Gramsci and Marxism," in *The Socialist Register*. London: Merlin Press, 1972, pp. 1-32.

Kosík, Karel. "Gramsci et la Philosophie de la Praxis," *Praxis*, 3:3 (1967), 328-332.

Lay, Giovanni. "Colloqui con Gramsci nel carcere di Turi," *Rinascita*, 22:8 (February 20, 1965), 21-22.

Lentini, Giacinto. *Croce e Gramsci*. Rome: Mori, 1967.

Leonetti, Alfonso. *Note su Gramsci*. Argalia: Urbino, 1970.

Lisa, Athos. *Memorie: In carcere con Gramsci*. Milan: Feltrinelli, 1973.

Lombardi, Franco V. *Idee pedagogiche di Antonio Gramsci*. Brescia: La Scuola, 1969.

Macciocchi, M.A. *Pour Gramsci*. Paris: Editions du Seuil, 1974.

Macciotta, Giorgio. "Rivoluzione e classe operaia negli scritti sull 'Ordine Nuovo,'" in *Gramsci e la cultura contemporanea*, 2 vols. Rome: Riuniti, 1969, vol. II, pp. 173-182.

Manacorda, Mario Alighiero. *Il Principio educativo in Gramsci*. Rome: A. Armando, 1970.

Martinelli, Alberto. "In Defense of the Dialectic: Antonio Gramsci's Theory of Revolution," *Berkeley Journal of Sociology*, 13 (1968), 1-27.

Matteucci, Nicola. *Antonio Gramsci e la filosofia della prassi*. Milan: Guiffre, 1951.

Merolle, Vincenzo. *Gramsci e la filosofia della prassi.* Rome: Bulzoni, 1974.
Merrington, John. "Theory and Practice in Gramsci's Marxism," in *The Socialist Register.* London: Merlin Press, 1969, pp. 145-176.
Morpurgo-Tagliabue, Guido. "Gramsci tra Croce e Marx," *Il Ponte*, 4:5 (May 1948), 429-438.
Mouffe, Chantal, and Anne S. Sassoon. "Gramsci in France and Italy," *Economy and Society*, 6 (February 1977), 31-68.
Nardone, Giorgio. *Il Pensiero di Gramsci.* Rome: De Donato, 1971.
Orfei, Roberto. *Antonio Gramsci, coscienza critica del marxismo.* Milan: Relazioni Sociali, 1965.
Ottino, Carlo. *Concetti fondamentalli nella teoria politica di Antonio Gramsci.* Milan: Feltrinelli, 1956.
Paggi, Leonardo. "Machiavelli e Gramsci," *Studi Storici*, 10:4 (October-December 1969), 833-876.
______. *Gramsci e il moderno principe.* Rome: Riuniti, 1970.
______. "Gramsci's General Theory of Marxism," *Telos*, 33 (Fall 1977), 27-70.
Pellicani, Luciano. *Gramsci e la questione comunista.* Florence: Vallechi, 1976.
Piccone, Paul. "Gramsci's Hegelian Marxism," *Political Theory*, 2:1 (February 1974), 32-45.
______. "Gramsci's Marxism: Beyond Lenin and Togliatti," *Theory and Society*, 3 (Winter 1976), 485-512.
______. "From Spaventa to Gramsci," *Telos*, 31 (Spring 1977), 35-65.
Piotte, Jean-Marc. *La Pensée Politique de Gramsci.* Paris: Anthropos, 1970.
Portelli, Hugues. *Gramsci et le Bloc Historique.* Paris: Presses Universitaires de France, 1972.
______. *Gramsci et la Question Religieuse.* Paris: Anthropos, 1974.
Pozzolini, A. *Antonio Gramsci: An Introduction to His Thought.* Trans. A.F. Showstack. London: Pluto Press, 1970.
Quercioli, Mimma Paulesu, ed. *Gramsci vivo.* Milan: Feltrinelli, 1977.
Ragionieri, Ernesto. "Gramsci e il dibattito teorico nel movimento operaio internazionale," in *Gramsci e la cultura contemporanea*, 2 vols. Rome: Riuniti, 1969, vol. I, pp. 101-147.
Salvadori, Massimo L. "Gramsci e la questione meridionale," in *Gramsci e la cultura contemporanea*, 2 vols. Rome: Riuniti, 1969, vol. I, pp. 391-438.
______. *Gramsci e il problema storica della democrazia.* Turin: Einaudi, 1970.
______. *Gramsci e l'organizzazione del lavoro nel periodo di transizione dal capitalismo al socialismo.* Turin: G. Giapplehelli, 1971.
Santhia, Battista. *Con Gramsci all' Ordine Nuovo.* Rome: Riuniti, 1956.
Scalia, Gianni. "Il Giovane Gramsci," *Passato e presente*, 9 (May-June 1959), 1132-1170.
Scuderi, Ermanno. *Cultura e Società nel Pensiero di Antonio Gramsci.* Catania: Muglia, 1974.
Spriano, Paolo. *Gramsci e "L'Ordine Nuovo."* Rome: Riuniti, 1965.
______. *Gramsci e Gobetti.* Turin: Einaudi, 1977.
______. *Gramsci in carcere e il partito.* Rome: Riuniti, 1977.

Stipcević, Nikśa. *Gramsci e i problemi lettarari.* Milan: Mursia, 1968.
Tamburrano, Giuseppe. *Antonio Gramsci. La vita, il pensiero, l'azione.* Manduria: Lacaita, 1963.
Texier, Jacques. *Gramsci.* Paris: Seghers, 1966.
———. "Gramsci, Théoricien des Superstructures," *La Pensée*, 139 (1969), 35-60.
Togliatti, Palmiro, et al. *Gramsci.* Rome: Rinascita, 1948.
———. "Gramsci sardo," *Il Ponte*, 7:9-10 (September-October 1951), 1085-1088.
———. *Gramsci.* Florence: Parenti, 1955.
———. "Il Leninismo nel pensiero e nell'azione di Antonio Gramsci," in *Studi Gramsciani.* Rome: Riuniti, 1958, pp. 418-444.
———. *La formazione del gruppo dirigente del PCI nel 1923-1924.* Rome: Riuniti, 1962.
Tosin, Bruno. *Con Gramsci.* Rome: Riuniti, 1976.
Trombetti, Gustavo. "'Piantone' di Gramsci nel carcere di Turi," *Rinascita*, 22:18 (May 1, 1965), 31-32.
Tronti, Mario. "Tra materialismo dialettico e filosofia della prassi: Gramsci e Labriola," in *La Città futura*, ed. A. Caracciolo and G. Scalia. Milan: Feltrinelli, 1959, pp. 139-162.
Vajda, Mihaly. Review of *Selections from the Prison Notebooks*, in *Telos*, 15 (Spring 1973), 148-156.
White, Stephen. "Gramsci and the Italian Communist Party," *Government and Opposition*, 2 (1972), 186-205.
Williams, Gwyn A. "The Concept of 'Egemonia' in the Thought of Antonio Gramsci: Some Notes on Interpretation," *Journal of the History of Ideas*, 21:4 (October-December 1960), 586-599.
———. *Proletarian Order.* London: Pluto Press, 1975.
Zucàro, Domenico. *Vita del carcere di Antonio Gramsci.* Milan: Avanti, 1954.
———. "Antonio Gramsci all'Università di Torino, 1911-1915," *Società*, 13:6 (December 1957), 1091-1111.

III. Other Sources

Agazzi, Emilio. *Il Giovane Croce e il Marxismo.* Turin: Einaudi, 1962.
Aloysio, Francesco de. *Studi sul pensiero di Antonio Labriola.* Rome: Carucci, 1976.
Althusser, Louis. "Marxism Is Not a Historicism," in Louis Althusser and Etienne Balibar, *Reading Capital.* Trans. B. Brewster. London: New Left Books, 1970, pp. 119-144.
Aquarone, Alberto, ed. *Mazzini nella cultura italiana.* Rome: Voce Republicana, 1965.
Arato, Andrew. "The Second International: A Reexamination," *Telos*, 18 (Winter 1973-74), 2-52.
Arfé, Gaetano. *Storia del socialismo italiano, 1892-1926.* Turin: Einaudi, 1965.
———, et al. *Socialismo e socialisti dal Risorgimento al Fascismo.* Bari: De Donato, 1974.
Avineri, Shlomo. *The Social and Political Thought of Karl Marx.* London: Cambridge University Press, 1968.

______. *Hegel's Theory of the Modern State*. London: Cambridge University Press, 1972.

Bellini, Fulvio, and Giorgio Galli. *Storia del partito comunista italiano*. Milan: Schwarz, 1953.

Bernstein, Eduard. *Evolutionary Socialism*. New York: Schocken Books, 1971.

Bernstein, Richard J. *Praxis and Action*. Philadelphia: University of Pennsylvania Press, 1971.

Bordiga, Amadeo. *Scritti scelti*. Ed. F. Livorsi. Milan: Feltrinelli, 1975.

Borkenau, Franz. *World Communism: A History of the Communist International*. Ann Arbor: University of Michigan Press, 1960.

Bukharin, Nicolai. *Historical Materialism: A System of Sociology*. Ann Arbor: University of Michigan Press, 1969.

Cambria, Rita. *I Liberali Italiani e il Socialismo*. Milan: Marzorati, 1974.

Carini, Carlo. *Benedetto Croce e il Partito Politico*. Florence: Olschki, 1975.

Carlo, Antonio, and Edmondo Capecelatro. *Contro la questione meridionale*. Rome: La Nuova sinistra, 1972.

Carr, H. Wildon. *The Philosophy of Benedetto Croce*. London: MacMillan, 1927.

Clough, Shepherd B. *The Economic History of Modern Italy*. New York: Columbia University Press, 1964.

Colletti, Lucio. "The Marxism of the Second International," *Telos,* 8 (Summer 1971), 84-91.

______. *From Rousseau to Lenin*. Trans. J. Merrington and J. White. New York: Monthly Review Press, 1972.

Cortesi, Luigi. "Palmiro Togliatti, la 'svolta di Salerno,' e l'eredità gramsciana," *Belfagor*, 30 (January 31, 1975), 1-44.

Coser, Lewis. "Marxism in the First Quarter of the Twentieth Century," *American Journal of Sociology*, 78 (July 1972), 173-201.

Croce, Benedetto. *What Is Living and What Is Dead of the Philosophy of Hegel*. Trans. D. Ainslee. London: MacMillan, 1915.

______. *A History of Italy, 1871-1915*. Trans. C. Ady. Oxford: Clarendon Press, 1929.

______. *Etica e politica*. Bari: Laterza, 1945.

______. *Teoria e storia della storiografia*. Bari: Laterza, 1954.

Dallmayr, Fred R. "Phenomenology and Marxism: A Salute to Enzo Paci," in *Phenomenological Sociology*, ed. George Psathas. New York: John Wiley, 1973, pp. 305-356.

DeClementi, Andreina. "La politica del Partito Comunista d'Italia nel 1921-22 e il rapporto Bordiga—Gramsci," *Rivista storica del socialismo*, 9:29 (September-December 1966), 61-94.

______. *Amadeo Bordiga*. Turin: Einaudi, 1971.

De Felice, Renzo. *Mussolini*. Turin: Einaudi, 1965.

Degras, Jane, ed. *The Communist International, 1919-1943*. 2 vols. London: Oxford University Press, 1956-1960.

Dupre, Louis. *Philosophical Foundations of Marxism*. New York: Harcourt, Brace and World, 1966.

Ferrara, Marcella, and Maurizio Ferrara. *Conversando con Togliatti*. Milan: Cultura Sociale, 1953.

Fleischer, Helmut. *Marxism and History*. Trans. E. Mosbacher. New York: Harper and Row, 1973.

Gay, Peter. *The Dilemma of Democratic Socialism*. New York: Columbia University Press, 1952.

Gentile, Emilio. *"La Voce" e l'età giolittiana*. Milan: Pan, 1972.

Gerratana, Valentino. "Marxismo ortodosso e marxismo aperto in Antonio Labriola," in *Annali Feltrinelli 1973*, vol. 15. Milan: Feltrinelli, 1974, pp. 554-580.

———. "Realtà e compiti del movimento socialista in Italia," in *Annali Feltrinelli 1973*, vol. 15. Milan: Feltrinelli, 1974, pp. 581-607.

Gerschenkron, Alexander. *Economic Backwardness in Historical Perspective*. New York: Holt, Rinehart and Winston, 1962.

Gobetti, Piero. *La Rivoluzione liberale*. Turin: Einaudi, 1964.

Gould, Carol. *Marx's Social Ontology*. Cambridge, Mass.: MIT Press, 1978.

Gruppi, Luciano. "Lenin e il concetto di egemonia," *Lenin teorico e dirigente rivoluzionario, Critica Marxista*, 4 (1968), 206-218.

Habermas, Jürgen. *Knowledge and Human Interests*. Trans. J. J. Schapiro. Boston: Beacon Press, 1968.

———. *Theory and Practice*. Trans. J. Viertel. Boston: Beacon Press, 1971.

Hegel, G. W. F. *The Phenomenology of Mind*. Trans. J. B. Baillie. New York: Harper and Row, 1967.

———. *The Philosophy of Right*. Trans. T. M. Knox. London: Oxford University Press, 1967.

Heller, Agnes. *The Theory of Need in Marx*. New York: St. Martin's Press, 1976.

Hobsbawn, E. J. *Primitive Rebels*. Manchester, England: Manchester University Press, 1959.

Hook, Sidney. *From Marx to Hegel*. Ann Arbor: University of Michigan Press, 1968.

Horowitz, Irving Louis. *Radicalism and the Revolt against Reason*. London: Routledge and Kegan Paul, 1961.

Hostetter, Richard. *The Italian Socialist Movement, Origins: 1860-1882*. Princeton, N.J.: Van Nostrand, 1958.

Hyppolite, Jean. *Studies on Marx and Hegel*. Trans. J. O'Neill. New York: Harper and Row, 1969.

Istituto Giangiacomo Feltrinelli. "Dalla fondazione della Seconda Internazionale alla rivoluzione in Russia," and "Lenin," in *Annali Feltrinelli 1972*, vol. 14. Milan: Feltrinelli, 1973, pp. 3-799.

Joll, James. *Intellectuals in Politics*. London: Weidenfeld and Nicolson, 1960.

———. *The Anarchists*. New York: Grosset and Dunlap, 1964.

———. *The Second International*. New York: Harper and Row, 1966.

Kautsky, Karl. *The Class Struggle*. Chicago: Charles H. Kerr, 1910.

Kellner, Douglas, ed. *Karl Korsch: Revolutionary Theory*. Austin: University of Texas Press, 1977.

Kitchen, Martin. "Thalheimer's Theory of Fascism," *Journal of the History of Ideas*, 34:1 (January-March 1973), 67-78.

König, Helmut. *Lenin und der italienische Sozialismus, 1915-1921*. Tubingen: Arbeitsgemeinschaft für Osteuropaforschung, 1967.

Korsch, Karl. *Marxism and Philosophy*. Trans. F. Halliday. New York: Monthly Review Press, 1970.

Labriola, Antonio. *Essays on the Materialistic Conception of History*. Trans. C. Kerr. Chicago: Charles Kerr, 1908.

______. *Socialism and Philosophy*. Trans. E. Untermann. Chicago: Charles Kerr, 1918.

______. *Lettere a Engels*. Rome: Rinascita, 1949.

______. *Saggi sul materialismo storico*. Ed. V. Gerratana and A. Guerra. Rome: Riuniti, 1964.

______. *Opere*. Ed. F. Sbarberi. Naples: Rossi, 1972.

Labriola, Arturo. *Storia di dieci anni, 1899-1909*. Milan: Il Viandante, 1910.

______. *Economia, socialismo, sindicalismo*. Naples: Società Editrice Partenopea, 1911.

______. *Studio su Marx*. 2nd edition. Naples: Morano, 1926.

Lefebre, Henri. *La Pensée de Lénine*. Paris: Bordas, 1957.

Lenin, V.I. *Selected Works*. 3 vols. New York: International Publishers, 1967.

Leonetti, Alfonso. *Da Andria contadina a Torino operaia*. Argalia: Urbino, 1974.

Lichtheim, George. *Marxism: An Historical and Critical Study*. New York: Praeger, 1961.

______. *Georg Lukács*. New York: Viking, 1970.

Livorsi, Franco. *Amadeo Bordiga, Il pensiero e l'azione politica 1912-1970*. Rome: Riuniti, 1977.

Lobkowicz, Nicholas. *Theory and Practice*. South Bend, Ind.: University of Notre Dame Press, 1967.

Lukács, Georg. *History and Class Consciousness*. Trans. R. Livingstone. Cambridge, Mass: MIT Press, 1971.

______. *Tactics and Ethics*. Trans. M. McColgan. New York: Harper and Row, 1972.

______. *The Young Hegel*. Trans. R. Livingstone. Cambridge, Mass.: MIT Press, 1976.

Luxemburg, Rosa. *Rosa Luxemburg Speaks*. Ed. M.A. Waters. New York: Pathfinder Press, 1970.

Lyttleton, Adrian. *The Seizure of Power: Fascism in Italy, 1919-1929*. London: Weidenfeld and Nicolson, 1973.

Mack Smith, Denis. *Italy: A Modern History*. Ann Arbor: University of Michigan Press, 1959.

______. *Victor Emanuel, Cavour, and the Risorgimento*. London: Oxford University Press, 1971.

Manacorda, Mario Alighiero. *Marx e la pedagogia moderna*. Rome: Riuniti, 1966.

Marramao, Giacomo. *Marxismo e Revisionismo in Italia*. Bari: De Donato, 1971.

Marx, Karl. *Correspondence, 1846-1895: A Selection*. London: Martin Lawrence, 1934.

______. *Selected Works*. 2 vols. Ed. V. Adoratsky. New York: International Publishers, 1935.

______. *Letters to Americans, 1848-1855*. New York: International Publishers, 1953.

______. *Basic Writings on Politics and Philosophy*. Ed. L. Feuer. Garden City, N.Y.: Doubleday, 1959.

______. *Writings of the Young Marx on Philosophy and Society*. Ed. L.D. Easton and K.H. Guddat. Garden City, N.Y.: Doubleday, 1967.

______. *Karl Marx on Colonialism and Modernization*. Ed. S. Avineri. Garden City, N.Y.: Doubleday, 1968.

______. *The Marx-Engels Reader*. Ed. R. Tucker. New York: W.W. Norton, 1972.

Mazzini, Giuseppe. *The Duties of Man*. Ed. T. Jones. London: J.M. Dent, 1955.

Mészáros, István. *Lukács' Concept of Dialectic*. London: Merlin Press, 1972.

Meyer, Alfred G. *Leninism*. New York: Praeger, 1965.

Michels, Robert. *Political Parties*. Glencoe, Ill.: Free Press, 1958.

Miliband, Ralph. *Marxism and Politics*. New York: Oxford University Press, 1977.

Miller, James. "Merleau-Ponty's Marxism: Between Phenomenology and the Hegelian Absolute," *History and Theory*, 15:2 (1976), 109-132.

Moore, Stanley. *Three Tactics*. New York: Monthly Review Press, 1963.

Mosca, Gaetano. *The Ruling Class*. Trans. H. Kahn. New York: McGraw-Hill, 1939.

Nettl, J.P. *Rosa Luxemburg*. 2 vols. London: Oxford University Press, 1966.

Nolte, Ernst. *Three Faces of Fascism*. Trans. L. Vennewitz. New York: Holt, Rinehart and Winston, 1966.

Ollman, Bertell. *Alienation*. London: Cambridge University Press, 1971.

Paci, Enzo. *The Function of the Sciences and the Meaning of Man*. Trans. P. Piccone and J.E. Hanson. Evanston, Ill.: Northwestern University Press, 1972.

Palmer, L.M., and H.S. Harris. *Thought, Action and Intuition as a Symposium on the Philosophy of Benedetto Croce*. New York: Georg Olms, 1975.

Pareto, Vilfredo. *The Mind and Society*. Trans. A. Bongiorno and A. Livingston. London: Jonathan Cape, 1935.

Piccone, Paul. "The Problem of Consciousness," *Telos*, 5 (Fall 1970), 178-187.

______. "Phenomenological Marxism," *Telos*, 9 (Fall 1971), 3-31.

______. "Labriola and the Roots of Eurocommunism," *Berkeley Journal of Sociology*, 22 (1977-78), 3-43.

Platone, Felice. "L'Ordine Nuovo," in *Trenta Anni di storia e di lotta del PCI*. Rome: Rinascita, 1951, pp. 35-40.

Poulantzas, Nicos. *Fascism and Dictatorship*. Trans. J. White. London: New Left Books, 1974.

______. *Political Power and Social Classes*. Trans. T. O'Hagan. London: New Left Books, 1976.

Procacci, Giuliano. "Antonio Labriola e la Revisione del Marxismo attraverso l'Epistolario con Bernstein e con Kautsky (1895-1904)," in *Annali Feltrinelli*, vol. 3. Milan: Feltrinelli, 1961, pp. 264-284.

Riccio, Peter M. *On the Threshold of Fascism*. New York: Casa Italiana, Columbia University, 1929.

Rosenberg, Arthur. *A History of Bolshevism*. London: Oxford University Press, 1934.

Rossi, A. *The Rise of Italian Fascism 1918-1922*. London: Methuen, 1938.

Rotenstreich, Nathan. *Basic Problems of Marx's Philosophy* Indianapolis, Ind.: Bobbs-Merrill, 1965.

Salomone, A. William. *Italy in the Giolittian Era*. Philadelphia: University of Pennsylvania Press, 1960.

______, ed. *Italy from the Risorgimento to Fascism*. Garden City, N.Y.: Doubleday, 1970.

Salvemini, Gaetano. *Scritti sulla questione meridionale (1896-1955)*. Turin: Einaudi, 1955.

______. *Mazzini*. Trans. I.M. Rawson. London: Jonathan Cape, 1956.

______. *The Origins of Fascism in Italy*. Ed. R. Vivarelli. New York: Harper and Row, 1973.

Santarelli, E. "Sorel e il sorelismo in Italia," *Rivista storica del socialismo*, 3:10 (May-August 1960), 289-328.

Sarti, Roland. *Fascism and the Industrial Leadership in Italy, 1919-1940*. Berkeley and Los Angeles: University of California Press, 1971.

Schorske, Carl E. *German Social Democracy, 1905-1917*. Cambridge, Mass.: Harvard University Press, 1955.

Secchia, Pietro. *L'azione svolta del partito comunista in Italia durante il fascismo 1926-1932*. Milan: Feltrinelli, 1970.

Soave, Emilio. "Appunti sulle origini teoriche e pratiche dei consigli de fabbrica a Torino," *Rivista storica del socialismo*, 7:21 (January-April 1964), 1-20.

Sorel, Georges. *L'Avenir socialiste des syndicats*. Paris: Librairie de l'art social, 1898.

______. *Saggi di critica del marxismo*. Ed. V. Racca. Palermo: Sandron, 1903.

______. *Le Décomposition du Marxisme*. Paris: Rivière, 1908.

______. *Matériaux d'une théorie du prolétariat*. Paris: Rivière, 1919.

______ *Reflections on Violence*. Trans. T.E. Hulme. New York: Collier, 1961.

Spriano, Paolo. *L'Occupazione della fabbriche, Settembre 1920*. Turin: Einaudi, 1964.

______. *Storia del partito comunista italiano*. 5 vols. Turin: Einaudi, 1967-1975.

______. "Lenin e il movimento operaio italiano," *Lenin teorico e dirigente rivoluzionario, Critica Marxista*, 4 (1968), 300-316.

Tarrow, Sidney G. *Peasant Communism in Southern Italy*. New Haven, Conn.: Yale University Press, 1967.

Taylor, Charles. *Hegel*. London: Cambridge University Press, 1975.

Terracini, Umberto. *Sulla svolta.* Milan: La Pietra, 1975.

Thayer, John A. *Italy and the Great War.* Madison: University of Wisconsin Press, 1964.

Togliatti, Palmiro, ed. *Trenta Anni di vita e di lotte del PCI.* Rome: Riuniti, 1952.

Viglongo, Andrea. "Momenti della lotta di classe nella primo metà dell 1920," *Il Ponte*, 26:10 (October 1970), 1303-24.

White, Hayden. "The Abiding Relevance of Croce's Idea of History," *Journal of Modern History*, 35:2 (June 1963), 109-124.

______. *Metahistory.* Baltimore: Johns Hopkins University Press, 1973.

Williams, Raymond. "Base and Superstructure in Marxist Cultural Theory," *New Left Review*, 82 (November-December 1973), 3-16.

______. *Marxism and Literature.* New York: Oxford University Press, 1977.

Wistrich, Robert S. "Leon Trotsky's Theory of Fascism," *Journal of Contemporary History*, 11:4 (October 1976), 157-184.

Wolfe, Bertram D. *Marxism: One Hundred Years in the Life of a Doctrine.* New York: Dial Press, 1965.

Wood, Allen W. "Marx's Critical Anthropology: Three Recent Interpretations," *Review of Metaphysics*, 26:1 (September 1972), 118-139.

Index

Compositor: In-House Composition
Printer: McNaughton & Gunn
Binder: McNaughton & Gunn
Text: Compset Times Roman
Display: Compset Times Roman
Cloth: Holliston Roxite A 50339
Paper: 50lb P&S offset